SOUND

TIMELESS LIFE LESSONS FROM 80S POP

ALAN GREEN

SOUND ADVICE

Timeless life lessons from 80s pop

S
SALT

CROMER

PUBLISHED BY SALT PUBLISHING 2025

2 4 6 8 10 9 7 5 3 1

First published in Great Britain in 2025 by
Salt Publishing Ltd
12 Norwich Road, Cromer, Norfolk NR27 0AX, United Kingdom

GPSR representative
Matt Parsons matt.parsons@upi2mbooks.hr
UPI-2M PLUS d.o.o., Medulićeva 20, 10000 Zagreb, Croatia

www.saltpublishing.com

Salt Publishing Limited Reg. No. 5293401

A CIP catalogue record for this book is available from the British Library

ISBN 978 1 78463 358 5 (Paperback edition)
ISBN 978 1 78463 359 2 (Electronic edition)

Typeset in Neacademia by Salt Publishing

Printed and bound in Great Britain by Clays Ltd, Elcograf S.p.A.

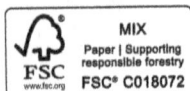

MIX
Paper | Supporting
responsible forestry
FSC
www.fsc.org
FSC® C018072

CONTENTS

THE INTRO
Notes   8

CHAPTER I
A brief history of rhyme (and the 1980s)   10
    The 1980s   12
    Technology   20

CHAPTER II
Unlocking lyrics   26

CHAPTER III
Themes   38

CHAPTER IV
Top 10   43

CHAPTER V
The lyrical advice   46
    Advice   47
    Ageing   51
    Alcohol   60
    Biology   64
    Change   67
    Destination   71
    Destiny   74
    Divorce   76
    Don't . . .   80
    Dreams   84

Drugs	96
Education	99
Environment	103
Evolution	107
Exercise	115
Fashion	123
Fortitude	131
Friends	134
Future	139
Greed	142
Holidays	146
Job	150
Knowledge	151
Loneliness	155
Love	160
Marriage	166
Meteorology	170
Mirrors	174
Mistakes	179
Money	184
New	191
Open-mindedness	195
Optimism	197
Parental Advice	200
Passion	202
Physics	206
Positivity	211
Q&A	217
Religion	221
Reputation	229
Respect	233

Self-reliance   235
Shakespeare   238
Society   242
Time   246
Truth   256
Unity   261
Wishes   264
Words   268
Work   274
Worry   283
Youthfulness   291

CHAPTER VI
The Outro

301

THE INTRO

GREEK philosopher Plato said that music gives soul to the universe, wings to the mind, flight to the imagination and life to everything. Fast forward 2,400 years, and welcome to your new musical life.[1] Your relationship with music and the way you allow its soul-affirming sound to flow through your life is unique, whether you use it as a pleasurable way to uplift your mood, relax and unwind, or a vital coping counterbalance to the challenges and complexities of modern life, or even as a portal to an entire identity and lifestyle ethos, where you marinate your whole life in music. Each person in the UK listens to an average of over 20 hours of music per week. This book explores how you can harness the immersive and enjoyable experience of listening to music into a tool for transformational and beneficial change.

How can music achieve this? Its intrinsic qualities enchant both heart and mind, producing a deeply profound and often obsessionally forceful effect on us that is unmatched by any other art form. Music from any genre, age or culture can enlighten, liberate and enthral to send shivers down your spine or move you to tears because it possesses a backstage 'access all areas' pass that can simultaneously stimulate and increase connections across all brain regions, including those tied to your emotional core. As Kylie Minogue noted,[2] music can bring happiness even when you feel blue; in doing so, it can help define who you are and what it means to be human.

From your first sensations of the rhythmic maternal heartbeat in

1   *Everybody Wants To Rule The World* by Tears For Fears. Written by Roland Orzabal, Ian Stanley and Christopher Hughes
2   *The Loco-Motion* by Kylie Minogue. Written by Gerald Goffin and Carol Klein

the womb to your choice of funeral music, the love of music remains an emotional and enduring joy. (Despite hearing being one of the last senses to fade at the end of life, you won't have the opportunity to listen to your funeral soundtrack; if you do hear it on that day or the muffled voice of someone saying 'Ashes To Ashes'[1] while you lie in a dark, confined space, bang on the sides of that wooden box as if your life depended on it, for it will.)

In *Radio Ga Ga*,[2] Queen sang of garnering all they needed to know by listening to the radio. In a similar vein, this book uncovers, reviews and applies nuggets of sound advice derived from panning song themes from top 10 pop hits from the 1980s (spanning 1 January 1980 to 31 December 1989) that will help you understand, guide and even transform your life by suggesting subtle shifts and positive interventions that help build good habits while dismantling harmful ones. Other themes, titles or even a single word from a song (taken out of context and used in a way that is always tenuous and usually frivolous, then shamelessly shoehorned into the text) are included to create new associations and connections with old songs, weaving a narrative designed to be fun and approachable. The more sober references serve as gateways to learning, developing and harnessing tools and techniques that introduce transformative advice into your life. You should enjoy the ride, even if your life is in perfect order.

Music can be revelatory,[3] particularly when it facilitates the uniquely human ability to mentally time travel. For those of a certain age[4] (as Tina Turner so delicately described it), 1980s music serves as both a launchpad and a cherished companion on a stroll down memory lane where you can rediscover, replay and recapture those heady days of youthful abandon and relive and revive specific memories banked from what seemed like a simpler place and time.

1 *Ashes To Ashes* by David Bowie. Written by David Jones
2 *Radio Ga Ga* by Queen. Written by Roger Taylor
3 *Into The Groove* by Madonna. Written by Madonna Ciccone and Stephen Bray
4 *I Don't Wanna Lose You* by Tina Turner. Written by Albert Hammond and Graham Lyle

You are most likely to draw comfort and significance from the nostalgic glow of the music that defined your emotionally charged adolescence – music imbued with uniquely meaningful moments, bottled and *Labelled With Love*.[1] Memories associated with music are called music-evoked autobiographical memories (MEAMs). Nostalgia harbours a widely held – albeit rose-tinted – belief that the pop music of yesteryear was somehow better. Music was different back then (and you were so much younger),[2] and memory is a naturally pliable reconstruction of a morphing mosaic of fragments rather than a perfectly pristine and immutable recording: your memory recall is more jazz improvisation than compact disc infallibility. In your resonant romanticism, your memory may have marginalised some less desirable aspects of that time. You will likely bestow your first record purchase with intense, emotionally resonant MEAMs to make it as unforgettable as your first sweet kiss.[3] By your early thirties, your musical taste will have expanded to encompass multiple genres, cooling your interest in contemporary music enough for you to seek comfort in the reassuring familiarity of music from your early teens to your early twenties. When music from your adolescence dovetails into your sonic synapses, its hold is tenacious.

As you accumulate years and develop tastes, you gain a broader perspective on life. This allows you to explore personal introspection and emotional archaeology, enabling you to sift through all that life has deposited on you along the way. Such excavations can add depth to your life and an extra dimension to the significance of familiar songs, helping you make sense of your present and shaping a more fulfilling future.

Other readers may ask of the tunes of the 1980s what Paul

1   *Labelled With Love* by Squeeze. Written by Glenn Tilbrook and Christopher Difford
2   *I Know Him So Well* by Elaine Paige and Barbara Dickson. Written by Göran Andersson, Timothy Rice and Björn Ulvaeus
3   *You Got It (The Right Stuff)* by New Kids On The Block. Written by Larry Johnson

McCartney did in *Once Upon A Long Ago:*[1] what do these songs have to do with me? First, they represent some of the best and most enduring pop music, covering timeless themes that still pulsate with relevance and meaning (explored further in Chapter III). Second, these themes emerge from a democratic platform – the UK top 10 (explored further in Chapter IV) – and from a decade many consider – albeit subjectively – a golden age of popular music. Music belongs to all and is non-elitist – you do not need to know how to read music or understand its theory or construction to enjoy, interact or benefit fully from listening to it. It is only relatively recently in our cultural history that music shifted from a creative, ritualistic and participatory activity to a more physically passive, contemplative audience listening pursuit, especially in adults. Analysing the top 10 pop songs from one decade in the twentieth century is no stranger than focusing almost all our musical attention on Western European music created from the mid-eighteenth century onwards, given the immense span of history over which human-created music has existed, as further explored in Chapter I.

Pop music's concise format transmits its message in a concentrated, entertaining and accessible way. Those unfamiliar with the tunes from the 1980s can appreciate them with fresh ears, free from biases that dictate a song or performer was either super cool or squarer (and less colourful) than a Rubik's cube. The focus of sound advice should always be on its quality, merit and relevance, not from whom, when, where or how it was created or delivered. It's not just the music you listen to that matters, but what you can take from what you hear, and the more you listen, the more you hear. Should you find sonic satisfaction from a song that helps keep you on track[2] or triggers an adjustment that makes you feel happier, you will double the dopamine hit, doubling the effect. Engaging with music-inspired advice, insight and lifestyle interventions will

1   *Once Upon A Long Ago* by Paul McCartney. Written by Paul McCartney
2   *The Slightest Touch* by Five Star. Written by Grover Morrow and Michael Margules

have more traction within your life than associating with other tools designed to help improve your life, such as scientific journals, wellness professionals or phone apps. Instead of spending every spare moment glued to your phone screen, listen to portal songs that can help you stay motivated, trigger positive adjustments or align with whatever message or thought the song delivers to you.

The advice, insights and lifestyle interventions presented in this book aim to create subtle changes for someone able to benefit from a gentle guiding hand.[1] Most lives benefit from a good airing; others need complete fumigation – a need recognised within songs: *The Look Of Love*[2] describes the feeling that something is missing, while *Change*[3] describes the loss of the essential lust for life,[4] where your excitement, energy, passion and purpose have been replaced by living in the autopilot torpor of an unfulfilling and numbing rut-like routine, rinsed and drained of any meaning beyond reaching the end of another week. When it feels like there's lead in your veins, it's easy to acknowledge that something is wrong,[5] something is holding you back, but you may be unable to articulate what has caused your once-sparkling pizzazz to diminish, your zest for life to fade and your essence to ebb away: you are alive but not living. The song themes and advice can help you to reoxygenate and recalibrate any flagging or stagnant aspects in your life. Initiating such action serves as a powerful, cleansing reset.

Individual stressors often combine, compound and amplify the collective harm they inflict, so it's wise to consider all the themes in your quest to restore equilibrium. If the environmental mantra is 'reduce, reuse and recycle', then the sonic equivalent is 'revisit, reinvent and refocus'. However, if you have a pre-existing physical

1 *Downtown '88* by Petula Clark. Written by Anthony Hatch
2 *The Look Of Love* by ABC. Written by Martin Fry, Mark White, Stephen Singleton, David Palmer and Mark Lickley
3 *Change* by Tears For Fears. Written by Roland Orzabal
4 *Animal* by Def Leppard. Written by Joseph Elliott, Philip Collen, Richard Savage, Robert Lange and Stephen Clark
5 *Too Shy* by Kajagoogoo. Written by Christopher Hamill, Steven Askew, Nicholas Beggs, Stuart Neale and Jeremy Strode

or mental health condition (an umbrella term, including addiction or clinical depression), you should first consult with a doctor, trusted healthcare provider or specialist for a diagnosis and a tailored clinical plan. You must seek medical advice before significantly changing your diet, exercise or other health-related regimes. While music can play a therapeutic role in the rehabilitation process that can help bolster resilience, harness fortitude, improve well-being, re-establish equilibrium and provide a great source of comfort to a fractured mind, it cannot alone undertake all the necessary repair work.

It's your life,[1] so the underlying reasons for reading this book will determine how you use it. For example, your desire to drop ingrained bad practices (such as a default negative inner voice) may be as important to you as your desire to adopt positive new habits, such as outdoor exercise or finding and following a passion. You'll need to dismantle the old as you create the new. Humans possess an innate drive and compulsion to improve, climb higher, push and probe further and harder at personal frontiers and try to build a better life for themselves and their families. The themes and advice within the featured songs can help you erect a personal scaffolding for growth and development as you pursue happiness, health, and productivity.

And now a spoiler alert: most good old-fashioned sound advice – including that fashioned out of sound itself – is so called because its guidance is timeless, sensible, reliable and evidence-based, gleaned from science, grounded in experience and stress-tested. As standalone sound advice is free from fashionable fads, it is rarely revolutionary, radical or miraculous, able to provide multiple a-ha moments. (Multiple A-ha moments were plentiful in the 1980s, courtesy of the Norwegian pop band and their eight UK top 10 hits.) Sound advice is rarely extreme advice; it instead focuses on practical and often simple, achievable guidance (much of which you will already be aware of but may have sidelined) through a series of small, manageable changes that you can embed into your life. Over

1   *High Life* by Modern Romance. Written by David Jaymes and Trevor Jones

time, these can consolidate to make a big, beneficial difference. You are more likely to act on advice that is easy to understand, requires minimal effort, and where the cost is low or even free (such as with breathing techniques, walking in daylight or following the basic hygiene of 'Hand, Face, Space' to reduce the risk of catching viruses). Sound advice can help you to make the right choices and crucially stick with them until they become habitual, all through the enjoyable medium of music.

You are unique. The depth and complexity of your life and the challenges you face will always surpass the themes covered in pop songs. The universal nature of some themes may render the advice simplistic. However, as described in *Beat Dis*,[1] you are about to embark on a voyage into sound where you can create a self-medicated, cherry-picked compilation playlist featuring a collection of personalised advice with personal significance that can help you achieve a full, rich and rounded life. You could freeze-dry any pertinent words or lines by writing them down to create daily personal affirmations or, better still, do what the record tells you[2] and bring the words to life by listening to the songs in their original form (which is also the most effective way to remember them). Elton John sang about how *Sad Songs (Say So Much)*,[3] especially from those words that manage to live on inside you. It is not only sad songs that possess this power. Music is deeply personal, so trust your instincts and choose the method and the songs that work for you. If you're unsure, experiment: for some, listening to music enhances their focus, while for others, it distracts. You can benefit from sound advice even if you're not a music fan. You can test the veracity of any advice against prevailing, objective science and the logic of common sense or philosophy, which is the multi-stranded approach taken towards the end of each theme after the words 'Sound advice?'. When presented with solid guidance,

1   *Beat Dis* by Bomb The Base. Written by Pascal Gabriel and Tim Simenon
2   *Twist And Shout* by Salt-N-Pepa. Written by Bertrand Berns and Philip Medley
3   *Sad Songs (Say So Much)* by Elton John. Written by Elton John and Bernard Taupin

most can make the right decisions. The personalised musical advice within this book is a simple extension of self-conditioning – using the groove to improve.[1]

Another advantage of using music as a catalyst for transformative change is that the tracks, like dream fragments, hold personal significance, uniqueness and relevance for you alone. No one needs to know why[2] you have chosen to listen to these tracks or what you wish to achieve through the songs' repurposed lyrics or secret prompts; the change you inspire can help you to be yourself (because, as Oscar Wilde quipped, everyone else is already taken).

Chapters I to IV provide a brief background history and an exploration of unlocking lyrics and themes, while Chapter V explores individual themes in greater detail.

Decoding the song themes delves into aspects of life that span the arc of human history. On this flight of music,[3] you will let the sound advice be music to your ears by allowing the music to free you.[4]

NOTES

Except for Elton John (Reginald Dwight), Paul McCartney (James McCartney), Freddie Mercury (Farrokh Bulsara), George Michael (Georgios Panayiotou), Roland Orzabal (Roland Orzabal de la Quintana) and Stevie Wonder (Stevland Judkins), the birth names of songwriters (sourced mainly from the discogs.com database) are listed in the footnote writing credits rather than stage names or aliases. This honours and acknowledges the true identity behind the songwriting process. Attach no significance to the order in which names appear in the writing credits.

Songwriters create songs to be heard, so the author's ears served as the primary tool for evaluating and selecting the more than 850 featured songs. Lyric websites, principally azlyrics.com and genius.com, were consulted only to clarify unclear enunciation (a regular occurrence).

The website officialcharts.com identified which songs were UK top 10 hits.

1   *Ant Rap* by Adam And The Ants. Written by Stuart Goddard and Marco Pirroni
2   *Breakfast In Bed* by UB40 with Chrissie Hynde. Written by Donald Fritts and Edward Hinton
3   *Street Tuff* by Rebel MC and Double Trouble. Written by Leigh Guest, Michael Tachie-Menson and Michael West
4   *Into The Groove* by Madonna. Written by Madonna Ciccone and Stephen Bray

The *Oxford English Dictionary* online (oed.com) and the *Oxford Dictionary of English* were used to check etymology.

The website theoi.com helped untangle the complex relationships webs within Greek mythology.

CHAPTER I

A brief history of rhyme (and the 1980s)

MUSIC has captivated humanity for millennia. The beauty of birdsong – especially the dawn chorus – has long enraptured our ears and captured our hearts. "Suppose the singing birds musicians" mused Shakespeare, *Et Les Oiseaux Chantaient (And The Birds Were Singing)*.[1] A male bird will serenade to seduce and impart information about his health, fitness and suitability as a mate. Birds also use their songs as sonic weapons to deter and intimidate rivals and delineate territories. With its ethereal beauty and virtuosity, this ancient avian orchestra must have sounded sublime to early humans, even inspiring replication.

While human-created music is more abstract than birdsong, it likely served similar purposes in early societies by defining territories and shaping social identities. Some argue that the joy we derive from melodic music is merely epiphenomenal – an extraordinary by-product of human intellect. However, for our chemically receptive brains, music feels more like an innate, visceral and primordial element of humanness than simply a cognitive adornment or a fortuitous offshoot of neural circuitry.

Music, like language, did not emerge from a single time or place but evolved independently across cultures. Our oldest musical 'instrument' is the human voice, arguably the most expressive form of music. The earliest discovered non-perishable musical instrument created by *Homo sapiens* is a small, lightweight and portable

[1]   *Et Les Oiseaux Chantaient (And The Birds Were Singing)* by Sweet People. Written by Maurice Morisod and Antonio D'Addario

bird-bone flute featuring five finger holes, dating back about 42,000 years. The connection to hollow bird bones may extend beyond practical construction, as these simple flutes produce sounds reminiscent of birdsong. Such instruments did not arise spontaneously but evolved in complexity from a succession of simpler predecessors, stretching back to the selection of stones (lithophones) or objects such as bones, used to create rhythmic sounds through banging, rattling or clapping.

Music evolved with ever-more complexity as a cognitive revolution continued to assemble an intricate mosaic of human culture and civilisation. Again, music likely served purposes akin to birdsong, such as marking tribal group identity, cementing social cohesion, communicating intra-group emotional states or signalling territorial boundaries to neighbouring groups.

Today, across all cultures, listening to music is one of the most popular ways to alleviate or reduce gatecrashing stress and tension. While other primates favour silence over music, humans enrich their lives through an incredible diversity of sound.

It's impossible to pinpoint when humans first added lyrics to music or (more likely) added music to service the development of vocalisations and protolanguages. The oldest surviving piece of written music that archaeo-musicologists can interpret and perform is a 3,400-year-old hymn to the goddess of orchards, composed for a nine-stringed lyre – a small U-shaped harp-like stringed instrument beloved by the ancients. Both music and language require biological evolution that involves a complex array of anatomical features, indicating they share a long and complex co-evolution. As academics and Rick Astley have pointed out, humans have been striving to express themselves for a long, long time.[1]

The etymology of 'music' and 'lyric' has more straightforward origins. 'Music' derives from the Greek word for the Muses, the nine goddess daughters of Zeus who presided over and inspired creative artists, while 'lyric', also from Greek, means 'of the lyre'.

1   *Hold Me In Your Arms* by Rick Astley. Written by Richard Astley

(One member of the lyre family – the *kithara*, from which the modern-day guitar draws its name and form – was once a part of an Olympic musical contest.) From about 2,500 years ago, lyrics were the poems sung to accompany the lyre. To be passed down through the generations, poems needed to be memorable, and one of the most effective ways to be memorable is to be melodic.

Love, a timeless theme in poems, remains the most prevalent subject in modern pop music. Love songs encapsulate age-old emotional experiences, reimagined for a new generation of eager listeners. Throughout history, the human need to express emotion through storytelling, music and song has remained constant, providing motivation, enhancing or altering our mood, paying homage to the divine or simply offering joy. Music will continue to have a place within our evolving cultures, and because we have music, we should use it.[1]

THE 1980S

Music is not created in isolation but reflects its time's cultural and social undercurrents. For the listener, music can capture specific moments, anchoring the people and place of that time deep within their mind and creating a lasting emotional connection to an era. Advertisers and film directors frequently tap into this nostalgia by employing contemporary soundtracks as a quick and cost-effective way to evoke a particular time. Music that opens your ears can unfasten your memory and mind.

Whether you regard pop songs as active drivers or passive recorders of social and cultural change, you need context to sift, decode and appreciate what you hear. Each generation expresses and imprints its unique perspective on culture in response to contemporary events. Enough years have elapsed since the 1980s to examine the decade objectively and offer proper perspective and insight. At the same time, it is still recent enough for any influence that filtered down to

1   *Word Up* by Cameo. Written by Larry Blackmon and Thomas Jenkins

linger in today's culture. Looking back to connect the dots becomes easier when you can see the bigger picture.

Despite being underrated and maligned by some critics, the appeal of much of the music and many of the stars from the 1980s has endured remarkably well. In *Anyone Can Fall In Love*,[1] listeners are asked how to stop the music from dying. One answer is to revisit, reappraise and reclaim these songs as work created by talented musical artists operating in their prime. While some deride and dismiss the decade as divisive, others champion it as a gold standard and a benchmark of pop music excellence – a decade *Too Good To Be Forgotten*.[2] Pre-1980s songs were often (lyrically) shunned in songs of the 1980s as being unwanted golden oldies.[3] However, when record companies re-released these classic tracks, many sold well. Likewise, some stars from the 1980s have successfully reinvented themselves (often multiple times) to stay relevant and continue to perform a generation later, both to their original fanbase and to a new generation of enthusiastic listeners who may have discovered them through digital platforms. (Take a bow, Madonna, the Bee Gees, David Bowie, U2 . . .) Some stars have grown to become cultural musical icons, with their musical footprint rediscovered and rebranded by the current generation of musical explorers. It is listeners who keep the songs they love alive, helping to create a resurgence of interest in the 1980s, such as through dedicated digital radio stations playing 1980s music. Pop songs persist when they remain relevant through their content or quality (ideally, both). Even vinyl, having been read the last rites, managed to cheat death. Fortunately, most of the lurid spandex from the 1980s remains deeply buried.

Clichés abound around the sound and legacy of the 1980s,

1   *Anyone Can Fall In Love* by Anita Dobson and The Simon May Orchestra. Written by Simon May, Leslie Osborne and Donald Blackstone
2   *Too Good To Be Forgotten* by Amazulu. Written by Barbara Acklin and Eugene Record
3   *I'd Rather Jack* by The Reynolds Girls. Written by Michael Stock, Matthew Aitken and Peter Waterman

depicting it as a socially selfish decade of decadence,[1] devoid of care and compassion. Tensions ran high as the world felt the chill of the cold war; fears of nuclear apocalypse blew like a keen wind through the early 1980s, reflected in songs like Nena's *99 Red Balloons*[2] and Frankie Goes To Hollywood's *Two Tribes*.[3] However, much like Katharine Hamnett's oversized, shouty sloganed T-shirts of the time, reducing the decade to a one-dimensional narrative overlooks any nuance.

Interwoven throughout the decade were a series of largely peaceful yet still transformative revolutions – social, economic, political, cultural and technological. One name bookended the decade: Margaret Thatcher (bestowed with various monikers, most famously the 'Iron Lady' thanks to her uncompromising political ideology). Thatcher made history by becoming the country's first woman Prime Minister (often described as the only man in her Cabinet), the longest-serving British Prime Minister of the 20th century and the dominant political figure of the decade. Having survived a deadly and audacious assassination attempt by the IRA – made with *A View To A Kill*[4] – during the Conservative Party conference at the Grand Hotel in Brighton in 1984, Thatcher had shown herself politically bombproof. Thatcher's policies made her a highly divisive presence and a target of blame for the pain and anxiety that change inevitably creates in its wake. For The Style Council, public enemy number one resided at Number 10.[5] For Tears For Fears, Thatcher, having achieved her third consecutive election win in 1987, was an idealistic grandmother, out of touch with how most think and feel.[6]

1   *D-Days* by Hazel O'Connor. Written by Hazel O'Connor
2   *99 Red Balloons* by Nena. Written by Jörn-Uwe Fahrenkrog-Petersen, Carlo Karges and Kevin McAlea
3   *Two Tribes* by Frankie Goes To Hollywood. Written by Peter Gill, William Johnson and Mark O'Toole
4   *A View To A Kill* by Duran Duran. Written by Simon Le Bon, Nigel Taylor, Roger Taylor, Andrew Taylor, Nicholas Bates and John Prendergast
5   *Walls Come Tumbling Down!* by The Style Council. Written by John Weller
6   *Sowing The Seeds Of Love* by Tears For Fears. Written by Roland Orzabal and Curt Smith

Thatcherite right-wing ideology advocated reduced state intervention in people's lives, emphasising self-reliance and hard work, both central tenets of individualism. Many global pop superstars embraced this shift towards individualism by embarking on successful solo careers away from their former bandmates: Michael Jackson (Jackson 5), George Michael (Wham!), Phil Collins (Genesis), Sting (The Police), Lionel Richie (Commodores), Tina Turner (Ike and Tina Turner) and Diana Ross (The Supremes) each typified this trend.

Those who danced to *The Time Warp*[1] needed to jump to the left before stepping to the right. Politically, Britain took a step to the right through monetarist policies (strategies used to regulate the money supply to help control inflation), privatisations of nationalised industries (such as British Gas and British Telecom) and legislation to curb trade union power. Although this political dance and free-market party was open to all, not everyone opted to join in or cash in. Marred by industrial decline, factory closures and recession, a simmering mix of repressed anger, despair and resentment boiled over into inner-city violence. Picket lines became fault lines that split some formerly united communities. In *Thunder In The Mountains*,[2] Toyah describes how anger can ignite from a single spark at a time when, on the ever-more combustible inner-city streets of powder keg[3] Britain, you could find a plentiful supply of youthful flint flakes kicking around. Sparks turned to flame[4] as riots erupted on the streets of Brixton and Toxteth, creating anxiety about multiculturalism, especially among those on the political right. Cracks in community cohesion and other challenges, such as freedom of artistic expression and religious (in)tolerance, were prised open later in the decade when Iran's Ayatollah Khomeini issued a fatwa on author Salman Rushdie for his depiction of the

1   *The Time Warp* by Damian. Written by Richard Smith
2   *Thunder In The Mountains* by Toyah. Written by Adrian Lee, Nigel Glockler and Toyah Willcox
3   *Total Eclipse Of The Heart* by Bonnie Tyler. Written by James Steinman
4   *Wake Me Up Before You Go-Go* by Wham! Written by George Michael

prophet Muhammad in his book *Satanic Verses*. Under 24-hour police protection, Rushdie spent nearly a decade in hiding. The fatwa was never formally rescinded. In 2022, Rushdie was stabbed more than a dozen times on stage in New York, resulting in the loss of the use of one hand and sight in one eye.

In the early 1980s, the number of unemployed surpassed three million. Youth unemployment (those under 25) reached nearly one in four, a statistical plight explored by UB40 (named after the unemployment benefit card issued to claimants) in *One In Ten*.[1] Some hatched an unconventional escape plan to avoid the dole: they turned to music. A new wave of bands began their phoenix-like emergence from the embers of the old industrial heartlands of Manchester, Sheffield, Birmingham, Coventry and Liverpool.

In 1985, the acrimonious year-long miners' strike against pit closures ended with victory for the Iron Lady, the eponymous iron presumably smelted before the widespread decommissioning of the foundries. As traditional manufacturing industries declined, a fresh entrepreneurial spirit emerged along with a new service economy, particularly in advertising and financial services. The country gradually shifted from production to consumption, fuelled by slick and increasingly sophisticated cross-marketing techniques within a growing media network.

Marketing makeovers extended to the music industry through music videos, film soundtracks, television brand extensions and new covers of old hits. Ambitious young models such as Samantha Fox and Nick Kamen seized the opportunity to leverage their looks and capitalise on their public exposure to market themselves as pop stars. As visual awareness increased and personal identity emerged as a marketable commodity, brands and bands became increasingly image-conscious. In *Radio Ga Ga*,[2] Queen suggested that you could see as much as hear how music changes.

1   *One In Ten* by UB40. Written by James Brown, Alistair Campbell, Earl Falconer, Norman Hassan, Brian Travers and Michael Virtue
2   *Radio Ga Ga* by Queen. Written by Roger Taylor

In 1984, rock's contemporary aristocracy coalesced to form the supergroup 'Band Aid', using the immediacy of pop culture to raise both awareness and hard cash to alleviate the devastating effects of famine in East Africa. *Do They Know It's Christmas?*[1] became the biggest- and fastest-selling single in chart history, raising over £8 million and securing the coveted Christmas number 1 spot. The subsequent Live Aid concert in July 1985, broadcast live from Wembley to over 1.5 billion viewers worldwide (from an estimated global population of 4.8 billion) in over 160 countries, created a global jukebox and was hailed as the day rock and roll changed the world. The limited number of media outlets helped bolster these viewing figures as Britain at this time still experienced real-time, shared national cultural moments through event television, such as Live Aid, a royal wedding (Queen central to both), the FA Cup final and Thursday evening's ritual viewing of *Top of the Pops*. These events provided a sense of unity, comfort, escapism and a chance to share your sofa with your family, and the nation.

Buoyed by the success of Band Aid but deflated after the holing of union power following the failed miners' strike, a new movement of openly politically motivated musicians (including Paul Weller and Billy Bragg) emerged in 1985 under the name 'Red Wedge' as a buttress against the relentless blue tide of Thatcherism. They sought to persuade and inspire young followers to engage in political activism and to support and vote for the far-from-fashionable ideology of the Labour Party. However, none of this activism was to change the election outcome, as Thatcher stormed her way to secure a third consecutive victory. The Red Wedge walls soon came tumbling down.

The 'Big Bang' of 1986 ignited financial deregulation in the City of London, paving the way for more modern money markets. Deregulation, in turn, helped spawn the swaggering yuppie, the

1   *Do They Know It's Christmas?* by Band Aid. Written by Robert Geldof and James Ure

1980s *Wide Boy*[1] (wide yes, deep no), Filofaxes, power-dressing, mobile telephony, share ownership, consumerism, homeownership, soaring property prices and homelessness. Some economists have directly implicated the deregulation initiated in the 1980s with what later exploded as the global financial crisis of 2008.

The music business also became big business, bolstered by the additional revenue that record companies generated from devoted fans who had to repurchase their favourite music during the transition from vinyl and cassette to compact disc. Big business is a *Dog Eat Dog*[2] world. One example came in 1987 when record company EMI re-released Nat King Cole's 1956 cover of *When I Fall In Love*[3] to thwart Rick Astley's cover of the same song from reaching the top spot. This tactical manoeuvre allowed EMI's Pet Shop Boys cover of *Always On My Mind*[4] to sneak down the chimney and deliver the decade's most unlikely Christmas number 1. This unexpected present likely left each of the Pet Shop Boys to wonder, *What Have I Done To Deserve This?*[5]

Rick Astley was one of several 1980s performers produced by a new *Starmaker*[6] machine in a hit-making factory run by Stock, Aitken and Waterman, who manufactured well-crafted pop songs characterised by their signature 'Hi-NRG' sound. They used their magic-bean formula to transform Australian TV soap actors Kylie Minogue and Jason Donovan into international pop stars. With a carefully marketed image and prefabricated sound, the Stock, Aitken and Waterman approach exemplified the late 1980s trend that prioritised style over substance, regularly outselling edgier,

1   *Wide Boy* by Nik Kershaw. Written by Nicholas Kershaw
2   *Dog Eat Dog* by Adam And The Ants. Written by Stuart Goddard and Marco Pirroni
3   *When I Fall In Love* by Nat King Cole. Written by Edward Heyman and Victor Young
4   *Always On My Mind* by Pet Shop Boys. Written by Wayne Head, Francis Zambon and John Christopher Jr
5   *What Have I Done To Deserve This?* by Pet Shop Boys with Dusty Springfield. Written by Neil Tennant, Christopher Lowe and Alta Willis
6   *Starmaker* by The Kids From Fame. Written by Bruce Roberts and Carole Bayer

more innovative artists who had characterised musical diversity earlier in the decade. In Thatcher's market economy, consumers were supposed to get what they wanted; the success of bubblegum pop demonstrated how producers could prime public taste to want what they were given, a sentiment echoed in The Jam's hit *Going Underground.*[1]

In the late 1980s, possibly in a backlash against the clean-cut assembly-line artists and their plastic pop-by-numbers sound, an underground, ragged-edged acid-house scene emerged. Accompanied by raves often held at post-industrial venues such as old factories or warehouses, this counterculture movement embraced hallucinogenic drugs and challenged social conformity. Ecstasy put the 'E' into the euphoria-enhanced eighties, while dance music, especially when experienced with a headful of sleep-depriving, delirium-inducing drugs,[2] helped shift the musical focus from bands to tracks, especially where digital technology permitted greater democratisation of music production, fostering a bedroom-based DIY ethos that put a new spin into old tunes. While pushing the boundaries of pop, this drugged-up descendant of disco experimented with digital doctoring, musical mingling and altogether liberal sampling[3] to create a new splice of grafted life from musical cuttings, often breaching copyright and thereby restricting this artistic expression to niche broadcasting.

Beyond Britain, revolutionary fervour swept the globe, most significantly with the collapse of communist totalitarianism. With the dismantling of the oppressive, divisive Berlin Wall (once again, *Walls Come Tumbling Down!*),[4] communist East Germany was able to turn to the West to find and reunify with its old capitalist friend,

1   *Going Underground* by The Jam. Written by John Weller
2   *It Is Time To Get Funky* by D Mob featuring LRS. Written by Daniel Poku, Basil Reynolds, Charles Scarlett and Courtney Coulson
3   *Doctorin' The House* by Coldcut featuring Yazz and The Plastic Population. Written by Yasmin Evans, Jonathan More and Matthew Cohn
4   *Walls Come Tumbling Down!* by The Style Council. Written by John Weller

West Germany.[1] Pro-democracy movements and demonstrations spread, even reaching as far as the red skies of Tiananmen Square in Beijing.

The nuclear threat from communism that clung to the 1980s like an oppressive, stifling fog came not from ideological weapons of warfare but from a malfunctioning power plant. When reflecting on the fall of the once-mighty hammer and sickle empire, Mikhail Gorbachev, the last leader of the Soviet Union, cited the nuclear disaster at the Chernobyl reactor in 1986 as a catalyst for change that ultimately led to the collapse of the Soviet Union. Now that's what you call nuclear fallout.

However beneficial, revolutions invariably bring about change and collateral damage in their wake.

TECHNOLOGY

On 1 August 1981, another revolution began with the launch of Music Television – MTV. Before MTV, music videos were occasionally aired on *Top of the Pops*, often as a substitute for musicians on tour. However, MTV's offering was unprecedented: a platform dedicated entirely to the slick imagery of rock music videos broadcasting 24 hours a day, seven days a week, enabling viewers to watch their favourite performers for hours on end.[2] Although it wouldn't reach the UK for another six years, MTV redefined the face and operation of the music industry by shifting the emphasis of attention from ear to eye. According to Red Box, adding sight to sound was an opiate.[3]

The first video broadcast on MTV was The Buggles' 1979 hit *Video Killed The Radio Star*.[4] Contrary to the pessimistic prediction in the provocative title, radio stars could now add new big-picture video imagery to enhance their music. These new fast-paced

1   *Nikita* by Elton John. Written by Elton John and Bernard Taupin
2   *Radio Ga Ga* by Queen. Written by Roger Taylor
3   *For America* by Red Box. Written by Simon Toulson-Clarke
4   *Video Killed The Radio Star* by The Buggles. Written by Geoffrey Downes, Trevor Horn and Bruce Woolley

promotional video 'commercials' elevated theatrical performance, production creativity and financial backing to unprecedented heights, exemplified by the release in 1983 of Michael Jackson's 14-minute long, $1 million short-film video for *Thriller*[1] and A-ha's ground-breaking rotoscoped video to *Take On Me*.[2] Early adopters of *Living On Video*,[3] such as Duran Duran, quickly realised the potential of regular exposure to an expanding global audience. Twenty-four hours a day is a long time to fill with three-minute videos, making some stars appear omnipresent, propelling them to new levels of fame and fortune. MTV transformed the aural into the visual, the message into an image, the star into a superstar, and the superstar into a megastar.

The 1980s also witnessed an expansion in terrestrial television, albeit from a baseline of only three channels at the decade's onset. A fourth channel, imaginatively named Channel 4, launched in 1982 with a remit to be disruptive, innovative and creative (much like the pop music of the time, reflected in its boundary-pushing music show *The Tube*) and to challenge the established broadcasters. Partly in response to the revolutionary spirit of this edgy new kid on the block promising more on the other side,[4] the established broadcasters revamped and expanded their schedules, introducing breakfast television and, by 1986, much to the delight of retirees, under-stimulated students and the unemployed, a full daytime schedule. The 1989 Broadcasting Bill further deregulated commercial television, paving the way to what was once only a remote possibility: channel surfing.

Technological advancements in music production involved far more than merely ushering in carefully curated pop promotions onto television screens. Ways to produce and consume music changed

1   *Thriller* by Michael Jackson. Written by Rodney Temperton
2   *Take On Me* by A-ha. Written by Magne Furuholmen, Morten Harket and Pål Waaktaar Gamst
3   *Living On Video* by Trans-X. Written by Pascal Languirand
4   *Starmaker* by The Kids From Fame. Written by Bruce Roberts and Carole Bayer

with the advent and widespread use of experimental sonic sculpting and manipulation created by a new electronic arsenal of affordable and programmable pop production staples such as synthesisers, samplers, sequencers and drum machines, all digitally recorded. Some musicians became inventive and pioneering electronic technicians, able to wield unprecedented control over a vast array of conjured sounds.

In 1982, ABBA became the first mainstream pop band to release an album on compact disc – the often melancholic *The Visitors*. Within 25 years, global CD sales topped 200 billion, many but not all of which were recorded by ABBA. With their light-splitting allure and futuristic look, shiny CDs were digital dynamite read with a laser beam, producing their distinctly 'clean', distortion-free and pristine sound and offering greater track capacity, increased durability (although rarely to the promised levels) and the convenience of skipping tracks and programming play order. This audio revolution created a lucrative market for back-catalogues as fans replaced vinyl collections, like-for-like, with CDs, providing a much-welcomed new revenue stream for record company coffers.

The relatively expensive CD (both discs and players) first had to usurp the audio cassette tape, which had undergone a revolution of its own making, fuelled by one of the must-have status symbols of the time: the Sony Walkman. The song *Wired For Sound*[1] celebrated the joy and freedom of having a portable, pocket-sized personal stereo and radio cassette player that delivered surprisingly high sound quality on the go. This portable technology made listening more insular, helping to decouple music from place and creating an interior space awash with a private soundscape. Some commentators attributed the marked increase in the popularity of walking as a form of exercise to the aptly named Walkman, which sold in the millions throughout the 1980s.

1   *Wired For Sound* by Cliff Richard. Written by Alan Tarney and Brian Robertson

My One Temptation.[1] The popularity of cassettes did, however, tempt formerly law-abiding citizens to partake in the all too easy but illegal thrill of 'pirate' home recording, particularly from Radio 1's weekly chart countdown, onto cheap blank cassettes. DJs were encouraged to talk over song outros to deter home recording and protect record label profits, part of which they used to find and fund new talent. Audio cassettes made it possible to record not only from the radio but also from vinyl, CDs and (using twin tape-deck technology on integrated hi-fi systems) other tapes, allowing listeners to weave music[2] and create personalised compilation mixtapes.

Inevitably, the Sony Discman skipped along in the footsteps of the Walkman. The slipped discman only found favour with chiropractors and osteopaths.

The miniaturisation of microelectronics during the 1970s paved the way for a new silicon dream[3] of affordable, user-friendly and (in a predominantly analogue age) futuristic personal/home computing. Rudimentary home computers, such as Clive Sinclair's ZX81 (in either kit or pre-assembled form), required a television set to display their black-and-white graphics and to produce the electronic beeping sounds.[4] This technology suited nascent programmers and video gamers more than aspiring musicians.

Computer Love.[5] By 1983, thanks in part to the BBC's schools computer literacy programme, Britain had fallen, bit by bit,[6] in love with computers, becoming the world leader in computer ownership, much to the delight of politicians keen to build and project a new, high-tech future. The decade that began with the likes of the Sinclair ZX81 ended with Tim Berners-Lee's visionary concept of

1   *My One Temptation* by Mica Paris. Written by Michael Leeson, Stephen Waters and Peter Vale
2   *Vienna* by Ultravox. Written by William Currie, Christopher Allen, James Ure and Warren Cann
3   *Eighth Day* by Hazel O'Connor. Written by Hazel O'Connor
4   *System Addict* by Five Star. Written by William Livsey and Gary Bell
5   *Computer Love* by Kraftwerk. Written by Ralf Hütter, Karl Bartos and Emil Schult
6   *Toy Soldiers* by Martika. Written by Marta Marrero and Michael Margules

a network of computers that would enable users to exchange and share information easily – the World Wide Web.

Burning Bridges (On And Off And On Again).[1] Aside from a few hardware glitches and the occasional software bug[2] requiring a reboot via the on/off switch, computerisation flourished, especially within the financial services sector, where electronic screen-based trading became a reality. Computers also transformed the newspaper industry as Fleet Street's unionised hot metal print production transitioned to modern screen-based offices in Wapping, enabling journalists to input their articles directly and quickly using a keyboard rather than through tangible typesetting arranged by the calloused fingers of unionised compositors. Although the story of the year-long printers' strike against these changes made front-page news,[3] it represented another failure for the unions at a time when print journalism still wielded enough influence to determine whether the litmus paper of the voting booth turned red or blue.

Throughout history, technology has driven change. Whether lithophone or smartphone, technology is a tool; its impact depends on how we use it. In the 1980s, most changes facilitated by technology within the music industry were a triumph: dynamic production techniques, improved sound quality with CDs, greater portability with devices such as the Walkman and global exposure through music video. Video didn't kill the radio star. On the contrary, those radio stars who combined sight and sound on video shone brighter thanks to the power of visual memory, which is even more intense than its auditory counterpart. However, others raised questions about the downsides to technology, the answers to which lie outside the scope of this book: Did the transfer of creative influence from musicians to producers go too far, creating non-musical pop stars? Did digitally manipulated production techniques

1   *Burning Bridges (On And Off And On Again)* by Status Quo. Written by Francis Rossi and Andrew Bown
2   *99 Red Balloons* by Nena. Written by Jörn-Uwe Fahrenkrog-Petersen, Carlo Karges and Kevin McAlea
3   *The Story Of The Blues (Part One)* by Wah! Written by Peter Wylie

24

mask vocal shortcomings, shifting the spotlight from great singers to great performers? Did the joy of listening to music become diluted by the distraction of watching slick music videos? Did the proliferation of stylised pop videos further objectify women? Did CDs sound too sanitised, too clinical? Did the smaller CD case diminish the quality of album artwork? Did personal, portable private headphones herald the decline of shared listening experiences? Did the proliferation and splintering of TV channels end the collective national viewing experience? Did the ubiquity of music video separate and alienate performers from their fans? Did technological advancements such as fast-forwarding or track skipping contribute to shrivelled song introductions and shorter attention spans?[1]

1 *You Can Call Me Al* by Paul Simon. Written by Paul Simon

CHAPTER II

Unlocking lyrics

U NLOCKING the cryptic qualities of a successful song requires several keys. A song needs to blend and balance various elements to engage, connect and captivate the listener: a scene-setting intro with a sharp, memorable hook; a catchy melody that flows effortlessly into your ears and stubbornly lingers in your memory; a singable lyric; a compelling chorus; and, if appropriate, a danceable rhythm. Songs often incorporate a 'bridge' where the melody and lyrics shift direction, tapping into our deep-seated instinct to pay attention to sudden change. Each genre has its distinct principles; for example, lullabies employ a slow, regular rhythm and a simple, repetitive melody (the instinctive urge to sing to babies aids language development, explaining the universal presence of lullabies across all cultures). The 1980s are often regarded as the last decade when many pop songs adhered to a loosely established formulaic structure: intro, verse, chorus, verse, chorus, bridge, verse, chorus and outro.

Listeners are drawn to relatable lyrics, whether as a source of joy, a refuge from distress, to address a contemporary societal issue or to explore the human condition. Crafting with eloquence a song that elicits powerful emotions (happiness, melancholia, inspiration, compassion, fear, indignation . . .) within the constraints of a three- to four-minute track takes great skill. It's akin to creating a super-material, where ordinary ingredients combine to form something stronger, more malleable and better than the sum of its parts. The second verse of Sly Fox's song *Let's Go All The Way*[1] demonstrates this holism by capturing in the lyrics the monotony and soul-sapping reality of production-line work, then alloying these words with a mechanical-sounding synth-pop beat that amplifies the intensity of both elements.

Arguably, the most compelling lyrics stem from songwriters who allow their strumming fingers to settle for long enough to take the pulse of contemporary life. These artists unapologetically mine and sieve not only through the documentation of their lives but also the collective bank of human experience. Their ability to distil and articulate thoughts and feelings goes beyond simply adding words to a tune; it can help to define a sense of personal identity. When wunderkind phenoms express themselves fluently in words and music about significant events, emotions and stories that have shaped their young lives, they find a natural affinity with a peer-group audience who can themselves feel besieged in their search for light from what they perceive as the menacing darkness in their lives,[2] seek rescue from inarticulacy (to share all that may be difficult to say),[3] require courage to express their true feelings or experience a sense of hopelessness and entrapment arising from poor circumstances.[4] One defining characteristic of pop music's appeal is the ease with which it can reach out and embrace its listeners with well-expressed, relatable emotions.

The Pasadenas' *Tribute (Right On)*[5] tells a simple, linear story. Storytelling has captivated humans since we first acquired the vocabulary and grammar necessary to communicate thoughts and feelings. Both music and stories allow the audience to peer into and experience the interior lives of others, facilitating social connectivity

1 *Let's Go All The Way* by Sly Fox. Written by Gary Cooper
2 *Steppin' Out* by Joe Jackson. Written by David Jackson
3 *Valentine* by T'Pau. Written by Carol Decker and Ronald Rogers
4 *Sanctify Yourself* by Simple Minds. Written by James Kerr, Charles Burchill and Michael MacNeil
5 *Tribute (Right On)* by The Pasadenas. Written by David Milliner, Aaron Brown, Andrew Banfield, Hamish Seelochan, Michael Milliner and William Wingfield

and helping to make sense of a complex world of thoughts and ideas. Allied with this innate desire to communicate is the ability to discern and find meaning in the words we hear. For decades, pop music fans have eagerly pored over lyrics to dissect, scrutinise and, in all likelihood, over-interpret the words of their favourite songs in pursuit of hidden depth, meaning or literary value. This analysis acquires an extra dimension when a songwriter uses allusion or deploys a freshly minted metaphor, an extended metaphor or a multi-layered metaphor to act as a lyrical lens. For example, when alerted to their presence, you may detect subtle heroin references shooting through the veins of *Golden Brown*;[1] this interpretation is only likely to become apparent after someone has injected that idea into your mind. (Were those peers who deemed this song worthy of an Ivor Novello award alert to this connection?) Similarly, the jaunty Bucks Fizz track *The Land Of Make Believe*[2] was said by co-writer Peter Sinfield to be virulently anti-Thatcher, with an air of menace created by ghostly shadows loitering in the garden. (The nastiest thing unseen lurking within many a suburban garden is sly fox poo.) It takes skill to slip into the elegant velvet glove of a song, an iron fist of a lyric.

The most effective way to deliver sound advice is plainly and explicitly, without deciphering. This book mainly uses literal interpretations, even in cases where this was not the intended aim of the lyricist. Some songwriters deliberately create duplicity and layers of meaning to be peeled back and discovered by the curious without this being essential to enjoy the song on a more superficial level. For example, when Phil Collins sang of the plight of a homeless woman who, despite her best efforts, is unable to walk because of blistered feet,[3] the listener may interpret this as either a literal medical reason for her inability to move on, or with the blisters acting as a metaphor

---

1   *Golden Brown* by The Stranglers. Written by Hugh Cornwell, Jean-Jacques Burnel, David Greenfield and Brian Duffy

2   *The Land Of Make Believe* by Bucks Fizz. Written by Andrew Hill and Peter Sinfield

3   *Another Day In Paradise* by Phil Collins. Written by Philip Collins

for the complex needs and conditions that commonly afflict homeless people, including drug or alcohol addiction, collapsed mental and physical health or the trauma of abuse. Similarly, Prince's *Little Red Corvette*[1] could be an innuendo-free song about an American car – a red Chevrolet Corvette – rather than a commentary about casual sex during a one-night stand. Hidden within the lines of a song,[2] the double entendre remains an effective and much-used device that allows songwriters to inject controversial themes while bypassing censorship.

Some literary devices are perfectly tailored for lyrics, while others, such as irony and sarcasm, are less well-suited. Black's song *Wonderful Life*[3] from 1987 displays an example of an ill-fitting literary device. Singer/Songwriter Black (Colin Vearncombe) was, at the end of 1985, in a dark and airless place in his failing life: he had survived a couple of car accidents, his mother was seriously ill, both his record company and his first wife had dropped him, he barely had enough money for food, and he was homeless. Life was far from wonderful. Vearncombe infused his words with sarcasm and his melody with melancholy when he wrote his song. Listeners, however, generally misconstrued his message and, in so doing, propelled it as an upbeat anthem to be an international top 10 hit. Given his straitened circumstances, Vearncombe could probably forgive his audience for misinterpreting his darker, intended message.

When lyrics such as Vearncombe's arise from intense personal experience, their heartfelt authenticity resonates well with audiences keen to hear performers reveal qualities such as vulnerability that transcend the ability to sing a song's words. However, even imagined scenarios can be powerfully persuasive if conveyed convincingly. Some performers have successfully created and maintained on-stage personas far from their off-stage identities. David Bowie's myriad on-stage personas exemplify this. Sometimes, fans project their

1   *Little Red Corvette* by Prince. Written by Prince Nelson
2   *The NeverEnding Story* by Limahl. Written by Giovanni Moroder and Keith Forsey
3   *Wonderful Life* by Black. Written by Colin Vearncombe

vision and ideals onto their idols; many Bruce Springsteen fans view him as a blue-collar icon, despite Springsteen never having lived or worked the Rust Belt life about which he so often sings.

As with life, what you take from a song depends on what you bring to it. When a lyric resonates with you emotionally or experientially, allowing you to imbue and attach personal meaning to the words, it can embed deeply into your mind, where it may reside for a lifetime. This phenomenon also applies to imagery – seeing an unearthed childhood photograph can instantly whisk you back to the moment of capture.[1] This highlights one of the limitations of music videos, as they impose a single visual interpretation of a song's narrative. For songwriters, creating a permeable and easily identifiable situation – such as a relationship breakdown – to which an audience can relate and return is essential in establishing a connection with the listener.[2]

In *Crazy Crazy Nights*,[3] rock band KISS expressed the need to release steam from life's pressures by proudly playing their brand of music, and playing it loud. A listener's ability to identify with, and to take personal ownership of, the emotional heft within a song as if it were written specifically for them helps explain the popularity of *Our Tune*, a daily mid-morning segment aired throughout the 1980s as part of DJ Simon Bates' Radio 1 show. Listeners submitted moving or sentimental stories – everything from a fleeting holiday romance to the tragedy of terminal illness – and the bassy-voiced Bates would broadcast their accounts (anonymised when necessary) over Nino Rota's classical love theme from Franco Zeffirelli's film *Romeo & Juliet*. After sharing (critics would say 'oversharing') a story, Bates would play the song that the letter writer felt was integral to their tale, often a popular tear-jerker such as *I'm Not In Love*[4] or *I Will Always Love You*.[5] For the millions who tuned in, *Our Tune* was a

1   *Marguerita Time* by Status Quo. Written by Bernard Frost and Francis Rossi
2   *Find My Love* by Fairground Attraction. Written by Mark Nevin
3   *Crazy Crazy Nights* by KISS. Written by Adam Mitchell and Stanley Eisen
4   *I'm Not In Love* by 10cc. Written by Eric Stewart and Graham Gouldman
5   *I Will Always Love You* by Dolly Parton. Written by Dolly Parton

shared distraction that allowed a connection with, and reflection on, a private, heartbreaking moment through words and music. For the letter writer, their chosen song was a way to capture and preserve a profound and personal moment from their life story – 'their' song, 'our' tune.[1] The ability to appropriate lyrical and emotional content and then project it onto one's own life represents an essential quality that a song needs to find a place within that busy life. Such songs, which operate along similar neurological pathways to the sense of smell, can lubricate the seized mechanisms of memory and unlock a gamut of powerful emotions anchored to a specific place and time buried deep within the recesses of the brain.

Songs have the power to create new mental states, allowing us to rewrite and reclaim the stories we tell ourselves about ourselves more positively, showing that our past and present circumstances do not make us prisoners of a predetermined future. The ability to change the trajectory of your narrative arc rests with you: *You're The Voice*[2] who decides how to narrate – or re-narrate (by choosing what to include or exclude) – your story based on the core facts of your life. By actively engaging in the cathartic editing of the stories and thoughts you tell yourself, you can alter how you think and feel. "Make not your thoughts your prisons" wrote Shakespeare in *Anthony and Cleopatra*. Throughout history, people have harnessed their voices to add texture and agency to their stories, helping to raise spirits, particularly during the frustration of forced separation from loved ones or through songs of lamentation when displaced from their homeland. When Britain dispatched its naval task force to reclaim the remote Falkland Islands from Argentine occupation in 1982, it did so amid a fervent chorus of patriotic songs sung from the docksides, creating a powerful narrative of victory on the media battleground.

Most music lovers recognise, appreciate and accept how music can subconsciously regulate mood (cheer you up, calm you down),

1   *Oh Yeah (On The Radio)* by Roxy Music. Written by Bryan Ferry
2   *You're The Voice* by John Farnham. Written by Anderson Qunta, Keith Reid, Marguerite Rider and Christopher Thompson

shape, modify and manipulate behaviour and convey personality traits, effectively moulding mindsets by priming your emotions.[1] Consider the background mood music played in shops designed to affect purchasing decisions subconsciously, or the music you would select (or, more tellingly, the physical albums/CDs you would hide – your musical guilty pleasures – to avoid adverse judgement) when trying to seduce an urbane sophisticate. The immediacy of musical messaging can signal a sudden shift in mood. While early silent films lacked a soundtrack and colour, they often featured live musical accompaniment to add aural complexion and drown out both the projector's incessant whir and the audience's incessant chatter (some things never change). The music set the emotional tone, helping the audience discern who was who (villain, hero, love interest) and guiding their reactions to the unfolding narrative (horror, comedy, romance). This magic melodic manipulation persists as an essential subliminal element in film-making, where the right score or song can conjure emotions and elevate a scene without the need for words; screechy, discordant violins may remind you of *Psycho*,[2] thanks to the power of Bernard Herrmann's score in Hitchcock's shocking shower scene. Similarly intense (and with a nod to Maurice Ravel) is the imminent threat of peril created by John Williams' simple yet ominous heart-pounding soundtrack to *Jaws*. There are good reasons why some within the film industry refer to the soundtrack as the 'emotion lotion'.

The ancient Greeks believed music could enhance athletic coordination, explaining why lyres were played during events such as the pentathlon. Today, athletes harness the uplifting power that high-tempo, upbeat music (about 120 beats per minute) and throbbing bass have on their heartbeat rates, helping them to enter the 'zone' of peak psychophysical performance. With less subtlety, boxers employ music not only to boost their confidence and alertness by absorbing

---

1   *Misfit* by Curiosity Killed The Cat. Written by Martin Volpeliere-Pierrot, Julian Brookhouse, Miguel Drummond, Nicholas Thorp and Tobias Andersen
2   *Somebody's Watching Me* by Rockwell. Written by Kennedy Gordy

the megawatt power and energy inherent in loud music,[1] but also to intimidate their opponent and land the first psychological punch before they enter the ring, displaying to their adversary that they are full of fight.[2] Boxers looking to *Hit That Perfect Beat*[3] choose powerful stadium rock anthems like *Eye Of The Tiger*[4] or *The Best*[5] for their ring walks.

If music sets the tone, the lyrics connect and communicate the emotional elements to build and propel the sound onward and upward. This fusion is more art than science. Songwriters rarely set out to give advice or be didactic, relying instead on statements, maxims, adages, truisms, homilies or proverbs rooted in wisdom and observation passed down through the generations to help convey their message. Most pop themes that involve life lessons stem from actions within the narrative – such as what can be learnt from a lost love – rather than being the song's *raison d'être*. Pop songs often tell stories that raise questions, much like how the Bible uses parables (simple stories that draw analogies) to illustrate moral points.

Despite its ephemeral nature, pop music retains its cultural significance, particularly for younger audiences who may feel alienated from more traditional 'adult' art forms or wider society. That's not to say that all music fans want to accept the invitation to contemplate lyrics, preferring instead the simple cocooning comfort of a musical blanket that feels familiar and predictable. This non-engagement can result in pop music akin to fast food: quick, cheap, unchallenging, momentarily enjoyable and satisfying at consumption but ultimately lacking sustenance. Ultra-processed pop gives rise to inane and clichéd lyrics. The 1980s witnessed a slew of high-selling, highly memorable and highly irritating novelty earworms that burrowed

1   *We'll Bring The House Down* by Slade. Written by Neville Holder and James Lea
2   *9 To 5* by Sheena Easton. Written by Florrie Palmer
3   *Hit That Perfect Beat* by Bronski Beat. Written by John Foster, Lawrence Cole and Steven Forrest
4   *Eye Of The Tiger* by Survivor. Written by Frank Sullivan III and James Peterik
5   *The Best* by Tina Turner. Written by Michael Chapman and Holly Erlanger

their way into public consciousness, such as *Agadoo*,[1] famously paro-died by Spitting Image in *The Chicken Song*[2] as a sound that is loud, grates and nauseates. While examining vapid, banal, facile, frothy, low-brow lyrics and themes can be momentarily entertaining, they lie diametrically opposed to the weighty, profound and enduring philosophy and advice that one would wish to integrate as one of the moving parts within a considered life.

For those unable to remember as far back as the ancient Greeks but who can recall Chapter I, some of the earliest lyrics were poems sung to accompany a lyre. Does this imply that modern pop song lyrics are a form of poetry? The poetic link continues to echo down the generations, particularly through the creations of some of the finest word-conscious songwriters – John Lennon, Paul McCartney, Bob Dylan, Leonard Cohen, Joni Mitchell, Lou Reed, Kate Bush and others, many of whom have had their lyrics published as collected works, where their words, even when left exposed and detached from their music, work well on paper[3] and certainly look and read in a way similar to poetry. For songwriters, the art lies in coupling their words with the more elusive elements of music.

In 2016, Bob Dylan won the Nobel Prize in literature, raising an eyebrow in the high-brow/low-brow debate that tends to elevate and inflate poetry and denigrate and deflate song lyrics. While songs and poems share common characteristics, they remain distinct crafts, each adhering to different rules and fulfilling different needs. Rhythm and rhyme may intertwine in a song to create an emotional musicality greater than the sum of its parts; poetry, on the other hand, emphasises intellectual richness, depth and complexity. In poetry, the words are the music, where the expression of feelings and ideas is given beauty and intensity through literary devices such as alliteration, onomatopoeia, imagery, rhyme and rhythm. A

1   *Agadoo* by Black Lace. Written by Mya Symille, Michael Delancray, Gilles Péram and Günther Behrie
2   *The Chicken Song* by Spitting Image. Written by Philip Pope, Robert Grant and Douglas Naylor
3   *Coming Around Again* by Carly Simon. Written by Carly Simon

song needs to be experienced as a complete package of its constituent parts, where the harmonious interplay of music and lyrics must deliver an immediate and comprehensible narrative, with each element embedded, entwined and enhancing the other. Songwriters create lyrics to be sung rather than read as disembodied words on a page. Lyrics can seem dry, unpalatable and difficult to digest without their accompanying music, much like eating cornflakes without milk.[1] Music adds a vital and distinct component to compensate for the lighter literary style of pop lyrics. The weight we assign to words within a rhyme enhances their impact, known as the 'rhyme-as-reason' effect: a pleasurably appealing and easily processed rhyming lyric (words that rhyme sound sublime) will be more memorable – and crucially perceived as more truthful, trustworthy and believable – than a non-rhyming one (so if you're seeking trust, rhyming's a must).

If you were an investor in culture from any decade over the last half-century, your return from popular music would far outperform that from the niche poetry market. When Tupac Shakur transformed his poetry into recitative rap, his message exerted more influence by reaching a much wider audience than it could have through words and thoughts jotted down on crumpled paper alone.[2] Broadly, the deep thought and analysis required to unlock poetry's intricate complexity can feel exclusive, even intimidating. In contrast, pop lyrics are inclusive, using easy-going words and melody that engage listeners more immediately.

It's time for a quick word association name game: who do you most closely associate with each of these popular poems?

If

I Wandered Lonely As A Cloud

Ode To A Nightingale

The Owl And The Pussycat

1 *The Rain* by Oran "Juice" Jones. Written by Vincent Bell
2 *The Living Years* by Mike + The Mechanics. Written by Brian Robertson and Michael Rutherford

The Raven

The authors are Rudyard Kipling, William Wordsworth, John Keats, Edward Lear and Edgar Allan Poe.

Now state the name you most closely associate with each of these popular songs released in the 1980s:

> *Tainted Love*
> *Red Red Wine*
> *Don't Leave Me This Way*
> *Girls Just Want To Have Fun*
> *Islands In The Stream*

The answers are Soft Cell (or Marc Almond), UB40, the Communards (Jimmy Somerville, Richard Coles or, for a bonus point, Sarah Jane Morris), Cyndi Lauper, and Kenny Rogers and Dolly Parton. Here's that same list with some different names:

> *Tainted Love*, Edward Cobb
> *Red Red Wine*, Neil Diamond
> *Don't Leave Me This Way*, Kenneth Gamble, Leon Huff and
>   Cary Gilbert
> *Girls Just Want To Have Fun*, Robert Hazard
> *Islands In The Stream*, Barry Gibb, Robin Gibb and Maurice
>   Gibb

In many people's minds, poems have a direct ownership link with the poets who created them. Songs, on the other hand, often spotlight the performers over the songwriters, who are frequently overlooked to the point of anonymity. The songwriters' names appear in the second version of the song list above. The Bee Gees maintained a connection with their prolific songwriting output by adding their distinctive backing vocals to many tracks they wrote and produced for other artists, such as that heard on Diana Ross's version of *Chain Reaction*.

Prosody – the musicality of patterns of rhythm and sound found in words in general and poetry in particular – enables listeners to sense the emotional state of the singer or speaker (such as being able to differentiate the quieter, slower, lower-pitched monotone sounds made by a sad, subdued voice from those made by cheerful, upbeat ones), even in an unfamiliar language. 'Prosody' has Greek origins, describing a song with an instrumental accompaniment (from *pros* meaning 'in addition to' and *oide* meaning 'song'). *Oide* is the source of 'ode', as in *Ode To A Nightingale* by Keats, a poem intended to be sung rather than read.

The ancient Greeks celebrated the deeds of heroes and gods with a song of praise – a *húmnos* – a word that arrived and lodged itself into sixteenth-century English as 'hymn' with the narrower meaning of a song in praise of God. Several poems have successfully transitioned into familiar hymns or songs, including *Auld Lang Syne* by Robert Burns, *Jerusalem* by William Blake and Christina Rossetti's poem *In The Bleak Midwinter*, which became a Christmas carol.

I Want To Break Free.[1] Occasionally, instead of lines of poems becoming songs or hymns, the reverse happens, and a lyrical line manages to break free from its melodic moorings to become a standalone expression (often reproduced as a T-shirt slogan or fridge magnet) and a part of everyday speech. From the top 10 of the 1980s, *Another Brick In The Wall*[2] and *Don't Worry, Be Happy*[3] are but two examples.

The camaraderie, invigoration and often hypnotic melding felt with synchronous singing of poems-cum-songs, whether in primary schools, on football terraces, on battlegrounds, in the choirs of churches and cathedrals or on the chilly streets at Christmas, is remarkably stirring, unifying and hormonally mood-enhancing. Singing – making music from within – can help you find your voice.

---

1 *I Want To Break Free* by Queen. Written by John Deacon
2 *Another Brick In The Wall (Part II)* by Pink Floyd. Written by George Waters
3 *Don't Worry, Be Happy* by Bobby McFerrin. Written by Robert McFerrin Jr

CHAPTER III

Themes

IN *The Sun And The Rain*,[1] Madness didn't doubt that the theme of their song was what life was about. Song themes endure because they reflect fundamental aspects of listeners' lives, becoming absorbed into the very fibres and fabric of collective experience as events and milestones relevant across generations: a baby born today will grow and change as it develops language, gains and loses friends, becomes educated and acquires knowledge, marvels at the world, carves out an identity, dreams, becomes a teenager, bends the truth, accepts or rejects religion, feels lonely, feels elated, has relationships (possibly marries, possibly divorces), makes mistakes, endures misfortune, worries, develops self-reliant, works, loses loved ones, ages and dies. These universal themes and events shape life, some more profoundly than others. Every society, past and present, has cultivated forms of music, words and religion to help channel these timeless themes. The inputs of life become the output of songs.

Love and relationships remains the dominant theme in pop songs and most other art forms. Songwriters explore the various facets and subsets of this theme, including courtship, declarations of love, romance, devotion, unrequited love, infatuation, rejection, fidelity, infidelity and heartbreak – in other words, all the staple ingredients in the often intense and emotionally charged times of a young (and not so young) life. During the 1980s, sentimental torch songs shone particularly brightly, a phenomenon common during darker socioeconomic times.

1   *The Sun And The Rain* by Madness. Written by Michael Barson

Other themes that helped paint a picture of life in the 1980s include (in no particular order) dancing ('grooving'), partying and nightlife, loneliness, dreams, praying (wishful thinking rather than religious obligation), drugs and alcohol (and addiction to both), protest (anti-Thatcher, anti-apartheid, anti-war, anti-patriarchy), social consciousness, film soundtracks and the annual festive cash-in from a sack load of songs from Christmases past. These recurring and relatable themes hold broad appeal as listeners can relate to and empathise with the issues; they remain susceptible to having their emotional strings[1] plucked by a tune. This broad appeal drives record sales when it reflects a lot of what life has to offer.[2]

Each generation emerging onto the cultural scene believes its ideas are new. This would amuse ancient civilisations who feasted on mythological tales, believing that all stories can fit into only seven archetypal categories (overcoming adversity; rags to riches; the quest; voyage and return; comedy; tragedy; and rebirth). Themes recycle and ideas circulate. However, what distinguishes each generation is the unique context of that time and its evolving attitudes. One example marked the end of the tenure of Legs & Co, an all-female, scantily clad and highly sexualised in-house dance troupe that performed regularly on *Top of the Pops*. At the dawn of the decade, their presence was considered acceptable for early evening – pre-watershed – television on BBC1. However, by the mid-1980s, artists like the Eurythmics (in conjunction with Aretha Franklin) were, on the same show, singing songs that celebrated female liberation.[3]

Despite the common stereotype surrounding status and visible wealth in the 1980s, this theme was less prevalent in songs than might be expected. However, it did emerge with greater prominence with the rise of the gangsta rap hip-hop movement with its raw portrayal of testosterone-steeped braggadocio in videos often featuring highly

1   *Victims* by Culture Club. Written by Roy Hay, George O'Dowd, Michael Craig and Jonathan Moss
2   *Master And Servant* by Depeche Mode. Written by Martin Gore
3   *Sisters Are Doin' It For Themselves* by Eurythmics and Aretha Franklin. Written by Ann Lennox and David Stewart

sexualised, scantily clad women. Without the wider exposure from music video, hip-hop depictions of status, wealth and objectified women might have remained confined to the neighbourhoods that initially spawned them.

Kim Wilde's song *You Came*[1] captures the change and exhilaration inherent in a new relationship, infusing the protagonist with newfound inspiration. While love and relationships inspire many songwriters to reflect inwardly, a select few looked outwards for inspiration or to promote causes about which they were passionate. Among the more unconventional themes featuring in the top 10 during the 1980s were alien life, the bombing of Hiroshima (alongside artwork created by survivors), sericulture (silkworm farming), the twelfth-century Middle-Eastern poem *Layla and Majnun* by Nizami, colonisation, *Kubla Khan*, Aboriginal reparation, the Highland Clearances, religious repression, Joan of Arc, informing for the FBI, Armageddon, racism, groupies, the Orinoco River, 1984 (Orwell's dystopian novel), *Don Quixote*, a spectral US marine, traffic congestion, rough sleeping and *Frankenstein*. The array of ideas that spark songs into life is virtually limitless. However, since the 1980s, the proliferation of other platforms (primarily online) for self-expression and activism has altered the role of pop music, leading to a narrower range of inward-focused themes. Nonetheless, the essential ingredients for a successful song remain consistent: a compelling and coherent story told using old words in a fresh, new and relatable way.

Songwriters are not restricted to a single subject or theme. Laurie Anderson's *O Superman*[2] is a cocktail of unusual themes inspired by (among others) Jules Massenet's 1885 opera *Le Cid*, telephone answering machines, a US Post Office motto (itself translated from the writing of ancient Greek historian Herodotus), and the Tao-te-Ching (The Book Of The Way), a foundational Taoist text. Anderson packed and rolled all these eclectic themes into an unsettling,

1   *You Came* by Kim Wilde. Written by Kim Smith and Richard Smith
2   *O Superman* by Laurie Anderson. Written by Laura Anderson

dream-like single (albeit unusually long) that reached number 2 on the UK charts in 1981.

As with *Golden Brown*[1] discussed in Chapter II, the themes in *O Superman* may not be immediately apparent. A song's genre, subgenre or microgenre may be equally obscure but is secondary to the central theme. *O Superman* is, unsurprisingly, tricky to categorise as it flies defiantly across the genre boundaries of electronic, post-modern, new wave and experimental music. And possibly many others. The 1980s witnessed a remarkable pace of musical experimentation and innovation, showcasing a diverse and vibrant array of styles – from ABBA to ZZ Top and Sinitta to Sinatra – that shone through the lingering, nebulous murk of the post-punk era. Among some of the many musical genres from the 1980s are disco, Hi-NRG, reggae, ska, country, synth-pop, rap, new wave, Brit funk, new romantic, house, acid house, sophisti-pop, new age and gangsta rap. And all without mention of 'rock'. This creative smorgasbord, where new fusions blurred the previously sharp borders of genre boxes, added interest and variety to the weekly chart across much of the decade, fostering some unlikely collaborations, such as Freddie Mercury's duet with opera singer Montserrat Caballé on *Barcelona*[2] and the fusion of hip-hop group Run DMC with rock band Aerosmith on *Walk This Way*.[3]

Following the success of Band Aid, the charity single emerged as another distinct category. Charity songs aimed to raise money to alleviate the effects of specific disasters, such as the Bradford City stadium fire, the sinking of the Herald of Free Enterprise and the Hillsborough Stadium tragedy, as well as supporting organisations addressing ongoing issues and broader causes and concerns, such as Comic Relief, Sport Aid, Childline and the Help a London

1   *Golden Brown* by The Stranglers. Written by Hugh Cornwell, Jean-Jacques Burnel, David Greenfield and Brian Duffy
2   *Barcelona* by Freddie Mercury and Montserrat Caballé. Written by Freddie Mercury and Michael Moran
3   *Walk This Way* by Run DMC and Aerosmith. Written by Anthony Perry and Steven Tallarico

Child Appeal. While the songs were not written to tackle directly the specific trials and challenges posed by the causes they championed, they served to remind listeners of the fragility and transience of human existence and the potential for positive change through collective action, even when that action involved little more than buying a record. This spirit of philanthropy challenges the stale cliché that this decade of individualism was uncaring and devoid of empathy or unpricked consciousness. Cynics might contend that compassion, like many facets of the 1980s, underwent its own form of privatisation and that the drive to create and sell charity records was an easy way for both the music industry and the public to assuage feelings of guilt linked to their extravagant lifestyles while sidestepping the underlying structural issues that contributed to creating the problem.

Occasionally, a pithy song title can effectively convey both the overarching theme and the specific advice, as seen in titles such as *You Can't Hurry Love*,[1] *Work That Body*,[2] *Self Control*,[3] *Don't Give Up*,[4] or *Just Say No*.[5] These titles deliver their message without the need to play the track itself. In the case of *Just Say No*, this is a bonus.

1   *You Can't Hurry Love* by Phil Collins. Written by Brian Holland, Lamont Dozier and Edward Holland
2   *Work That Body* by Diana Ross. Written by Diana Ross, Paul Jabara and Ray Chew
3   *Self Control* by Laura Branigan. Written by Stephen Piccolo, Giancarlo Bigazzi and Raffaele Riefoli
4   *Don't Give Up* by Peter Gabriel and Kate Bush. Written by Peter Gabriel
5   *Just Say No* by Grange Hill Cast. Written by Al Gorgoni and George McMahon

CHAPTER IV

Top 10

W HY limit the exploration of themes to just the top 10 songs on the UK singles chart? The aim is to examine themes that tap into the collective consciousness via the mass appeal of mainstream music. While the top 10 ruthlessly reflects the 'pop' in 'pop music', popularity is not synonymous with simplicity or shallowness. However, confining the selection to the top 10 singles does not guarantee the winnowing away of all the chaff to leave only the finest grains of music or sound advice. Some entirely forgettable hits made the top 10, while other tracks deserving of acclaim languished in obscurity, barely leaving a mark on the top 100. What the top 10 does ensure is that the musical message successfully connects with and entertains the minds of a large audience, thereby serving as a kind of natural selection that preserves advantageous ideas and emotions, allowing them to endure across generations. Their popularity also makes top 10 hits easily accessible.

For a song to ascend the chart rungs and reach the top 10, it must be a commercial sales success; the purchasers serve as the ultimate arbiters. In the introduction to *So Emotional*,[1] Whitney Houston admits liking what she likes without knowing why. Some songs, like some aspects of life, defy deconstruction and analysis – you just enjoy them for what they are. While marketing efforts can boost sales, the top 10 serves as an objective measure of sales success (albeit from a skewed demographic) rather than subjective critical acclaim.

1   *So Emotional* by Whitney Houston. Written by William Steinberg and Thomas Kelly

For instance, Bob Dylan, bestowed with high praise for his lyrical content, saw his three UK single releases in the 1980s peak at 90, 96 and 98, respectively, demonstrating that even legendary talent does not always translate into sales success, something about which Mr Dylan was probably not so emotional.

The chart compilation process underwent significant change during the 1980s. With the advent of new-fangled computer terminals, compilers could gather sales data electronically, expanding the number of retail outlets permitted to register their sales to approximately 500 (previously, it was not uncommon for record companies to dispatch individuals to buy records from retailers known to feed sales figures to the chart compilers). Stricter rules also banned manipulative marketing tactics, such as giving away merchandise at the point of sale. These improvements made the UK charts the fastest and most accurate in the world. While the UK top 10 singles chart has never pretended to be a definitive barometer of musical merit, the profits generated by popular songs helped sustain the entire pop music industry, including those talented and critically acclaimed artists who were unlikely to trouble the top 10 with mainstream, commercially successful hits.

Today, the ubiquitous smartphone permits instant access to an extensive song catalogue. However, despite this convenience, something intangible has been lost. In the 1980s, buying 'physical' music was an anticipatory, elaborate experience requiring planning, effort and a trip to visit a high-street bricks-and-mortar shop to browse the racks (adding a slight urban bias – alongside the youthful one – to the charts). This investment of time, effort and money bestowed the charts with great significance among its adolescent followers. Consequently, the weekly chart show became essential appointment listening for many, with the anticipation of the ups and downs on the chart merry-go-round[1] becoming almost an obsession for some and a personal validation that their musical taste was in tune with their peers. In the grappling quest for confidence in identity and the

1   *All Night Long (All Night)* by Lionel Richie. Written by Lionel Richie

desperate desire for peer acceptance, finding allegiance among other like-minded souls and being seen as relevant – knowing that you belong[1] – fostered a priceless sense of connection and communion with other kindred spirits.

Timing a song's release goes a long way to achieving top-10 success. One of the best examples of capturing the zeitgeist during the 1980s was the poignant social commentary and haunting melody of *Ghost Town*[2] by The Specials. Released in 1981 amid the discontent that had ignited riots on the streets of inner-city Britain, the song's sparse lyrics foretold in an eerily prescient way about a sense of dislocation and social disquiet stemming from high unemployment and a government seemingly prepared to brush aside the nation's youth, all of which culminated in an outpouring of public anger. However, *Ghost Town* did not directly reflect the events of 1981 because it was written a year earlier, inspired by a different but parallel set of circumstances, including widespread civil unrest and rioting. In the 1980s, the lengthy process of conceiving, writing, refining, recording and releasing a song made it difficult to ride a short-lived trend or land a hit on a moving target. However, success becomes almost inevitable when a great song aligns with a perfectly timed release – such as that which propelled *Ghost Town* into a strong social tailwind.

1   *Feel So Real* by Steve Arrington. Written by Steven Arrington and India Arrington
2   *Ghost Town* by The Specials. Written by Jeremy Dammers

CHAPTER V

The lyrical advice

I N the words of Odyssey[1] (the disco group, not the Homeric poem), it's time to recharge your soul. Just as a well-crafted album features a thoughtful selection of songs, the self-selecting thematic advice presented here exhibits common threads. As with any advice, it may be familiar or fresh, serious or playful, inspiring or eye-rolling, take it or leave it.

The themes are arranged alphabetically within broad category headings rather than specific topics, so it's 'alcohol' rather than 'wine'. Naturally, many themes will overlap and interlink, such as alcohol and regret.

In *Papa Don't Preach,*[2] the protagonist pleads for good advice, while the egotist in *I'm A Wonderful Thing, Baby*[3] suggests starting with the A's. Following this sound alphabetical advice provides the perfect launchpad, complemented by Freddie Mercury's call in *Barcelona* to let the songs and music begin.[4] To move your life to its next stage, it's time to turn the page.[5]

1   *Going Back To My Roots* by Odyssey. Written by Lamont Dozier
2   *Papa Don't Preach* by Madonna. Written by Brian Elliot and Madonna Ciccone
3   *I'm A Wonderful Thing, Baby* by Kid Creole and The Coconuts. Written by Thomas Browder and Peter Schott
4   *Barcelona* by Freddie Mercury and Montserrat Caballé. Written by Freddie Mercury and Michael Moran
5   *Nobody's Diary* by Yazoo. Written by Genevieve Moyet

ADVICE

You should always make room for sound advice, regardless of who you are or what you do. Those actively seeking or open and receptive to guidance are much more likely to benefit from shared experiences and knowledge than those passively bombarded with well-intentioned but unsolicited advice (as regularly encountered by pregnant women).

Song lyrics often provide contradictory advice. In *Billie Jean*,[1] Michael Jackson's relationship advice is always to think twice, whereas Ottawan[2] suggest never doing so. Elsewhere, some lyrics urge you to live for now, while others advise you to make plans.

Swing Out Sister lamented having their heads filled with others' opinions.[3] Some mistake the opportunity to offer sound advice for a chance to promote their opinions – which often border on the tedious, self-righteous or disrespectful – to their captive audience. These individuals perceive themselves as serial problem solvers, convinced that their crude or simplistic binary worldview (usually devoid of nuance) is correct; they seem equally eager to exert control and pass judgement, often motivated more by ego than a genuine desire to help or support others. If you receive advice that leaves you feeling unheard, defensive or demotivated, seek a fresh perspective from a trusted, supportive person with whom you have a good rapport and who has your best interests at heart. Unsurprisingly, individuals with high emotional intelligent are rare, so cherish them.

Other advice suggests you find a recreation[4] or passion and pursue it with dedication and devotion.[5] Sisters Mel and Kim's advice was to look after number one[6] – a sentiment reflecting the

1 *Billie Jean* by Michael Jackson. Written by Michael Jackson
2 *Hands Up (Give Me Your Heart)* by Ottawan. Written by Daniel Bangalter and Jean Kluger
3 *Surrender* by Swing Out Sister. Written by Andrew Connell, Corinne Drewery and Martin Jackson
4 *London Nights* by London Boys. Written by Ralf-René Maué
5 *Walk Of Life* by Dire Straits. Written by Mark Knopfler
6 *That's The Way It Is* by Mel and Kim. Written by Michael Stock, Matthew Aitken and Peter Waterman

decade's leanings towards individualism. Similarly, in *The Edge Of Heaven*,[1] Wham! suggest the only things that matter are your own needs. Selfishly looking after *Numero Uno*[2] differs from self-care, which involves establishing behaviours to protect and enhance your well-being and happiness.

Sound advice? In *The Rain*,[3] the narrator can offer nothing more than advice to his girlfriend, while A-ha seek insights that could be helpful.[4] Thanks to alphabetical fortuitousness, advice is the first theme explored, which is significant because of the inherent danger that someone might heed your advice and even share it with others. Advice to think twice (especially before giving away your heart),[5] find a recreation, be dedicated and devoted, and remember that the more you give to life, the more you will get from it,[6] are all sound.

When receiving advice, it's essential to evaluate both the guidance and any motives driving it, especially when monetised professionally for a fee. Salubrious advice – notably quick fixes dished up online over the latest saintly, exotic and often expensive superfood – is particularly predisposed to unpalatable myth, fallacious fad and marketing hype, usually based on the limited experience of those promoting it rather than objective scientific evidence. With this in mind, consider the following advice universal: if it sounds too good to be true,[7] it probably isn't true. Solid nutritional advice remains simple but effective: eat less; diversify your diet with high-quality, locally sourced seasonal whole food grown and produced in environmentally sustainable ways; eat more fibre; stay hydrated; consume alcohol in moderation; cut out (or cut down to no more than a pinch of) salt and refined sugar; and avoid or minimise highly or

1 *The Edge Of Heaven* by Wham! Written by George Michael
2 *Numero Uno* by Starlight. Written by Valerio Semplici, Mirko Limoni and Daniele Davoli
3 *The Rain* by Oran "Juice" Jones. Written by Vincent Bell
4 *I've Been Losing You* by A-ha. Written by Pål Waaktaar Gamst
5 *Faith* by George Michael. Written by George Michael
6 *Start!* by The Jam. Written by John Weller
7 *Can't Take My Eyes Off You* by Boys Town Gang. Written by Robert Crewe Jr and Robert Gaudio

ultra-processed foods (which often contain a cocktail of chemicals among their multiple ingredients).

Should it fall on your shoulders to deliver well-intentioned, help-ful and necessary advice that the recipient may not want to hear,[1] think carefully about your delivery (and rehearse it mentally) to avoid causing offence. Focus on addressing the problem, not criticising the individual. One effective strategy to deal with someone who may not want to hear what you say[2] is to begin with a positive point, gently back up all you say with evidence and examples, and then offer constructive, easy-to-follow steps toward a solution. Consider an activity-based approach, such as a walk-and-talk, to minimise face-to-face confrontation (especially among men who may need to offload their frustration). The more open-minded the recipient, the easier it is to deliver valuable but hard-to-hear advice.

What should you do if your sound advice meets a closed mind, goes unheeded[3] or falls on deaf ears?[4] People disregard advice for various reasons, often centred on the relationship (the trust, respect and rapport) that exists between adviser and advisee. In a perfect world, life is too valuable and short to play mind games,[5] but play a part they often do, particularly when there is a lack of respect for the adviser or when the unsolicited advice is preachy or condescending. In extreme cases, the strain on the elasticity of the relationship may stretch beyond the point of return.

In other cases, an advisee may actively seek advice (as when a child asks a parent) but then choose to ignore that advice or adopt an opposing viewpoint in a defiant display of independence – often to show the adviser who is in control. An advisee may also deny their need for change, may fear (or be mentally unprepared for) the

1   *Good Thing* by Fine Young Cannibals. Written by Roland Gift and David Steele
2   *An Innocent Man* by Billy Joel. Written by William Joel
3   *(Keep Feeling) Fascination* by The Human League. Written by John Callis and Philip Oakey
4   *Someone's Looking At You* by The Boomtown Rats. Written by Robert Geldof
5   *Perfect* by Fairground Attraction. Written by Mark Nevin

potential flow of success that good advice could unleash, or they may prefer to arrive at a solution they consider their own. Others delay acting on what they know deep down is sound advice until they reach a breaking point, by which time it may be too late to have any beneficial effect. Finally, even the soundest advice may fall short if the advisee needs to tackle deeper, long-term underlying issues rather than looking for a short-term or one-off solution to a specific symptom. When called on for advice, aim to provide both actionable one-off advice and the mental tools and techniques to help the advisee meet future challenges.

Using top 10 songs as a source of advice offers multiple, easily digestible perspectives. By creating a playlist tailored to your needs, the advice can simultaneously look you in the eye and whisper directly into your ear. The more bespoke the advice, the more applicable and persuasive it becomes. Most people need different guidance across the various phases and the changing circumstances of their life. A fortunate few may find a single song – even a single snippet – perfectly encapsulates a personal motto or message, containing all the advice or motivation they need. These one-hit wonders act as a catalyst, prompt, fillip or aide-memoire that can be carried around and used to maintain motivation or remind the listener to change the way they think, feel and live, or help them to stay on track after they have made changes until those changes become habitual. Most people will, however, require a whole compilation album of supportive and interconnected themes. Songs resonate with different people with different needs.[1] Although easy answers to complex questions remain as elusive as ever, music can serve as a valuable, engaging tool to help build good rhythms and habits and a way to maintain control over how you think and feel.

They Don't Know.[2] Incomplete knowledge or a lack of an overview of the back story (not divulging or disclosing information helps the advisee protect their privacy and avoid unwelcome incursions that

1   *People Are People* by Depeche Mode. Written by Martin Gore
2   *They Don't Know* by Tracey Ullman. Written by Kirsty MacColl

breach personal boundaries) means that you may be forced to give advice that, albeit grounded in truth, is simplified or generalised. Your advice may help form a part of the solution without being the whole solution. For instance, advising an alcoholic to quit drinking, a gambler to stop betting or the anxious to cease worrying is all sound advice, but it overlooks a deeper exploration of the options, a breakdown of the specific practical 'how-to' steps or the benefits of taking such action. To avoid the shortcomings of generalised advice, ask compassionate, open, non-judgemental and clarifying questions, then listen actively and without judgement. If appropriate, share your experiences and then grant the advisee the time and space to imagine themselves in the same or a similar situation, allowing them to mentally explore the options available and the benefits that a change in their behaviour could elicit.

Zeno of Citium, the founder of the Stoic school in Athens, noted that we have two ears and one mouth, reminding us of the ratio with which we should use them. Often, those in need want two open ears of empathy offering listening support rather than one busy tongue telling them right from wrong.[1] Good listeners create a safe space for others to share their stories (or offload their frustrations) without feeling obliged to fix everything with an immediate solution. Try to engage in gentle, healing conversations. When asked for direct, actionable advice, remember that the easiest option (advising people to do what they want to do) may not always be the best option. When you offer relevant and appropriate information alongside some gentle guidance and advice, you empower others to make the right decisions for themselves.

AGEING

In Greek mythology, Eos, the goddess of the dawn, fell for and whisked off handsome Tithonus. Eos asked Zeus to bestow immor-

1   *Goody Two Shoes* by Adam Ant. Written by Stuart Goddard and Marco Pirroni

tality on mortal Tithonus but forgot to ask for eternal youth and vigour. Tithonus' endless life became unbearable. Fame may allow you to live for ever,[1] but to avoid a fate similar to Tithonus, you'll need to know how to age well.

Skipping forward to Shakespeare's time, tinker Christopher Sly observed in *The Taming Of The Shrew* that, as time slips by, "we shall ne'er be younger". Indeed, you do not get younger[2] and will never be younger than you are today,[3] which is one compelling reason to make every day deliver.[4] Although ageing is a normal, natural and inevitable part of life's progression, it is not a theme on which young, image-conscious pop stars dwell. Ageing is a subtle process that slowly sneaks up upon you, barely noticed at first, starting as early as puberty.

You will know that the years are beginning to show[5] when, now and again, bits of your body start to fall apart.[6] The traditionally dispiriting drawbacks of ageing include creaky weak knees,[7] hair that loses both its colour (*Fade To Grey*)[8] and its foothold[9] (although regularly reappearing in unexpected places), myopia (where the closer things are the better they look),[10] diminished balance and hearing (falls on deaf ears),[11] expanding waistlines that you cannot let go,[12]

1   *Fame* by Irene Cara. Written by Dean Pitchford and Michael Gore
2   *The Tunnel Of Love* by Fun Boy Three. Written by Terence Hall, Neville Staple and Lynval Golding
3   *Help!* by Bananarama and Lananeeneenoonoo. Written by John Lennon and Paul McCartney
4   *A Night To Remember* by Shalamar. Written by Charmaine Sylvers, Dana Meyers and Nidra Beard
5   *Don't Know Much* by Linda Ronstadt featuring Aaron Neville. Written by Barry Imberman, Cynthia Weil and Thomas Snow
6   *Total Eclipse Of The Heart* by Bonnie Tyler. Written by James Steinman
7   *Love Train* by Holly Johnson. Written by William Johnson
8   *Fade To Grey* by Visage. Written by William Currie, Christopher Payne and James Ure
9   *Ashes To Ashes* by David Bowie. Written by David Jones
10 *I Get The Sweetest Feeling* by Jackie Wilson. Written by Alicia Evelyn and Van McCoy
11 *Out In The Fields* by Gary Moore and Phil Lynott. Written by Gary Moore
12 *Hard To Say I'm Sorry* by Chicago. Written by David Foster and Peter Cetera

an unreliable memory (forgetting what you came here for)[1] and an inelastic bladder (*Wee Rule*).[2] None makes for an appealing song theme. Naturally, you should love your body as it grows older[3] and focus on the compensatory upsides, such as feeling confident, wiser and comfortable within your slightly looser-fitting skin, using this bonus storage space for your expanded vocabulary.

As you age, life's cellular collateral damage, like drops of water slowly filling a bath, begins to accumulate before manifesting as, for instance, lines in the mirror.[4] Songs referencing lines and mirrors may allude to cocaine usage, a drug that reduces the opportunity for ageing via its ability to hasten mortality. All drugs, including alcohol, accelerate rates of cellular ageing. In a tragically perverse way, lifestyle choices that result in an early grave help to keep pop stars forever young.

Iron Maiden gave the fatalism of senescence a brutally prophetic edge with their biblically inspired thought that, from the moment you're born, you begin to die.[5] However, this bleak prognosis overlooks the body's remarkable capacity for cellular regeneration (even neurogenesis) through activities such as exercise. Despite our relatively modest size among mammals, humans exhibit inexplicable longevity.

Sound advice? The relative youthfulness of most lyricists and performers skews the song themes towards subjects directly in line with their 20/20 vision; the young see ageing as distant and hazy.

When it comes to *Holding Back The Years*,[6] try the holistic approach that combines practical self-care advice for vitality, graceful ageing and a longer, healthier life: eat a natural plant-based Mediterranean-style diet rich in a variety of fruits, vegetables, nuts, seeds,

1   *Nobody's Diary* by Yazoo. Written by Genevieve Moyet
2   *Wee Rule* by Wee Papa Girl Rappers. Written by Charles Cochrane, Hamish MacDonald, Samantha Lawrence and Sandra Lawrence
3   *Welcome To The Pleasuredome* by Frankie Goes To Hollywood. Written by Peter Gill, William Johnson, Mark O'Toole and Brian Nash
4   *Bedsitter* by Soft Cell. Written by David Ball and Peter Almond
5   *The Clairvoyant* by Iron Maiden. Written by Stephen Harris
6   *Holding Back The Years* by Simply Red. Written by Michael Hucknall

berries, wholegrains, beans, pulses and extra virgin olive oil; consume microbe-rich fermented foods such as 'live' yoghurt, kombucha, kimchi and kefir; engage in regular physical activity to stay mobile and help maintain muscle mass, bone health and maintain a healthy weight point; moderate your alcohol intake; never smoke (even if it's your only vice);[1] sleep well; manage stress (fewer responsibilities and obligations with age naturally help achieve this); find and cultivate purpose, passion and a reason to go on[2] (these are likely to evolve with age); maintain cognitive stimulation; seek and embrace novelty, variety and curiosity (engage with the Arts); cultivate social engagement and a sense of belonging (older people can devote more time to building and deepening social connections); read avidly; feel gratitude; laugh; start a pension; and kick that crippling dependency on illicit drugs. These recommendations may seem at odds with the perceived image of fast-paced pop stardom. Why bother saving for a pension when you have repeatable and reasonably predictable royalties rolling in? (For those without the luxury of annual royalties from a Christmas hit – the ultimate gift that keeps giving – you receive tax relief on your pension contributions.) The sounds may still be alive,[3] but, sadly, too few stars who lived through the 80s get to live through their 80s.

A dissolving memory is one of the most distressing and cruellest aspects of ageing, often accompanied by the fear, agitation and frustration of becoming a stranger in your own life. Memory and lived experience are as central to identity and personality in older age as is the discovery of that identity in the young. Hearing the sound of a distant song[4] from your formative years for the first time

1   *Lay All Your Love On Me* by ABBA. Written by Göran Andersson and Björn Ulvaeus

2   *Since Yesterday* by Strawberry Switchblade. Written by Jill Bryson and Rose McDowall

3   *Tribute (Right On)* by The Pasadenas. Written by David Milliner, Aaron Brown, Andrew Banfield, Hamish Seelochan, Michael Milliner and William Wingfield

4   *Fade To Grey* by Visage. Written by William Currie, Christopher Payne and James Ure

in decades can trigger a Proustian or Pavlovian response that may ring a sentimental bell within your memory.[1] Music can disinter and stimulate long-buried tubers of deep, dormant memory and emotion, allowing vivid blooms of recall infused with the sweet scent of familiarity to flower once again. One of the top notes of this nostalgic aroma serves as a reminder of youthful dreams, as such thoughts seem to attach to and linger around the songs, the recall of which, having seeped and absorbed their way into the core of your mind, can remain word-perfect despite the absence of any conscious effort to memorise them. The ability to reawaken, recollect and reconnect with these deeply imprinted musical moments from the time of their planting can unlock and rekindle other positive life-affirming memories tied to that time and that somehow defy the leakage of forgetfulness, even in those who suffer from the degeneration of archived memories or other cognitive decline. Clearing away the accumulated grime from the grooves etched into musical memory so that those memories are free to live once more[2] can help bolster and brighten a gradually fading identity, allowing people to connect with themselves and communicate with the wider world through their love of music. All this potential is possible because musical memories may be discrete and deeper than other memory circuits. Some memory pathways overlap and connect with the olfactory cortex – the brain region that processes signals from smell receptors – making your sense of smell a powerful trigger for memory recall. Exploring musical memory is a simple (often not even requiring language in cases where speech is problematic), cheap, accessible and non-pharmacological intervention that can help loosen the grip of neurodegenerative conditions and unlock and allow positive experiences to resurface without unintended consequences or the usual long list of unpleasant side effects.[3]

Aerobic exercise, such as dancing, helps maintain or increase

1 *A Kind Of Magic* by Queen. Written by Roger Taylor
2 *Memory* by Elaine Paige. Written by Andrew Lloyd Webber and Trevor Nunn
3 *Alphabet St.* by Prince. Written by Prince Nelson

the volume of your hippocampus, a small structure nestled within the brain that's involved in memory conversion. Exercise may help enhance and strengthen memory and ward off the demons of dementia (a word that's a sentence). Additionally, exercise, the benefits and importance of which increase with age, improves sleep quality, which plays a crucial role in memory consolidation.

Why don't you remember?[1] Not all memories are destined to last. The ability to forget – especially to relinquish painful memories – is a healthy sign of evolved human ageing. The young undergo synaptic pruning of the neural pathways they no longer need, and post-partum mothers regularly forget the intense pain and discomfort of childbirth. The flipside of pruning is tuning, a process whereby you can strengthen neural connectivity.

Growing old happens to everyone all the time.[2] While you cannot stop ageing, you can influence and manage some of the biological processes underpinning it. Never let others underestimate you or use your age solely to define who you are.

Ageing is neither a battle against the accumulation of biological and societal problems nor a disease against which you constantly fight but never win. Learning to embrace ageing positively with appropriate thinking, language and changes to your lifestyle[3] will help to ensure that your chronological age (measured by the number of birthday cake candles) is always higher than your biological age (how well your body functions relative to your chronological age). Ageing is living; your aim is to adopt healthy lifestyle habits that decelerate the ageing process by reducing the accumulation of cellular, linguistic and societal toxins.

Bonnie Tyler's concern in *Total Eclipse Of The Heart*[4] is that her prime years are behind her. She needn't worry as research suggests

1 *I Feel Love* by Bronski Beat with Marc Almond. Written by Giovanni Moroder, Peter Bellotte and LaDonna Gaines
2 *Waiting For A Train* by Flash And The Pan. Written by Johannes van den Berg and George Young
3 *I Beg Your Pardon* by Kon Kan. Written by Barry Harris and Joseph Souter
4 *Total Eclipse Of The Heart* by Bonnie Tyler. Written by James Steinman

that, for many, happiness, satisfaction and fulfilment increase during the riper, golden years from the second half of life: as you draw upon your knowledge, experience and perspective to master life's themes in a calmer, more centred way, your life gets better.[1] When the alternatives to an improved quality of life via healthy ageing are as unpalatable as ageing badly, physical incapacitation or dying young, you need to use the wisdom that age bestows upon you to look at how to improve and optimise the ageing process. External advances, such as personalised diets (uniquely tuned for your microbiome, metabolism and age) and medication (including personalised musical medication), will help alleviate, if not cure, disease even in those who view medical intervention as only necessary when prevention has failed. Sound advice dictates that active prevention is always better than reactive cure; for example, it is easier to prevent weight gain than to shed weight when you are older. Although advances in allies of healthy ageing – such as healthcare and technology – will help, life comes with the guarantee that something will get you in the end. A good, varied and balanced lifestyle (one in which you take care of your physical, intellectual and social well-being) and an updated sense of purpose and engagement with life will, however, reduce the list of harmful practices that can lead to preventable, non-communicable illnesses, effectively helping you to age better and live longer. And what is better for the individual through slower ageing, longer independent living and reduced disease occurrence is better (and more cost-effective) for society as a whole.

Musical talent and longevity are both influenced by genetic good fortune, but genes are far from the sole determinant of a long life. For ageing and exceptionally long life, genes may account for only between 5 and 40%, leaving between 60 and 95% attributable to establishing and developing healthy lifestyle choices (ideally across your lifetime, or for as long as possible) that remain under your

[1]   *Wee Rule* by Wee Papa Girl Rappers. Written by Charles Cochrane, Hamish MacDonald, Samantha Lawrence and Sandra Lawrence

control. It is not a battleground of nature versus nurture; they interact, influence and complement each other.

Time will inevitably play its tune, blunting the once razor-sharp physical and mental edge of youthfulness, so ensure you make the most of life before the Grim Reaper pays you a visit.[1] Try focusing on what ageing leaves behind – an enhanced sense of perspective, acumen and freedom (from, for instance, the hollowness of material-ism[2] or many other concerns and obsessions you once held precious in your youth)[3] – rather than what it takes from you. Ageing enhances your ability to navigate life's challenges and inevitable headwinds and to appreciate those more intangible themes (such as education, friendships, fortitude, love, optimism, open-mindedness, passion, self-respect, self-reliance, truth) that are essential in leading a full and contented life. As your remaining time becomes limited, it becomes easier to prioritise, embrace and enjoy life more fully by living in the moment.

Post-retirement, you should have the time (and with tax-efficient retirement planning, the financial freedom) to enjoy and pursue your interests and the aspects of life that mean the most to you, perhaps with a return to dormant or neglected interests (especially those squeezed out by the constant demands of work) or with the acquisition of new skills as part of a personal reinvention. Other benefits of ageing are increased independent thinking and caring less about what others think of you and your choices, making this the ideal opportunity to engage fully in what you've always wanted, which can, in turn, lead to a longer and healthier life.

If post-retirement days become too grey, monotonous or silent[4] or you feel empty and cut adrift since dismantling the structure and direction provided by the world of work, establish what you valued

1 *Let's Go Crazy* by Prince And The Revolution. Written by Prince Nelson
2 *Could It Be I'm Falling In Love* by David Grant and Jaki Graham. Written by Melvin Steals and Mervin Steals
3 *You Came* by Kim Wilde. Written by Kim Smith and Richard Smith
4 *Everyday Is Like Sunday* by Morrissey. Written by Steven Morrissey and Stephen Street

about that previous structure and then build a new framework incorporating those elements. You may find that you can dedicate time (and your unique skill set) to engage in regular prosocial activities, such as charity volunteering that benefit others or improves the wider community, while concurrently re-establishing the purpose, responsibility, duty, pattern, social engagement and physical movement that was retired along with you. If you feel you still have much to give, give it.

No Regrets.[1] Regret can weigh heavily upon you. Psychological studies show that, over a lifetime, regret for the things you have never done[2] is stronger and lingers for longer than regret for something you attempted but failed. Even at the risk of failure, choosing to act is more rewarding than facing the regret of a missed opportunity. Some fear tarnishing their reputation or appearing foolish when, in reality, others may fail to notice or care about your actions.

Instead of accumulating regret, keep your spirits buoyed so that you feel *Young At Heart*[3] (most older people feel younger than their chronological age); this will help maintain your sense of gratitude, curiosity and playfulness and even help keep your heart young. Challenge the negative ageing stereotypes: growing older does not compel you to drop anchor and let your life become like a boat in a harbour.[4] Your expansive and flexible brain loves the challenge of learning new creative skills – including expanding your musical choices – which helps to build, explore and solder new neural pathways. You'll find life's horizons expand even if physical limitations arise.

Will you grow old?[5] Yes, and with a bit of luck and some sensible lifestyle choices, you can accept, embrace and celebrate with gusto and positivity the opportunity to live, grow older and wear the signs

1   *No Regrets* by Midge Ure. Written by Tom Rush
2   *Town Called Malice* by The Jam. Written by John Weller
3   *Young At Heart* by The Bluebells. Written by Robert Hodgens and Siobhan Fahey
4   *Blue Monday* by New Order. Written by Gillian Gilbert, Peter Hook, Stephen Morris and Bernard Sumner
5   *Live To Tell* by Madonna. Written by Madonna Ciccone and Patrick Leonard

of ageing with the pride of a life well-lived. A positive psychological outlook on ageing can extend your healthy lifespan – your healthspan, the years free from frailty and disease – by beneficially altering cellular chemistry. Conversely, you could begin to feel twice as old[1] if you harbour negative beliefs and use negative words about your ageing centred on decline, frailty and decrepitude – the age reservations[2] repeatedly perpetrated in many modern societies.

How you think, feel, talk about and act as you age profoundly affects the quality of your ageing. As you mature, your core – the essence of who you are – can align more closely with the person you want to be. You will, at last, be free to be you[3] and be entirely secure and content within yourself to live authentically.

ALCOHOL

The human-alcohol connection stretches back at least 9,000 years to Neolithic times; the alcohol-music association likely dates back just as far. Both offer relaxation and a way to unwind. In modern societies, alcohol's legality, social and cultural acceptance (even glamorisation), relative affordability and ready availability (music venues are usually licensed venues) have not always served pop stars – and other lesser mortals – well. Despite its widespread and casual use, alcohol remains one of the world's deadliest and most devastating drugs. Early death from alcohol abuse may perversely help to embalm the legend and physical attributes of a rock/pop star; however, choking to death on alcohol-induced vomit is neither a dignified nor desirable way to exit life.

What's this poison that runs through your veins?[4] Etymologically,

1   *Embarrassment* by Madness. Written by Lee Thompson and Michael Barson
2   *Labelled With Love* by Squeeze. Written by Glenn Tilbrook and Christopher Difford
3   *Can I Play With Madness* by Iron Maiden. Written by Adrian Smith, Paul Dickinson and Stephen Harris
4   *Poison* by Alice Cooper. Written by Vincent Furnier, John Barrett and John McCurry

'poison' refers to something drinkable, related to both 'potion' and 'potable'. 'Intoxication' signifies the injection of poison. Chemically, yeasts produce ethyl alcohol as a toxin to kill competing microorganisms. It's no surprise that regular or excessive consumption of society's socially sanctioned drug of default is detrimental to health, increasing the risk of cardiovascular problems, at least seven types of cancer and organ damage that can make your liver quiver.[1] A long-term, heavy daily drinking habit[2] is a cocktail of avoidable risks that can shorten life expectancy, while alcohol's psychoactive properties can dilute mental health, leading to wasted days in a hangover haze and sleep-disrupted nights.[3] Age amplifies sensitivity to any adverse effects of alcohol on sleep, while alcohol-induced sedation disrupts natural, restorative sleep cycles, so forgo any nightcaps. At any age, alcohol saps your energy. If you find that the Devil brews an irresistible potion[4] that has you over a barrel – transforming potential benefits into harm – it is wiser to end the relationship entirely and choose mindful no- and low- ('NoLo') alcohol alternatives rather than make repeated but failed attempts at moderation. The *Ant Rap*[5] suggests that sobriety can be neat, especially in today's world of highly palatable NoLo drinks and with society's increasingly accepting (less suspicious and judgemental) attitude toward sobriety. Abstinence is not a character flaw.

Given the long association with this intoxicant, there must be upsides to mixing life with alcohol. Surprisingly, one is health-related: in early agrarian communities, drinking alcohol was safer than drinking water. Another health-related upside was conviviality.

1   *It Is Time To Get Funky* by D Mob featuring LRS. Written by Daniel Poku, Basil Reynolds, Charles Scarlett and Courtney Coulson
2   *What Have I Done To Deserve This?* by Pet Shop Boys with Dusty Springfield. Written by Neil Tennant, Christopher Lowe and Alta Willis
3   *Is This Love* by Whitesnake. Written by David Coverdale and John Sykes
4   *That Ole Devil Called Love* by Alison Moyet. Written by Allan Roberts and Doris Fisher
5   *Ant Rap* by Adam And The Ants. Written by Stuart Goddard and Marco Pirroni

Alcohol acts as a social lubricant, an ice-breaking tool[1] that boosts confidence and sociability, helping drinkers to feel at ease and engage in free-flowing conversations. As a lyrical lubricant, alcohol has undoubtedly encouraged the spilling of inventive words and ideas onto the page. Flirtatiousness often follows loquaciousness as alcohol loosens social inhibitions; however, as alcohol further dissolves the bonds of cohesive life, it can impair judgement and increase impulsiveness, where you may end up doing what is out of (sober) character.[2] More moderate drinkers may simply savour the temporary respite that alcohol brings, helping them to relax, bond socially and unwind. The problems begin when the alcohol you use to unwind causes you to unravel.

Alcohol consumption can all too easily cross invisible boundaries, moving from a pleasant social activity into a habit, and from habit to dependency. When sober reality returns, you might want to follow the example in *Johnny Come Home*[3] and ask yourself some reflective questions that explore the underlying causes that allow alcohol to seep into the cracks of your fractured life. Those who want to drown their sorrows[4] or drink to forget[5] must pay the price when the effects from their *Happy Hour*[6] fade because alcohol amplifies feelings of miserableness.[7] If oblivion is what you crave,[8] and any time is margarita time,[9] it's time to seek help.

Sound advice? There's much to drink in, particularly for musicians who work in musical bars and who have alcohol in their blood.

1   *Ashes To Ashes* by David Bowie. Written by David Jones
2   *Push It* by Salt-N-Pepa. Written by Hurby Azor and Ray Davies
3   *Johnny Come Home* by Fine Young Cannibals. Written by David Steele and Roland Gift
4   *Mad World* by Tears For Fears. Written by Roland Orzabal
5   *Dancing With Tears In My Eyes* by Ultravox. Written by William Currie, Christopher Allen, James Ure and Warren Cann
6   *Happy Hour* by The Housemartins. Written by Paul Heaton and Ian Cullimore
7   *Heaven Knows I'm Miserable Now* by The Smiths. Written by Steven Morrissey and John Maher
8   *Addicted To Love* by Robert Palmer. Written by Robert Palmer
9   *Marguerita Time* by Status Quo. Written by Bernard Frost and Francis Rossi

For some people, life is too short; for others, life is two shorts. A curious, if not entirely palatable, cocktail of advice results, some of which may go to your head.[1]

The problem lies not with alcohol per se (many enjoy drinking sensibly without falling into alcohol's wasp trap) but in its misuse and overuse. *Celebration*.[2] It's advisable to refrain from using alcohol for every celebration, every commiseration and everything else in between. Set unbreachable personal boundaries and ensure you have at least two – but preferably more – consecutive alcohol-free days each week. This weekly restraint will allow your body time to recuperate and help prevent weight gain from the empty (nutrition-less) calories of alcohol and any associated, non-inhibited eating (aka 'the munchies'). The debate about 'safe' thresholds and the potential health benefits of alcohol continues; however, assume any level of alcohol consumption is harmful to health, a view of the WHO (the World Health Organization, not the instrument-smashing rock band).

If the sound of clinking ice is more enticing than sound advice, consider switching to a glass of polyphenol-rich *Red Red Wine*,[3] taken at mealtimes. Small quantities of red wine may offer some protection against cardiovascular problems and provide substances of interest to your gut microbiome.

Finally, what *Message In A Bottle*[4] does alcohol send? What appears to love you will slowly turn you blue.[5]

1   *Gimme All Your Lovin'* by ZZ Top. Written by William Gibbons, Joseph Hill and Frank Beard
2   *Celebration* by Kool And The Gang. Written by Roland Bell, Claydes Smith, George Brown, James Taylor, Robert Mickens, Earl Toon Jr, Dennis Thomas, Robert Bell and Eumir De Almeida
3   *Red Red Wine* by UB40. Written by Neil Diamond
4   *Message In A Bottle* by The Police. Written by Gordon Sumner
5   *Party Fears Two* by Associates. Written by William MacKenzie and Alan Rankine

BIOLOGY

From the Greek *bios*, meaning life, biology is the study of living organisms; it includes the processes underpinning song themes such as ageing, love, evolution, exercise and youthfulness, and the 37 trillion cells that make you who you are.

Your emotions, including those stirred by music, are rooted in biology; they enable you to differentiate living from existing. Inside your brain, primordial neurotransmitters like dopamine (the 'happy hormone'), oxytocin (the 'love hormone'), serotonin (the 'feel-good hormone'), noradrenaline (associated with 'fight or flight') and endorphins (natural opioids for pain-relief and a well-being reward for listening to music you like) all play vital roles. You'll want these multitasking chemical messengers to appear regularly on your brain's guest list.

The Pasadenas sang that songs were in their blood,[1] while The Jacksons stated that, through human brotherhood, the blood within them is the same as that within you.[2] While the latter is generally true – adults have about five litres of blood coursing through 60,000 miles of vessels, about 400 miles of which are within the brain, transporting red blood cells produced in your bone marrow at the staggering rate of about two million per second – not all blood is the same or interchangeable. Blood groups exist for biologically sound – if not fully understood – reasons, probably linked to resistance against infectious diseases.

For your precious blood to fulfil its circulatory fetch-and-carry duties, it relies on a muscular organ revered in many cultures as the seat of love, courage and strength: the heart. Those *Addicted To Love*[3] hear that hearts sweat, which, biologically, they don't. Hearts

1   *Tribute (Right On)* by The Pasadenas. Written by David Milliner, Aaron Brown, Andrew Banfield, Hamish Seelochan, Michael Milliner and William Wingfield
2   *Can You Feel It* by The Jacksons. Written by Michael Jackson and Jackie Jackson
3   *Addicted To Love* by Robert Palmer. Written by Robert Palmer

pump to the beat with such efficiency that there's no requirement for pulsatile heart deodorant.

Kiss Me,[1] urges Stephen Duffy, with your mouth. By definition, this is the only way to kiss. If, while kissing (or at any other time), someone's lips start to turn green,[2] arrange for immediate medical assistance.

Turning the biological spotlight on to animals (some of which spend their entire lives immersed in sound), Will To Power wondered how fireflies shine.[3] It's bioluminescence.

Moving into what Tight Fit describe as the quiet jungle, we learn that this is where *The Lion Sleeps Tonight.*[4] However, most lions typically inhabit savannah, grassland or scrub, which form their natural hunting grounds and where – usually by day – the pride sleeps for up to 15 hours. The feline kings of the jungle are tigers, jaguars and some leopards. And animals living among dense vegetation communicate through sound, so a healthy jungle is always alive with noise, thanks to the relentless jungle call.[5]

Sound advice? Despite living in a *Wonderful World,*[6] Sam Cooke admitted to knowing little about biology. Lyrically, he's not alone. Notwithstanding this, our biology has equipped us with the most complex natural structure in the known universe, the pinnacle of millions of years of evolution that you are currently using to comprehend this sentence, and everything else in your life: the human brain. Jermaine Stewart suggests that, instead of removing

1   *Kiss Me* by Stephen "Tin Tin" Duffy. Written by Stephen Duffy
2   *Start Me Up* by Rolling Stones. Written by Michael Jagger and Keith Richards
3   *Baby, I Love Your Way/Freebird Medley (Free Baby)* by Will To Power. Written by Larkins Collins Jr, Peter Frampton and Ronald Van Zant
4   *The Lion Sleeps Tonight* by Tight Fit. Written by Hugo Peretti, Luigi Creatore, George Weiss, Albert Stanton and Solomon Linda
5   *Welcome To The Pleasuredome* by Frankie Goes To Hollywood. Written by Peter Gill, William Johnson, Mark O'Toole and Brian Nash
6   *Wonderful World* by Sam Cooke. Written by Lester Adler, Herb Alpert and Samuel Cooke

clothing, an equally good time can be had with some brain stimulation,[1] so, with some figures ahead,[2] here goes: with a volume of less than 1,500 cubic centimetres, your blood-rich watery brain weighs about 1.35 kilograms, houses about 86 billion neurons and has 100 trillion synaptic connections. This neuron-rich organ allows you to understand the very biology that created it. Your brain's thoughts largely determine your choices, habits, behaviours and actions, more than your encoded genes. All your experiences feed back into your brain, reshaping its structure through unique neural pathways.

One way your brain communicates with your body (and internally among discrete neural regions) is through electrical impulses.[3] For example, your ear transforms vibrating air molecules into electrical signals that travel along your auditory nerve to your brain's cerebral cortex, where you perceive it as music, making you a live wire.[4]

One fundamental biological imperative is survival for long enough to reproduce and perpetuate your genes. By extrapolating the sonic connection between animals and mating, Charles Darwin noted how we can charm one another with music. Pop music across the decades amply reflects this primal drive for reproduction while your biology compels you to engage in activities that help you to stay and feel alive.[5]

Much of your biology mirrors the intricacies of life itself. Its complexity and interconnectedness mean that much could go wrong, yet, day to day, it functions in perfect working order without your conscious awareness. By embracing sound advice and making informed choices, you can enhance both your biology and your life.

1 *We Don't Have To Take Our Clothes Off* by Jermaine Stewart. Written by Michael Walden and Preston Glass
2 *These Dreams* by Heart. Written by Bernard Taupin and Martin Page
3 *(Hey You) The Rock Steady Crew* by Rock Steady Crew. Written by Budd Dixon, Ruza Blue and Stephen Hague
4 *The Slightest Touch* by Five Star. Written by Grover Morrow and Michael Margules
5 *Rio* by Duran Duran. Written by Simon Le Bon, Nigel Taylor, Roger Taylor, Andrew Taylor and Nicholas Bates

CHANGE

The opening lines to *Up Where We Belong* reflect on the uncertainty of tomorrow.[1] While an undetermined future is uncertain, one natural and inevitable constant is change. Paul Young reminds us that *Everything Must Change*[2] because nothing lasts for ever,[3] nothing stays the same[4] in the changing times[5] of a changing world.[6] However, agreement about the nature of change varies. In *Hymn To Her*,[7] The Pretenders say that while some things change, others stay the same (it can certainly feel that way), a sentiment echoed by A-ha, who noted that, despite changes, everything remains the same.[8] In contrast, Carly Simon declares that nothing stays the same.[9]

Despite these differences, Tears For Fears' message is that you can change yourself[10] and it's *Never Too Late*[11] to instigate or embrace positive change.

Those who have read Karl Marx[12] may know that he wrote about how philosophers only interpret the world when their real purpose should be to change it. Billy Joel sang about how some people

1   *Up Where We Belong* by Joe Cocker and Jennifer Warnes. Written by Bernard Nitzsche, Beverly Sainte-Marie and Wilbur Jennings
2   *Everything Must Change* by Paul Young. Written by Paul Young and Ian Kewley
3   *Everybody Wants To Rule The World* by Tears For Fears. Written by Roland Orzabal, Ian Stanley and Christopher Hughes
4   *In Your Eyes* by George Benson. Written by Daniel Hill IV and Michael Masser
5   *Purple Rain* by Prince And The Revolution. Written by Prince Nelson
6   *Every Loser Wins* by Nick Berry. Written by Simon May, Stewart James and Bradley James
7   *Hymn To Her* by The Pretenders. Written by Meg Keene
8   *The Living Daylights* by A-ha. Written by Pål Waaktaar Gamst and John Barry
9   *Coming Around Again* by Carly Simon. Written by Carly Simon
10 *Change* by Tears For Fears. Written by Roland Orzabal
11 *Never Too Late* by Kylie Minogue. Written by Michael Stock, Matthew Aitken and Peter Waterman
12 *When Will I Be Famous?* by Bros. Written by Nicholas Graham and Thomas Watkins

accept the world as they find it.[1] In contrast, mercurial musician Paul Weller, known for his ever-changing moods,[2] was typically forthright about trying to change the world for the better rather than accepting the way you find it.[3] Your challenge is not to initiate change just for the sake of it but to strive to make yourself or the world (ideally both) better.

Whether found or lost, love is often a potent catalyst for change, frequently falling under the collective banner of *Love Changes Everything*.[4] As time passes, love transforms and deepens as relationships evolve.

Sound advice? The lyrical message is unmistakable: the world always changes,[5] just as it has always done. Greek philosopher Heraclitus was one of the first to record that change is a constant, perpetual and essential aspect of life, noting that you can never step into the same river twice, for you are not the same person, and it's not the same river. While pop stars and their music can act as influential external agents of change, the most significant transformative change originates from within.

As change propels progress, it banishes stagnation. Attempts to put chains on change are typically futile. However, not all change follows a predictable, gradual and upward trajectory, such as the abrupt and unpredictable change accompanying natural or man-made crises. Yet, even in times of stressful adversity, change often reveals the best in people. One evolutionary theory of change posits that the best in apes evolved to become the distinctly bigger-brained, more intelligent early humans, driven by a rapidly changing and increasingly fragmented environment, particularly the volcanicity and fluctuating climate experienced in East Africa's Great Rift

1   *An Innocent Man* by Billy Joel. Written by William Joel
2   *My Ever Changing Moods* by The Style Council. Written by John Weller
3   *Walls Come Tumbling Down!* by The Style Council. Written by John Weller
4   *Love Changes Everything* by Michael Ball. Written by Andrew Lloyd Webber, Donald Blackstone and Charles Hart
5   *Cherish* by Kool And The Gang. Written by Robert Bell, Ronald Bell, James Bonnefond, George Brown, Charles Smith, James Taylor and Curtis Williams

Valley. Part of our evolutionary success as a species may hinge on our ability to see, adapt to and capitalise on opportunities created by change.

You can either actively seek change or passively accept it. In either case, you must decide to accept and cope with change, then adapt and respond accordingly. Incorporating frequent yet small, incremental changes into your lifestyle, such as improving your diet, increasing your exercise regime or learning relaxation techniques, can cumulatively reach a critical mass of collective 'marginal gains' that spark a whole self-sustaining *Chain Reaction*,[1] resulting in permanent and beneficial change. Minor improvements to lifestyle and thinking patterns are easier to implement than radical attempts to overhaul deeply ingrained habits.[2]

However, it can be hard to change your mind,[3] especially those long-standing, recurrent negative thought patterns or addictive behaviours, such as drinking, smoking or gambling. Lasting change requires time and patience,[4] desire and determination.

Girl Crazy band Hot Chocolate craved personality in potential partners.[5] Personality traits, including those that some perceive to be character flaws, are not immutably fixed at some point in your past. Research indicates that, on average, most personalities, as measured by the 'big five' personality traits (openness to new experiences, conscientiousness, extroversion, agreeableness and neuroticism), naturally change with age, even without conscious effort. Even if change fails to yield your desired outcome, it can still move you closer to your goal, and the benefits you reap along the way can spur continued perseverance.

Searching for love that lets you feel that you are once again living[6]

1   *Chain Reaction* by Diana Ross. Written by Barry Gibb, Robin Gibb and Maurice Gibb
2   *Sledgehammer* by Peter Gabriel. Written by Peter Gabriel
3   *Only When You Leave* by Spandau Ballet. Written by Gary Kemp
4   *Got My Mind Set On You* by George Harrison. Written by Rudolph Clark
5   *Girl Crazy* by Hot Chocolate. Written by Lester Brown
6   *You Can't Hurry Love* by Phil Collins. Written by Brian Holland, Lamont Dozier and Edward Holland

is a common theme in pop songs. It also raises a deeper question: given the opportunity, would you choose to relive your life as it is, or would you change anything?

While the world will change throughout your life,[1] you may decide it's not your responsibility to try to shape global change.[2] Always choose your battles wisely (ditch the minor or inconsequential) so that you prioritise and focus your limited resources on change that holds meaning for you. This targeted approach is far more effective than expending time and energy trying to change countless external minutiae in pursuit of an unattainable, perfect world.[3] It's essential to recognise that some aspects are beyond your control,[4] such as the thoughts and actions of others. Instead, focus on what lies within your sphere of influence – what you can control (your thoughts, attitude and behaviour) and what you can do differently to improve outcomes. By intentionally changing and controlling what resides within your mind,[5] you enhance your *Self Control*.[6] For example, while you can't change today's weather, you can decide to adapt to it by dressing appropriately.

Change often takes time. For some, the wheels of societal change turn too slowly, but turn they eventually do, especially when given an encouraging prod from the handle of a sweeping new broom,[7] such as that accompanying a change in political ideology. Belief in your ability to align your internal and external worlds will motivate you to effect such change, while remaining flexible and adaptable to new ideas is crucial for overcoming challenges and improvising

1   *Nothing's Gonna Change My Love For You* by Glenn Medeiros. Written by Gerald Goffin and Michael Masser
2   *A New England* by Kirsty MacColl. Written by Stephen Bragg
3   *Hold Me Now* by Thompson Twins. Written by Thomas Bailey, Alannah Currie and Joseph Leeway
4   *Can't Stay Away From You* by Gloria Estefan and Miami Sound Machine. Written by Gloria Estefan
5   *Listen To Your Heart* by Sonia. Written by Michael Stock, Matthew Aitken and Peter Waterman
6   *Self Control* by Laura Branigan. Written by Stephen Piccolo, Giancarlo Bigazzi and Raffaele Riefoli
7   *The King Of Rock 'N' Roll* by Prefab Sprout. Written by Patrick McAloon

solutions in response to changing circumstances. You've been adept at adapting since the day you were born.

DESTINATION

"Life's a journey, not a destination" runs the well-worn maxim, emphasising the importance of living in the present, fully experiencing this moment[1] where you live for now,[2] without being tethered to the past or fixated on an uncertain future destination. Mindfulness counters mindlessness and raises a question: what if your hopes and dreams involve a bigger, brighter, better destination than your current reality? Your life unfolds in the eternal present - a continually forward-flowing fulcrum of experience and expectation - that can spur you onward towards your destination.

Every destination requires a journey. If you find yourself drifting down a *Road To Nowhere*,[3] it might be time to seek inspiration.[4] Seventeen-year-old George Michael reportedly found the inspiration to write *Careless Whisper*[5] while travelling on a bus in Bushey. According to Stevie Wonder, moving forward with positivity can lead you to the brightest (and guiding) star.[6]

Sound advice? If you can strike the right balance between journey and destination, then yes, all of life is out there waiting to be found.[7] Your unique life itinerary will present you with many possible and equally valid paths to your destination: there's no right or wrong way. However, if you set out without a clear destination, it can be

1 *Need You Tonight* by INXS. Written by Andrew Farriss and Michael Hutchence
2 *Every Loser Wins* by Nick Berry. Written by Simon May, Stewart James and Bradley James
3 *Road To Nowhere* by Talking Heads. Written by David Byrne
4 *Chain Reaction* by Diana Ross. Written by Barry Gibb, Robin Gibb and Maurice Gibb
5 *Careless Whisper* by George Michael. Written by George Michael and Andrew Ridgeley
6 *Master Blaster (Jammin')* by Stevie Wonder. Written by Stevie Wonder
7 *Up Where We Belong* by Joe Cocker and Jennifer Warnes. Written by Bernard Nitzsche, Beverly Sainte-Marie and Wilbur Jennings

challenging to identify favourable conditions or to recognise if (or when) you have arrived at your desired spot.

Everyone's life journey is a one-way ticket,[1] ending at the same terminal destination: we are all destined to die.[2] In the 3 minutes and 46 seconds of *Let's Go Crazy* (which delivers this stark message), an average of about 400 people worldwide would have breathed their last. For the faithful, this is a necessary step toward a spiritual home. For the non-religious, the steps in the throes of grief are to mourn a journey without destination, with no prospect of an eternal afterlife, where the departed is only an echo that resonates in the hollow space they once filled in the lives and memories of those who remain.

A subtle and sober reminder of our inevitable destination is often depicted in paintings (particularly in the aptly named 'still life') that display symbols of death and decay, such as skulls, clocks, hourglasses, decomposing fruit, candle stumps or ruins, collectively known as memento mori ('remember you must die'). Artists incorporate memento mori not to frighten but to remind, inspire and evoke reflection in viewers about the relentless passage of time and the brevity and finite nature of existence. Memento mori serve as visual cues to remind the viewer to kick-start their life back into reality and to find meaning and appreciation in the present. Much of the remaining physical evidence of ancient civilisations exists solely through their obsession with the artefacts of death and the often elaborate provisions they made for the afterlife, such as the Egyptian practice of placing musical instruments in tombs to ward off death's endless silence. Your bespoke *Sound Advice* playlist can function as an auditory memento mori, allowing music to help you find yourself (or reveal a new side of yourself) and lose yourself.

How to begin?[3] The first step towards any destination is literal: take that first step. Having a clear destination or goal in mind and a series of closer, more achievable stop-off points instils a sense of

1   *When The Going Gets Tough, The Tough Get Going* by Billy Ocean. Written by Wayne Brathwaite, Barry Eastmond, Robert Lange and Leslie Charles
2   *Let's Go Crazy* by Prince And The Revolution. Written by Prince Nelson
3   *Silver Dream Machine* by David Essex. Written by David Cook

direction and purpose into your peregrination. Creating a simple plan – even an easy-to-remember rough sketch – adds structure and control, helping steer you toward your desired destination. Setting sail without a clear destination or map to chart your course will soon see you adrift in a sea of uncertainty, vulnerable to the whims of wind and current.

Life is for living, not just planning. The unexpected twists and turns experienced along the way may excite and help you reimagine the speed and direction of your onward voyage. Therefore, keep your mind open, flexible and adaptable. Many performers and musicians who managed to fulfil their professional ambitions were changed by their creative travels. Similarly, the history of human exploration is rich with explorers who set out to find new land or routes only to stumble upon something entirely unexpected as they ventured forth. Embrace spontaneity and explore possibilities along the way – progress is not always linear. Remember that giant leaps for both you and mankind need to be broken down into smaller, more manageable steps. Reaching a milestone or stop-off point is a sign of progress and achievement, reinforcing your confidence and fueling the optimism and determination to continue discovering who you are.[1]

Edging ever closer to a destination naturally creates distance from your past. A destination is about where you're heading, not where you started. While you cannot control the circumstances of your birth and upbringing, you can choose how to respond to them. Don't let your circumstances define who you are: rise above them. If you have faced adversity, view this formative experience as a source of fortifying strength: having navigated rough waters, you will be more psychologically resilient, self-reliant and adept at manoeuvring through challenging situations than those who have sailed only on smooth seas. Overcoming adversity or trauma can be as transformative and valuable as the destination itself, leaving a

1   *Living In America* by James Brown. Written by Daniel Hartman and Charles Kaufman

legacy that may include a greater appreciation for the preciousness of life, stronger relationships, a new or renewed sense of meaning and purpose, and greater self-knowledge. *Kintsugi* is the traditional Japanese art of mending broken ceramics by filling the cracks with gold lacquer, highlighting the repairs, celebrating beauty within an object's history and giving it a new lease of life. Embracing a kintsugi mindset can help you make sense of and repurpose any fracturing experiences, allowing you to generate and channel energy, cultivate resilience and fuel positive change within yourself and those around you. In doing so, you may inspire others to discover beauty in their pasts.

DESTINY

In Greek and Roman mythology, three goddess sisters known as the Fates were believed to determine the course of birth, life and death. Life's destiny was fabricated by fate[1] at birth,[2] with the thread of life spun out by Clotho, measured out by Lachesis and cut to its designated length by Atropos (Greek for a Thatcher-like 'not turning' or 'unchangeable'). This mythology aligns with the programmed theory of ageing and death, which suggests our lifespan is predetermined at birth. (For an opposing view, see the theme on *Ageing*.)

In modern usage, destiny often carries a positive connotation, hinting at desirable outcomes and a degree of personal agency. By contrast, fate is associated with inevitable, uncontrollable outcomes, as reflected in phrases such as 'tempting fate'[3] and 'twist of fate',[4]

---

1   *Something About You* by Level 42. Written by Michael Lindup, Philip Gould, Mark King, Rowland Gould and Waliou Badarou

2   *A Boy From Nowhere* by Tom Jones. Written by Michael Farr and Edward Seago

3   *What's The Colour Of Money?* by Hollywood Beyond. Written by Jamie Rose and Mark Rogers

4   *With Or Without You* by U2. Written by Paul Hewson, Adam Clayton, David Evans and Laurence Mullen Jr

making people 'resigned' to their fate,[1] primarily through genetic predisposition and age-related fatalism.

Within pop songs, destiny frequently intertwines with love and relationships, usually portraying the object of desire as an inevitable part of one's destiny,[2] whether through a calling,[3] a close friendship with,[4] or simply having faith in destiny.[5]

Sound advice? The advice lacks crystal-clear consistency. Some songs adopt the classical view that destiny unfolds in a predetermined way, while others assert that our destiny is unknown.[6] What should you believe? Start by rejecting the blind surrender of your future fortunes to fate[7] or any guardian angel of destiny.[8] Fate is not the keyholder to unlocking life,[9] or love; it isn't justification for what was meant to be,[10] and the Fates did not conspire against you at birth. Believing yourself to be a mere marionette, manipulated by mysterious and invisible strings[11] controlled by higher hands and unseen forces of destiny, is delusional and self-centred. You are the architect of your destiny through your choices and actions, echoing the paraphrased words of Cassius in Shakespeare's *Julius Caesar* – our destiny lies not in the stars but within ourselves. Life's too

1   *Come On Eileen* by Dexys Midnight Runners and The Emerald Express. Written by Kevin Rowland, James Paterson, Kevin Adams and Michael Billingham

2   *You Gave Me Love* by Crown Heights Affair. Written by Ida Reid

3   *Together Forever* by Rick Astley. Written by Michael Stock, Matthew Aitken and Peter Waterman

4   *You're History* by Shakespears Sister. Written by Siobhan Fahey, Marcella Detroit, Richard Feldman and Patrick Seymour

5   *Incommunicado* by Marillion. Written by Derek Dick, Mark Kelly, Ian Mosley, Steven Rothery and Peter Trewavas

6   *Never Gonna Give You Up* by Musical Youth. Written by Dennis Seaton, Kelvin Grant, Michael Grant, Patrick Waite and Freddie Waite

7   *The Living Years* by Mike + The Mechanics. Written by Brian Robertson and Michael Rutherford

8   *Requiem* by London Boys. Written by Ralf-René Maué

9   *Every Loser Wins* by Nick Berry. Written by Simon May, Stewart James and Bradley James

10   *Never Never* by The Assembly. Written by Vincent Martin

11   *Victims* by Culture Club. Written by Roy Hay, George O'Dowd, Michael Craig and Jonathan Moss

short[1] and precious to passively entrust it to destiny, fate or heavenly compulsion. And, in the search for your destiny,[2] examining lines in a song is likely to be a better predictor than examining lines on your palms.

The Latin phrase 'amor fati', meaning 'love of one's fate', encourages you to enthusiastically embrace everything that happens in your life rather than simply accept it, a philosophy championed by Friedrich Nietzsche. Recognising that external events lie beyond your control can free you from regret and the burden of *If Only I Could*[3] thoughts.

Your destiny is too important to leave to the whims of the Fates, coincidence or chance.[4] Believing everything will work out simply because it's your destiny is a comforting but dangerous illusion. Instead, take charge, make conscious choices and actively craft your desired future.

DIVORCE

When a married couple is living together but living apart,[5] and the gap in compatibility between them has grown too wide to bridge,[6] it may be time to end all the fuss and fighting,[7] the stress and resentment, the contempt and criticism, and seriously consider divorce. With love and relationships being the most enduring song

1 *Walking In The Rain* by Modern Romance. Written by David Jaymes and Michael Mullins
2 *Whatever I Do (Wherever I Go)* by Hazell Dean. Written by Michael Stock and Matthew Aitken
3 *If Only I Could* by Sydney Youngblood. Written by Claus Zundel, Michael Staab, Sydney Ford and Ralf Hamm
4 *Breakout* by Swing Out Sister. Written by Andrew Connell, Corinne Drewery and Martin Jackson
5 *Hard Habit To Break* by Chicago. Written by Steven Kipner and John Lewis Parker
6 *I Know Him So Well* by Elaine Paige and Barbara Dickson. Written by Göran Andersson, Timothy Rice and Björn Ulvaeus
7 *Hold Me Now* by Thompson Twins. Written by Thomas Bailey, Alannah Currie and Joseph Leeway

theme, it's no surprise that breaking the vows you once made[1] is a topic explored in songs.

Marriage is like fire: when harnessed correctly, it can be beneficial and transformative, providing warmth, comfort and security. However, when fuelled by highly combustible unresolved conflict – when love goes up in flames[2] – it can flare up and burn uncontrollably, becoming highly destructive and capable of consuming everything in its path. While it's unrealistic to expect marriage to be entirely spark-free (expectation levels within marriage are often unreasonably high), many couples wait until the friction of conflict ignites into a dangerous conflagration before reading the message from the smoke signals[3] or installing preventative detectors. Once the love upon which you built your marriage burns to nothing,[4] the options for repair and rebuild become limited, even with professional help. All that rises from the ashes is divorce, the more detrimental, complex and costly adult version of the simple break-up. Divorce proceedings can reveal deeper truths about both parties. Such truths can burn.[5]

In the 1980s, when no-fault divorce was not an option, couples had to establish grounds for dissolving their marriage, often citing 'unreasonable behaviour' – a term closely associated with the everyday antics of rock stars. Some songwriters maintained their reasonableness and channelled the raw pain, anger, despair and frustration of an acrimonious divorce into searing pop lyrics, as Phil Collins did when he sang about the lies underpinning his marriage.[6]

Challenges, tensions and ructions are inevitable in any relationship, be it a marriage or a musical collaboration, and they have a

1   I Can't Stand Up For Falling Down by Elvis Costello And The Attractions. Written by Allen Jones and Homer Banks
2   Take My Breath Away by Berlin. Written by Thomas Whitlock and Giovanni Moroder
3   Tarzan Boy by Baltimora. Written by Maurizio Bassi and Naimy Hackett
4   Alive And Kicking by Simple Minds. Written by James Kerr, Charles Burchill and Michael MacNeil
5   I Just Don't Have The Heart by Cliff Richard. Written by Michael Stock, Matthew Aitken and Peter Waterman
6   In The Air Tonight by Phil Collins. Written by Philip Collins

reliable habit of exposing and scratching away at any weak spots. Balancing the demands of public life as a band with the private life of a marriage can double the potential for internecine trouble. Band of gold group ABBA originally comprised two married couples. The poignant message in their song *One Of Us*[1] was that one of them had to go. Soon after, they were two divorced couples before they untied their musical knot and disbanded.

If you are talking divorce before marriage,[2] you're either thoroughly preparing for all eventualities or already in a doomed relationship. (Spoiler: it's probably the latter.) While it's sensible to have candid, premarital discussions about potential sources of conflict, practical obstacles, sacrifices and challenges (such as childcare responsibilities or finances), it's hardly romantic.

Sound advice? Despite the optimism at the time of saying 'I do' in songs like *I Just Can't Stop Loving You*,[3] things can and do go wrong; love can fade or slip away[4] and married life can fail to live up to the ideal of happy ever after.[5] As people change (as they always do),[6] harmony can descend into marital discord as couples may no longer get along.[7]

To manage escalating conflict, refrain from reacting impulsively or emotionally to your partner's aggressive criticism or attempts to shoot you down in flames.[8] Instead, try to analyse criticism objectively. As time helps effectively disperse concentrated moments

1   *One Of Us* by ABBA. Written by Göran Andersson and Björn Ulvaeus
2   *On My Own* by Patti LaBelle and Michael McDonald. Written by Burt Bacharach and Carole Bayer-Sager
3   *I Just Can't Stop Loving You* by Michael Jackson featuring Siedah Garrett. Written by Michael Jackson
4   *All The Love In the World* by Dionne Warwick. Written by Barry Gibb, Maurice Gibb and Robin Gibb
5   *All Of My Heart* by ABC. Written by Martin Fry, Mark White, Stephen Singleton and David Palmer
6   *Being With You* by Smokey Robinson. Written by William Robinson Jr
7   *That's The Way Love Is* by Ten City. Written by Byron Stingily, Byron Burke and Herb Lawson
8   *Don't Break My Heart* by UB40. Written by Deborah Banks, Alistair Campbell, Terence Wilson, Brian Travers, Earl Falconer, Norman Hassan, James Brown, Michael Virtue and Robin Campbell

of anger,[1] consider counting to ten[2] to allow the pressure and heat from the chamber of hurt and anger to dissipate and cool rather than erupt as explosive emotional outbursts. By remaining calm and composed, you avoid spewing out harmful and unhelpful retorts that you may later regret.[3] Maintaining civility in communication is always helpful. Rational thinking – such as pressing your personal pause button – is far easier said than done at the moment of rupture, but keeping a level head and staying open-minded may allow you to hear some hard-to-hear truths that no one else has said – or would dare to say – to you before.[4]

Unfortunately, some problems, obstacles and grievances feel insurmountable, deepening the chasm of an unhappy marriage. The drivers of divorce are as unique and varied as those behind the initial desire to commit publicly to part only upon death. One pop song trope is to portray divorce (or a break-up not involving marriage) as a harmful, stressful and destructive failure. However, a low point can also become a turning point. Some post-divorce couples feel immensely liberated after escaping a stifling, unfulfilling and slowly sinking marriage. The end of a marriage can signal the start of personal recovery (although it can take many months to reach this onset), involving a rediscovery of identity and a revival, rebuilding and refocusing of a formerly wilting life via an injection of newfound independence, vitality and clarity.

Marriage is intended to be a life-changing, life-long commitment, not a disposable commodity. Releasing negative emotions attached to a failing or low-quality marriage can bring relief. Divorce, however, harbours its own set of stresses, strains and upheaval, especially where children create an emotional backdraught. If love's *Eternal*

1   *Mirror Mirror (Mon Amour)* by Dollar. Written by Trevor Horn and Bruce Woolley
2   *Tom Hark* by The Piranhas. Written by Rupert Bopape and Robert Grover
3   *Glory Of Love* by Peter Cetera. Written by David Foster, Diane Nini and Peter Cetera
4   *All Around The World* by Lisa Stansfield. Written by Andrew Morris, Ian Devaney and Lisa Stansfield

Flame[1] fails to live up to its billing and burns out (most divorces result from a slow burn rather than a rapid flashover), it may be time to consider the possibility of moving on.[2] Just take care not to get scorched by the glowing embers of divorce.

DON'T . . .

The contraction 'don't' is a staple in many themes and song titles, valued for its blunt and emphatic instructional nature. Psychologically, negatively framed advice exerts a strong influence because humans are loss-averse – we feel the pain of losing something we already have more acutely than we appreciate the gain of something of equal magnitude. The Kids From Fame try to measure what they have lost during the star-making process.[3] Consequently, we tend to dwell more on the risks and uncertainties of life than on the potential benefits, which can lead to overly cautious behaviour.

The lyrical list of what not to do is long and varied, suggesting that you don't: give in or give up,[4] settle for second best,[5] look down,[6] look back,[7] be macho,[8] tell lies,[9] regret anything,[10] underestimate

1   *Eternal Flame* by The Bangles. Written by William Steinberg, Susanna Hoffs and Thomas Kelly
2   *How 'Bout Us* by Champaign. Written by Dana Walden
3   *Starmaker* by The Kids From Fame. Written by Bruce Roberts and Carole Bayer
4   *Rage Hard* by Frankie Goes To Hollywood. Written by Peter Gill, William Johnson, Brian Nash and Mark O'Toole
5   *Express Yourself* by Madonna. Written by Madonna Ciccone and Stephen Bray
6   *Wonderful Christmastime* by Paul McCartney. Written by Paul McCartney
7   *Walk Right Now* by The Jacksons. Written by Sigmund Jackson, Michael Jackson and Steven Jackson
8   *Beat It* by Michael Jackson. Written by Michael Jackson
9   *The Edge Of Heaven* by Wham! Written by George Michael
10 *I Knew You Were Waiting (For Me)* by Aretha Franklin and George Michael. Written by Simon Climie and Dennis Morgan

others' views,[1] hesitate,[2] procrastinate,[3] waste emotions,[4] deceive yourself,[5] be shy,[6] lose control,[7] deceive,[8] close your mind,[9] chase polar bears (or run after cars),[10] loiter where trouble lurks,[11] hide behind a cause[12] or get duped into believing everything you see or hear.[13]

Don't Talk To Me About Love.[14] Yet, love is a recurring topic (don't blame me[15] or look surprised)[16] because, as with many themes, it's often easier to articulate what you don't want than to specify or express what you do want. Love-related song titles that capture this sentiment include *Don't Break My Heart*,[17] *Please Don't Make*

1   *Cherish* by Madonna. Written by Madonna Ciccone and Patrick Leonard
2   *Baby, I Love Your Way/Freebird Medley (Free Baby)* by Will To Power. Written by Larkins Collins Jr, Peter Frampton and Ronald Van Zant
3   *Sexual Healing* by Marvin Gaye. Written by Marvin Gaye Jr and Odell Brown Jr
4   *Lay All Your Love On Me* by ABBA. Written by Göran Andersson and Björn Ulvaeus
5   *Love Action (I Believe In Love)* by The Human League. Written by Philip Oakey and Ian Burden
6   *Breakfast In Bed* by UB40 with Chrissie Hynde. Written by Donald Fritts and Edward Hinton
7   *The Loco-Motion* by Kylie Minogue. Written by Gerald Goffin and Carol Klein
8   *Oh Julie* by Shakin' Stevens. Written by Michael Barratt
9   *Criticize* by Alexander O'Neal. Written by Alexander O'Neal and Garry Johnson
10 *Waterfalls* by Paul McCartney. Written by Paul McCartney
11 *Saddle Up* by David Christie. Written by Philo Robinson and Jacques Pépino
12 *Out In The Fields* by Gary Moore and Phil Lynott. Written by Gary Moore
13 *New Song* by Howard Jones. Written by John Jones
14 *Don't Talk To Me About Love* by Altered Images. Written by Clare Grogan, John McElhone, Stephen Lironi and Anthony McDaid
15 *Shut Up* by Madness. Written by Christopher Foreman and Graham McPherson
16 *All Cried Out* by Alison Moyet. Written by Genevieve Moyet, Steven Jolley and Anthony Swain
17 *Don't Break My Heart* by UB40. Written by Deborah Banks, Alistair Campbell, Terence Wilson, Brian Travers, Earl Falconer, Norman Hassan, James Brown, Michael Virtue and Robin Campbell

Me Cry,[1] *I Don't Wanna Get Hurt,*[2] *Don't Leave Me This Way,*[3] *I Don't Want To Talk About It,*[4] *Don't You (Forget About Me)*[5] and *Don't Go.*[6]

Don't Tell Me[7] that all the 'don'ts' in song titles relate to love because, well, they don't: *Don't Stop The Music,*[8] *I Don't Wanna Dance,*[9] *Don't Stand So Close To Me,*[10] *Don't Waste My Time*[11] and *Don't Worry, Be Happy.*[12]

In the mid-1980s, the UK government's 'Don't Die of Ignorance' campaign effectively used negative framing to address the emergence of a big disease with a small label:[13] AIDS. This powerful slogan is equally applicable to other aspects of life. While some individuals have an inherent aversion to authority and find it hard to live under top-down rules,[14] seeing them as a threat to personal freedom, there are times when curbing individual choice becomes necessary for the greater good, such as the *Just Say No*[15] anti-drug campaign or initiatives promoting the wearing of seatbelts (which became mandatory in 1983). Such campaigns protect lives and ease the burden on taxpayer-funded services like the NHS. 'Don't' messages risk

1   *Please Don't Make Me Cry* by UB40. Written by Winston Tucker
2   *I Don't Wanna Get Hurt* by Donna Summer. Written by Michael Stock, Matthew Aitken and Peter Waterman
3   *Don't Leave Me This Way* by The Communards with Sarah Jane Morris. Written by Kenneth Gamble, Leon Huff and Cary Gilbert
4   *I Don't Want To Talk About It* by Everything But The Girl. Written by Daniel Whitten
5   *Don't You (Forget About Me)* by Simple Minds. Written by Keith Forsey and Steven Schiff
6   *Don't Go* by Yazoo. Written by Vincent Martin
7   *Don't Tell Me* by Blancmange. Written by Neil Arthur and Stephen Luscombe
8   *Don't Stop The Music* by Yarbrough & Peoples. Written by Jonah Ellis, Alisa Peoples and Lonnie Simmons
9   *I Don't Wanna Dance* by Eddy Grant. Written by Edmond Grant
10 *Don't Stand So Close To Me* by The Police. Written by Gordon Sumner
11 *Don't Waste My Time* by Paul Hardcastle. Written by Paul Hardcastle
12 *Don't Worry, Be Happy* by Bobby McFerrin. Written by Robert McFerrin Jr
13 *Sign O' The Times* by Prince. Written by Prince Nelson
14 *Talk Of The Town* by The Pretenders. Written by Christine Hynde
15 *Just Say No* by Grange Hill Cast. Written by Al Gorgoni and George McMahon

backlash and accusations of creating an overprotective 'nanny' state (few crave more government interference or intrusion in their lives). Nevertheless, these messages serve an important role in educating the public (especially relevant in the context of the stigma, fearmongering and misinformation surrounding AIDS) and in guiding behaviour that prevents harm.

Sound advice? It's easy to let restrictive and fearful 'don'ts' dominate your thoughts and words rather than illuminate the more liberating and motivating 'dos', but *Je Ne Sais Pas Pourquoi*[1] (I don't know why).[2] Try to adopt a positive and motivating outlook by expressing and cultivating what you want rather than negatively ruminating on what you don't want. Leave alone or challenge those who try to define you only by what you don't have, such as a job, partner or children.

Some omissions are conspicuous by their absence: don't be afraid to live your life; don't fear change; don't overcomplicate what's simple; don't try to be someone you're not; don't expect to please all of the people all of the time; don't worry about what others may think of you; don't delegate major decisions; don't allow life to end before it ends; don't add negativity to a bad situation; don't suffer imaginary troubles; don't put off or prolong challenging tasks; don't hold grudges or seek revenge (don't become like the person who wronged you); don't override or neglect your body's deep biology (your need for sleep, movement and a healthy diet); don't treat your body as a biological bin; don't take time for granted and don't shy away from taking calculated risks or making mistakes. While the lyrical advice may lack detailed reasoning or step-by-step guidance, its core message is sound. Remember that gratitude is a positive acknowledgement of what you already have, not what you don't have.

1   *Je Ne Sais Pas Pourquoi* by Kylie Minogue. Written by Michael Stock, Matthew Aitken and Peter Waterman

2   *Good Thing* by Fine Young Cannibals. Written by Roland Gift and David Steele

DREAMS

Lionel Richie had an awesome dream.[1] According to Roman mythology, dreamers like Richie owe their experiences to Morpheus, the god of dreams and son of Somnus (the god of sleep, who gave his name to its infuriating absence – and the most common thief of night-time sleep[2] – insomnia). Morpheus can take any form as he ventures on his nightly invasions inside your somnolent head.[3] For centuries, dreams and the sleep from which they arose were seen as divine gifts.

This dream theme explores both unconscious nocturnal concoctions and conscious daytime aspirations. Pop songs often depict dreams as being broken (usually in a dramatic-sounding way, such as in *Shattered Dreams*),[4] fulfilled, wild, sweet or nostalgic. Both types of dreams have the potential to transform your life.

First, those night-time dreams. In the chorus to *These Dreams*, Heart tells us how, during each second of their nightly escapades, they live a different life.[5] To live those dreams[6] sounds enticing, especially through lucid dreaming – a form of parasomnia where you control the unfolding events, raising the possibility of a dream within a dream[7] (from Edgar Allan Poe's titular poem). While it's true that you dream every night, you don't dream for every second of the night. Sleep involves a series of complex, multi-phase brainwave cycles, each lasting approximately 75 to 90 minutes, so you will typically transition through five or six cycles when sleeping seven-and-a-half hours (an ideal minimum reached by far too few) to nine hours. If most days feel like an endless groggy struggle to stay

1   *Say You, Say Me* by Lionel Richie. Written by Lionel Richie
2   *Do What You Do* by Jermaine Jackson. Written by Larry Ditomaso and Ralph Palladino
3   *Something's Gotten Hold Of My Heart* by Marc Almond featuring Gene Pitney. Written by Frederick Cook and Roger Greenaway
4   *Shattered Dreams* by Johnny Hates Jazz. Written by Clark Datchler
5   *These Dreams* by Heart. Written by Bernard Taupin and Martin Page
6   *Relax* by Frankie Goes To Hollywood. Written by Peter Gill, William Johnson and Mark O'Toole
7   *Running In The Family* by Level 42. Written by Mark King, Waliou Badarou and Philip Gould

awake or sufficiently alert or focused, you may be playing hostage to nothing more than sleep deprivation.

These sleep cycles resemble the path traced by a deep-diving whale as it descends from the surface (representing consciousness) through the oceanic zones to feed close to the seabed (the equivalent sleep phase is restorative, non-dreaming deep sleep) before resurfacing every 90 minutes or so. Each stage within the sleep cycle has a role and may have evolved to allow us to check for dangers during this vulnerable, non-conscious time. Your most intense, frequent and memorable dreams occur during short bursts of frantic brain activity in the rapid eye movement (REM) phase in the 'light' zone closest to the surface of the ocean/consciousness. The first REM phase typically begins after about 90 minutes and then repeats after subsequent 90-minute intervals. Consequently, you can expect to experience five vivid, discrete dreams each night, accounting for only about 20-25% of your night's sleep.

Dreams are not always idyllic. In the *Mad World* of Tears For Fears, the duo describe how their best dreams are those in which they believe they are dying[1] (a phenomenon common among terminally ill patients), while Iron Maiden's *Infinite Dreams* describes the torment some dreams evoke.[2] Dreams involving a sensation of choking may be a manifestation of obstructive sleep apnoea, the brief cessation of normal breathing while asleep caused by the relaxing and narrowing of throat muscles around the trachea (windpipe), which is common in snorers and may feed peril into dreams. Singing (which strengthens throat muscles), sleeping on your side, avoiding overtiredness and quitting the bad-boy trio of alcohol, smoking, and tranquilising drugs may help alleviate this condition. Even without sleep apnoea, fear – such as that which accompanies the common and recurring examination anxiety dream – remains the most common emotion experienced in dreams, which may indicate unresolved emotional issues or the remnants of trauma.

1   *Mad World* by Tears For Fears. Written by Roland Orzabal
2   *Infinite Dreams* by Iron Maiden. Written by Stephen Harris

Matthew Wilder pondered the symbolic meaning of his strange dreams.[1] The ancients viewed mysterious dreams as a form of prophecy. Building on the voluminous writings of Greek diviner Artemidorus, the more modern theories of psychoanalyst Sigmund Freud sought to interpret, analyse and decode dreams, usually as windows into the unconscious mind that mirror desires (typically repressed sexual desires), fears and challenges present in our waking life. Before following Billy Joel's advice to share all his crazy dreams[2] with his partner, remember that not everyone (bar your Freudian psychoanalyst) will be interested in hearing about them.

Several top 10 songs from the 1980s were said to have been directly inspired by dreams. However, it remains exceedingly rare for non-musicians to hear music while dreaming.

The second dream theme is aspirational – the dreams that, in a good sense, keep you awake at night. These often youthful dreams[3] are the ones you methodically construct when you take a series of small steps (such as selecting subjects to study to pursue your desired career) that, over time, help bring you closer to achieving a more significant, long-term goal – referred to lyrically as building a dream.[4] The clearer your dream – the more precise you are about the specifics of what you want – the easier it is to determine the necessary steps you'll need to take. (Note, however, that aspirational dreams can shift with age as your priorities and circumstances change.) If you don't have a well-defined, ready-made dream to guide you, try vividly visualising what your ideal life would look, sound and feel like. Without such a dream, how will you know if your dream comes true?[5]

---

1 *Break My Stride* by Matthew Wilder. Written by Matthew Weiner and Gregory Prestopino
2 *Tell Her About It* by Billy Joel. Written by William Joel
3 *I Want It All* by Queen. Written by Brian May, Freddie Mercury, John Deacon and Roger Taylor
4 *Burning Bridges (On And Off And On Again)* by Status Quo. Written by Francis Rossi and Andrew Bown
5 *Happy Talk* by Captain Sensible. Written by Oscar Hammerstein and Richard Rodgers

According to *Love Of The Common People,*[1] it's hard to live on dreams alone. Keeping a dream alive[2] requires self-belief and action, while regularly revisiting dreams can motivate you to stay on track. Those whose dreams remain unfulfilled commonly cite how other demands of everyday life get in the way,[3] leading to the neglect, relegation or sidelining of their dreams. If negative thoughts hinder your dream fulfilment, it's within your remit to overcome or circumnavigate them.

Sound advice? A whole world of dreams[4] resides in the unconscious mind for everyone every night and, for daydreamers, throughout moments during their waking hours. Daydreaming is natural and commonplace, offering a calm and constructive escape that promotes relaxation, improves concentration and focus and can help you create or revisit perfect moments throughout imperfect days. Provided you don't allow daydreams to become intrusive, distracting or too focused on the past, they can help unleash innate creativity and encourage flights of fancy by connecting unrelated thoughts.

Some fear that the constant hyper-connectivity of today's digital world impinges on any spare moments to such a degree that we no longer have or create any daily unallocated free time to simply sit with our thoughts, recharge or allow our minds to wander and indulge in reverie. *It Doesn't Have To Be This Way.*[5] Just five minutes of intentional daily daydreaming (or shorter, more frequent microbreaks) can counteract this and help you dare to believe in creative possibilities and prime your subconscious to incubate and deliver positive outcomes. Electronic devices, with their vampire-like drain on your time and attention, also emit short-wavelength blue light to which your body's receptors are sensitive and can disrupt your brain's

1 *Love Of The Common People* by Paul Young. Written by John Hurley and Ronnie Wilkins
2 *Alive And Kicking* by Simple Minds. Written by James Kerr, Charles Burchill and Michael MacNeil
3 *A New England* by Kirsty MacColl. Written by Stephen Bragg
4 *The Best* by Tina Turner. Written by Michael Chapman and Holly Erlanger
5 *It Doesn't Have To Be This Way* by The Blow Monkeys. Written by Bruce Howard

ability to produce melatonin, the hormone of darkness essential for sleep. To avoid electronic overstimulation before bedtime, put down your screens and pick up a printed book (which also improves retention of what you've read).

Hold On Tight[1] to your aspirational dreams, as they can help transform your life. Continue to dare to dream and define what your dreams look like, but try not to delude yourself about the practicalities of life by over-sweetening illusory dreams.[2] Pursuing your dreams with the passion, desire and determination that comes with purposeful hard work (aspiration usually involves perspiration)[3] will help turn your dream into reality.[4] Ambitious, aspirational dreams (and subsequent actions) have shaped much of our culture and society, leaving lasting legacies that continue to shine long after the light of the initial dreamer has flickered its last.

As old as advanced consciousness, dreams have always held a deep fascination. However, if perfect dream recall were advantageous because dreams played a significant or survival role in our waking existence, we would have evolved perfect dream recall. Our actual evolved trait may be our inability to remember dreams as a form of protection against what is, after all, not real.[5] In *I've Never Been To Me*, Charlene is confident that you, like many others, dream about what you'll never do.[6] As dreams exist only in *The Land Of Make Believe*,[7] it's possible (among many other possibilities) that dreaming allows us to confront our internalised anxieties, permitting us to explore various strategies and mentally rehearse opportunities to

1   *Hold On Tight* by Electric Light Orchestra. Written by Jeffrey Lynne
2   *One Vision* by Queen. Written by Brian May, Freddie Mercury, Roger Taylor and John Deacon
3   *Push It* by Salt-N-Pepa. Written by Hurby Azor and Ray Davies
4   *Happy Birthday* by Stevie Wonder. Written by Stevie Wonder
5   *Hold Me Now* by Johnny Logan. Written by Seán Sherrard
6   *I've Never Been To Me* by Charlene. Written by Kenneth Hirsch and Ronald Gould
7   *The Land Of Make Believe* by Bucks Fizz. Written by Andrew Hill and Peter Sinfield

meet with unusual situations, unlikely people[1] or even imaginary creatures in odd or unusual settings, all within the safe space of a dream. The threat simulation theory extends this idea to explain the evolution and function of nightmares that, once again, allow the sleeper to rehearse how to deal with the fears, threats and unfamiliar encounters (common to our early ancestors) before encountering similar events in waking life. You could stretch this idea further and apply it to the access afforded when listening to songs, where you can hear, think about and explore the intimate and illuminated interiors of emotion and raw honesty expressed within a song, all free of real-life consequences.

For Shakespeare's Macbeth, sleep was the chief nourisher in life's feast. The dreams that feed off sleep serve as a vital source of artistic inspiration. Creative artists like Salvador Dali and Edgar Allan Poe have incorporated free-thinking, hallucinatory fragments from the rich surrealistic sights[2] and often chaotic imagery of their micro-nap dreams – particularly from the fleeting transition between wakefulness and sleep known as hypnagogia – into their work. As you begin the gentle slide into the arms of sleep, try to convince yourself that you will remember your dreams. Much like successful pop songs, dreams comprise emotions[3] rather than simply replaying mundane events. In about one in five dreams, you can generate creative and unbounded mental imagery or fantasy – where you can dream the impossible.[4] You will need to act quickly to capture and retain these thoughts as the gentle warmth from the first rays of morning light[5] swiftly evaporates these delicate, watery images long before they have had the chance to leave a trace on your waking mind.

1   *Come Live With Me* by Heaven 17. Written by Glenn Gregory, Ian Craig Marsh and Martyn Ware
2   *Echo Beach* by Martha And The Muffins. Written by Mark Gane
3   *It's A Miracle* by Culture Club. Written by Roy Hay, George O'Dowd, Michael Craig, Jonathan Moss and Philip Pickett
4   *Shattered Dreams* by Johnny Hates Jazz. Written by Clark Datchler
5   *First Time* by Robin Beck. Written by Gavin Spencer, Thomas Anthony and Terence Boyle

For some, a short nap of between 15 and 30 minutes can effectively reset their energy and alertness levels after the natural post-lunch dip. Naps are about quality, not quantity; longer naps may tip you into a deep sleep phase that triggers sleep inertia (grogginess) or interferes with your night-time sleep (so no napping after 3pm; insomniacs shouldn't nap at all). A strong coffee immediately before a nap – sometimes dubbed a 'nappuccino' – can help counteract any grogginess, as the rapidly absorbed caffeine takes about 20 minutes to start mounting its blockade of the sleep-inducing adenosine receptors in your brain. Caffeine, the world's most widely consumed psycho-active substance present in coffee, some teas, colas and chocolate, is commonly used to counteract the same sleep deprivation and fragmentation that it often causes; caffeine halts the decline in how attentive you would otherwise feel from the daily accumulation of adenosine, a sleep-inducing chemical that builds up daily within your brain. Short naps or micro-sleeps can yield vivid, creative dreams, help consolidate memories and learning, boost psychological well-being, improve coordination and reaction times and recharge general performance and productivity for many hours after waking. Furthermore, what's good for your brain is good for your heart (and vice versa), and you should always cherish A Good Heart.[1] The biggest challenge within a busy schedule is carving out the time and space to incorporate your forty winks.[2]

The sense of empowerment you feel when controlling a lucid dream can be brought to waking life,[3] boosting your confidence to take charge of real-life situations. (If you don't experience lucid dreams, instead write about those moments where you felt empowered and full of confidence, which can help you relive those moments.) Likewise, trusting your creative imagination while awake can help give you the charismatic confidence to visualise leading your ideal life and allow you to rehearse and role-play any tricky situations.

1 A Good Heart by Feargal Sharkey. Written by Maria McKee
2 I Won't Let The Sun Go Down On Me by Nik Kershaw. Written by Nicholas Kershaw
3 Living On Video by Trans-X. Written by Pascal Languirand

Your aim is to become the writer, producer, director and star of your dreams.

Similarly, motor imagery, where you mentally rehearse physical actions like playing a musical instrument or striking a ball through vivid visualisation, enhances and fine-tunes the neural connections between your brain and muscles, mirroring the real action and improving your performance. Likewise, to induce sleep onset, try embarking on a detailed but imaginary walk.

Roman author Pliny told the tale of a young shepherd named Epimenides who fell asleep in a cave, failed to hear his alarm go off and overslept for 57 years. Upon waking, he found he possessed enough wisdom to become a poet and priest. Sleep plays a vital role in learning and processing information, so it's sound advice to sleep on an important decision or when trying to solve a problem. However, despite the positive outcome of Epimenides' legendary oversleep and the prevalence in medieval myths and tales of those who have fallen asleep, dreamt and awoken to find themselves blessed with newfound and mystical powers, chronic oversleeping – hypersomnia – is too much of a *Good Thing*[1] and detrimental to your health by increasing the risk of all-cause mortality. The medical advice is clear: once rested, get up,[2] and a blast from Black Box may be just what you need to kick-start your day.

Some argue that dreams and music are both examples of epiphenomena – mere by-products of brain activity. While the complete biological purpose of sleep continues to elude science, the importance of good quality sleep as the bedrock of physical and mental health in everything from tissue repair to memory consolidation is indisputable. When asleep, your body performs its quotidian housekeeping duties, including a good sweep-out of harmful neurotoxic metabolic waste debris, such as beta-amyloid and tau proteins, which, if left to accumulate within your brain, contribute to neurodegenerative

1   *Good Thing* by Fine Young Cannibals. Written by Roland Gift and David Steele
2   *Ride On Time* by Black Box. Written by Daniel Hartman, Daniele Davoli, Mirco Limoni and Valerio Semplici

diseases. The amount of sleep needed for peak cognitive performance and non-irritability varies between individuals and with age: babies can sleep for a cat-like 17 hours a day, while very young children may wake soon after some 'net lagged' nocturnal teenagers – whose circadian rhythms have been shunted forward by two or three hours – finally settle into bed, where they subsequently need nine to ten hours' sleep. Sleep is as essential for survival as food and water.

In fulfilling its role as part of the American dream, New York is a city that never sleeps.[1] The rest of our fast-paced world seems determined to adopt this unforgiving approach; reported levels of feeling 'TATT' ('tired all the time') continue to rise. Those genetically rare individuals who can function on only a few hours of sleep – most famously Margaret Thatcher – often wear their lack of sleep as a badge of strength and success. However, don't be bullied into thinking that sleep is the preserve of lazy wimps. Rest, relaxation and sleep are highly productive and essential in allowing both mind and body to recalibrate and recuperate; time sleep is always well spent, not wasted. There are no short cuts to achieving restorative sleep: it's the natural thing to do.[2] You must rest to maintain your body and brain at its best.

I Go To Sleep.[3] As a third-of-your-life recharging necessity rather than a dispensable lifestyle luxury, prioritise and treat your sleep with the respect it deserves by establishing a 'sleep hygiene' routine that you look forward to completing each night, helping you to smooth the path to sleep and perchance to dream. Completing such a routine (even if you only pretend to be tired) primes your brain to relax and wind down. Although essential and probably the best predictor of the quality of your waking life, remember to embrace, relish and luxuriate in the natural indulgence of rest[4]

1   *Theme From New York, New York* by Frank Sinatra. Written by Fred Ebb and John Kander
2   *Tonight, I Celebrate My Love* by Peabo Bryson and Roberta Flack. Written by Gerald Goffin and Michael Masser
3   *I Go To Sleep* by The Pretenders. Written by Raymond Davies
4   *Sledgehammer* by Peter Gabriel. Written by Peter Gabriel

and the creative powers and possibilities that dreams can awaken.

The idiom that you should sleep as soundly as a log[1] is only likely if you make your bedroom a sanctuary of rest and contemplation – cool, dark and quiet. Avoid turning your bedroom into a private cinema, an office extension, a digital shopping centre or a place you associate with any activity requiring full wakefulness. If you share a mattress with a partner who snores or fidgets and who likes to toss and turn throughout the night[2] or play *Night Games*[3] such as duvet tug-of-war – and thus constantly disturbs and interrupts your slumber – and you have the luxury of a spare bedroom, then lie back and think of separate beds. Sleeping apart may enhance the quality and quantity of your sleep and even improve your relationship by reducing the resentment, frustration and irritability that arise from disturbed sleep. If you don't have a spare bedroom but need to reduce your partner's snoring, encourage them to lose any excess weight, ditch nicotine and forgo using alcohol as a sedative; sedated sleep is fragmented sleep.

So Cold The Night.[4] Whether master or spare, aim to keep your well-ventilated bedroom cooler than other rooms (ideally about 18 degrees Celsius; keep your feet warm for quicker sleep onset), clutter-free and brightly lit only in the morning (naturally or artificially). In the evening, dimming your bedroom lights is a better way to illuminate[5] than using bright, short-wavelength digital blue light from an end-of-day doom-scrolling session. Low, calm and warm light entices your body to release melatonin. By using curtains, blackout blinds or an eye mask, external light should not find you[6]

---

1 *The Beatles' Movie Medley* by The Beatles. Written by John Lennon and Paul McCartney
2 *The Rain* by Oran "Juice" Jones. Written by Vincent Bell
3 *Night Games* by Graham Bonnet. Written by Edwin Hamilton
4 *So Cold The Night* by The Communards. Written by Richard Coles and James Somerville
5 *Baby I Don't Care* by Transvision Vamp. Written by Nicholas Sayer
6 *Everybody Wants To Rule The World* by Tears For Fears. Written by Roland Orzabal, Ian Stanley and Christopher Hughes

so that, when the lights go out,[1] you can switch off in a restful room darker than a Goth's Vantablack overcoat. If your bedroom isn't dark, your sleep will be light.

Just Can't Get Enough?[2] If you struggle to fall asleep within 20 minutes of your head hitting the pillow, try some of the following techniques. To help regulate your biological body clock (this master clock resides within your brain's hypothalamus) and improve cardiovascular health, aim to go to bed at about the same time every night; the optimal bedtime appears to be in the hour after 10pm, a time when the body's core temperature naturally drops by about one degree Celsius. A scheduled, consistent bedtime helps you to wake up naturally at about the same time each morning without relying on sunrise-mimicking smart lights or the stressing jolt of an audible alarm. Try avoiding the de-synchronising jet lag effects of shift work. Restrict eating a large meal to about three/four hours before bedtime to allow your body to prepare for sleep rather than digestion; forgo mindless sofa or intra-meal snacking. Reading a physical book can be calming by reducing stress, lowering your heart rate and easing muscle tension. Engage in some simple deep breathing exercises for a few minutes as you prepare to fall asleep, along with a body scan where you focus on – and, in turn, relax – each body part, starting with your toes and working up to the top of your head. Try falling asleep in a foetal position on your non-dominant side. If you listen to music as you drift off into your world of sleep,[3] choose sounds that soothe and relax, with rhythms of about 60 to 80 beats per minute to match and mirror your resting heartbeat. If you listen to music via a mobile device, place it just beyond arm's reach to avoid a sneak peek. Technology is likely to play an increasing role in helping to alleviate sleep disorders by allowing monitoring to move from sleep laboratories into the convenience of your bedroom. Finally, allow enough time (between six and twelve hours for most

1   *Walls Come Tumbling Down!* by The Style Council. Written by John Weller
2   *Just Can't Get Enough* by Depeche Mode. Written by Vincent Martin
3   *Song For Whoever* by The Beautiful South. Written by Paul Heaton and David Rotheray

metabolisms) for any caffeine consumed during the day to lose its lingering and blockading grip on you and your brain.[1]

Creating an environment conducive to good sleep (which extends to taking daily exercise) to aid the natural benefits that quality sleep and dreaming yields is always worthwhile. While it may not be romantic to sleep apart from your dream partner, the alternative – severe chronic sleep deprivation caused by lost slumber[2] – is far less appealing. In the short term, a lack of good quality sleep will disrupt your emotional regulation (making you irritable), sap your energy, loosen your self-control (sleep-deprived people often crave calorie-rich snacks) and thus dampen your ability to perform cognitively – creatively or productively – at your highest level. Poor sleep (less than six hours per night or fragmented) in the longer term is linked to an elevated risk of a host of adverse physical and psychological outcomes, all of which you will want to avoid, especially the nightmare of Alzheimer's, diabetes (also associated with an increased risk of developing dementia), cardiovascular disease, obesity and cancer, all things you can do without.[3] Chronic snorers rarely treat this common problem – and twice as common in men – with the seriousness it deserves, despite contributing to sleep deprivation, depression and the destabilisation of relationships (often cited as a contributory factor in divorce proceedings). Snorers are often blissfully unaware of the problem or play down its significance and are thus disinclined to try remedial measures.

We Take Mystery (To Bed).[4] A duvet of doubt shrouds much of our understanding of dreams and the sleep from which they arise; beware those beckoning siren songs that try to lure you away from the incredible benefits of both.

1   *Don't Tell Me* by Blancmange. Written by Neil Arthur and Stephen Luscombe
2   *Call Me* by Spagna. Written by Giorgio Spagna, Ivana Spagna and Alfredo Pignagnoli
3   *Shout* by Tears For Fears. Written by Roland Orzabal and Ian Stanley
4   *We Take Mystery (To Bed)* by Gary Numan. Written by Gary Webb

DRUGS

For Bobby Brown, the world was a trip.[1] Drugs, despite their well-documented physical and mental harms – ranging from irreversible liver damage to mind-bending psychosis – make users feel good – albeit a heaven wrapped in hell. This religious metaphor leads us to the entheogenic theory, which posits that the use of mind-altering psychedelics by early communities sparked mystical experiences that, in turn, sowed the seeds for the development of religion. Substances such as cannabis and alcohol have been a part of human history for nearly 10,000 years, providing users with an escape from the harsh realities of life.

The connection between drugs and music is also far from new. In modern culture, drugs are regularly sandwiched between sex and rock 'n' roll. Musicians and lyricists have long experimented with stimulants, especially psychedelics, to alter their consciousness, experience the world anew, and gain fresh perspectives on life.[2] Brain activity and perception can be distorted by surging with stimulants (like waking up to a blast of amphetamine)[3] or dampened by depressants. The more recent potted history of soft drugs and hard rock (and hard drugs and soft rock) often highlights the grim toll that drug abuse has on those who live fast and die young.[4] One often unfelt danger[5] for users searching for musical inspiration is that drugs can blunt all life's edges and feelings, creating a life devoid of meaning[6] beyond the craving for yet more drugs, as increasing tolerance turns users into lifeless addicts. All too easily, drugs take

1   *My Prerogative* by Bobby Brown. Written by Robert Brown, Edward Riley and Gene Griffin
2   *The Living Years* by Mike + The Mechanics. Written by Brian Robertson and Michael Rutherford
3   *Beat Surrender* by The Jam. Written by John Weller
4   *The Message* by Grandmaster Flash And The Furious Five. Written by Clifton Chase, Edward Fletcher, Melvin Glover and Sylvia Vanterpool
5   *One More Try* by George Michael. Written by George Michael
6   *Do Nothing* by The Specials featuring Rico with The Ice Rink String Sounds. Written by Lynval Golding and Jeremy Dammers

control of users' lives, impairing and blurring reality with their deceptive hallucinations that can dislocate the senses.[1] When users reach the point where they've become human pincushions willing to inject anything,[2] or they cannot untangle illusion from reality,[3] it's time for urgent professional help.

At the start of the 1980s, drug references needed to be cryptic to retain a song's presence on the all-important radio playlists. *Golden Brown*,[4] with its subtle titular nod to heroin, exemplifies this. As the decade progressed and the significance of radio playlists waned, these veiled drug references began to fade, especially with the advent of the less socially stigmatised, pill-popping acid house scene.

Hooked On Classics.[5] Music can be addictive and mind-altering – although more *A Kind Of Magic*[6] than a kind of mushroom. From the high of performing to the compulsive desire created by activating and manipulating the brain's pleasure and reward centres, this musical drug is more catnip than cocaine, unlikely to cauterise your neural reward circuitry. Nowadays, many are hooked to digital devices and the dopamine hit they receive from social media interactions. Whether addiction is substance-based or behavioural, the underlying problem remains: you give in to what you cannot give up.[7]

Addicted To Love.[8] Love, particularly the thrilling high of first love, can feel like another hard-to-quit addiction[9] and is often

---

1   *There Must Be An Angel (Playing With My Heart)* by Eurythmics. Written by Ann Lennox and David Stewart
2   *Wood Beez (Pray Like Aretha Franklin)* by Scritti Politti. Written by Paul Strohmeyer
3   *In The Army Now* by Status Quo. Written by Robert Bolland and Ferdinand Bolland
4   *Golden Brown* by The Stranglers. Written by Hugh Cornwell, Jean-Jacques Burnel, David Greenfield and Brian Duffy
5   *Hooked On Classics* by Royal Philharmonic Orchestra. Arranged by Louis Clark
6   *A Kind Of Magic* by Queen. Written by Roger Taylor
7   *Cry Wolf* by A-ha. Written by Pål Waaktaar Gamst and Magne Furuholmen
8   *Addicted To Love* by Robert Palmer. Written by Robert Palmer
9   *Don't Go* by Yazoo. Written by Vincent Martin

portrayed as such in pop songs such as *Classic*,[1] *Love Is A Stranger*,[2] *Hard Habit To Break*,[3] *Dancing On The Floor (Hooked On Love)*[4] and *My One Temptation*.[5]

Sound advice? Within the tolerant culture of the music industry, where drugs and the literal *High Life*[6] are more accessible than for the general population, substance use is widespread. Grandmaster & Melle Mel deliver forceful and explicit sound advice against drug use with intravenous effectiveness; their double dose of 'don't' in *White Lines (Don't Don't Do It)*[7] serves not as a double negative but as doubly emphatic in a song that emphasises the high personal and financial costs of drug addiction.

Whether ancient or designer, legal or illegal, drugs taken to ease pain often end up causing more of it. Thrills and pills[8] become especially problematic when people (users and those in the supply chain) start dying for drugs. Hard drugs increase users' exposure to risks and troubles, including violent behaviour, relationship breakdowns, infectious diseases, poor decision-making and criminal activity to fund addiction. Even softer drugs can harm mental and physical health, and they impose societal costs through impaired cognition (and the increased risk of accident and injury), lost or unproductive time and the general depletion of human potential. Addiction is non-discriminatory; it always takes more than it gives and is far easier to start than stop.

The soundest advice is always to reduce or eliminate toxins from

1   *Classic* by Adrian Gurvitz. Written by Adrian Gurvitz
2   *Love Is A Stranger* by Eurythmics. Written by Ann Lennox and David Stewart
3   *Hard Habit To Break* by Chicago. Written by Steven Kipner and John Lewis Parker
4   *Dancing On The Floor (Hooked On Love)* by Third World. Written by William Clarke
5   *My One Temptation* by Mica Paris. Written by Michael Leeson, Stephen Waters and Peter Vale
6   *High Life* by Modern Romance. Written by David Jaymes and Trevor Jones
7   *White Lines (Don't Don't Do It)* by Grandmaster & Melle Mel. Written by Melvin Glover and Sylvia Vanterpool
8   *Let's Go Crazy* by Prince And The Revolution. Written by Prince Nelson

your life, whether from external sources such as air pollution, food additives (organic helps minimise exposure to chemicals), cosmetics or social media, or from internal sources, such as the voices in your head.[1]

Chasing the high life often involves dealing with lowlifes. Drug dealers don't deal in hope, but they will cost you plenty of money and time.[2] The only needle-and-arm you should contemplate is the turntable that injects inspirational music into your life, not fleeting chemical escapism into your veins. The sound advice from the end of this line,[3] and upon which you can never overdose, is clear: avoid drugs.

EDUCATION

Everybody's Got To Learn Sometime.[4] Education is life's great enabler, transforming the lives of the young (and the not-so-young) by opening doors to opportunities and careers and serving as a valuable vehicle for social mobility. Yet, for many, the oppressive stress and pressure of education feels more stifling than liberating. "Unwilling to school", wrote Shakespeare.

Successful songwriters explore universal themes, and education (especially secondary education) is a universal theme among young music enthusiasts because everyone has to go to school.[5] These artists are acutely aware of the uniform tribulations of standardisation and suppressed individuality – the thought control and the feeling

1   *Gloria* by Laura Branigan. Written by Umberto Tozzi, Giancarlo Bigazzi and Trevor Veitch
2   *True Faith* by New Order. Written by Gillian Gilbert, Stephen Hague, Peter Hook, Stephen Morris and Bernard Sumner
3   *Paradise City* by Guns N' Roses. Written by Saul Hudson, William Rose, Jeffrey Isbell, Michael McKagan and Steven Adler
4   *Everybody's Got To Learn Sometime* by The Korgis. Written by James Warren
5   *Holiday Rap* by MC Miker and DJ Sven. Written by Brian Bennett, Curtis Hudson, Bruce Welch, Lisa Stevens, Lucien Witteveen and Sven van Veen

of being just *Another Brick In The Wall*[1] - that comes with, and is exacerbated by, the tyranny of educational micromanagement, including rigid timetables, the endless ringing of bells,[2] homework, detentions, uniforms, prescribed hairstyles, rote learning, cramming for high-stake exams and (especially in the 1980s) unappetising school meals. It's no wonder that Toyah exclaimed *I Want To Be Free*.[3]

Songs about education are often sour with resentment rather than sweet with nostalgia. What - if anything - did songwriters learn from their time in education? Madness learnt to bend rather than break arbitrary rules,[4] the Pet Shop Boys learnt purity in their thinking, language and actions[5] (with limited success), Dexys Midnight Runners felt academically uninspired,[6] Sam Cooke retained little knowledge of history, biology, science, French . . .'[7] (*C'est La Vie*),[8] while The Specials left their school with an 'O' level in art, which did little for them.[9] Some students feel that there is much they do not want to learn,[10] believing instead that success requires little more than a street degree[11] from the University of Life.

Lessons in Love.[12] The Police investigate classroom dynamics awash with sexuality and erotic fixation in their song *Don't Stand*

1   *Another Brick In The Wall* (Part II) by Pink Floyd. Written by George Waters
2   *Food For Thought* by UB40. Written by James Brown, Alistair Campbell, Robin Campbell, Earl Falconer, Norman Hassan, Brian Travers, Michael Virtue and Terence Wilson
3   *I Want To Be Free* by Toyah. Written by Toyah Willcox and Joel Bogen
4   *Baggy Trousers* by Madness. Written by Graham McPherson and Christopher Foreman
5   *It's A Sin* by Pet Shop Boys. Written by Neil Tennant and Christopher Lowe
6   *Geno* by Dexys Midnight Runners. Written by Kevin Archer and Kevin Rowland
7   *Wonderful World* by Sam Cooke. Written by Lester Adler, Herb Alpert and Samuel Cooke
8   *C'est La Vie* by Robbie Nevil. Written by Robert Nevil, Duncan Pain and Mark Holding
9   *Rat Race* by The Specials. Written by Roderick Byers
10 *One More Try* by George Michael. Written by George Michael
11 *Girlfriend* by Pebbles. Written by Kenneth Edmonds and Antonio Reid
12 *Lessons In Love* by Level 42. Written by Waliou Badarou, Mark King and Rowland Gould

So Close To Me.[1] In matters of the heart, love and relationships are meant to be your teachers, not with your teachers.

Sound Advice? What's the lyrical lesson taught by education?[2] You are unlikely to learn all of life's essentials (though you will learn a lot of maths) within a flawed, tick-box production-line educational system that relies on snapshot examination results as its primary sorting mechanism. Karel Fialka wondered whether his young son would learn to live, and live and learn.[3] The value of education extends beyond the struggle for official recognition conferred by a paper qualification earned through a rigid curriculum of goal-oriented targets (the national curriculum, 'key stages' and an element of school choice were all introduced under the Education Reform Act 1988). Academic subjects rarely recognise the importance of independence, resourcefulness, adaptability, tenacity, confidence, cooperation, creativity or critical thinking, despite all these transferable skills being crucial for navigating adulthood and the world of work.

Should schools prioritise teaching societal values or focus on high-stakes examinations that allow society, other educational establishments and potential employers to evaluate academic achievement? In a 'comprehensive' education system, students should be exposed to all facets of learning to become well-rounded, informed citizens. The idea of a comprehensive or universal education is not new. Jan Amos Komenský (1592-1670), known as Comenius and the father of modern education, believed that everyone should learn about everything to improve our understanding and tolerance of each other. Greek philosopher Aristotle (a pupil of Plato, who in turn was a pupil of Socrates) advocated for young people to be educated in music and PE. Discuss.

Teachers wield considerable control over their charges, so avoid upsetting the teacher[4] or wasting their time (or, as they describe it,

1   *Don't Stand So Close To Me* by The Police. Written by Gordon Sumner
2   *Mad World* by Tears For Fears. Written by Roland Orzabal
3   *Hey, Matthew* by Karel Fialka. Written by Karel Fialka
4   *The Circus* by Erasure. Written by Vincent Martin and Andrew Bell

wasting your time). Teachers should be authoritative figures who inspire intellectual exploration by igniting omnivorous curiosity. If a teacher asks you to ingest morsels of information to regurgitate for an exam, but you find these gristly gobbets are more likely to get stuck in your throat than in your memory, try learning through self-testing or imagine explaining the material in a way understandable to an imaginary child, or a real one if you happen to have one handy (it's their time you're wasting). As sleep plays a crucial role in helping you retain and consolidate what you have learnt, always resist the temptation to cram *All Night Long.*[1]

Much of what you learn during the first quarter of life will forever stay with you. The most important lesson (aside from not running in corridors while carrying scissors) is to keep feeling fascination[2] and foster a lifelong love of learning that cultivates and pursues relentless curiosity. Such an approach nurtures personal growth and development. And the data show a high probability that if you refresh those lapsed maths skills you will improve your physical and mental health and earning potential throughout your extended life.

Education imparts essential social skills and core knowledge, such as arithmetic and grammar. Learning should begin before formal schooling (such as learning the alphabet through song) and continue long after your last day in education or your first day in the working world. Today, students remain in full-time education for much longer than in the 1980s (in 1980, only 15% stayed after age 18, rising to 25% by 1990 and doubling again by 2018).

By engaging in mentally challenging learning, you can alter the structure and build new neural pathways within your brain through a remarkable process called neuroplasticity. If you start learning later in life, you may call yourself an 'opsimath'. If this word is new to you, regard it as your first step.

Regardless of your age or stage of life, one quality remains a

1   *All Night Long* by Rainbow. Written by Written by Richard Blackmore and Roger Glover

2   *(Keep Feeling) Fascination* by The Human League. Written by John Callis and Philip Oakey

central starting point for success in education, learning and life: *Desire.*[1] You will continue to learn about aspects of who you are through the lessons in life's curriculum.

ENVIRONMENT

Environmental awareness, spurred by urgent wake-up calls including acid rain, pollution, deforestation, desertification, the population boom,[2] nuclear concerns, and the Antarctic ozone hole, helped define the 1980s.

On 26 April 1986, a catastrophic explosion at the three-year-old Chernobyl nuclear reactor in Ukraine released vast quantities of contaminating radiation that drifted *sans frontières*[3] across Europe, reaching the UK. Highly visible pollution incidents – such as the devastating 1989 oil spill from the Exxon Valdez into the fragile Alaskan ecosystem – and the invisible but increasingly detectable threats from the something-in-the-air[4] peril of radiation or colourless, odourless gases such as the ozone-depleting chlorofluorocarbons (CFCs) followed. Sleep deprivation (see the theme on *Dreams*) was a common denominator and significant causal factor at Chernobyl and aboard the Exxon Valdez.

As the 1980s advanced, environmental awareness and activism gained momentum, migrating from the margins to become more mainstream, thanks, in part, to several speeches from a most unexpected advocate: Margaret Thatcher. Whether the green that seeped into her blue heart[5] was driven by political expediency or genuine concern is debatable, especially given her government's reliance on

---

1   *Desire* by U2. Written by Paul Hewson, Adam Clayton, David Evans and Laurence Mullen Jr
2   *Too Much Too Young* by The Specials featuring Rico. Written by Jeremy Dammers and Lloyd Tyrell
3   *Games Without Frontiers* by Peter Gabriel. Written by Peter Gabriel
4   *Dance Yourself Dizzy* by Liquid Gold. Written by Adrian Baker and Edward Seago
5   *Red Red Wine* by UB40. Written by Neil Diamond

the substantial revenues from North Sea black gas.[1] While words alone are no solution to pollution,[2] environmental issues did begin to gain traction.

Some pop songs reflected broader concerns about turning our back on Mother Nature,[3] such as the Pet Shop Boys' cover of *It's Alright*[4] (deforestation and desertification) and UB40's *The Earth Dies Screaming.*[5]

Sound advice? Given the magnitude of the existential threat facing our planet's environment, it's no surprise that some songs were flecked with toxic darkness. Songwriters correctly recognised that humanity was not merely a passive observer but an active agent in environmental degradation.

Sydney Youngblood sang about how – if he could – he'd like to make the world a better place.[6] The good news is that it's now easier than ever to open that *Green Door*[7] and instigate positive change through simple choices that can play a significant role in helping to turn around the world,[8] especially when you place the environment at the forefront of your thinking. This includes the food you eat (opt for local, seasonal, organic and plant-based, and be creative to eliminate waste); the funds you invest in (you know you should save);[9] travel (opt for greener, healthier modes of transport and minimise flying;

1   *Two Tribes* by Frankie Goes To Hollywood. Written by Peter Gill, William Johnson and Mark O'Toole

2   *Wordy Rappinghood* by Tom Tom Club. Written by Martina Weymouth, Charlton Frantz and Steven Stanley

3   *Everybody Wants To Rule The World* by Tears For Fears. Written by Roland Orzabal, Ian Stanley and Christopher Hughes

4   *It's Alright* by Pet Shop Boys. Written by Paris Robinson, Marshall Jefferson and Duane Pelt

5   *The Earth Dies Screaming* by UB40. Written by James Brown, Alistair Campbell, Robin Campbell, Earl Falconer, Norman Hassan, Brian Travers, Michael Virtue and Terence Wilson

6   *If Only I Could* by Sydney Youngblood. Written by Claus Zundel, Michael Staab, Sydney Ford and Ralf Hamm

7   *Green Door* by Shakin' Stevens. Written by Robert Bunyan Davie III and Marvin J. Moore

8   *Holiday* by Madonna. Written by Curtis Hudson and Lisa Stevens

9   *All She Wants Is* by Duran Duran. Written by Simon Le Bon, Nigel Taylor and Nicholas Bates

where flying is unavoidable, choose economy class and offset your carbon emissions – but not your responsibility – through reputable, thought-through schemes); the clothes you wear (put on a jumper before you put on the heating, and put your heating on a green tariff); your consumption habits (aim to reduce, reuse and recycle); and ensure that your democratic vote counts. Collectively, individual choices matter, as we are each a product and a part of – not apart from – our natural environment. Nature sustains and protects us; in return, we must nurture, protect and enhance it.

Despite some notable early environmental successes – such as the 1987 Montreal Protocol to phase out CFCs and the establishment in 1988 of the Intergovernmental Panel on Climate Change (IPCC) – significant challenges remained and continue to persist.

If you long for freedom and the call of the wild[1] over life in the asphalt urban jungle,[2] step outside (but tread lightly,[3] ensuring no trace is left)[4] and relish the soothing, nourishing beauty that natural green spaces offer. Iron Maiden called for a sense of wonder,[5] which you will often find in physically expansive landscapes. When immersed in the landscapes and connected to the rhythms of the natural world within which you evolved, you may feel an innate, deep sense of love for and affinity with nature – known as biophilia. Engaging with the natural environment has elevating and therapeutic powers and benefits that soothe busy, over-stimulated minds, shifting the focus away from introspection. This mind relief[6] enhances self-esteem and feelings of calm (by lowering cortisol levels), aids immunity and improves memory and concentration. Reconnecting

---

1   *La Isla Bonita* by Madonna. Written by Madonna Ciccone, Patrick Leonard and Bruce Gaitsch
2   *Let's Go All The Way* by Sly Fox. Written by Gary Cooper
3   *Rapture* by Blondie. Written by Deborah Harry and Christopher Stein
4   *Temptation* by Heaven 17. Written by Glenn Gregory, Ian Craig Marsh and Martyn Ware
5   *Can I Play With Madness* by Iron Maiden. Written by Adrian Smith, Paul Dickinson and Stephen Harris
6   *Sexual Healing* by Marvin Gaye. Written by Marvin Gaye Jr and Odell Brown Jr

with the seasons' reassuringly predictable cycles and rhythms will help you feel better in the moment and over the longer term.

How can you make a dull day brighter?[1] Even on a dull, overcast day, light levels outdoors far exceed those under indoor lighting, so spending time outside will naturally regulate and reset your biological master clock. You can magnify these positive effects by heading outside within a couple of hours of waking up, as the bright morning light helps melt away melatonin, uplifts serotonin levels and enhances your mood. Sunlight on your skin stimulates the production of vitamin D, helping to improve bone health and your autoimmune system while lowering blood pressure. (Vitamin D is both a para-hormone created by epidermal alchemy and an ingested nutrient found in certain foods such as mushrooms, vegetables, dairy products and oily fish.) Additionally, spending time outdoors can help enhance your problem-solving skills. Any form of outdoor, year-round exercise in a green environment for 20-30 minutes a day generates multiple benefits.

We have amassed unparalleled insight and understanding of our environment, including knowledge that current rates of animal extinction are higher than at any time in the last 10 million years, and thousands of times higher than the natural baseline rate. As a small part of the universe's evolved consciousness, it is incumbent on each of us to protect, preserve and enhance our environment and the life it sustains, not only for the good of our own physical and mental well-being but also for the good of current and future generations of all species. We are an integral part of, shaped by and are mutually dependent on the continuing good health and interconnectedness of the thin skin of the natural environment, which, despite some unconscionable treatment from human actions, continues to bestow upon us its priceless and irreplaceable life support systems.

Scientists expect Chernobyl to remain uninhabitable for human occupation for thousands of years. To address global environmental

---

[1]   *Love Resurrection* by Alison Moyet. Written by Genevieve Moyet, Steven Jolley and Anthony Swain

challenges requires that we summon unwavering collective political will to ensure that humanity safeguards its survival and that of all other lifeforms.

EVOLUTION

Chapter I touched on music's role in our biological and cultural evolution. While traces of music's evolutionary origins remain elusive, ethnomusicology does show that every society has music as a fixture, usually paired with storytelling. Humans have evolved advanced social intelligence, including complex language skills (the meaning of words also evolves, including the word 'evolution', which originally described the action of unrolling a scroll) and empathetic listening, all shaped by observation and personal experience. Most primates show little interest or ability in music – aside from some chimpanzees that drum out aural messages on tree-root buttresses, behaviour reminiscent of the drummers referenced in *Money For Nothing*.[1] A few humans also lack the necessary neural connectivity to experience the intense frisson and thrill of the chill from musical goosebumps (aka piloerection, the enjoyable version of feeling fear) despite possessing functional reward circuitry.

Our ancestors may have used synchronised movement in the rhythm of their feet[2] to aid in stalking their prey,[3] honing their capability to isolate and identify non-synchronous sounds. The ability to feel and fall into a rhythm created with others lives on today in the social bonding and unalloyed delight felt (by some, at least) in bouncing along in unison at festivals, concerts, raves or on dance floors to a rhythmic musical beat – a process known as entrainment: we evolved to be collective movers and shakers. Other activities, such as foraging, walking or even watching a sunset,[4]

1. *Money For Nothing* by Dire Straits. Written by Mark Knopfler and Gordon Sumner
2. *All Night Long (All Night)* by Lionel Richie. Written by Lionel Richie
3. *The Love Cats* by The Cure. Written by Robert Smith
4. *Echo Beach* by Martha And The Muffins. Written by Mark Gane

further dissolve the boundaries between self and others, connecting us on a fundamental level to our peers and our evolutionary roots.

The miracle of life[1] is born, in part, by the sheer improbability that a culmination of coincidences piled one on top of another delivered existence on either a cosmic level (the Earth orbits a stable, ideally sized star within the habitable 'Goldilocks zone' of temperature and pressure) or a genetic level (the coupling of your parents, grandparents, great-grandparents ...). While evolution via natural selection seems inevitable once life is up and running (figuratively speaking), the origin of complex life seems far less probable, leading some to look for a pattern, a plan or even divine intervention[2] – a Father of Creation.[3] Along more Darwinian lines, some say that only the strong survive[4] (a phrase first used by Herbert Spencer after reading Charles Darwin's seminal book from 1859, *On The Origin Of Species*; in the first edition, one word was conspicuous by its absence: evolution). Bob Marley echoed Spencer's view in lyrics about the survival of the fittest.[5]

Humans evolved to be mobile, using our legs[6] in a highly efficient and uniquely perpendicular way: bipedalism. Some six million years ago, our ancestors made a giant leap from the gnarly tree of evolution to stand on two feet,[7] affording our early upstanding ancestors hands-free mobility, reduced exposure to the scorching midday equatorial sun and the highest vantage point from which

1   *Heaven Is A Place On Earth* by Belinda Carlisle. Written by Richard Nowels Jr and Ellen Shipley

2   *All She Wants Is* by Duran Duran. Written by Simon Le Bon, Nigel Taylor and Nicholas Bates

3   *One Love/People Get Ready* by Bob Marley and The Wailers. Written by Robert Marley and Curtis Mayfield

4   *Body And Soul* by Mai Tai. Written by Eric van Tijn and Jochem Fluitsma

5   *Could You Be Loved* by Bob Marley and The Wailers. Written by Robert Marley

6   *Brass In Pocket* by The Pretenders. Written by Christine Hynde and James Honeyman-Scott

7   *Sisters Are Doin' It For Themselves* by Eurythmics and Aretha Franklin. Written by Ann Lennox and David Stewart

their eyes could see.[1] Throughout evolution, successive generations have stood on the broad Atlantean shoulders of our ancestors so that we may see further.

Stand And Deliver.[2] Standing delivered freedom. With liberated limbs and opposable thumbs, it was now in our hands[3] to pick fruit, light fires, carry the young, throw projectiles, communicate by gesture and craft objects. Some 60,000 years ago, legs and feet caught up with hands and minds and, step by step,[4] *Homo sapiens* walked out of Africa, venturing forth to colonise virtually the entire globe. When our ancestors' legwork propelled them to higher latitudes, skin became paler, allowing continued vitamin D synthesis in environments with limited daylight. Sadly, in our modern sedentary times, many have forgotten the remarkable advantages bestowed on us by evolution from little more than the way we walk.[5]

Evolution both poses fundamental questions and provides straightforward answers to lyrical inquiry. For instance, perched in the branches of their evolutionary tree, why do birds sing so beautifully?[6] asked a curious Diana Ross. Songbirds evolved a specialised vocal organ, the syrinx (from Greek and named after the cylindrical reeds of shepherd's pipes; syrinx, in turn, evolved into the word 'syringe'), as an adaptive function that enabled them to convey distinct messages – much like today's pop songs. *Dear Prudence*[7] suggests birds sing about how you are a part of all things: genetically, through the kinship of DNA, and biochemically, through the periodic table, the birds are right.

Given music's capacity to alter iris size, it's no surprise that eye

1   *Alive And Kicking* by Simple Minds. Written by James Kerr, Charles Burchill and Michael MacNeil
2   *Stand And Deliver* by Adam And The Ants. Written by Stuart Goddard and Marco Pirroni
3   *Love Is Contagious* by Taja Sevelle. Written by Nancy Richardson
4   *Toy Soldiers* by Martika. Written by Marta Marrero and Michael Margules
5   *Candy Girl* by New Edition. Written by Larry Johnson and Michael Johnson
6   *Why Do Fools Fall In Love* by Diana Ross. Written by Franklin Lymon and Moishe Levy
7   *Dear Prudence* by Siouxsie And The Banshees. Written by John Lennon and Paul McCartney

colour remains a popular song subject. *Blue Eyes*[1] are the result of a genetic mutation that, within the iris, switches off genes for melanin (the pigment that creates darker skin also makes eyes naturally brown; the word 'melancholy' reflects this darkness) and, as with lighter-coloured hair and skin, likely evolved around the Baltic Sea between 6,000 and 10,000 years ago. All blue-eyed people share a single, common ancestor. Despite conferring no known evolutionary advantage, blue eyes persist within both populations and pop songs. Perhaps it's how we wear our blue genes.[2] If both parents have sky-blue eyes,[3] genetics suggests a high likelihood that their offspring will inherit eyes of blue or green (where the production of melanin is turned down rather than off and has subsequently rinsed the colour from the eyes)[4] but not brown. Therefore, blue-eyed parents with a brown-eyed newborn may wish to deal with this pain behind the eyes[5] by taking a DNA test.[6] Genetics has a remarkably reliable habit of *Running In The Family*.[7]

Sound advice? After nearly four billion years, evolution's genetic jigsaw has created a picture of where you've come from[8] rather than where you're heading. Understanding evolution helps explain some behaviours, although Darwin failed the sound advice test on genetic diversity by marrying Emma Wedgwood, his first – and presumably perfect – cousin.[9] Genetic diversity ensures uniqueness within the

---

1   *Blue Eyes* by Elton John. Written by Elton John and Gary Osborne
2   *Something 'Bout You Baby I Like* by Status Quo. Written by Richard Goodman
3   *Sweet Child O' Mine* by Guns N' Roses. Written by Steven Adler, Michael McKagan, Jeffrey Isbell, William Rose and Saul Hudson
4   *I've Been Losing You* by A-ha. Written by Pål Waaktaar Gamst
5   *Private Investigations* by Dire Straits. Written by Mark Knopfler
6   *Annie, I'm Not Your Daddy* by Kid Creole and The Coconuts. Written by Thomas Browder
7   *Running In The Family* by Level 42. Written by Mark King, Waliou Badarou and Philip Gould
8   *Buffalo Soldier* by Bob Marley and The Wailers. Written by Robert Marley and Noel Williams
9   *My Perfect Cousin* by The Undertones. Written by Stephen O'Neill and Michael Bradley

same general wrapping;[1] we are not clones of our parents for sound genetic reasons.

Natural selection, evolution's principal mechanism, is fuelled by beneficial genetic mutations that confer advantages in the face of environmental change, leading to their retention and transmission to subsequent generations. Natural selection accelerates in response to rapid environmental change, as was evident 66 million years ago following the asteroid strike that triggered the extinction of non-avian dinosaurs, allowing our small, burrowing mammalian ancestors the opportunity to exploit and flourish in new ecological niches.

Genetically evolved traits, including the emotions interwoven into modern pop songs, persist to serve important purposes. For example, the physiological fight-or-flight response is a legacy indicating the presence of danger. When it comes to evolution and its genetic underpinning, you cannot run from the past[2] because your genes ensure that what is beneficial is preserved. Evolution, however, has primed us for a radically different world from today's rapidly changing one, especially the profound change witnessed over the past five generations, where cultural evolution has far outpaced its biological equivalent. The result is an evolutionary mismatch and a subsequent rise in lifestyle diseases and conditions of modernity, requiring us to recalibrate aspects of our lives to align more closely with our evolved nature.

Some attribute their behaviour to this evolutionary mismatch, seeing themselves as hostages to genetic inheritance. For example, for sound evolutionary reasons honed over aeons of our hunter-gatherer history, most people enjoy eating high-calorie food thanks to neural reward pathways that create pleasurable sensations – it simply tastes good.[3] Our bodies evolved to readily store the excess energy from this abundance of food as fat, another useful evolutionary adaptation for

1 *Reward* by The Teardrop Explodes. Written by Alan Gill and David Balfe
2 *Running In The Family* by Level 42. Written by Mark King, Waliou Badarou and Philip Gould
3 *Alphabet St.* by Prince. Written by Prince Nelson

times when feast turns to famine. Despite modern-day dieters' best efforts, brains and bodies have evolved to guard against excessive weight loss in preparation for times of shortage by adjusting the body's basal metabolic rate. Karel Fialka asked whether what you see is famine or feast;[1] the problem is that many see a biscuit-shaped world[2] where feast turns not to famine but into yet another feast, topped off with sugar-laden cola and cookies.[3] When it comes to taking the biscuit, you will likely take another,[4] succumbing to the *Sweet Surrender*[5] of edible comfort.

Fast food, slow death? Our urge to overindulge in addictively sugary, fatty and calorie-dense ultra-processed foods (check the ingredients and watch out for items like emulsifiers that are more at home in a chemistry lab than a kitchen) will not end well. The problems multiply when paired with our modern sedentary lifestyle – where the chairs are all worn out.[6] (Despite our need to conserve energy, our hunter-gatherer bodies didn't evolve for excessive sitting, creating a possible connection to increases in cardiovascular problems, musculoskeletal pain, diabetes and even some cancers.) In contrast, movement and exercise create positive feedback loops for both brain and body, thus forming a fundamental part of what it means to be human: to clear your mind, *Work That Body*.[7] As a minimum, try to stand up and stretch two to three times each hour. If you can't be bothered to move,[8] you defy your evolutionary legacy and risk living slowly and dying young.

With a helping hand from – or, more accurately, the sticky fingers of – Prometheus, said to have stolen fire from the gods to

1 *Hey, Matthew* by Karel Fialka. Written by Karel Fialka
2 *Senses Working Overtime* by XTC. Written by Andrew Partridge
3 *Americanos* by Holly Johnson. Written by William Johnson
4 *Chocolate Box* by Bros. Written by Luke Goss and Matthew Goss
5 *Sweet Surrender* by Wet Wet Wet. Written by Graeme Clark, Thomas Cunningham, Neil Mitchell and Mark McLachlan
6 *Gold* by Spandau Ballet. Written by Gary Kemp
7 *Work That Body* by Diana Ross. Written by Diana Ross, Paul Jabara and Ray Chew
8 *Wee Rule* by Wee Papa Girl Rappers. Written by Charles Cochrane, Hamish MacDonald, Samantha Lawrence and Sandra Lawrence

give to humans, our ability to harness fire and effectively extract nutrients and calories from a wide range of food through cooking (which helps kill pathogens and turn the inedible into the digestible) is likely to have played a significant role in shaping the evolution and growth of our energy- and nutrient-hungry brains. To combat old eating urges in our new world, try consciously appreciating and relishing food by doing so in the present to make eating an enjoyable, multi-sensory experience: delight in the sight of its presentation and colour – a plateful of naturally polychromic 'rainbow' foods, such as the orange, yellows and purples from naturally carotenoid-rich fruit and vegetables, is a good indicator of nutrient and micro-nutrient diversity, all gratefully received by the 100 trillion or so microbes that comprise your microbiota (collectively weighing more than your brain, they are a living catalyst directly influenced by your diet and lifestyle and are involved in producing chemicals that help you to digest food), which are thought to play a positive role in good mental health; take in the smells, notice textures, savour flavour and enjoy the sounds of your eating by chewing thoroughly ('noisy' food draws attention to the sensations within the mouth, heightening satisfaction). To consume fewer calories and eat more slowly (a variety of textures help with this), keep track of what you eat, and avoid mindless distractions such as staring at a screen. You may, however, eat to the beat and listen to soul-feeding music, although pop music may cause faster eating. Sharing meals with companions helps foster connections, ticking another evolutionary box (a 'companion' is, etymologically, someone with whom you share your bread, a practice dating back at least 14,000 years from a time when sharing food diluted the risk of starvation to any individual). When you take a little time[1] to enjoy the pleasure of food, you will help your body to recognise the natural cues for feeling full. "Best is water", stated Pindar, a renowned lyric poet from ancient Greece; drinking a glass before or during meals will add to your feelings of fullness without contributing to your calorie count.

1   I Want To Know What Love Is by Foreigner. Written by Michael Jones

Good food is not the enemy, nor is it the cause of overeating (which is more likely if you rely on soft, addictive, hyperpalatable ultra-processed foods – designed for quick consumption through the manipulation of texture and taste – that disrupt and deny your hunger-regulating hormones from doing their job). Overeating – eating beyond your natural appetite and failing to stop when satiated – is often a symptom of an underlying issue. In *Bedsitters*,[1] Soft Cell cooked their meals to fill an emptiness inside them. Overeaters frequently turn to food not to stave off starvation but as a mechanism to escape from feeling anxious, lonely, bored, frustrated or when they eat as part of a reward system. Try to address these realities, as consuming more calories than you burn leads to weight gain. You may find it easier to control your food environment than your appetite: try to establish regular meal times (to help stabilise blood sugar levels, maintain energy and focus, and avoid becoming irritable and snappy[2] following a glucose crash), store unhealthy salt- and sugar-laden hyper-processed snacks out of sight (while keeping their high-fibre fruit and protein-packed nut substitutes more visible and accessible), serve food on smaller plates and drink alcohol from smaller, taller glasses to reduce your intake. Make breakfast a literal break fast to ensure your digestive tract has at least 12 hours' rest after your last meal. Try to start your day with a sense of purpose, exposure to bright light and a glass of water, and stay hydrated throughout the day; taking half a dozen or so trips to fill your glass and empty your bladder – use the appropriate room for each – will also help you to keep moving naturally and fend off lethargy, poor focus and prevent the confusion that sometimes exists between hunger and thirst.

Evolution's greatest marvel sits in silence[3] and darkness inside your skull. Your brain is primarily responsible for governing your

1   *Bedsitter* by Soft Cell. Written by David Ball and Peter Almond
2   *Stutter Rap (No Sleep Til Bedtime)* by Morris Minor And The Majors. Written by Anthony Hawksworth
3   *You're The Voice* by John Farnham. Written by Anderson Qunta, Keith Reid, Marguerite Rider and Christopher Thompson

food choices and activity levels, not some fatalistic string of genetic code (which merely brackets a range of probabilities and possible outcomes rather than being deterministic). Tune in to your body's innate evolved signals and act accordingly – drink when you start feeling thirsty and rest when you start feeling tired. Despite the modern disconnection that many people feel from the natural world, evolution has equipped us to endure and survive life's significant challenges.

EXERCISE

Odyssey suggest you make your body busy.[1] Our bodies evolved to be physically active throughout our lives, as movement was essential for survival of our hunter-gatherer ancestors. Today, listening to upbeat, high-tempo music during exercise is a simple, proven way to elevate your mood and boost energy by minimising the perception of effort, especially during endurance training, allowing you to keep running.[2] Music distracts your mind from any thoughts of fatigue or physical discomfort, enhancing your enjoyment of exercise – and, yes, you can enjoy exercise, especially in outdoor settings. As with many aspects of exercise and sport, the race you run is in your head.[3]

Why running?[4] First, your heat-dissipating body has evolved to move in a highly efficient and effective way, making you a natural bipedal endurance runner, able to relentlessly pursue quadruped prey to the point of its exhaustion and collapse. Secondly, exercise is a vital component of a healthy and balanced lifestyle, with regular cardiovascular activity providing physical and psychological benefits such as improved muscle tone, stronger bones, a lower risk of

1   *Use It Up And Wear It Out* by Odyssey. Written by Lawrence Russell Brown and Sandford Linzer
2   *The Land Of Make Believe* by Bucks Fizz. Written by Andrew Hill and Peter Sinfield
3   *The Race* by Yello. Written by Hans-Rudolf Strickler and Dieter Meier
4   *Too Much* by Bros. Written by Matthew Goss, Luke Goss and Nicholas Graham

heart disease, improved sleep, elevated mood, a fortified mental state and cognitive clarity. A healthy circulatory system supports your brain's vasculature, allowing oxygen, hormones and nutrients to run through your head,[1] boosting neural efficiency and preventing cognitive decline.

If a run is beyond you, try to walk and walk and walk[2] instead. Hippocrates – the Father of Medicine – regarded walking as the best medicine, as it promotes physical fitness, creative inspiration and spiritual well-being. A brisk 20 to 30-minute daily walk (even when split into two or three 10-minute walks) – ideally within two hours of waking, but any time is a good time – can yield significant health benefits. The rhythm of motion helps align body and mind, helping you to manage anxiety, overcome setbacks and adversity, become more adept at sweeping away any demons residing within your head[3] and improve your problem-solving ability by allowing your unleashed brain the freedom to explore new neural pathways.

Peripatetic, derived from Greek, originally referred specifically to the teaching-while-walking practice favoured by Aristotle. Similarly, Charles Darwin sought and found inspiration on his thrice-daily walks around his 'thinking path' at his home in Down House. Other well-known figures who regularly used walking as a catalyst to unleash creativity include Beethoven (one among many classical composers), Wordsworth, Nietzsche and Dickens. Walking is a simple, effective, freely accessible and low-impact exercise that allows you to take a leaf out of the books of creative thinkers and take everything in your stride.[4]

The first 20 minutes of exercise yield the greatest benefits but are generally the toughest. Fortunately, exercise creates a virtuous

1   *Ghostbusters* by Ray Parker Jr. Written by Ray Parker Jr
2   *Do Nothing* by The Specials featuring Rico with The Ice Rink String Sounds. Written by Lynval Golding and Jeremy Dammers
3   *I Guess That's Why They Call It The Blues* by Elton John. Written by Elton John, Bernard Taupin and David Johnstone
4   *Mama Used To Say* by Junior. Written by Robert Carter and Norman Giscombe Jr

cycle: as you improve your fitness, exercise becomes easier, as does your motivation to stay fit.

Despite the boom in popularity of home workout videos and aerobic exercise in the 1980s, few songs from that era reflect this trend. Sporting a sweatband and leotard, Olivia Newton-John's video to *Physical*[1] might look and sound like a gym anthem, but the lyrics hint at a desire to satisfy a more horizontal interest in *Body Talk*.[2] Viewed positively, this still counts as exercise and helps to enhance mood and relieve stress.

Diana Ross's motivation to work her body was pragmatic: to offset the cake-calorie indulgence from the night before.[3] With a typical slice of cake averaging approximately 300 calories, Ross would need to loop the upbeat five-minute *Work That Body* track and heed its sound titular advice somewhere between 12 and 15 times to burn off those calories. Consuming calories is quick and easy; working them off is slow and arduous.

One surprising way to increase the calorie burn from cake is to pair it with coffee, a beverage high in fibre and polyphenols. When consumed approximately one hour before exercise, coffee may improve performance and endurance while stimulating your brown fat to burn more calories. However, as with any addictive substance, it's crucial to strike the right balance between the potential benefits (which, in the case of bioactive-rich tea, can be multiple) and any possible drawbacks. To avoid disrupting night-time sleep, limit your intake of caffeinated drinks to three/four per day, starting after breakfast and stopping by mid-afternoon. For maximum benefits, enjoy your coffee in the morning.

Sound advice? Despite the perennial need to be match-fit to enjoy a full life, exercise is a neglected theme in 1980s pop songs.

1   *Physical* by Olivia Newton-John. Written by Steven Kipner and Terry Shaddick
2   *Body Talk* by Imagination. Written by Ashley Ingram, Leslie John, Steven Jolly and Anthony Swain
3   *Work That Body* by Diana Ross. Written by Diana Ross, Paul Jabara and Ray Chew

Nevertheless, lifestyles across that decade afforded more opportunities for physical movement than in today's digitally connected world.

The soundest exercise advice emanates from scientists rather than lyricists. A daily, year-round and life-long commitment to both aerobic activities (which enhance the efficiency of your cardiovascular system, such as with running, walking or cycling) and resistance training (which, by resisting gravity, strengthens your musculoskeletal system, such as when performing press-ups) is an essential piece of the jigsaw for the good of your health.[1] Other vital pieces that help build a balanced picture come in the shape of sleep (nature's best performance enhancer), diet and attitude. It is always sound advice to ease into exercise gradually and progressively build on your achievements by increasing the intensity and duration over time rather than risking burnout by adopting an all-or-nothing approach.[2]

Exercise is equally beneficial for flexing your mind's mental muscles as it is for your body's physical ones. Together, they burn excess energy and angst. The 'use it or lose it' principle applies to both physical and mental muscle (your brain does not maintain neural pathways that are little used or which it can commandeer for more pressing executive function). Post-exercise, the release of serotonin and endorphins lifts your mood and reduces anxiety, making you feel naturally good. Endorphins activate your body's opiate receptors, which help mask any post-exercise discomfort caused by the microtears that all exercise inflicts on your body. These post-exercise repair processes regenerate, rebuild and strengthen your muscles and bones.

Also, post-exercise, avoid being caught in the trap[3] of reward-

1   *April Skies* by The Jesus And Mary Chain. Written by William Reid and James Reid
2   *We Don't Need Another Hero (Thunderdome)* by Tina Turner. Written by Terence Britten and Graham Lyle
3   *Lost In Music* by Sister Sledge. Written by Nile Rodgers and Bernard Edwards

ing yourself with an indulgent meal far exceeding the calories you burned while exercising. Counterintuitively, exercise seldom leads to weight loss, but it can help control and moderate hormone and stress levels, thus reducing your cravings for unhealthy (usually high-calorie) comfort foods. As the Greek philosopher Socrates noted, eat to live, not live to eat. Once again, it's about striving for appropriate balance.

To maintain appropriate physical balance and improve core strength, posture, coordination and confidence, allocate short daily pockets of time (for example, during mundane tasks such as washing your pots and pans)[1] to stand on one leg. Improving balance reduces the frequency of falls, which are particularly problematic where decreased bone density increases the risk of sustaining fractures; fractures, in turn, significantly increase morbidity in older adults, often marking life's outro – the beginning of the end. Loss of balance is a marker of accelerated ageing, particularly from middle age onwards; older people may compensate for poor balance by shuffling their feet.[2] If these prospects make you think, *I Ain't Gonna Stand For It*,[3] you can adopt a literal, simple and effective one-legged stand. If you balance while listening to a song – perhaps *I'm Still Standing*[4] – swap your standing leg halfway through the track; the ultimate challenge is to try balancing (but only if safe to attempt) with your eyes shut. While this exercise improves the link between your inner ear and balance, it may impair your ability to wash up.

Back with your feet on the ground,[5] you can combine exercise with other techniques to enhance your life. On a run or walk, you can either move on autopilot (provided you can maintain the pace), thereby freeing your mind to think about something entirely

1   *Americanos* by Holly Johnson. Written by William Johnson
2   *The Message* by Grandmaster Flash And The Furious Five. Written by Clifton Chase, Edward Fletcher, Melvin Glover and Sylvia Vanterpool
3   *I Ain't Gonna Stand For It* by Stevie Wonder. Written by Stevie Wonder
4   *I'm Still Standing* by Elton John. Written by Elton John and Bernard Taupin
5   *Blow The House Down* by Living In A Box. Written by Albert Hammond and Marcus Vere

unrelated, or focus completely on the moment, paying attention to everything you see, hear and smell along the way, including the rhythmic sound of your footfall and the maintenance of correct posture. You'll usually feel happier when you fully engage in whatever you do. Engaging your brain also helps increase blood flow, creating another virtuous cycle.

Kid Creole and The Coconuts' inspired advice was to ensure that you breathe[1] ('inspire' literally means 'to breathe' or 'to blow breath into'). Many find the harmonious blend of physical and meditative exercises within yoga, especially the powerful cleansing purity and focus that accompanies conscious deep breathing exercises known as pranayama (from the Sanskrit, meaning 'breath control'), to be a beneficial way to increase flexibility, balance and stress-coping mechanisms. A mindful Dennis Waterman claimed he could help you breathe.[2] To flood your cells with revitalising oxygen, try inhaling deeply through your nose for four seconds, holding your breath for seven, then exhaling deeply and evenly for eight, ideally while sitting with your eyes closed and both feet on the ground (you can also use this technique to hasten the onset of sleep when lying in bed); repeat this cycle. Alternative patterns include three-four-five or four-four-four, which you can combine with alternate nostril breathing. (All involuntary – autonomic – breathing should be channelled through your nostrils, the natural way to humidify, warm and filter the air entering your lungs and keep your mouth moist and healthy.) Breathing reflects and affects your mental state, so learning to calm and control your breathing enables you to calm and control your thoughts, giving your brain a mini reset. Try to incorporate brief 'pockets' of yoga (where, for example, you dedicate five minutes to conscious breathing, a few minutes to tense and relax various muscle groups and a couple of minutes each hour for stretching) into your daily routine or during any spare moments as a beneficial alternative

1   *I'm A Wonderful Thing, Baby* by Kid Creole and The Coconuts. Written by Thomas Browder and Peter Schott
2   *I Could Be So Good For You* by Dennis Waterman. Written by Gerard Kenny and Patricia Waterman

to mindlessly checking your phone. Focusing on breathing and relaxation is an excellent way to start and end your day.

You can also improve your breath control by learning to sing, while the oscillations from humming can help clear your sinuses. Dancing is an enjoyable way to put your best foot forward, combining your favourite music with exercise and even a hint of escapism. Singing and dancing often involve a social dimension, combining exercise and enjoyment with the mental benefits of connecting with others. And don't forget that while listening to music is a gentle mental exercise that engages your brain, playing (or, best of all, learning to play) an instrument will give your brain a full workout as it simultaneously activates multiple brain regions that will improve cognitive function, such as auditory processing and fine motor skills. Brains love music's complexity.

Madness were sane to think they had a chance if they moved around.[1] With movement and exercise, it is *Never Too Late*[2] to begin or to reap the benefits. Regardless of your age or current fitness, do what you can to let your body move,[3] and then keep on moving.[4] It's better to be an old runner than an ex-runner or non-runner. All movement counts, whether low-intensity domestic chores or highly rewarding gardening. Choose an exercise you enjoy and can commit to regularly, ideally scheduled daily, and then do what you can.[5] Time spent exercising should be fun, with any benefits a bonus. Set exercise goals that are small, achievable and motivating. For some, focusing on a personal target, particularly when fatigue strikes, can sharpen their resolve and improve physical performance; however, exercise is more than just a competition against yourself or others.

1   *Tomorrow's (Just Another Day)* by Madness. Written by Michael Barson and Carl Smyth
2   *Never Too Late* by Kylie Minogue. Written by Michael Stock, Matthew Aitken and Peter Waterman
3   *Street Dance* by Break Machine. Written by Frederick Zarr, Henri Belolo, Jacques Morali and Keith Rodgers
4   *Break My Stride* by Matthew Wilder. Written by Matthew Weiner and Gregory Prestopino
5   *Beat It* by Michael Jackson. Written by Michael Jackson

Combining aerobic and resistance exercise is most beneficial as each targets and challenges a different group of muscles and bones. If you feel resistance[1] to resistance exercise or you see formal, structured aerobic activity as intimidating, stick to a daily brisk walk (ideally post-meal and unplugged from your phone) or build more movement into your daily routine where you will not think of it as exercise, such taking the stairs (both up and down), adding some confidence-boosting kitchen dance while cooking or alighting public transport a stop early and briskly walking the final leg of your journey. Because you'll feel better just by the simple act of moving your feet,[2] you should try to redesign aspects of your daily life to do so at a pace and time that suits you. If, for example, you need to exercise your dog, split your walks into two/three shorter sessions; this will benefit you and your dog. National travel surveys repeatedly show that nearly a quarter of journeys are less than one mile – perfect for a walk or cycle ride that will boost your health and well-being, save you money (and possibly time and stress), improve local air quality and ease local traffic congestion.

An inextricable link exists between exercise and good health: blood-pumping exercise will help you to live longer (by slowing ageing and delaying or even preventing the onset and accumulation of some chronic diseases), live stronger (by reducing chronic inflammation and increasing muscle strength and bone density), sleep more soundly and increase energy levels. All exercise helps lower blood pressure, especially (and again counterintuitively) isometric exercises (exercise without movement) such as squats or the 'plank' posture, which can help engage core muscles, improve posture and alleviate lower back problems. With any exercise, you'll feel better within yourself and about yourself, making it worthwhile to overcome any barriers.

Music and health are symbiotic: music can move you emotionally

1   *Living In A Box* by Living In A Box. Written by Marcus Vere and Steve Pigott
2   *Church Of The Poison Mind* by Culture Club. Written by Roy Hay, George O'Dowd, Michael Craig and Jonathan Moss

and physically. If you want to give your exercise routine an extra edge or put a skip in your step, find an inspiring track that elevates your heart rate, then *Pump Up The Volume*.[1]

FASHION

The emergence of MTV in the 1980s gave silky-voiced pop stars unprecedented visibility to dazzle their audiences with strutting displays of fashionable plumage and rampant, unabashed vanity. The dandy highwayman in *Stand and Deliver*[2] proudly declared that he spent his ill-gotten gains on ostentation to collar your attention.

The Look[3] adopted by performers is usually tied to the musical message they wish to send.[4] Fashion – even anti-fashion – is rarely neutral, conveying non-verbal cues that instantly signal and identify markers of culture, ethnicity, religion, class, sexual orientation and allegiance to ideals, all of which extend beyond the civilising function and practical utility of clothing. Fashion can foretell a musical style before a note is played – for instance, compare the look and subsequent sound difference between heavy metal and new romantics. Despite fashion's superficial wrapper, the tone set by your first impression will last, even if fickle fashion fads change with the seasons.

Shocking new fashion often intentionally aims to provoke, designed to make people stop and stare.[5] The message, marker or identifier – shocking, daring or otherwise – that characterised 1980s fashion is commonly portrayed by gold lamé suits, the spandex ballet,

1   *Pump Up The Volume* by M/A/R/R/S. Written by Martyn Young and Steven Young
2   *Stand And Deliver* by Adam And The Ants. Written by Stuart Goddard and Marco Pirroni
3   *The Look* by Roxette. Written by Per Gessle
4   *Tell It To My Heart* by Taylor Dayne. Written by Ernest Goldberg and Seth Swirsky
5   *The Sun Goes Down (Living It Up)* by Level 42. Written by Michael Lindup, Mark King, Philip Gould and Waliou Badarou

shimmery sequins, oversized shoulder pads, designer labels and voluminous hair, all reflecting a distinctive – albeit strange – fashion.[1] Gender boundaries became more fluid, allowing cross-dressing to emerge as a pop-culture theme. Women following the 'dress-for-success' mantra donned 'power suits' (central to 'power dressing'), complete with pronounced shoulder pads, to project a harder, more masculine silhouette associated with authority and confidence. Concurrently, men's casual suits became more 'relaxed' in both cut and colour. Dazzling neon, as loud as the amplified music it accompanied, found favour among the young.

Some performers decided that this was the time and place to cross over,[2] to position themselves in the middle-ground by deploying a new exterior[3] androgynous look, exemplified by the likes of Annie Lennox, Grace Jones, Boy George and Pete Burns. To both enhance and transform identities, performers employed extensive use of make-up; from the neck up, big hair and eyeliner became de rigueur, even among hard rockers, often counterbalanced from the waist down by distressingly tight-fitting trousers, squeezing the 'pain' into painted-on jeans.[4]

Sporting detective headwear, the Thompson Twins sensed something suspicious about a gloved left hand.[5] Occasionally, pop stars could leverage their influence and exposure to start a fashion trend, especially if the fashionable item was pointlessly decorative or impractical, both common traits throughout sartorial history. A few pop performers during the 1980s used accessories as visual signatures (here deliberately sidestepping the Grolsch bottle tops attached to Dr Martens boots or shoes, à la Bros, or Cameo's codpiece). A single

1   *The Riddle* by Nik Kershaw. Written by Nicholas Kershaw
2   *This Is Not A Love Song* by Public Image Ltd. Written by John Lydon, Keith Levene and Martin Atkins
3   *Sisters Are Doin' It For Themselves* by Eurythmics and Aretha Franklin. Written by Ann Lennox and David Stewart
4   *Caribbean Queen (No More Love On The Run)* by Billy Ocean. Written by Leslie Charles and Keith Alexander
5   *We Are Detective* by Thompson Twins. Written by Thomas Bailey, Alannah Currie and Joseph Leeway

white sequined glove? Michael Jackson. A lacey fingerless glove? Madonna. A glove, eyepatch or anything else in purple? Prince. Prince, for whom purple reigned perpetually, penned The Bangles' hit *Manic Monday*,[1] which blames the tardy start to the working week on indecision over what to wear. You can significantly cut the cognitive load and time spent on your manic Monday morning routine by limiting your wardrobe selection, thereby minimising too many choices,[2] purple or otherwise.

Fashion retains its importance for pop stars and their impressionable, youthful fanbase keen to be seen to fit in (rather than stand out in any peculiar way) with their peers and potential partners. The songs, however, frequently champion the importance of individuality and display indifference to mindlessly and slavishly following the herd of popular fashion, instead urging listeners to look beneath the exterior carapace to see the unique substance and characteristics within everyone. For example, The Specials questioned the sense of being a follower of fashion[3] (their subsequent advice to wear a cap[4] was contraceptive rather than sartorial), Toyah didn't want others telling her what to wear,[5] Bros lamented being slaves to fashion,[6] and Deniece Williams was unfazed that her boyfriend was not a good dresser[7] – a partner sentiment shared by *Girl Crazy*[8] Hot Chocolate and image-conscious Milli Vanilli.[9] Even with his penchant for flamboyant pantomime costumes,

1 *Manic Monday* by The Bangles. Written by Prince Nelson
2 *West End Girls* by Pet Shop Boys. Written by Neil Tennant and Christopher Lowe
3 *Do Nothing* by The Specials featuring Rico with The Ice Rink String Sounds. Written by Lynval Golding and Jeremy Dammers
4 *Too Much Too Young* by The Specials featuring Rico. Written by Jeremy Dammers and Lloyd Tyrell
5 *I Want To Be Free* by Toyah. Written by Toyah Willcox and Joel Bogen
6 *When Will I Be Famous?* by Bros. Written by Nicholas Graham and Thomas Watkins
7 *Let's Hear It For The Boy* by Deniece Williams. Written by Thomas Snow and Dean Pitchford.
8 *Girl Crazy* by Hot Chocolate. Written by Lester Brown
9 *Girl You Know It's True* by Milli Vanilli. Written by William Pettaway Jr, Sean Spencer, Kevin Liles, Rodney Holloman and Kayode Adeyemo

Adam Ant was adamant that following fashion would be absurd.[1]

Sound advice? Despite the subject material, there's surprisingly little flannel, making pop music and fashion a good fit. The cutting-edge worlds of pop music and fashion naturally cross-pollinate, explaining why many fashion show catwalks (and some showcased garments) seem to take their inspiration directly from *Top of the Pops*. Success in both industries requires the weaving of creativity into commercial viability.

Historically, sumptuary laws enforced rigid dress codes, reinforcing social hierarchies by limiting personal expenditure on goods, including fashionable clothing. In modern times, fashion trends reflect social change, such as how economic fortunes influence the rise and fall of hemlines, revealing hopes, aspirations and thighs. Art history shows how the female form – thighs and all – has been subject to the fashionably fleshy ebb and flow of beauty ideals. Similarly, religious doctrine dictated what was considered acceptable attire (for women), often emphasising sexual modesty to temper male desire.

The rapid expansion of high-street clothing retailers in the 1980s brought consumers a wide range of affordable and desirable fashion. Marketeers principally targeted young women's disposable incomes with slick style-over-substance advertising that generated desire beyond necessity for ever-more disposable fashion items.[2] The aptly named Style Council highlighted one hidden cost of inexpensive popular fashion through commonplace clothing chains: shop windows and the high streets they lined all began to look the same.[3] Meanwhile, luxury fashion brands hinted at lifestyle possibilities well beyond the clothes they promoted in their glossy campaigns.

Neneh Cherry took the stance that looking good is just a state

---

1   *Goody Two Shoes* by Adam Ant. Written by Stuart Goddard and Marco Pirroni

2   *Americanos* by Holly Johnson. Written by William Johnson

3   *Shout To The Top* by The Style Council. Written by John Weller

of mind,[1] emphasising that it doesn't matter what you wear[2] - your purchasable external sense of fashion - as much as how you wear it - your unpurchasable internal sense of style. There may be only a few ways to be fashionable, but there are myriad ways to be stylish. Using your style[3] requires confidence and comfort in your skin, for you alone bring life to what you wear. Having body confidence and poise (the New Kids On The Block claimed they could see this in little more than the way you walk)[4] can undoubtedly add elegance and a dash of debonair to what you wear, so be mindful of your posture and try to stand and walk tall with your head held up[5] and your shoulders back. Beyond relief from 'tech neck' caused by endlessly staring down at your phone, you may experience a positive outcome from simply looking upwards.[6] Good posture (to keep standing tall[7] imagine being stretched upwards by a string attached to the top of your head) projects signals of confidence, helping you feel better about yourself and improving general health, including your core muscle strength (reducing the likelihood of neck or upper back pain), breathing and blood circulation. If you can wear and carry off with conviction an air of insouciance, you can pull off any look; others may even bestow upon you that most coveted but elusive of tags: cool. Even in times of looser dress codes, dressing to fit your shape and personality can convey more about your self-control, competence and confidence than adorning yourself in the latest status-symbol designer trends, especially if you are trying to use the cachet of vanity

1   *Buffalo Stance* by Neneh Cherry. Written by Neneh Karlsson, Cameron McVey, James Morgan and Philip Ramacon
2   *Dancing In The Street* by David Bowie and Mick Jagger. Written by Marvin Gaye Jr, William Stevenson and George Hunter
3   *Brass In Pocket* by The Pretenders. Written by Christine Hynde and James Honeyman-Scott
4   *You Got It (The Right Stuff)* by New Kids On The Block. Written by Larry Johnson
5   *Good Tradition* by Tanita Tikaram. Written by Tanita Tikaram
6   *Wings Of A Dove* by Madness. Written by Graham McPherson and Cathal Smyth
7   *Glory Of Love* by Peter Cetera. Written by David Foster, Diane Nini and Peter Cetera

fashion to mask underlying insecurities. Sound advice dictates that you shouldn't judge a book by its cover;[1] others, however, may well read the shorthand commentary sent through clothing to jump to quick conclusions and make snap judgements about your character, credibility and allegiances rather than using your fashion sense as a springboard to discover more about who you are. From dust jackets to *The Lady In Red*,[2] fashion allows wearers to express or conceal their personalities, showing how we cover ourselves reveals much.

Imagine a free and always fashionable magical cloak that is simple, quick and easy to don that sends an instant, powerful and positive non-verbal, first-impression signal that you're likeable, competent, trustworthy, courteous and thus generally more attractive. And what if this universal, always-on-trend, all-weather, infinitely versatile garment also had multiple health benefits woven into its fabric that could elevate your emotional state, lower your heart rate and reduce your blood pressure. Additionally, its twice-daily cleaning requirement yields positive health benefits, such as eliminating harmful bacteria. How do you get to wear this magic cloak? Put on a smile.[3] Although corny,[4] the positive effects conjured up by a magical smile[5] are measurable, particularly the neurological fireworks ignited when you smile.[6] Positive feedback mechanisms allow you to convince your brain that all is well when you go with a smile.[7] These embodied mechanisms work equally well in reverse, so remove any unbecoming frowns.[8] If you struggle to muster the motivation to spread joy

1   *The Look Of Love* by ABC. Written by Martin Fry, Mark White, Stephen Singleton, David Palmer and Mark Lickley
2   *The Lady In Red* by Chris de Burgh. Written by Christopher Davison
3   *Don't Worry, Be Happy* by Bobby McFerrin. Written by Robert McFerrin Jr
4   *Rockin' Around The Christmas Tree* by Mel Smith and Kim Wilde. Written by John Marks
5   *Girl I'm Gonna Miss You* by Milli Vanilli. Written by Frank Farian, Peter Bischof-Fallenstein and Dietmar Kawohl
6   *Don't Get Me Wrong* by The Pretenders. Written by Christine Hynde
7   *Batdance* by Prince. Written by Prince Nelson
8   *Say Hello, Wave Goodbye* by Soft Cell. Written by Peter Almond and David Ball

with a smile,[1] consider forcing your facial muscles into an artificial 'plastic' smile[2] by holding a pencil lengthways between your teeth. According to the James-Lange theory of emotion, your brain will interpret this smile as a sign of genuine happiness. You can deceive your brain with other temporary 'fake-it-until-you-make-it' ploys, such as acting as if you are highly motivated, pretending to be tired before going to sleep or using powerful creative visualisation to imagine yourself leading a better life, which your primed brain can then help turn from thought into reality. However, maintaining a long-term, full-pretence facade can be exhausting, especially if you're not waving but drowning; ultimately, it's better to be yourself and feel it rather than simulate it. In the 1980s, some of the biggest pop stars – including Freddie Mercury, Michael Jackson, Prince and David Bowie (who had a hit called *Fashion*)[3] – used fashion to help create elaborate, extroverted and often flamboyant stage personas as suits of shining armour[4] to protect their naturally introverted *Shy Boy*[5] selves.

What is in fashion can quickly drop out of fashion.[6] With a few decades tucked under the belt of time, some crazier clothes[7] and fashions from the 1980s have aged far faster than the songs they helped adorn, many of which feature interwoven themes cut from the timeless cloth of the human condition. Some fashion trends and pop songs are intentionally designed to be ephemeral, offering a fleeting moment of fun before moving on. The sweat-shop pop production factories of the late 1980s that churned out their one-size-fits-all lyrical content and performance style were the antithesis of

1   *Do They Know It's Christmas?* by Band Aid. Written by Robert Geldof and James Ure
2   *It's A Miracle* by Culture Club. Written by Roy Hay, George O'Dowd, Michael Craig, Jonathan Moss and Philip Pickett
3   *Fashion* by David Bowie. Written by David Jones
4   *Emotional Rescue* by The Rolling Stones. Written by Michael Jagger and Keith Richards
5   *Shy Boy* by Bananarama. Written by Steven Jolley and Antony Swain
6   *Echo Beach* by Martha And The Muffins. Written by Mark Gane
7   *You Better You Bet* by The Who. Written by Peter Townshend

the celebrated bespoke individuality of bands and performers who brought heart-on-the-sleeve personal experience and creative energy to the diverse UK singles chart earlier in the decade. Although bespoke themes and lyrical advice cannot fit all the people all the time, they still manage to fit enough of the time to be wearable, as most people think and act the same way;[1] it's just that some are more frayed at the edges than others.

Regardless of whether or not you dress to a T[2] and wear clothes in vogue,[3] your approach to clothing and fashion is an integral part of how you *Express Yourself*.[4] However, when fashion becomes out of kilter within a balanced life, it risks becoming another tiresome obsession on a path to personal dissatisfaction.

Despite the industrial scale of the fashion sector in the 1980s, manufacturers largely disregarded sustainability. In subsequent years, the high price that all paid for the environmental and social threads that held together this damaging cycle of cheap, overproduced, quickly superseded, disposable 'fast fashion' began to unravel and fall apart at the seams.[5] Nowadays, there's a growing emphasis towards more sustainable 'slow fashion', encouraging consumers to be more thoughtful and buy fewer higher-quality clothes of timeless style – statement staples that outlive fleeting trends. The 'buy once, buy well' mantra allows manufacturers to make things last longer,[6] can be worn more often (and across multiple seasons), are repairable and, ultimately, are recyclable. However, according to the UN, the fashion industry remains one of the world's most environmentally damaging sectors, consuming vast amounts of pesticides and over 200 trillion litres of water per year, often extracted from regions

1 *See You* by Depeche Mode. Written by Martin Gore
2 *Rapper's Delight* by Sugarhill Gang. Written by Guy O'Brien, Henry Jackson, Michael Wright and Sylvia Vanterpool
3 *Ooh To Be Ah* by Kajagoogoo. Written by Christopher Hamill
4 *Express Yourself* by Madonna. Written by Madonna Ciccone and Stephen Bray
5 *The Look Of Love* by ABC. Written by Martin Fry, Mark White, Stephen Singleton, David Palmer and Mark Lickley
6 *Only When You Leave* by Spandau Ballet. Written by Gary Kemp

already suffering from water scarcity. A cotton T-shirt has over 3,000 litres of water embedded in its production. The alternatives to cotton frequently use non-biodegradable fossil fuel-derived materials that shed bioaccumulating microfibres into the environment.

The fashion industry has traditionally recycled trends more enthusiastically than it has its garments. Only a few fashion items are direct escapees from the 1980s. Some garments of function, such as leggings and the pairing of denim jeans with training shoes, managed to become garments of fashion, but they remain the exception. At the decade's end, the carefree spirit of the rave new world of acid house (no connection with denim's 'acid wash') had seeped into the mainstream. Sartorially, ravers prioritised practical dressing down rather than the exotic dressing up that defined early 1980s club culture. The relentless and often frenetic nature of 'house' dancing, frequently performed on improvised, uneven surfaces, necessitated functional, loose-fitting and comfortable clothing matched with sensible trainers. This relaxed look remained after the acid scene had all but dissolved.

Patented in 1873, Levi's hard-wearing, long-lasting 501 denim jeans (requiring about 10,000 litres of water to produce) achieved the rare feat of embedding themselves in the culture of the 1980s, using the eternal tagline 'Quality never goes out of style'. Thankfully for all, the once-fashionable mullet remains condemned to the cutting room floor.

FORTITUDE

When The Going Gets Tough, The Tough Get Going.[1] Fortitude is the persistent strength of mind and character that enables you to draw on inner resources such as courage, resilience and steadfastness to overcome adversity or setbacks, face challenges or conquer

1   *When The Going Gets Tough, The Tough Get Going* by Billy Ocean. Written by Wayne Brathwaite, Barry Eastmond, Robert Lange and Leslie Charles

fear. Fortitude is that strength that flows within you,[1] a force that allows you to rise up and win,[2] all of which music can facilitate. Labi Siffre's song (*Something Inside) So Strong*[3] captures the essence of fortitude: no matter the obstacles that arise, your inner strength will always shine through.

During the 1980s, Britain served as a crucial base for the anti-apartheid movement, as the ongoing brutality of the South African regime forced apartheid up the political agenda. While boycotts of South African products and sports teams raised awareness and elevated the profile of the anti-apartheid movement, it was the 'soft power' of pop music, especially the clarion call from the 1984 hit *Free Nelson Mandela*,[4] that grabbed the attention of a younger generation to Mandela's plight and the cause for which he fought and was imprisoned. Although incarcerated in body, Mandela's mind remained free. Protest songs amplified the call for change. The 1988 BBC broadcast of the Nelson Mandela 70th Birthday Tribute concert from Wembley Stadium reached over 600 million viewers worldwide. Momentum grew, as did the sense that the tide would turn.[5] And turn it did. In 1990, after serving 27 years in prison, Mandela walked free. Four years later, he became South Africa's first democratically elected President.

Madonna advocated for cherishing your inner strength,[6] while Iron Maiden (the rock band, not the Prime Minister) asked for the strength to hold up their heads.[7] Heaven 17 observed that those lacking fortitude are rarely free.[8]

Sound advice? Yes. To build relationships, fight injustice and

1 *Rock The Boat* by Forrest. Written by Waldo Holmes
2 *Rage Hard* by Frankie Goes To Hollywood. Written by Peter Gill, William Johnson, Brian Nash and Mark O'Toole
3 *(Something Inside) So Strong* by Labi Siffre. Written by Claudius Siffre
4 *Free Nelson Mandela* by The Special AKA. Written by Jeremy Dammers
5 *Gimme Hope Jo'anna* by Eddy Grant. Written by Edmond Grant
6 *Cherish* by Madonna. Written by Madonna Ciccone and Patrick Leonard
7 *Can I Play With Madness* by Iron Maiden. Written by Adrian Smith, Paul Dickinson and Stephen Harris
8 *Come Live With Me* by Heaven 17. Written by Glenn Gregory, Ian Craig Marsh and Martyn Ware

strive to reach your potential, fortitude is indispensable in attaining what you want.[1] Fortitude helps transform our inner strength into outer success. As descendants of multiple generations of the strongest – those with the will to survive[2] (and reproduce) – fortitude is a part of our genetic inheritance and a desirable character virtue.

Instead of allowing setbacks, trauma, prejudice or general adversity – especially that encountered early in life – to justify a poor or stagnant personal situation, use these experiences as invaluable opportunities to cultivate fortitude and realise new skills (such as perseverance, resilience and how best to understand and learn from such events) into all areas of life to help you to grow and soldier on to do what only can do.[3] The incidents and accidents[4] that shaped our planet's history illustrate a remarkable capacity to recover from and adapt to adversity. The Giant Impact Hypothesis proposes that about 4.5 billion years ago, a wandering Mars-sized planet called Theia delivered a glancing blow to proto-Earth with enough force to knock Earth's perpendicular axis to its current tilt of 23½ degrees. This seemingly catastrophic event contributed to the formation of our now ideal-sized planet (complete with a fortified iron core that generates a protective magnetic field), our relatively stable climate, the cyclical beauty of the four seasons and an opportunity to marvel at our disproportionately large Moon, thought to have accreted from the dust and debris propelled into space following the impact. When geochemistry turned to biochemistry and life emerged, it adapted to the prevailing conditions and rhythms – such as the tides, our 24-hour circadian rhythm and the seasons.

On a human level, what matters is not what impacts you but how you respond – and the need to focus and keep your reactions

1 *Absolute Beginners* by The Jam. Written by John Weller
2 *Eye Of The Tiger* by Survivor. Written by Frank Sullivan III and James Peterik
3 *St. Elmo's Fire (Man In Motion)* by John Parr. Written by David Foster and John Parr
4 *You Can Call Me Al* by Paul Simon. Written by Paul Simon

under control.[1] Effectively managing negative emotions (jealousy, resentment, anger) is essential in preventing a bad situation from becoming worse. Fortitude is a gatekeeper to your mind, enabling you to stay resolute; many find music helpful in sustaining their strength and determination. Returning to the story of our early planet, emerging life continued to do what it had evolved to do: live. With a backbone of fortitude, so can you.

FRIENDS

In Book 8 of *Ethics*, Aristotle identifies three broad types of friendship: those based on utility (mutual benefit, as in a business relationship), pleasure (such as wit) and, best of all, goodness. This reciprocal *I Feel For You*[2] goodness is the desire in friends to share, appreciate and rejoice in each other's merits and virtues.

With A Little Help From My Friends.[3] Two thousand years later, friendship remains a celebrated song theme, often as a subset of love and relationships. For poet Lord Byron, friendship was love without wings. As in a successful romantic relationship, true friendship allows you to be yourself, accepted the way you are,[4] free from pretence and judgement. Such connections can help enrich and even prolong your life. Family may also love you for who you are, but you cannot choose your family as you do your friends. As with your music selections, you should not solely delegate your choice of friends to the closed loop of algorithms.

True friends are there for you through thick and thin,[5] celebrating

1 *The Time Warp* by Damian. Written by Richard Smith
2 *I Feel For You* by Chaka Khan. Written by Prince Nelson
3 *With A Little Help From My Friends* by Wet Wet Wet. Written by John Lennon and Paul McCartney
4 *Nothing's Gonna Change My Love For You* by Glenn Medeiros. Written by Gerald Goffin and Michael Masser
5 *Big Fun* by The Gap Band. Written by Lonnie Simmons and Rudolph Taylor

and sharing in the good times[1] and commiserating, consoling and supporting you through vulnerable, tougher times, much like a lighthouse guides a ship[2] safely to harbour. Popular lyrics remind us that it is during the roughest, most challenging conditions that you most need a friend[3] as a guiding light and a reliable source of emotional support, trust, companionship, warmth and uplift, as someone who truly understands you,[4] who you can lean on[5] and who can help pick you up if you suffer a fall.[6] Sound advice from a friend carries extra weight during fraught times. While a comforting song can provide emotional support and sound advice, the words are one-sided. In contrast, the support and companionship from flesh-and-blood friends is an uplifting, interactive exchange.

Sound advice? As a prosocial species, we are attuned to living in small, close-knit groups, so having a good friend who you can rely on,[7] trust implicitly and look to as a source of support and candid advice is natural (and in Aristotle's view, essential), not needy. However, even with the best intentions, friends may offer advice they might not heed themselves, especially when they cannot see – or you deliberately restrict the full view of – the bigger picture or if they fail to consider the unintended consequences of their well-meaning suggestions. Nevertheless, a fresh, candid perspective from a trusted and loyal friend can help you to make better, more informed decisions, especially if you recognise any biases in their advice.

Even casual friendships bring significant health benefits, such as improved cardiovascular health. Those who nurture robust social

---

1   *Celebration* by Kool And the Gang. Written by Roland Bell, Claydes Smith, George Brown, James Taylor, Robert Mickens, Earl Toon Jr, Dennis Thomas, Robert Bell and Eumir De Almeida
2   *There It Is* by Shalamar. Written by Charmaine Sylvers, Dana Meyers and Nidra Beard
3   *I Don't Want A Lover* by Texas. Written by John McElhone and Sharleen Spiteri
4   *Say You, Say Me* by Lionel Richie. Written by Lionel Richie
5   *Lean On Me* by Club Nouveau. Written by William Withers
6   *You Came* by Kim Wilde. Written by Kim Smith and Richard Smith
7   *Coming Up* by Paul McCartney. Written by Paul McCartney

networks consistently exhibit the lowest levels of damaging stress hormones.

Should all friends remain friends until the end?[1] Not necessarily. Friendships are fluid and dynamic, changing as they mature. Some friendships deepen and strengthen with age, while you naturally outgrow others[2] that, having run their course, wither and decay. It's normal to experience a certain level of churn in your friendships as your life is in many ways likely to change,[3] such that the person you were as a youngster and the person you are as an adult may be as different as the caterpillar is from its butterfly. While the memory of moments shared[4] – especially youthful first-time, formative or milestone moments – can enhance social bonds, friends may drift apart as they enter new chapters in their lives and priorities shift more towards romantic partners and the mounting responsibilities of building a family and career. Sometimes, changes in ideology, personality or personal circumstances can lead to conflict or divergence, making it healthier for both parties to go their separate ways.[5] A wearisome friend who consistently depletes you can become a corrosive, life-sapping drain on your energy[6] and well-being, even increasing your likelihood of developing a chronic illness. If this imbalance persists, execute the 'end' in 'friend' and let them go. Aristotle noted that friendships based on utility and pleasure are the least enduring, as these factors change over time. With time, effort and an open, inquisitive mind, you can start afresh to nurture new friendships with those who share traits, values and interests beyond mere coincidental childhood connections of age and location.

1   *Barcelona* by Freddie Mercury and Montserrat Caballé. Written by Freddie Mercury and Michael Moran
2   *Starmaker* by The Kids From Fame. Written by Bruce Roberts and Carole Bayer
3   *Help!* by Bananarama and Lananeeneenoonoo. Written by John Lennon and Paul McCartney
4   *Cat Among The Pigeons* by Bros. Written by Nicholas Graham and Thomas Watkins
5   *Valentine* by T'Pau. Written by Carol Decker and Ronald Rogers
6   *Jive Talkin'* by Boogie Box High. Written by Barry Gibb, Robin Gibb and Maurice Gibb

The pattern of making new friends resembles that of discovering new music. During early years, friendships form naturally as you develop skills such as cooperation and conflict resolution (albeit play-ground-based). In your teens and early twenties, shared experiences, common locations, educational establishments and youth culture passions – particularly contemporary music – all play a significant role in building bonds. The freedom afforded in early adulthood is a golden time for forging friendships. However, in your thirties and through middle age, responsibilities tied to settling down, family obligations and work commitments often restrict the opportunities for new friendships to the social gatherings that these events spawn. The greater the overlap with another person (personality, hobbies and interests, musical preferences, sense of humour, personal situation, beliefs and outlook . . .), the closer and more robust the friendship is likely to feel. Where the attachment bond forged between you is securely locked (as it often is in early adulthood), you can effortlessly reconnect from where you last left off, regardless of how much time has elapsed.

Maxi Priest prays you'll find many friends in the *Wild World*.[1] Investing in friendships requires care. What matters are the qualities and traits of your friends (fun, playful, optimistic, light, supportive, understanding, dependable, honest, loyal, respectful . . .), not the number. Some anthropologists (particularly Robin Dunbar) and some apps try to count the number of friends you have, which diagrammatically resembles the concentric circles of an archery target – with a central bullseye representing an essential core of one to five of the most meaningful and life-partner relationships, increasing in number but diminishing in importance to the outer-most ring, totalling about 150 (the 'Dunbar number'). Intriguingly, 150 aligns with the typical size of populations of both hunter-gatherer communities and villages recorded in the Domesday Book of 1086. The number of friends will vary from person to person, naturally contracting with age as more time and energy are devoted to those

1   *Wild World* by Maxi Priest. Written by Steven Georgiou

central, deep-core friendships at the expense of the more superficial and peripheral ones.

Melodies were F. R. David's best friends.[1] If you lack close friendships (whether two- or four-legged), emotionally supportive songs can help share your troubles,[2] offering the solace of an auditory hug. Songs as friends are consistent, available, patient and willing to repeat themselves endlessly, although they can never fully replace deep bi-directional interpersonal relationships. No song can replicate simple friendship pleasures, such as sharing a meal or drink or enjoying a walk and a talk.

Ain't No Pleasing You.[3] One important friendship to cultivate is with your keenest critic and the person hardest to please: yourself. The best way to overcome you against you[4] is to develop self-compassion (not the tough-love approach), which allows you to celebrate your victories and be less judgemental of others. Keep your internal dialogue positive and uplifting, and if it turns negative and self-limiting, mentally command it to *Stop!*[5] Reflect on whether this critical voice is rooted in reality or echoes an external source, such as an overly critical parent, teacher or colleague. If your internal voice were made into a song, would it be so packed with vibrancy, excitement and positivity that you (or anyone else) would want to listen to it? Neurologists suggest that an excellent way to keep your brain in fine fettle is to learn and practise a new language (especially musical notation), so learning to speak a new internal language should yield multiple lifelong benefits. Physically, try lightly stroking the back of your hands to stimulate nerves and reduce stress; this technique also works on others, provided you have their consent.

1   *Words* by F.R. David. Written by Eli Fitoussi
2   *Sad Songs (Say So Much)* by Elton John. Written by Elton John and Bernard Taupin
3   *Ain't No Pleasing You* by Chas & Dave. Written by Charles Hodges and David Peacock
4   *Burning Heart* by Survivor. Written by Frank Sullivan III and James Peterik
5   *Stop!* by Sam Brown. Written by Bruce Brody, Samantha Brown and Gregg Sutton

According to *The Only Way Out*,[1] the only way in is through you. Embracing your inner self – imperfections and all – does not contradict leading a meaningful, altruistic life; instead, it will better equip you to spread kindness, happiness and support to others.

FUTURE

Henceforth to eternity, the time ahead of the ever-unfolding present is the perpetually revealing future. The future is shaped by both the present and the past, underscoring why history is so significant to the themes within this book; as Bob Marley suggests, while the future may be full of promise, you should not forget the past.[2]

The 1980s technological revolution enabled pioneering synth-pop producers and musicians like Gary Numan to explore and create a new range of sounds with a distinctly futuristic edge. The era's lyrics often portrayed the future as something to be predicted, anticipated, found,[3] built and even owned.

Futuristic outlooks often oscillate between optimism and pessimism. For some who lived through the 1980s, this was a time clouded by anxiety from the looming threat of nuclear annihilation, casting a menacing shadow across personal and political outlooks and permeating into some songs. Prince's declaration that everyone had a bomb – meaning death could drop in any day[4] – overstated the reality as only about 3% of countries possessed nuclear capability (although still more than enough to trigger a global nuclear holocaust). The future is inherently uncertain, shaped by events beyond your control. However, before the darkness drowns you[5] with the belief that the

1   *The Only Way Out* by Cliff Richard. Written by Ray Martinez
2   *No Woman, No Cry* by Bob Marley and The Wailers. Written by Vincent Ford and Robert Marley
3   *I Want It All* by Queen. Written by Brian May, Freddie Mercury, John Deacon and Roger Taylor
4   *1999* by Prince. Written by Prince Nelson
5   *Dolce Vita* by Ryan Paris. Written by Pierluigi Giombini and Paul Mazzolini

future lacks a brightness,[1] the prevailing mood in the 1980s leaned more towards hope and optimism.

Sound advice? The broadly optimistic outlook on the future proved correct: humanity has survived and thrived in the intervening years.

As the future is uncharted territory, replete with unknowns, it can only be imagined and anticipated. While attempting to predict every twist and turn is futile, it is prudent to plan for and expect opportunities and challenges to arise and to remain adaptable and flexible, ready to improvise in the face of the unexpected. The Roman philosopher Seneca warned that expectation is the greatest obstacle to living because, by fixating on the anticipation of tomorrow, you risk losing sight of today, and every day should count.

Both language and anatomy dictate that you think of the future as an expanse stretching out in front while you perceive the past as somewhere behind you. Danish philosopher Søren Kierkegaard observed that you can only live your life forwards, while you can only understand it by looking backwards. Howard Jones sang how people prefer to discuss the future, not dwell on the past.[2] With these viewpoints in mind, coming to terms and making peace with your past can help you move forward; as Shakespeare's Lady Macbeth (a woman whose present is overwhelmed by the past) reminds us, what's done is done and cannot be undone. To help leave the past behind,[3] allow the constant slipstream created by life's perpetual forward motion[4] to gently carry away any unwanted thought dust deposited by lingering regrets or painful memories that you do not wish to settle upon you. While your past is a unique narrative that has helped shape your identity, your focus should be on

1   *Shattered Dreams* by Johnny Hates Jazz. Written by Clark Datchler
2   *Like To Get To Know You Well* by Howard Jones. Written by John Jones
3   *I Don't Wanna Get Hurt* by Donna Summer. Written by Michael Stock, Matthew Aitken and Peter Waterman
4   *The Sun Goes Down (Living It Up)* by Level 42. Written by Michael Lindup, Mark King, Philip Gould and Waliou Badarou

living today,[1] savouring the present and anticipating an even better forward-thinking future.[2] Knowing everything about your future would diminish your purpose of living in the present.

The past can serve as a valuable resource for reflecting on and incorporating the most beneficial elements into your present, allowing you to craft your desired future. However, your future can be more than just an extension of your current or past experiences. Sound advice suggests you don't rely solely on the rear-view mirror while driving. Instead, use the lessons from the past to guide you towards a brighter and more fulfilling future.

You are the best-placed person to be both planner and architect of your future[3] – from the drawing board to undertaking some of the heavier construction work. Remember that your life is a continual work in progress, happening here and now,[4] so appreciate what you have today (so often you will fail to value what you have until it has gone,[5] which is especially true of health, fitness, love and relationships, youthfulness, and fulfilling work). Creating a plan helps reel in the future towards the shore of the here and now.[6]

Some songs invite us to hold on to every grain of hope,[7] as hope represents the future.[8] The sharper your imagination, the crisper your vision of the future will be, and the more resourceful you'll become in your endeavours and priority-setting. Once you establish

1   *Music And Lights* by Imagination. Written by Ashley Ingram, Leslie John, Steven Jolley and Anthony Swain
2   *Coming Up* by Paul McCartney. Written by Paul McCartney
3   *Love Changes Everything* by Michael Ball. Written by Andrew Lloyd Webber, Donald Blackstone and Charles Hart
4   *Up Where We Belong* by Joe Cocker and Jennifer Warnes. Written by Bernard Nitzsche, Beverly Sainte-Marie and Wilbur Jennings
5   *Hard Habit To Break* by Chicago. Written by Steven Kipner and John Lewis Parker
6   *Back To Life (However Do You Want Me)* by Soul II Soul featuring Caron Wheeler. Written by Trevor Romeo, Caron Wheeler, Paul Hooper and Simon Law
7   *Can't Stay Away From You* by Gloria Estefan and Miami Sound Machine. Written by Gloria Estefan
8   *Rage Hard* by Frankie Goes To Hollywood. Written by Peter Gill, William Johnson, Brian Nash and Mark O'Toole

the right direction, the necessary momentum should follow, driven by preparation and planning.

While lyricists don't claim to be oracles, seers or prophets, listening to music from the past[1] can inspire and shape a better future. Reflecting on the past can help propel you with purpose and focus into the future. The future is inevitable – there's a tomorrow[2] – and tomorrow matters because that is where life, with all its exciting potential and boundless possibilities, will take you, stemming from today's thoughts and actions. While you may not always be able to shape the future for yourself, you can shape yourself for the future.

GREED

"Greed is good" runs the infamous truncated mantra from the 1987 film *Wall Street*, leading some to brand the 1980s as the 'Decade of Greed'. In music, Queen released a song encapsulating the allure and culture of personal ambition, reflecting the era's unbridled economic bingeing: *I Want It All*.[3]

Some argue that greed's relentless take, take, take[4] is a primary motivating driver of economic growth, personal ambition and even the "upward surge of mankind", as posited by Gordon Gekko in *Wall Street*. During the 1980s, conspicuous consumption and competitive flaunting gained social acceptability, particularly among the upwardly mobile who found lucrative employment in the newly deregulated City of London, catering to a new class of ordinary investor eager for a slice of the profit pie.

These cycles of perpetual overconsumption align with the 'Diderot effect', a concept coined by anthropologist Grant McCracken in 1988.

1 *Tribute (Right On)* by The Pasadenas. Written by David Milliner, Aaron Brown, Andrew Banfield, Hamish Seelochan, Michael Milliner and William Wingfield
2 *Lean On Me* by Club Nouveau. Written by William Withers
3 *I Want It All* by Queen. Written by Brian May, Freddie Mercury, John Deacon and Roger Taylor
4 *Say Say Say* by Paul McCartney and Michael Jackson. Written by Paul McCartney and Michael Jackson

The term refers to French philosopher and writer Denis Diderot (1713-1784), who received a luxurious new red dressing gown as a gift. Rather than bringing happiness, the gown accentuated how worn and in urgent need of upgrade were Diderot's other possessions. The gown became a catalyst for a new and disruptive pattern of consumptive greed driven by an obsession for complementary unity, harmony and coherence in his possessions; this was about crafting personal identity, not fulfilling rational functionality. *Master And Servant*.[1] Diderot felt trapped and consumed by greed and the need to allocate more resources and effort to buy the possessions with which he wished to identify, describing himself as "master of my old dressing gown . . . a slave to my new one".

For Seneca, poverty was not about having too little but craving too much. Modern-day economists attribute greed to unadulterated capitalism, while psychologists view the need for greed – the unquenched desire to have, do and want more, more, more[2] – as comforting compensatory and identity-projecting behaviour in the search for validation stemming from fears of scarcity, loss, anxiety, vulnerability or low self-esteem. Many consumers attempt to fill a devouring void of discontent or to mask personal inadequacies, leading to an obsessive quest to overstep, engorge and accumulate, wanting too much for too long,[3] and exceeding excess.[4] Such personal impoverishment can disrupt the proper functioning and balance of individuals and societies, leading to selfish, unethical or exploitative behaviour and contributing to environmental overexploitation and degradation. Unsurprisingly, avarice is one of the seven deadly sins; the Bible warns that you cannot serve two masters – God and Mammon (a term St Augustine identified as greed). Greed exposes humanity's uglier underside by eroding generosity and empathy; it is neither good nor godly.

1 *Master And Servant* by Depeche Mode. Written by Martin Gore
2 *Rebel Yell* by Billy Idol. Written by William Broad and Steven Schneider
3 *I Know Him So Well* by Elaine Paige and Barbara Dickson. Written by Göran Andersson, Timothy Rice and Björn Ulvaeus
4 *Wide Boy* by Nik Kershaw. Written by Nicholas Kershaw

Two masters of pop – the duo Tears For Fears – were no fans of Thatcherite economic ideology that demanded more and more,[1] singing of their desire to end both need and the politics of greed.[2] Depeche Mode sang of rampant corporate rapaciousness – primarily unleashed by the free-market policies of the era – grabbing all it could in a world where *Everything Counts*[3] in ever-larger amounts.

Sound advice? When it comes to greed, how much do you need?[4] Lyrical handouts of sound or practical advice were more subtle than generous. Cynics might argue that the unbridled hedonism and general profligacy of 1980s pop culture, especially the breezy opulence flaunted in many music videos, contradicted any critical messaging and could attract accusations of hypocrisy.

John Lennon urged us to imagine a world where there was no need for greed.[5] To escape a life tarnished by endless greed and a perpetual focus on personal gain,[6] learn to recognise indicators of greedy behaviour: don't take for take's sake – only take what you need.[7] Consider redirecting your attention towards what you can give rather than always presenting a hand that takes.[8] When your hand gives freely with pleasure, pleasure is your reward.

Just Can't Get Enough.[9] With an ever-shifting finishing line, pernicious greed entices you to grasp what's just beyond reach,[10] distorting and devaluing your appreciation for what you already hold. Roman poet Ovid observed that the harvest always appears more

1   *Pale Shelter* by Tears For Fears. Written by Roland Orzabal
2   *Sowing The Seeds Of Love* by Tears For Fears. Written by Roland Orzabal and Curt Smith
3   *Everything Counts* by Depeche Mode. Written by Martin Gore
4   *West End Girls* by Pet Shop Boys. Written by Neil Tennant and Christopher Lowe
5   *Imagine* by John Lennon. Written by John Lennon and Yoko Ono
6   *Harvest For The World* by The Christians. Written by Ernest Isley, O'Kelly Isley Jr, Ronald Isley, Rudolph Isley, Marvin Isley and Christopher Jasper
7   *Stand Up For Your Love Rights* by Yazz. Written by Yasmin Evans and Timothy Parry
8   *O Superman* by Laurie Anderson. Written by Laura Anderson
9   *Just Can't Get Enough* by Depeche Mode. Written by Vincent Martin
10 *Holding Out For A Hero* by Bonnie Tyler. Written by James Steinman and Dean Pitchford

bountiful in another's field, a sentiment more commonly expressed as the grass is always greener on the other side.[1] Our modern consumer culture, amplified by extensive use of social media, promotes greed by flaunting surface-level, attention-seeking materialism. Although visually seductive, addictive and constant comparison can leave those who already have more than enough to feel outperformed, inadequate and in need of yet more to elevate their status. Greed and gullibility often go hand in hand. Such comparison depletes your gratitude account, stoking inequality and breeding envy and jealousy. If you must indulge in comparison, opt to compare yourself with the have-nots rather than with the world's privileged one-percenters living in a bubble of highly curated, lurid ostentation. Such comparison should leave you feeling grateful for what you already have (both materiality and spiritually) rather than lamenting what you think you ought or deserve to have. Lightening the burdensome weight of needless materialism allows your spirit to rise.

Give me more.[2] Feeding the insatiable furnace of greed leads to perpetual dissatisfaction. For the Buddha, greed was one of three fires that must be extinguished on the path to nirvana (the other two being hatred and delusion). To help extinguish greed, define what 'enough' means to you (where greed thrives, it's usually a yearning for more where you can never get enough[3] because too much is never enough:[4] brazen greed has an all-consuming appetite). Set specific (quantifiable), realistic (achievable) and measurable goals within a defined time frame, all expressed in action-oriented positive language – focusing on what you want to achieve, not what you wish to avoid. You'll discover riches when you recognise you already have enough.

1   *Chocolate Box* by Bros. Written by Luke Goss and Matthew Goss
2   *Special Brew* by Bad Manners. Written by Douglas Trendle, Louis Cook, David Farren, Paul Hyman, Christopher Kane, Andrew Marson, Alan Sayag and Martin Stewart
3   *Requiem* by London Boys. Written by Ralf-René Maué
4   *Fame* by Irene Cara. Written by Dean Pitchford and Michael Gore

HOLIDAYS

On *Holiday*,[1] even if you only escape the shackles of everyday routine for a day, Madonna suggests you celebrate. Chicago (the rock band, not the municipal tourist board) sang about the need for time away.[2] Pop songs offer escapism – near-instant, carbon-free internal flights of fancy capable of whisking you away to another world, even a personal *Wonderland*,[3] far outside yourself.

During the 1980s, the largest fillip for the travel industry came from deregulation and technological advancements, leading to a slew of low-cost (and low authenticity) package holidays with enticing promises of sun, sand and fun,[4] particularly on the shores of southern Spain.[5] These changes enabled a whole new generation to sign up for a slice of life in a foreign land[6] and clock up a previously unimaginable number of air miles. *One Day I'll Fly Away*.[7] Virgin Atlantic and Ryanair first took to the freedom of the skies in 1984, ushering in a new *International Jet Set*[8] lifestyle. In the 1980s, to help alleviate the frazzling stress and the time-dragging boredom inherent in international travel, smokers could light up their duty-free cigarettes at the back of the aeroplane, making it hard to see through the smoky air.[9] There was no option to smoke outside.

What transformative tips did contemporary pop songs offer for the intrepid traveller? Don't be misled by the photographs in

1   *Holiday* by Madonna. Written by Curtis Hudson and Lisa Stevens
2   *Hard To Say I'm Sorry* by Chicago. Written by David Foster and Peter Cetera
3   *Wonderland* by Big Country. Written by William Adamson, Mark Brzezicki, Anthony Butler and Bruce Watson
4   *Wipe Out* by The Fat Boys and The Beach Boys. Written by Robert Berryhill, Patrick Connolly, James Fuller and Ronald Wilson
5   *The Chicken Song* by Spitting Image. Written by Philip Pope, Robert Grant and Douglas Naylor
6   *In The Army Now* by Status Quo. Written by Robert Bolland and Ferdinand Bolland
7   *One Day I'll Fly Away* by Randy Crawford. Written by Joseph Sample and Wilbur Jennings
8   *International Jet Set* by The Specials. Written by Jeremy Dammers
9   *Crazy For You* by Madonna. Written by John Bettis and Jonathan Lind

sun-filled brochures, advised *Left To My Own Devices*.[1] 'Left to my own Devizes' could be the title to a self-guided tour around a quaint Wiltshire market town – in April or the summertime[2] – but given that it was now easier to travel anywhere[3] and that you could choose to go wherever you wanted,[4] from where across the seven seas[5] did the songs suggest for that escape-from-it-all[6] holiday? *Funkytown?*[7] *Love Town?*[8] *Paradise City?*[9] A taste of paradise[10] is always enticing, but what if you want something more immersive than an ego trip?[11]

Belsize Park?[12] Muswell Hill?[13] The brief was more seven seas than Seven Sisters, so how about holidaying somewhere you've never been,[14] somewhere far, far away?[15]

Inner City suggested taking you somewhere they knew you

1   *Left To My Own Devices* by Pet Shop Boys. Written by Neil Tennant and Christopher Lowe
2   *Close (To The Edit)* by Art Of Noise. Written by Anne Dudley, Gary Langan, Jonathan Jeczalik, Paul Morley and Trevor Horn
3   *Living In America* by James Brown. Written by Daniel Hartman and Charles Kaufman
4   *The Safety Dance* by Men Without Hats. Written by Ivan Doroschuk
5   *Sweet Dreams (Are Made Of This)* by Eurythmics. Written by Ann Lennox and David Stewart
6   *Robert De Niro's Waiting* by Bananarama. Written by Sara Dallin, Siobhan Fahey, Keren Woodward, Steven Jolley and Anthony Swain
7   *Funkytown* by Lipps Inc. Written by Steven Greenberg
8   *Love Town* by Booker Newberry III. Written by Leonard Barry and Eli Tatarsky
9   *Paradise City* by Guns N' Roses. Written by Saul Hudson, William Rose, Jeffrey Isbell, Michael McKagan and Steven Adler
10 *Girl I'm Gonna Miss You* by Milli Vanilli. Written by Frank Farian, Peter Bischof-Fallenstein and Dietmar Kawohl
11 *My Prerogative* by Bobby Brown. Written by Robert Brown, Edward Riley and Gene Griffin
12 *Kayleigh* by Marillion. Written by Mark Kelly, Ian Mosley, Steven Rothery, Peter Trewavas and Derek Dick
13 *Driving In My Car* by Madness. Written by Michael Barson
14 *The Power Of Love* by Jennifer Rush. Written by Gunther Mende, Wolfgang Detmann, Heidi Stern and Mary Applegate
15 *(Just Like) Starting Over* by John Lennon. Written by John Lennon

wanted to go[1] – and it's very far away:[2] a holiday to the Milky Way.[3] While a fine place,[4] you might prefer to keep your feet on more solid ground,[5] so anywhere more *Down To Earth?*[6]

Day Trip To Bangor (Didn't We Have A Lovely Time)?[7] and all for less than a pound. Unbeatable value and undoubtedly a *Fantastic Day*[8] out, but anything not only for the day?[9]

How about over the sea to Skye[10] to a mountain hideaway?[11] If you've recently travelled from the Isle of Skye,[12] you may crave a destination where the sun warms the sky,[13] not forgetting Roman poet Horace's observation that those who rush across the sea may change their sky but not their soul (Seneca, too, spoke of those who change the spectacle but are unable to escape themselves).

How about a place where no one's been before[14] or a visit to an

1   *Good Life* by Inner City. Written by Kevin Saunderson, Shanna Jackson and Roy Holmon

2   *Road To Nowhere* by Talking Heads. Written by David Byrne

3   *Hands Up (Give Me Your Heart)* by Ottawan. Written by Daniel Bangalter and Jean Kluger

4   *Downtown '88* by Petula Clark. Written by Anthony Hatch

5   *And The Beat Goes On* by The Whispers. Written by Leon Sylvers, Stephen Shockley and William Shelby

6   *Down To Earth* by Curiosity Killed The Cat. Written by Martin Volpeliere-Pierrot, Julian Brookhouse, Miguel Drummond, Nicholas Thorp and Tobias Andersen

7   *Day Trip To Bangor (Didn't We Have A Lovely Time)* by Fiddler's Dram. Written by Deborah Cook

8   *Fantastic Day* by Haircut One Hundred. Written by Nicholas Heyward

9   *The Captain Of Her Heart* by Double. Written by Felix Haug and Kurt Meier

10 *The Skye Boat Song* by Roger Whittaker featuring Des O'Connor. Written by Harold Boulton

11 *Is There Something I Should Know?* by Duran Duran. Written by Simon Le Bon, Nigel Taylor, Roger Taylor, Andrew Taylor and Nicholas Bates

12 *Donald Where's Your Troosers?* by Andy Stewart. Written by Andrew Stewart and Neil Grant

13 *La Isla Bonita* by Madonna. Written by Madonna Ciccone, Patrick Leonard and Bruce Gaitsch

14 *Jump (For My Love)* by Pointer Sisters. Written by Gary Skardina, Martha Sharron and Stephen Mitchell

ultra-exclusive club where *The Sunshine Of Your Smile*[1] is the only membership requirement?[2] Nice. If you have already been to Nice,[3] why not consider somewhere north of Kathmandu,[4] Waikiki,[5] or the legendary Avalon?[6] For those seeking a destination that exudes exotic dream-like magnificence and luxury, a place so grand that nobody dares to go, consider Xanadu.[7]

Sound advice? Holidays offer a brief but valuable chance for change, and a change is as good as a rest. *Sound Advice* recommends visiting – or revisiting – the 1980s for its transformative music rather than its ideas about holiday destinations.

Poorly planned holidays can be just as stressful as the toil you're escaping from, while the cost and inconvenience of travel can sometimes outweigh the benefits. The added pressure to present an unrealistic facade of bliss on social media can exacerbate the burden of expectation to unsustainable levels.

Research your destination's culture, cuisine, sights and sounds to ensure a fulfilling holiday. Set a budget, create an itinerary (with some flexibility) and consider your safety – tourists can inadvertently attract unwanted attention. Use a packing list to travel smart. Remember that visiting a country is different from experiencing it, so strive to look beyond what you are directed to see, relax and savour your well-deserved holiday. Upon return, you should feel refreshed, recharged and enriched by your experience. Your return presents an ideal opportunity to start cultivating new and beneficial habits.

1   *The Sunshine Of Your Smile* by Mike Berry. Written by Leslie Cooke and Liliah Ray
2   *Club Tropicana* by Wham! Written by George Michael and Andrew Ridgeley
3   *I've Never Been To Me* by Charlene. Written by Kenneth Hirsch and Ronald Gould
4   *Nobody Told Me* by John Lennon. Written by John Lennon
5   *Agadoo* by Black Lace. Written by Mya Symille, Michael Delancray, Gilles Péram and Günther Behrle
6   *Orinoco Flow* by Enya. Written by Enya Brennan and Roma Ryan
7   *Xanadu* by Olivia Newton-John and Electric Light Orchestra. Written by Jeffrey Lynne

JOB

While the Pet Shop Boys may have never worked in a pet shop, they sang of wanting a job and working for a living.[1] Despite sharing a workspace, 'job' and 'work' are not quite synonyms. A job typically refers to a specific role or task – such as retailing pet products – in return for pay. Work encompasses a broader pursuit, often contributing to a larger goal that brings personal fulfilment, advancement and satisfaction, such as a passion for working with animals. While a job is a form of work, it primarily represents a means to an end rather than a fulfilling end in itself.

For Gwen Guthrie, no job meant no chance of a relationship with her as she avoided the unemployed.[2] Blunt talk. As a theme, the songs often do not equate jobs with leading a happy, harmonious and balanced life. Morrissey sought and found a job, yet still felt miserable;[3] a job you hate can be hard work. Tethered to technology, Five Star felt their free will ebbing away as they tapped their keyboards.[4] Robbie Nevil's job required that he work night and day in a relentless cycle of clocking in and out, leading him to question whether this was all that life had to offer.[5]

Sound advice? Tracy Chapman's job paid the bills.[6] The songs acknowledge that a job can cover the rent, buy food and even secure a partner's affection but that perpetually living a hand-to-mouth existence comes at the cost of happiness. The constant striving to make ends meet[7] can compromise, blur and diminish any meaningful

1   *What Have I Done To Deserve This?* by Pet Shop Boys with Dusty Springfield. Written by Neil Tennant, Christopher Lowe and Alta Willis
2   *Ain't Nothin' Goin' On But The Rent* by Gwen Guthrie. Written by Gwendolyn Guthrie
3   *Heaven Knows I'm Miserable Now* by The Smiths. Written by Steven Morrissey and John Maher
4   *System Addict* by Five Star. Written by William Livsey and Gary Bell
5   *C'est La Vie* by Robbie Nevil. Written by Robert Nevil, Duncan Pain and Mark Holding
6   *Fast Car* by Tracy Chapman. Written by Tracy Chapman
7   *You're The Voice* by John Farnham. Written by Anderson Qunta, Keith Reid, Marguerite Rider and Christopher Thompson

purpose to living. When your focus is constantly locked on survival,[1] there's little opportunity for life to flourish.

For others, however, a regular, fixed-hours job (even where everyone is working overtime)[2] makes more sense than a demanding, stress-laden, long-hours, health-sapping career where endless work commitments leave little or no time for your family, friends or leisure activities.

KNOWLEDGE

Is There Something I Should Know?[3] What you need to know[4] is that knowledge exists in various forms. One binary division is between explicit knowledge (easily conveyed through words and numbers, like learning physics from a textbook) and tacit knowledge (challenging to explain and express with words and numbers, such as intuition, emotional intelligence or learning to play a musical instrument). Whether inherited or self-discovered, knowledge enriches our comprehension of the world, yet it remains inherently incomplete, as no mere mortal is omniscient. We pride ourselves on what we know, yet we all have much to learn. Interestingly, you already know far more than you need to know, yet despite our formidable intellect, no one knows why.

Applying our intellect to analyse pop lyrics reveals that the most sought-after knowledge pertains to love and relationships – questions like *I Want To Know What Love Is*[5] or *How Will I Know*[6] if she/

1   *Karma Chameleon* by Culture Club. Written by Roy Hay, George O'Dowd, Michael Craig, Jonathan Moss and Philip Pickett
2   *Living In America* by James Brown. Written by Daniel Hartman and Charles Kaufman
3   *Is There Something I Should Know?* by Duran Duran. Written by Simon Le Bon, Nigel Taylor, Roger Taylor, Andrew Taylor and Nicholas Bates
4   *Da Da Da* by Trio. Written by Stephan Remmler and Gert Krawinkel
5   *I Want To Know What Love Is* by Foreigner. Written by Michael Jones
6   *How Will I Know* by Whitney Houston. Written by George Merrill, Shannon Rubicam and Michael Walden

he loves me? Occasionally, ignorance is bliss,[1] such as with your partner's relationship history. Respecting others' personal space and privacy can alleviate the rumination or discomfort that comes with the burden of possessing full knowledge. Similarly, many intentionally choose to ignore uncomfortable truths or harsh realities regarding their health or finances, preferring to bury their heads in the sands of ignorance – known as the ostrich effect (although ostriches don't bury their heads in the sand) – rather than confront unpalatable facts and the need for change.

Sting, a former teacher, sang about the importance of tacit knowledge wrapped up in life experience – lessons not explicitly taught in college.[2] Recognising the distinction between knowledge and information is important. Information is the raw factual data collected, organised and categorised, while knowledge emerges from processing that information to develop deeper insight. Knowledge enables high-level thinking, informed decision-making, improved problem-solving and connects seemingly unrelated disciplines to create new ideas or concepts. You acquire knowledge through study, experience and reflection.

Sound advice? It's all part of the great unknown.[3] Plato described knowledge as the food of the soul. It's highly prized – Faust sold his soul to the Devil in return for knowledge. As a song theme, knowledge may leave you unsatiated – Hungry Like The Wolf[4] – making music more of a soul-soothing balm than brain food.

How do you know what you need to know? Cultivating natural curiosity drives discovery and creativity, making the desire to discover and acquire knowledge and understanding more significant than merely accumulating a hoard of facts. During the 1980s, knowledge about domestic and global events was funnelled mainly through

1   Annie, I'm Not Your Daddy by Kid Creole and The Coconuts. Written by Thomas Browder
2   Wrapped Around Your Finger by The Police. Written by Gordon Sumner
3   Waterfalls by Paul McCartney. Written by Paul McCartney
4   Hungry Like The Wolf by Duran Duran. Written by Simon Le Bon, Nigel Taylor, Roger Taylor, Andrew Taylor and Nicholas Bates

the narrow straits of journalism, which supplied a filtered, readily understandable perspective amid a world full of problems[1] (war, famine, terrorism). Bad news, particularly powerfully photogenic, visceral headline-making events, sells by tapping into the natural human negativity bias, which focuses your attention on warnings, threats and dangers; societal shortcomings often reflect those of individual human nature. However, there was – and still is – an abundance of underreported good news that gradually unfurls to transform the world, such as rising global educational levels, decreasing poverty rates, more affordable renewable energy, lower infant mortality and, since 1900, a more than doubling of life expectancy (not merely adding extra life, but adding a whole extra life). Expanding the scope and quality of your knowledge base broadens your horizons. Additionally, it helps reduce fear of the unknown, so keep an open mind that remains receptive to information from diverse sources. Where knowledge fails to replace fear of the unknown, faith or conspiracy theory has a habit of creeping in to fill the void.

Madonna suggests we spread the word.[2] Knowledge naturally disseminates and is at its most valuable when widely shared. When the candle of knowledge ignites another candle, they together illuminate what was once darkness. Once lit, the candle of knowledge burns brighter rather than down, becoming increasingly difficult to extinguish. Similarly, sound advice exists to inform, guide and be shared among enlightened listeners.

Knowledge can be transported and transferred; wisdom lies in knowing how to use that knowledge, a realisation that accumulates in the sediment of experience deposited by the river of passing years. The philosopher Socrates, considered the wisest man in Greece by the oracle at Delphi, viewed himself as a mere midwife of thought, saying that all he knew was that he knew nothing (the more you know, the more it dawns on you how little you know), a sentiment

1   *Master Blaster (Jammin')* by Stevie Wonder. Written by Stevie Wonder
2   *Holiday* by Madonna. Written by Curtis Hudson and Lisa Stevens

echoed by the protagonist in *It Ain't What You Do,*[1] who thought himself clever only to realise he didn't know much about life. This realisation applies to those who should know better, having been around the block a few times.[2] While age brings experience, it does not automatically confer wisdom because wisdom stems from the ability to discern what matters from what doesn't and knowing what you can control and change from what you can't. Wisdom is about knowing how and when to effectively integrate, assimilate and apply your accumulated knowledge, experience, understanding and judgement in a balanced and proportionate manner. When you can draw inspiration and ideas from diverse sources and synthesise the fragments of your knowledge from seemingly unrelated disciplines (adding in a dash of creative imagination), you may discover new, unexpected or deeper connections or patterns emerging. Your brain is naturally wired to seek patterns that make sense of the world, helping to render the random, chaotic or uncertain seem more predictable. Creating something new using the amalgamation of knowledge is known as recombinant innovation. The emergence of a new theory, such as Darwinian evolution, may require you to relinquish what you once thought of as the truth. Evolution lacks foresight, instead relying on recombining existing traits to meet new challenges in an ever-changing world – a DNA remix. Societies, communities and businesses all benefit from recombinant ideas, knowledge and perspectives from the neurodiversity inherent in those who dance to the beat of a different drum.[3]

Unlike the transient lives of those who discover it, knowledge endures, accumulates and evolves. Science (which etymologically means knowledge) and technology – such as the ability to peer in real-time into the brain's functioning via magnetic resonance

1   *It Ain't What You Do* . . . by Fun Boy Three and Bananarama. Written by Melvin Oliver and James Young
2   *This Time I Know It's For Real* by Donna Summer. Written by LaDonna Gaines, Michael Stock, Matthew Aitken and Peter Waterman
3   *I Eat Cannibals (Part I)* by Toto Coelo. Written by Barry Green, Paul Greedus and Roy Nicolson

imaging – will continue to build upon, refine and supersede some of the facts forming the foundational knowledge bedrock of the sound advice within this book.

The ever-accelerating velocity of our modern-day digital information age compels many users to communicate continually.[1] (The unending desire among contemporary pop stars to interact with their fans through digital channels may have lifted the shroud of mystique under which their 1980s counterparts could craft and maintain a musical myth.) Some consumers of digital content feel obligated to react to the constant bombardment of information raining upon them, leaving them feeling battered, saturated and overwhelmed. Now more than ever, it's essential to set boundaries, limit your exposure and be able to discern and deliberate useful, high-quality information from the avalanche of what is available. Learning to differentiate the real from the fake, the profound from the superficial, the beneficial from the fad and the permanent from the transient helps you to transform information into usable knowledge. Apply the same rigour in scrutinising evidence, methods, views and conclusions that support and align with your beliefs as you do to those that challenge them.

LONELINESS

Fairground Attraction use the metaphor of a boat at sea[2] to portray loneliness. Pop songs frequently depict a world full of lonely people[3] adrift in a sea of solitude. As social beings, our innate need for connection is profound, reflected in Queen's desire not to live alone,[4] Madonna's mathematical musing that one is a lonely number[5] and

1   *Tell Her About It* by Billy Joel. Written by William Joel
2   *Find My Love* by Fairground Attraction. Written by Mark Nevin
3   *Too Many Broken Hearts* by Jason Donovan. Written by Michael Stock, Matthew Aitken and Peter Waterman
4   *I Want To Break Free* by Queen. Written by John Deacon
5   *Open Your Heart* by Madonna. Written by Madonna Ciccone, Gardner Cole and Peter Rafelson

Duran Duran's realisation that solitude isn't a great deal of fun.[1] Enforced loneliness and social isolation can strike during any stage of life: in childhood and adolescence (especially for taciturn boys or those bullied for being different),[2] through middle age (in-work loneliness can range from literal remote working to the perfunctory and superficial interactions common in open-plan offices or resulting from the cult of perpetual busyness among professionals) and extending into older age, with the stereotypical image of the lonely pensioner.[3]

Whitney Houston reminded us that living alone isn't easy.[4] Loneliness, whether persistent or occasional, is a complex emotion often stemming from loss: examples include the disintegration of a relationship, leaving (or moving) home, loss of employment (including retirement), within-marriage isolation (where the loss of love can result in *Separate Lives*)[5] or at-home isolation (through motherhood, physical remoteness, infirmity - especially following sensory loss or deterioration - or grief after bereavement). None of these events constitutes a personal failing. For those for whom loneliness is an interfering, disruptive and unwelcome interloper, it is one of the toughest roles you will ever have to take on.[6] If, when loneliness calls,[7] it's allowed to linger unaddressed, it can lead to significant chronic physical and mental health problems, such as an increased likelihood of depression and anxiety, compromised

1   *Save A Prayer* by Duran Duran. Written by Simon Le Bon, Nigel Taylor, Roger Taylor, Andrew Taylor and Nicholas Bates

2   *Smalltown Boy* by Bronski Beat. Written by Steven Forrest, James Somerville and Lawrence Cole

3   *One In Ten* by UB40. Written by James Brown, Alistair Campbell, Earl Falconer, Norman Hassan, Brian Travers and Michael Virtue

4   *Saving All My Love For You* by Whitney Houston. Written by Gerald Goffin and Michael Masser

5   *Separate Lives* by Phil Collins and Marilyn Martin. Written by Stephen Bishop

6   *Candle In The Wind* by Elton John. Written by Elton John and Bernard Taupin

7   *I Wanna Dance With Somebody (Who Loves Me)* by Whitney Houston. George Merrill and Shannon Rubicam

immunity, increased inflammation, cognitive decline and jumping blood pressure.[1] These often hidden costs and afflictions affect both individuals and society. Jimmy Nail sang how all could see the loneliness within him.[2] However, in an increasingly self-absorbed world, few notice the cracks in others' internal lives, leaving the lonely to feel invisible in plain sight, reinforcing the claim in *The Great Pretender*[3] that the lonely feel so without anyone being able to tell.

Although loneliness isn't a disease, the 'cure' promoted by pop songs (often targeted at the young) is to find love: no more lonely days[4] means *No More Lonely Nights*[5] (feelings of loneliness and vulnerability often intensify at night, a time when quiet reflection is common and the absence of daylight may reflect a lack of hope). For those for whom love – or anyone – is a stranger[6] unlikely to come knocking at their door,[7] this is no time to stay at home[8] feeling lonely.[9] Instead, take the initiative[10] and actively build social networks and increase social interactions by, for example, joining local clubs and societies, supporting local shops, chatting to strangers, participating in community events or volunteering in areas that align with your interests and will increase the likelihood of social engagement. Each meaningful interaction, even if only a token gesture of kindness, a brief chat or simply sharing a smile,[11] can beneficially boost

1   *Really Saying Something* by Bananarama and Fun Boy Three. Written by Norman Whitfield, William Stevenson and Edward Holland Jr
2   *Love Don't Live Here Anymore* by Jimmy Nail. Written by Miles Gregory
3   *The Great Pretender* by Freddie Mercury. Written by Samuel Ram
4   *The Way You Make Me Feel* by Michael Jackson. Written by Michael Jackson
5   *No More Lonely Nights* by Paul McCartney. Written by Paul McCartney
6   *Love Is A Stranger* by Eurythmics. Written by Ann Lennox and David Stewart
7   *So Lonely* by The Police. Written by Gordon Sumner
8   *Rhythm Of The Night* by DeBarge. Written by Diane Warren
9   *Saddle Up* by David Christie. Written by Philo Robinson and Jacques Pépino
10   *Back To Life (However Do You Want Me)* by Soul II Soul featuring Caron Wheeler. Written by Trevor Romeo, Caron Wheeler, Paul Hooper and Simon Law
11   *I'll Be Satisfied* by Shakin' Stevens. Written by Berry Gordy III and Roquel Davis

well-being, making everyone feel better, more appreciated and connected, often for hours afterwards.

Health is more than the absence of illness, success is more than the absence of failure, and loneliness is more than the absence of people: even when surrounded by others, you can still feel a world away.[1] Loneliness entails a sense of social and emotional disconnection, a condition many social commentators believe has reached unprecedented levels (one in three regularly report feeling lonely) despite our technologically interconnected world, where the majority now live in densely populated urban areas. Even success and celebrity can bring isolation. ABBA spotlighted this loneliness paradox in *Super Trouper*, asking how anyone can feel lonely when faced with a sea of twenty thousand people?[2] Similarly, Bananarama commented on crowded city life while they were on their own,[3] with everyone a stranger.[4] The bottled-up message from The Police was that they were not alone in feeling alone.[5] The advent of modern social media exacerbates this paradox by being both inclusive – connecting like-minded people (often outside the mainstream) – and exclusive, creating invisible loneliness. This invisibility disproportionately affects younger people, with one in four regularly reporting feeling lonely. Despite being surrounded by their peers, some youngsters feel alone on their phone, as do those of all ages who view but do not interact directly with social media. Whether in a city or online, people who appear fully connected can still feel alone in a crowd[6] because the absence of quality, meaningful interactions can turn populous places into deserts of social connectivity. Loneliness remains subjective and self-defined.

Physical loneliness emerged relatively recently in human history

1   *Crazy For You* by Madonna. Written by John Bettis and Jonathan Lind
2   *Super Trouper* by ABBA. Written by Göran Andersson and Björn Ulvaeus
3   *Cruel Summer* by Bananarama. Written by Sara Dallin, Siobhan Fahey, Steven Jolley, Anthony Swain and Keren Woodward
4   *Turning Japanese* by The Vapors. Written by David Fenton
5   *Message In A Bottle* by The Police. Written by Gordon Sumner
6   *Blow The House Down* by Living In A Box. Written by Albert Hammond and Marcus Vere

following changes to the structure of communities, settlements and the multi-generational architecture of family households. In sidestepping loneliness, our ancestors sacrificed their privacy. The option to lead a life apart was primarily the domain of religious anchorites, which, by any measure, is an extreme position to take. The evolving shape of societies and increased life expectancy will amplify the potential for loneliness to hit home.

Sound advice? Enforced loneliness is toxic to mental and physical health. Songs may offer comfort and reassurance to those who feel alone in pursuing love, self-discovery or meaning, particularly during adolescence. As ABBA confirmed, it's not about how lonely you appear but how lonely you feel.

External social support and internal self-care (such as adopting an open and outward-looking attitude and cultivating meaning and purpose through helping others) can help alleviate or reverse some aspects of loneliness. The value of social connectedness to measurable health, longevity and happiness to those denied it is such that GPs and healthcare professionals now dispense social prescribing (aka community referral), referring patients to non-clinical community activities such as creative arts, gardening or sport, all as part of a complementary personalised care plan. Unusually, this is an outward-looking approach to healthcare.

Loneliness in songs is often wrapped in negative connotations, suggesting that being alone is worse than anything.[1] However, some cherish being and living alone without experiencing loneliness. The Smiths ask whether it is wrong to want to live alone, concluding that it's not.[2] Some feel better on their own,[3] actively seeking out, embracing and treasuring their solitude, using it as precious time to contemplate, replenish their energy and build and cultivate fortitude. Amid the clamour of an increasingly busy, noisy and interconnected world, finding true peace, solitude and quiet can be challenging.

1   *A Good Heart* by Feargal Sharkey. Written by Maria McKee
2   *Sheila Take A Bow* by The Smiths. Written by John Maher and Steven Morrissey
3   *I Quit* by Bros. Written by Nicholas Graham and Thomas Watkins

If you crave time alone[1] but struggle to find it within a hectic, people-saturated world, carve out guilt-free time alone in your daily routine for activities such as exercising (running, cycling, walking, yoga, Pilates), listening to music on headphones, reading for pleasure and writing either a diary of gratitude (see *Positivity*) or expressing your innermost thoughts on paper.

It doesn't hurt (and may even be beneficial) to spend time alone,[2] provided it's a valued, intentional choice (some thrive in the anonymity of city living) rather than an unintended default. The more comfortable, connected and confident you are with yourself and your thoughts, the more comfortable and connected others will feel in your presence.

LOVE

What's Love Got To Do With It?[3] Love is arguably the most profound word in the English language. If you've arrived here alphabetically, you will have noticed how this complex, deep and multi-faceted emotion has permeated into the heart of many songs to become the dominant theme. UB40 noted how love inspires song,[4] explaining why songwriters have for centuries served up lyrical love to a hungry audience.[5]

In *Love Train*,[6] Holly Johnson likens his love interest to a work of art, perhaps reflecting on how love and the symbols of music coexist on canvas in many of the world's most celebrated paintings. The unique yet easily relatable dynamics of love – especially the heart-wrenching drama of lost love – enable songwriters to capture

1   *Sister* by Bros. Written by Matthew Goss, Luke Goss and Nicholas Graham
2   *Love On Your Side* by Thompson Twins. Written by Thomas Bailey, Alannah Currie and Joseph Leeway
3   *What's Love Got To Do With It* by Tina Turner. Written by Terence Britten and Graham Lyle
4   *Breakfast In Bed* by UB40 with Chrissie Hynde. Written by Donald Fritts and Edward Hinton
5   *If I Was* by Midge Ure. Written by Daniel Mitchell and James Ure
6   *Love Train* by Holly Johnson. Written by William Johnson

broad-stroke emotions on to which listeners can then add their fine-brush personalised details. Often, what makes someone special to you resides in a collection of minor, seemingly inconsequential idiosyncrasies in their personality that endear them to you, even if you struggle to put your finger on what exactly it is they're doing right.[1]

I Want To Know What Love Is.[2] Okay, so *What Is Love?*[3] Evolutionary psychology suggests love's function is to attract and retain a mate committed to both reproduction and cooperative child-rearing. *The Power Of Love*[4] suggests love transcends biology to become an energy. Sometimes, love's energy is constant and everlasting, or it can quickly drain the amatory batteries and fizzle away, leaving behind powerless and redundant hardware. Despite millennia of contemplation and countless lines of simile and metaphor, love's enduring strength, intensity and intimacy remain difficult to define[5] as it's hard to encapsulate the mutual bond of understanding, connectedness, joy, happiness, passion and sexual desire that most recognise love to be. Plugging back into the energy concept, *The Power Of Love*[6] features as a song title three times in the top 10 of the 1980s, twice reaching number 1. The power of the ballad, this time from Robin Beck and again evoking the idea of electrical flow, suggests that when something real but mysterious happens to you that defies definition, this is when you know you are in love.[7] Perhaps music

1   *Something 'Bout You Baby I Like* by Status Quo. Written by Richard Goodman
2   *I Want To Know What Love Is* by Foreigner. Written by Michael Jones
3   *What Is Love?* by Howard Jones. Written by John Jones and William Bryant
4   *The Power Of Love* by Frankie Goes To Hollywood. Written by William Johnston, Peter Gill, Mark O'Toole and Brian Nash
5   *What Am I Gonna Do (I'm So In Love With You)* by Rod Stewart. Written by Roderick Stewart, Anthony Brock and Jay Davis
6   *The Power Of Love* by Frankie Goes To Hollywood. Written by William Johnston, Peter Gill, Mark O'Toole and Brian Nash / *The Power Of Love* by Jennifer Rush. Written by Gunther Mende, Wolfgang Detmann, Heidi Stern and Mary Applegate / *The Power Of Love* by Huey Lewis and The News. Written by Hugh Cregg III, Christopher Hayes and John Colla
7   *First Time* by Robin Beck. Written by Gavin Spencer, Thomas Anthony and Terence Boyle

first arose – and continues to exist – thanks to its ability to give voice to an indescribable connection.

The ancient Greeks viewed love with nuance, rationally categorising it into distinct realms: *eros* – still familiar today and the root of words such as 'erotic' – was the Greek god of love and fertility and represented the intense passion, romance and sexual desire regularly portrayed in pop songs; *philia* encompassed the affection and fondness of friendship, which philosopher Plato considered greater than eros, leading to the notion of platonic love; *agape* was the unconditional, selfless love extended to all people; *storge* was familial love; *mania* emerged when the excessive inspired frenzy of love transforms into unhealthy obsession; *ludus* (from Latin rather than Greek) described playful, non-committal love, covering 'ludicrous' behaviour such as flirting at every opportunity;[1] *pragma* represented the practical, 'pragmatic' approach to love, evident in the 1980s when closeted gay artists were married off in public displays of heteronormativity to avoid alienating their fan base; and *philautia* was self-love, closer to self-esteem than self-stimulation.

Regardless of definition, there's no mistaking or denying passionate love when its infatuating arrow lodges deep within your heart. Love's overarching presence within multiple song themes highlights how *Love Changes Everything*.[2] According to this song, taken from the stage musical *Aspects Of Love*, love alters your entire life, affecting how you live and die and how you perceive time, the intensity of words, the intensity of pain, and the future. Love is quite the multitasker.

According to Donna Allen, love's *Joy and Pain*[3] go hand in hand: what brings happiness can also bring sadness. Love's intensity can turn a break-up into a highly charged and negative experience, especially in the short term when painfully raw emotions such

1   *Really Saying Something* by Bananarama and Fun Boy Three. Written by Norman Whitfield, William Stevenson and Edward Holland Jr
2   *Love Changes Everything* by Michael Ball. Written by Andrew Lloyd Webber, Donald Blackstone and Charles Hart
3   *Joy And Pain* by Donna Allen. Written by Howard Beverly

as anger, rejection and anxiety (love's loss can leave you feeling vulnerable and insecure) are exposed. Marinating in the melancholic or suppressing emotions that need letting out[1] (suppression often festers as tension) can harm mental health, especially when over-whelming sadness folds in on itself to become depression. Music can provide a reflective space to process these emotions and serve as a helpful reminder that you don't have to suffer your plight alone; for the heartbroken, *Sad Songs (Say So Much)*.[2] Such songs can help you push the emotional reset button (by aiding the processing of emotions that arise when sharing the torment of loss and the sting of rejection), helping to bring a sense of perspective, consolation and connectedness. Elton John sings about sharing troubles and pain through a sad song and how if someone has suffered enough to commit their feelings to music, then those songs are worth having in your life. Melancholic songs and music, often composed in the darker, more ominous and manipulative minor key, may reflect how emotions such as sadness and thoughtfulness feel to the listener, creating a natural and elemental affinity. While this may help explain why those caught in the throes of searing heartbreak find relief and solace in sad songs, what about those who enjoy bathing in the beauty, peace and self-comforting pleasure of melancholic songs *sans* needing to soothe any obvious heartache? Various explanations exist, including the desire to process our feelings by stirring the sediment of deep-seated memories of lost love or by allowing a song to act as a proxy to fill any void of emptiness.[3] Like a lucid dream, a sad song may help you anticipate and mentally rehearse the emotional navigation required after a loss, all within the 'safe' confines of a song.

An alternative explanation suggests that the hormonal response evoked by sad music – measurable through analysing listeners' tears – offers soothing, cathartic benefits. When processing the grinding

1   *Shout* by Tears For Fears. Written by Roland Orzabal and Ian Stanley
2   *Sad Songs (Say So Much)* by Elton John. Written by Elton John and Bernard Taupin
3   *Human* by The Human League. Written by James Harris and Terry Lewis

pain of grief, allowing sadness to find its natural voice enables you to adapt to the inevitable change in trajectory that the loss of a loved one brings. Sad songs can help you navigate and function through the swirling, disorienting fog of loss and help you to return once again to the bountiful joys that love can bestow, wiser for your experience. Grief, yearning and sadness are all a natural part of the human experience and are testaments to our capacity to love and care deeply; they give depth, weight and value to mortal life. These universal yet deeply personal feelings do not exist to be cured or neatly resolved subject to a predetermined timetable or by following steps on a linear path of recovery. Instead, they exist for you to feel, acknowledge and even embrace and treasure in their own time so that they remain with you long after the presence of absence is lost to time. No loved one is lost to time while their memory lives on in the hearts and minds of those still living.

While empathetic sad songs often highlight how cruel love can be,[1] they also teach that love's not about possession.[2] What other *Lessons In Love*[3] are there to learn in the eternal quest to maintain stable, supportive and lasting relationships? *Express Yourself*[4] (your thoughts, feelings and concerns) honestly and courageously, which has never appeared difficult for Madonna, who further says that you deserve the best that life offers, so settling for second best will not empower you. Less forceful advice comes from The Three Degrees: be less demanding and more understanding,[5] as empathy and compromise are crucial for resolving relationship conflict. Phil Collins, known to have passed through love's emotional shredder, reminds us that love doesn't always come

1 *Say I'm Your No.1* by Princess. Written by Michael Stock, Matthew Aitken and Peter Waterman
2 *She's Out Of My Life* by Michael Jackson. Written by Thomas Bahler
3 *Lessons In Love* by Level 42. Written by Waliou Badarou, Mark King and Rowland Gould
4 *Express Yourself* by Madonna. Written by Madonna Ciccone and Stephen Bray
5 *My Simple Heart* by The Three Degrees. Written by Dominic King and Frank Musker

easy; its intricacies and challenges require both give and take.[1]

Sound advice? In another song proclaiming how *Love Changes (Everything)*,[2] duo Climie Fisher explore love's unique power to shake, make or break you. The prevalence of love-themed lyrics underscores the importance of open, honest and two-way communication, along with tolerance, empathy and compromise in relationships. However, no single slice of sound advice from this grand symphony can capture love's infinite complexity.[3] Indeed, some idealised imagery and romantic notions of fairy-tale love, especially those foisted on impressionable teenagers, are often misleading and nonsensical, such as the existence of only 'the one'[4] perfect partner for you. Likewise, the idea that ecstatic, infatuated love remains forever fixed, unable to evolve into a deep connection characterised by peace, serenity and mutual support that comes with intense trust, respect, kindness and compassion, is equally misguided. Like the lives they touch, love and relationships have their ups and downs,[5] punctuated with tears of laughter and heartache, neither requiring chemical analysis to differentiate one from the other. Love rarely flows smoothly, so effort and commitment are required to maintain and enhance your relationship. Love and life can endure even after flaws and weaknesses – such as infidelity – have been laid bare, as shown throughout history.

Although each love is unique, the emotions experienced resonate with many. Empathetic lyrics offer comfort and remind us that others have endured emotional turmoil and lived to retell their tales.[6] When love is lost, new possibilities and opportunities may emerge from the cleansing break-up process: hope, positivity, resilience, personal

1   *You Can't Hurry Love* by Phil Collins. Written by Brian Holland, Lamont Dozier and Edward Holland
2   *Love Changes (Everything)* by Climie Fisher. Written by Dennis Morgan, Simon Climie and Robert Fisher
3   *Drama!* by Erasure. Written by Vincent Martin and Andrew Bell
4   *Suddenly* by Angry Anderson. Written by Gary Anderson, Andrew Chicon and Kevin Beamish
5   *Joy And Pain* by Donna Allen. Written by Howard Beverly
6   *Shout* by Tears For Fears. Written by Roland Orzabal and Ian Stanley

growth and empowerment. When love endures intact or strengthens, it can bring lasting happiness, health and life satisfaction. The Greek concept of *philautia* should remind you to love the life you choose to create.

MARRIAGE

Following hard on the heels[1] of *Love* comes marriage, an institution to which Western societies have long been wedded. Marriage, a ceremony in which a couple take a legally recognised public vow to be together,[2] is often accompanied by romanticised (and increasingly Disneyfied) imagery and dreams of living happily and healthily ever after. The reality reflected in many songs, however, frequently challenges this ideal.

Pre-marriage tensions may arise when one party seeks only some fun while the other envisions a permanent one.[3] Just as music is at its best when it introduces new dimensions that enhance the experience of, and engagement with, life, marriage is intended as a binding, life-long commitment to another; it's not an opportunity to rectify any perceived personality flaws in a partner. Building a successful marriage requires solid foundations built on mutual love, compatibility, interdependence, respect, trust, kindness, acceptance, support and a shared sense of purpose and meaning, each of which will help sustain a couple through countless smaller days beyond the one big day.

During a new relationship's initial short-lived but thrilling infatuation phase, opposites may attract[4] (known as heterophily). However, a happy, solid and long-lasting marriage is served better by homophily – where a compatible couple shares a vision of their

---

1   *Heart And Soul* by T'Pau. Written by Carol Decker and Ronald Rogers
2   *That's The Way Love Is* by Ten City. Written by Byron Stingily, Byron Burke and Herb Lawson
3   *Wedding Bells* by Godley & Creme. Written by Kevin Godley and Laurence Crème
4   *What's Love Got To Do With It* by Tina Turner. Written by Terence Britten and Graham Lyle

core needs, wants, values and interests and possesses complementary attributes, skills and temperaments; in brief, they are a perfect combination.[1]

What if the combination is less than perfect? When shortcomings arise, open, honest and constructive dialogue, delivered thoughtfully at the right moment, can enable a couple to deepen their understanding and tackle head-on any underlying issues and concerns without fear or judgement or the need for erosive bickering, toxic festering and caustic contempt. Too often, willingness to communicate and share thoughts and feelings is lopsided, as explored in *Everything She Wants*,[2] where the expectation that marriage involves give and take becomes strained by a partner who exhibits an ample ability to take without any requisite giving.

The Specials' song *Too Much Too Young*[3] addresses birth control or, more significantly, the repercussions of its absence (marriage and parenthood instead of pursuing fun). Having too much too young (during the 1980s, with parental consent, you could marry at 16) is also a theme explored by Wham! in *Young Guns (Go For It)*,[4] which cautions that fatherhood by the age of 21 is only fun only if a nappy can make you happy. The song's dramatic conclusion is that the loss of freedom and weight of responsibility feels like death via matrimony.

Sound advice? Unlike much of the pop music of the time, marriage in the 1980s was exclusively a heterosexual affair. Although many closeted stars remained hidden behind an opaque veil of marketing heteronormativity, some, notably Bronski Beat - particularly with the themes addressed in their 1984 hit *Smalltown Boy*[5] - emerged as explicitly gay in sound, style and video content. The marriage

1 *Rise To The Occasion* by Climie Fisher. Written by Dennis Morgan, Simon Climie and Robert Fisher
2 *Everything She Wants* by Wham! Written by George Michael
3 *Too Much Too Young* by The Specials featuring Rico. Written by Jeremy Dammers and Lloyd Tyrell
4 *Young Guns (Go For It)* by Wham! Written by George Michael
5 *Smalltown Boy* by Bronski Beat. Written by Steven Forrest, James Somerville and Lawrence Cole

between gayness and pop seemed a match made in heaven until the arrival of a devastating interloper: AIDS. To placate any mainstream backlash against the gay community, pop marketers reverted to a straighter path.

The lyrical message that implies matrimony for the young is a joyless trap that involves sacrificing some of the freedom and all of the fun misses the essence of marriage. Marriage should centre on love, companionship, security and commitment with someone with whom you can be yourself,[1] and where both partners willingly give each other the space and freedom to be who and what they want to be.[2]

Marriage is a life-long commitment. Prince described 'life' as an electric word meaning for ever, which he helpfully explains is a long time.[3] For those who marry young,[4] the sheer length of a modern marriage – potentially lasting for seven decades or more – can be daunting. As Kylie Minogue said, with her *Hand On Your Heart*,[5] falling in love is one thing; making love last is quite another. One of humankind's most impressive recent achievements is the steady increase in global life expectancy, which has doubled since about 1900, having seen little change in the preceding 10,000 years. The approximate two-year increase in life expectancy across the 1980s is typical of the trend across the decades. In Shakespearean times, high mortality rates meant that a marriage lasted, on average, only about a decade before one partner became betrothed to death's eternal darkness. Within a generation since the start of the 1980s, the average age at which both sexes choose to marry has risen by approximately a dozen years.

Now that we are more adept at evading the cold gaze of the Grim

1 *Like To Get To Know You Well* by Howard Jones. Written by John Jones
2 *What Is Love?* by Howard Jones. Written by John Jones and William Bryant
3 *Let's Go Crazy* by Prince And The Revolution. Written by Prince Nelson
4 *Young At Heart* by The Bluebells. Written by Robert Hodgens and Siobhan Fahey
5 *Hand On Your Heart* by Kylie Minogue. Written by Michael Stock, Matthew Aitken and Peter Waterman

Reaper, we are better equipped to realise how we change over the years of our ever-longer lives. The narrative divisions of modern-day life now closely resemble Shakespeare's seven ages – infancy, schooling, teenagehood, early adolescence, middle age, old age and dotage – rather than the previous pinch points of education, work and retirement. A marriage must adapt to meet the changing needs of our extended lives. Adapting is worth the effort as studies show that a loving, supportive marriage can add years to your life; conversely, a mismatched or troubled union can have significant physical and mental repercussions. At any age, untying the multi-threaded knot of marriage can be challenging (see *Divorce*).

The practical realities of marriage can muddle a relationship, so it's wise to have 12 to 18 months before committing to a life-long union to allow enough time for the first flush of infatuation to fade and for any unseen traits to surface and be addressed.

The (often extravagant) splendour of a traditional *White Wedding*[1] in a picturesque old church does not guarantee ever-lasting happiness because, much like the structural fabric of an ancient church, marriage is susceptible to decay and requires ongoing effort and maintenance to ensure that everything holds together, is watertight and remains in proper working order. Should you choose to walk down the aisle (note that moonwalking is always disrespectful), slip a band of gold[2] around your finger, and indulge in eating a giant cake,[3] it would be wise to select with care from any of the tracks mentioned within this theme as your choice for a first-dance song, no matter how much you feel married to the beat.[4]

1   *White Wedding* by Billy Idol. Written by William Broad
2   *Wrapped Around Your Finger* by The Police. Written by Gordon Sumner
3   *Happy Birthday* by Altered Images. Written by Anthony McDaid, Bryan Keegan, Clare Grogan, Gerard McElhone, John McElhone and Michael Anderson
4   *The Sun Goes Down (Living It Up)* by Level 42. Written by Michael Lindup, Mark King, Philip Gould and Waliou Badarou

METEOROLOGY

Under low pressure, it can not only rain but pour.[1] The defining meteorological event of the 1980s (the enduring, uprooted effects of which are still evident lying in woodlands across south-east England decades later) was one to blow you away: the 953-millibar 'Great Storm' that struck over the night of 15/16 October 1987. Its hurricane-force winds claimed 18 lives and flattened 15 million trees.

Weather can affect lives in less dramatic but still forecastable ways. From mood swings to stock market movements (the infamous 'Black Monday', a day of dramatic falls on world stock markets, occurred on 19 October 1987, just days after the Great Storm), there's a link between extreme weather events and human behaviour. For instance, rainy days lower crime rates and affect voting outcomes. There's also a link between increased suicide rates and heatwaves/droughts and between heatwaves and excess deaths, particularly in vulnerable elderly populations. Extreme heat is a silent killer.

The stifling heat[2] of a long, hot *Cruel Summer*[3] can quickly start to disrupt sleep (it is too hot to think of sleeping),[4] derail rational thought (it is too hot to think of thinking)[5] and heighten irritability (it is too hot to stop tempers fraying),[6] all of which can escalate aggressive behaviour, fuelling the threat of further combustion, especially when people use alcohol to rehydrate and start to congregate in the streets.[7] The eruption of riots on the streets of Toxteth in July 1981 and Brixton and Handsworth in September 1985 coincided

1   *Under Pressure* by Queen and David Bowie. Written by Roger Taylor, Freddie Mercury, John Deacon, Brian May and David Jones
2   *Wouldn't It Be Good* by Nik Kershaw. Written by Nicholas Kershaw
3   *Cruel Summer* by Bananarama. Written by Sara Dallin, Siobhan Fahey, Steven Jolley, Anthony Swain and Keren Woodward
4   *Running With The Night* by Lionel Richie. Written by Lionel Richie and Cynthia Weil
5   *Someone's Looking At You* by The Boomtown Rats. Written by Robert Geldof
6   *The Circus* by Erasure. Written by Vincent Martin and Andrew Bell
7   *One More Try* by George Michael. Written by George Michael

with temperatures that reached 21 degrees Celsius. Nevertheless, it seems harsh to attribute it all to the sunshine,[1] especially when the weather is pleasantly balmy. The rising barometer of civil unrest was not the product of a few days' incubation but the culmination of many years of living under the pressure of simmering resentment and suppression. The correlation between rising temperatures and rising tempers does, however, reach a peak before plateauing as lethargy and languor set in. Rising temperatures might help explain why cars go up in flames,[2] but rioting mobs do not set them alight out of a desire to keep warm.

Given humanity's long dependence on favourable meteorological conditions for survival, finding a correlation between weather and mood is unsurprising. Artwork regularly portrays weather as a metaphor – happiness with sunshine, hope with blue skies and rainbows, anger with thunder, uncertainty with fog, and pensiveness with dark skies. In *Here Comes The Rain Again*,[3] the rain falling within Annie Lennox's head symbolises the internal storm[4] that is depression, a word with meaning in both medicine and meteorology. Although rain often carries negative associations within art and pop songs, it has many benefits, such as helping to cleanse particulate matter out of the air (wind also helps disperse pollution) while filling it with an abundance of negative ions created by the collision of water and air molecules. These ions help super-oxygenate both the air you breathe and the blood in your veins, aiding immunity and boosting your mood and general health. Mud, too, is rich in mood-enhancing microbes and organic compounds (such as geosmin) that are released after rain, giving off the characteristic earthy smell known as petrichor (from 'petro' meaning rock and 'ichor',

1 *Blame It On The Boogie* by Big Fun. Written by David-John Jackson-Rich, Michael Jackson-Clark and Elmar Krohn
2 *Hey, Matthew* by Karel Fialka. Written by Karel Fialka
3 *Here Comes The Rain Again* by Eurythmics. Written by Ann Lennox and David Stewart
4 *Alive And Kicking* by Simple Minds. Written by James Kerr, Charles Burchill and Michael MacNeil

the blood-like fluid in the veins of the gods of Greek mythology). To benefit from *Walking In The Rain*[1] while avoiding being soaked to the skin,[2] invest in some warm waterproofs.

Cold day?[3] The chill in songs reflects an internal coldness[4] (of the blood, heart, sweat, eyes, mind and emotions). When managed with care and appropriate attire, meteorological coldness can enhance aerobic exercise by preventing overheating, allowing you to walk, run and cycle further and faster.

As Champaign noted, some can hold their life together through adverse weather.[5] Sensitivity to life's emotional and meteorological storms[6] varies between individuals. You can weather both by donning suitable clothing, literal and metaphorical.

Chaos theory applies to complex systems like meteorology and life. Outcomes are highly sensitive to minor changes in inputs, so a slight variation (for example, in temperature, wind direction or a chance encounter) can give rise to significant consequences: turn *A Different Corner*[7] and life could change for good. Such unpredictability often fuels a belief in powerful but unseen forces (see *Destiny*), from the thermal uplift from having the wind beneath your wings[8] to the swirling vortex of despair.

Come *Rain Or Shine*,[9] a deluge of meteorological, metaphorical nonsense falls from some songs, including clouds of whey and a

1 *Walking In The Rain* by Modern Romance. Written by David Jaymes and Michael Mullins
2 *The Sun And The Rain* by Madness. Written by Michael Barson
3 *New Moon On Monday* by Duran Duran. Written by Simon Le Bon, Nigel Taylor, Roger Taylor, Andrew Taylor and Nicholas Bates
4 *One More Try* by George Michael. Written by George Michael
5 *How 'Bout Us* by Champaign. Written by Dana Walden
6 *This Ole House* by Shakin' Stevens. Written by Carl Hamblen
7 *A Different Corner* by George Michael. Written by George Michael.
8 *Wind Beneath My Wings* by Bette Midler. Written by Larry Henley and Jeff Silbar
9 *Rain Or Shine* by Five Star. Written by William Livsey and Peter Sinfield

sun of pie,[1] daisy-chain clouds,[2] *Purple Rain*[3] and the man-maiming, street-splattering horror show of *It's Raining Men*.[4] No wonder Mr Howard Jones didn't want to discuss the weather.[5]

Sound advice? How's the weather?[6] Whether you live under the weather or on cloud nine, it's a mixed lyrical forecast with an uncertain outlook.

I Think It's Going To Rain Today,[7] but what if you need to know for sure?[8] Who can predict and explain the thunder and rain?[9] Meteorologists with supercomputers (both work with their heads in the cloud)[10] would be a good starting point. However, be careful if all you seek is a quick answer to a simple question, such as that asked by Diana Ross: why does the rain fall from above?[11] (Spoiler: it's not because clouds shed tears, but instead involves the supercool Bergeron-Findeisen theory.)

Ongoing climate change increases the likelihood of extreme weather, as demonstrated by the number of record-breaking meteorological events occurring since the end of the 1980s. Warmer air holds about 7% more moisture for each degree of temperature rise, increasing rainfall intensity and heightening flood risk. More intense storms in one area can result in less rainfall elsewhere, adding to the possibility of more extreme storms and climatic tipping points, with more frequent and intense flash floods, heatwaves, droughts and wildfires.

1   *Senses Working Overtime* by XTC. Written by Andrew Partridge
2   *Dear Prudence* by Siouxsie And The Banshees. Written by John Lennon and Paul McCartney
3   *Purple Rain* by Prince And The Revolution. Written by Prince Nelson
4   *It's Raining Men* by The Weather Girls. Written by Paul Jabara and Paul Shaffer
5   *Like To Get To Know You Well* by Howard Jones. Written by John Jones
6   *Clouds Across The Moon* by RAH Band. Written by Richard Hewson
7   *I Think It's Going To Rain Today* by UB40. Written by Randall Newman
8   *Prove Your Love* by Taylor Dayne. Written by Seth Swirsky and Arnold Roman
9   *Don't Get Me Wrong* by The Pretenders. Written by Christine Hynde
10 *Wouldn't Change A Thing* by Kylie Minogue. Written by Michael Stock, Matthew Aitken and Peter Waterman
11 *Why Do Fools Fall In Love* by Diana Ross. Written by Franklin Lymon and Moishe Levy

Pop musicians strive to capture lightning in a song. Much of the thunder from the 1980s emanated from overblown pop song production, further intensified by potent and turbulent teenage hormonal jet streams containing enough punch to propel emotions high into the stratosphere.

MIRRORS

The original mythological *Mirror Man*,[1] Narcissus, was the beautiful youth who fell in love with his watery reflection. Meanwhile, Echo, the besotted mountain nymph with an unrequited love-at-first-sight crush on Narcissus, was cursed to repeat only the last words spoken to her, offering a possible (albeit cryptic) explanation for why, in Dollar's song, the mirror echoes.[2]

Adam And The Ants suggest we try using a mirror.[3] Zoologists employ the mirror test to gauge self-awareness – an animal's ability to recognise its reflection rather than perceive it as a rival – a defining trait of high cognition. Remarkably, some ants pass this mirror test. As for Adam and his fellow humans, *The Mirror In The Bathroom*[4] is used more for vanity and self-image than exploring identity and perception. In today's world, egos are further massaged where smartphones serve as digital mirrors, selectively presenting your best side that you wish others to see.

Status Quo open *Ol' Rag Blues*[5] with a question: what do you see when you look in the mirror? Some, particularly the young, can fall into a crack in the mirror[6] by seeing a reflection they struggle

1   *Mirror Man* by The Human League. Written by Philip Oakey, John Callis and Ian Burden
2   *Mirror Mirror (Mon Amour)* by Dollar. Written by Trevor Horn and Bruce Woolley
3   *Stand And Deliver* by Adam And The Ants. Written by Stuart Goddard and Marco Pirroni
4   *Mirror In The Bathroom* by The Beat. Written by Roger Charlery, Andrew Cox, Everett Morton, David Steele and David Wakeling
5   *Ol' Rag Blues* by Status Quo. Written by Alan Lancaster and Keith Lamb
6   *Abacab* by Genesis. Written by Anthony Banks, Philip Collins and Michael Rutherford

to identify with, experiencing disassociation from their self-image. More commonly, those who scrutinise their appearance in the mirror fixate on perceived physical imperfections that usually go unnoticed by others. Looking beyond the skin-deep, some compare their external behaviours against an internal set of model standards about how they ought to live. If you are such a person, and you wish to take charge of your potential, change your destiny and accept yourself for who you are, you will need to realise that what lies beneath your skin and within your control are your thoughts, words, actions, reactions and attitude.

Level 42's protagonist noticed a likeness in a potential partner that reminded him of himself.[1] The synchrony of interpersonal mirroring, learnt in infancy through imitation – monkey see, monkey do[2] – continues into adulthood, demonstrates traits of empathy and compassion, and enables you to understand another's viewpoint – to see from the other side[3] and to feel what others feel by imagining walking in someone else's shoes.[4] This aids individual and group bonding. The brain cells within social species that facilitate this beneficial mimicry are known as mirror neurons.

Mirroring as an empathetic technique is employed (exploited) by salespeople and negotiators who mirror patterns in your breathing, movement, posture and the words, pitch and speed of your speech such that, as with the voice of Echo, you may hear the last three words you uttered working their way back to you: *Working My Way Back To You*.[5] Effective mirroring requires establishing a natural, easy rapport with your subject, respecting their perspective and displaying dignity, compassion, empathy, tolerance and curiosity about them. Reading fiction allows you to lift the lid on and peer into

1 *The Sun Goes Down (Living It Up)* by Level 42. Written by Michael Lindup, Mark King, Philip Gould and Waliou Badarou
2 *Wishing Well* by Terence Trent D'Arby. Written by Terence Trent Howard and Sean Oliver
3 *Like To Get To Know You Well* by Howard Jones. Written by John Jones
4 *Wouldn't It Be Good* by Nik Kershaw. Written by Nicholas Kershaw
5 *Working My Way Back To You* by The Spinners. Written by Dennis Randell and Sandford Linzer

the lives (vulnerabilities and all) of characters, thereby sharpening your social skills by compelling your brain to create a mental image of the inner worlds of others.

Mirroring helps explain why we are naturally drawn to, and bond more readily with, those who look, sound, act and view the world as we do, creating familiarity and the feeling that the other person is one of your kind,[1] even one of your kin (we often share more DNA with close friends and soulmates than with a random sample of people). As mentioned in the theme on *Marriage*, this mirroring is known as homophily ('love of the same', from the Greek). Should you spot a likeness[2] in your long-term partner, it is not because long-standing couples grow to look more alike, but that *The Look Of Love*[3] that you initially experienced reflects what you see daily in the mirror, which raises the question: do you love that person for their unique attributes or are you captivated by a reflection of what you see in yourself?

A downside to finding someone a lot like you[4] is that this tendency can extend to your entire social circle (including social media choices), enforcing a belief that we're all the same.[5] This conformity can warp normal, objective and rational thinking as your brain seeks shortcuts that filter and fill any gaps from what it expects to find, thereby confirming and reinforcing established patterns of thinking, beliefs and values that are consistent with its preconceived model of the world; this denies you the opportunity to challenge and stretch how you see and think. The tendency to seek out and pay attention to information that supports your existing beliefs (simultaneously disregarding evidence that contradicts

1   *Need You Tonight* by INXS. Written by Andrew Farriss and Michael Hutchence
2   *Wishful Thinking* by China Crisis. Written by Gary Daly and Edmund Lundon
3   *The Look Of Love* by ABC. Written by Martin Fry, Mark White, Stephen Singleton, David Palmer and Mark Lickley
4   *St. Elmo's Fire (Man In Motion)* by John Parr. Written by David Foster and John Parr
5   *Ever Fallen In Love* by Fine Young Cannibals. Written by Peter McNeish

them) is known as 'confirmation bias'. The increasing reliance on predictive algorithms may exacerbate the downsides to mirroring because they cater to and prioritise existing preferences, reinforcing and reheating previous decisions and options – or those made by people 'like you' – to offer you choices that start to trap you in ever-narrowing loops.

For those who frequented the notorious 1980s cocaine-fuelled club scene, seeing your face in a mirror was more likely a nod to illicit nose candy than narcissistic eye candy. Soft Cell used the mirror for counting lines and noticing the marks from the high times.[1] Mirrored nightclubs served as a natural habitat for the grandiose, drug-taking, self-elevating narcissist as much as for those who enjoyed the melting pot of subcultural music, fashion and fluid sexuality. Attendees of nightclubs and other less steamy venues who enjoy moving to the groove know that prancing and dancing[2] are also forms of mirroring. The more formal the dance, the more mirroring is necessary; get the rhythm right, and you might even become lovers.[3]

Sound advice? Beyond any smoke-and-mirrors, people have long looked to the arts and culture to reflect their world experience. The desire for a clearer picture of the inner self is well served within the songs. Alas, for Narcissus, the story didn't end well.

Above the entrance to the temple of Apollo at Delphi was carved the overarching maxim *Gnothi Seauton* – 'Know Thyself'. Engaging in honest self-reflection during difficult times can empower you to confront reality and learn from your mistakes. A mirror can be unforgiving (blame the harsh lighting, mirror angle and tint), but it's a good place to start understanding, assessing and planning how to act in ways that best align with your goals, standards and values. Reflect on questions such as, "Who am I?" and "What truly matters to me, and why?" Embracing self-forgiveness allows

1   *Bedsitter* by Soft Cell. Written by David Ball and Peter Almond
2   *Don't Stop The Music* by Yarbrough & Peoples. Written by Jonah Ellis, Alisa Peoples and Lonnie Simmons
3   *Into The Groove* by Madonna. Written by Madonna Ciccone and Stephen Bray

you to cast aside any negative, judgemental feelings that you may harbour about yourself being the problem rather than the solution; self-forgiveness enables you to move on.

Using self-reflection to analyse 'negative' emotions can help transform them into positive actions. Nietzsche, for example, argued that envy reflects a deep-seated desire. Deconstructing envy will reveal the source of your insecurity, helping you learn what inspires, drives and motivates you. You can then follow this analysis with intentional action to help guide you from where you are to where you want to be.

Likewise, if you constantly pick yourself apart when you look in the mirror,[1] or if you seek your reflection in every shiny or reflective surface to the point where it becomes an unhelpful addiction or obsession that leaves you feeling demotivated or full of self-loathing, try using constructive self-reflection to promote positive action. For instance, if you are overweight, view what you see in the mirror as motivation to adopt healthier eating and to increase your physical activity. Sometimes, however, you'll need to turn the mirror into a window that allows you to glimpse a world beyond yourself.

Madonna sang that true beauty resides within.[2] Once you recognise that beauty shines out from your deep inner qualities and attributes (such as your actions and choices), you will find little need for checking the mirror[3] other than to ensure that your superficial appearance is socially presentable.

As a part of a social species, we become more aware of our actions and how others perceive them when mirrors are present, resulting in more socially appropriate and cooperative behaviour. Your approach and attitude towards others reflects directly into your life. If you are kind, compassionate and courteous to others as they go about the business of trying to do their best, and you genuinely wish others well,[4] this uplifts the recipients and buoys your spirits

1   *Lately* by Stevie Wonder. Written by Stevie Wonder
2   *Live To Tell* by Madonna. Written by Madonna Ciccone and Patrick Leonard
3   *Dancing In The Dark* by Bruce Springsteen. Written by Bruce Springsteen
4   *A Winter's Tale* by David Essex. Written by Michael Batt and Timothy Rice

(through, among other things, the release of endorphins), enhancing your well-being. The benefit of spreading this social feel-good factor through simple, small and sometimes anonymous acts of kindness is that it provides an internal reward that can create a wider ripple effect that may encourage others to participate and replicate similar acts of kindness. Being kind, supportive, compassionate and empathetic to others through your conscious choice of words or deeds are learnable attributes that can help you to be kinder to yourself. Although reciprocity should never be your motivation, your actions will reflect positively on you (or, if acting under anonymity, will give you a warm glowing feeling inside),[1] which in turn should help to make you feel happier, more energised, less anxious and more engaged and connected to others. If the formula for kindness were that the more you give, the better and longer you'll live, how generous would you choose to be?

MISTAKES

Within songs, mistakes – and their offspring, 'regrets' (covered in *Ageing*) – frequently stem from the bookends of a relationship: either the initial decision to get together (itself often arising from the mistaken belief that any relationship is better than none) or the decision to split up, followed by the realisation that this was a big mistake.[2] Spandau Ballet capture the serial and cyclical nature of these errors by asking how many times must they repeat their mistakes before learning their lesson.[3] This repetition reveals either a failure to face the truth[4] or an inability to recognise recurrent patterns of behaviour despite, at the outset, promising not to make the same mistake as before.[5]

1   *I Feel For You* by Chaka Khan. Written by Prince Nelson
2   *Hard Habit To Break* by Chicago. Written by Steven Kipner and John Lewis Parker
3   *Only When You Leave* by Spandau Ballet. Written by Gary Kemp
4   *Dreamin'* by Cliff Richard. Written by Alan Tarney and Gerard Sayer
5   *We Don't Need Another Hero (Thunderdome)* by Tina Turner. Written by Terence Britten and Graham Lyle

Mistakes are an inevitable consequence of growth and learning, a more optimistic view than that expressed in *Human*,[1] which asserts that we were born to make mistakes. When you view mistakes negatively, they can foster fear and anxiety, particularly when you repeatedly internalise mistakes that have an external cause (beyond your control) and then unfairly pin those mistakes on yourself.

Song lyrics rightly distinguish mistakes from failures, treating mistakes as temporary and rectifiable detours or stumbles on a journey – described by Gloria Estefan as the tendency to be misguided, to lose our way[2] – and failure as irreparable and permanent, where you should abandon any attempt to rejoin and continue along your original path. What matters is not the mistakes that may temporarily nudge you off course but how you respond, interpret and react to what has happened so that you can benefit and bounce back wiser, more creative and better informed (or reformed). Acknowledging mistakes as natural steps towards learning and success can enrich your life by allowing you to grow, explore and discover more about yourself and others.

Howard Jones expressed to his mother the need for freedom to make his own mistakes[3] (it's natural for parents to want to spare their children from making the same mistakes as they did). However, acknowledging that mistakes are inevitable does not absolve you from responsibility or accountability for your actions, particularly those with irreversible consequences. You'll still have to face the music.[4] Serious transgressions have severe repercussions (you get locked up),[5] a stark reminder of the mistakes you cannot afford to make. Let your internal moral compass guide your actions.

According to the chorus of *Perfect*,[6] everything has to be, well,

1   *Human* by The Human League. Written by James Harris and Terry Lewis
2   *Don't Wanna Lose You* by Gloria Estefan. Written by Gloria Estefan
3   *Look Mama* by Howard Jones. Written by John Jones
4   *Running In The Family* by Level 42. Written by Mark King, Waliou Badarou and Philip Gould
5   *Bad* by Michael Jackson. Written by Michael Jackson
6   *Perfect* by Fairground Attraction. Written by Mark Nevin

perfect. Sound advice suggests otherwise. Instead of pursuing unrealistic, mistake-free and idealistic perfection, it may be more appropriate to strive for excellence and find fulfilment in knowing that you have done the best you can.[1] Accepting that perfection isn't a prerequisite for starting a task will make it easier and more enjoyable to begin that task, helping generate momentum to help keep you moving forward and making consistent progress in a way that slower attempts at seeking perfection will stifle.

The second category is the factual error. In *Pride (In The Name Of Love)*,[2] we learn that, early morning, April 4, the sound of a gunshot pierced the skies of Memphis. This describes the assassination of civil-rights leader Martin Luther King in 1968, murdered as he stood on the balcony of room 306 at the Lorraine Motel at just after 6pm. Early evening, April 4 . . .

Was (Not Was) describe how (not why) 40 million years ago it was possible to *Walk The Dinosaur*,[3] despite the extinction of non-avian dinosaurs some 26 million years earlier.

We Are The World[4] tells us that God turned stone into bread. Really? When? Where?

If lyricists can warp world history, perhaps we should instead turn to the precision of numbers, allowing the mathematician to be someone we can count on.[5] Let us look up to Heaven 17, where the narrator informs us that he was 37, his girlfriend 17, making

1   *Joanna* by Kool And The Gang. Written by Robert Bell, Ronald Bell, James Bonneford, George Brown, James Taylor, Charles Smith, Clifford Adams and Curtis Williams
2   *Pride (In The Name Of Love)* by U2. Written by Paul Hewson, Adam Clayton, David Evans and Laurence Mullen Jr
3   *Walk The Dinosaur* by Was (Not Was). Written by David Weiss, Donald Fagenson and Randall Jacobs
4   *We Are The World* by USA For Africa. Written by Michael Jackson and Lionel Richie
5   *Joanna* by Kool And The Gang. Written by Robert Bell, Ronald Bell, James Bonneford, George Brown, James Taylor, Charles Smith, Clifford Adams and Curtis Williams

her half his age.[1] *Come Live With Me* and help with innumeracy?

How about geography? Kim Wilde announces that across America – from New York to east California – a new wave is coming.[2] The largest cities in California are Los Angeles, San Diego, San José and San Francisco, all in west California, as all *Kids In America* know.

Do They Know It's Christmas?[3] also makes inaccurate geographical claims by forecasting a barren, snowless Christmas in Africa, a land devoid of rain or flowing rivers. Africa, the second-largest continent, comprises over 50 countries, some of which boast luxuriant foliage, plentiful rainfall and mighty river flow, including the world's longest river, the 6,650km Nile, the Blue Nile tributary of which originates in Ethiopia, at the heart of the famine. And snow regularly falls at Christmas in high-altitude regions, such as in the Atlas Mountains or on Mount Kilimanjaro. (Incidentally, in Greek mythology, the fallen Titan, Atlas, was condemned by Zeus, the king of the gods, to bear the firmament – the sky and heavens above – upon his shoulders for eternity; it is thus a mistake perpetrated over centuries by publishers of atlases to portray Atlas as carrying the world upon his shoulders.)[4] Do they know it's careless? While the lyrics perpetuated stereotypic and misleading impressions of homogeneity across this vast and diverse continent into people's minds, they did serve the greater purpose of raising a lot of money (over £140 million and counting) and public awareness, which was the point of the exercise.

Staying with *Africa*[5] and Kilimanjaro, Toto tell us that this extinct volcano rises like Olympus above the Serengeti. Only it doesn't. The Serengeti lies about 200 miles away from this impressive mountain. Another 'mistake' (probably dismissed as poetic licence)

1   *Come Live With Me* by Heaven 17. Written by Glenn Gregory, Iain Craig Marsh and Martyn Ware
2   *Kids In America* by Kim Wilde. Written by Reginald Smith and Richard Smith
3   *Do They Know It's Christmas?* by Band Aid. Written by Robert Geldof and James Ure
4   *I Want To Know What Love Is* by Foreigner. Written by Michael Jones
5   *Africa* by Toto. Written by David Paich and Jeffrey Porcaro

surrounds the simile. Mount Kilimanjaro in northern Tanzania is, at 5,895 metres, Africa's highest mountain. Mount Olympus in north-east Greece is, at 2,917 metres, about half Kilimanjaro's height (take note, Heaven 17). In other words, the song suggests that a large mountain rises like another mountain only about half its size: plain nonsense. Mount Olympus was home to the 12 greater gods of ancient Greek mythology, so perhaps Kilimanjaro was meant to rise like Zeus? Or was it meant to rise like the 12-metre-tall ivory and gold statue of Zeus at Olympia, one of the Seven Wonders of the Ancient World? Despite these mistakes, *Africa* remains one of the most streamed songs from the 1980s.

Sound advice? The song *Starting Together*[1] rightly suggests that we are all bound to make some mistakes. Equally, there is also *Something About You*[2] (and everyone else) that means making mistakes is a part of life, especially when you try to grow by stepping beyond the reassuringly safe and secure perimeter of your comfort zone. Mistakes are often simply the price you pay for daring to challenge yourself and venture beyond this boundary.

Obsessing over mistakes is a mistake. It is always better to try, risk making mistakes or fail than being too shy to try[3] out of fear. Treat each mistake as a valuable lesson that helps you avoid making the same – or similar – missteps again. Anticipating mistakes before they manifest is a hallmark of wisdom. Mistakes often play a central role in scientific understanding, opening doors to unexpected discoveries. Adopting a growth mindset involves acknowledging, accepting and taking ownership of your mistakes (and, where possible, creating a plan to avoid or rectify them); this makes mistakes progressive by allowing you to move on.[4] Experiencing failure or having others highlight your mistakes is rarely pleasant, so consider them essential

1   *Starting Together* by Su Pollard. Written by Susan Pollard
2   *Something About You* by Level 42. Written by Michael Lindup, Philip Gould, Mark King, Rowland Gould and Waliou Badarou
3   *Open Your Heart* by The Human League. Written by Philip Oakey and John Callis
4   *Funkytown* by Lipps Inc. Written by Steven Greenberg

in enriching the soil from which success can grow. Throughout history, one of the biggest drivers of innovation is failure, and usually a lot of it, so if at first you don't succeed, you'll learn. Cultivating a constructive feedback mechanism is more positive and productive than wasting your time and effort trying to escape from the messy entanglement of blame (where you criticise and accuse others to absolve yourself of responsibility for what went wrong) that often follows in the wake of a mistake.

While analysing what went wrong to learn from mistakes is worthwhile, it's equally important to recall, learn from and celebrate successes, achievements and positive experiences. Failure to do so is a mistake because it becomes difficult to identify effective strategies and replicate success in other areas of life without recognising these moments.

Danny Wilson admitted to past carelessness.[1] To avoid imperfections and carelessness in factual matters – lyrical or otherwise – apply a little pride in the name of accuracy by fact-checking from primary sources. Whether dealing in facts or otherwise, how you approach any task reflects how you approach every task, or, as Wham! extol about their approach to life, if you're going to do something, ensure you do it right.[2]

The final words rest with the philosopher Friedrich Nietzsche: "Without music, life would be a mistake."

MONEY

If you buy into the lyrical notion that money makes the world go round[3] then having ready cash would, in the world of Fiddler's Dram, be grand.[4] Thatcherite free-market capitalism liked to measure value

1 *Mary's Prayer* by Danny Wilson. Written by Gary Clark
2 *I'm Your Man* by Wham! Written by George Michael
3 *Loadsamoney (Doin' Up The House)* by Harry Enfield. Written by Henry Enfield, Charles Higson, William Wainwright and Paul Whitehouse
4 *Day Trip To Bangor (Didn't We Have A Lovely Time)* by Fiddler's Dram. Written by Deborah Cook

monetarily. However, it was not until the rise of male-dominated rap and hip-hop that artists began to boast openly and regularly about money, wealth and name-dropping high-status luxury brands while showcasing grossly excessive peacock-tailed lifestyles of conspicuous consumption. Money symbolises vanity and prestige for the effete preening pavonisers who use public display to express and impress.

Pop stars adept at converting musical notes into pound notes could often amass substantial amounts of *Brass In Pocket*.[1] However, beneath the glitz and glamour of many successful pop careers lies economic hardship and struggle, either experienced first-hand or witnessed in the precarious early years during the climb from dark obscurity into the spotlight of fame and fortune.[2] *Money for Nothing*[3] originated as a blue-collar critique of music-industry excess, not a hip-hop brag.

The Message is that it is all about money.[4] Money is an abstract social construct, a necessary lubricant invented to facilitate the smooth functioning of human societies. As a limited resource with an agreed and standard value that is both portable and durable, money enables the exchange of goods and services between buyer and seller so that life's basic survival needs, such as food, shelter and healthcare, can be met. For the wealthy, money brings freedom and acts as a protective, insulating cushion of comfort against the cold, hard slab of poverty. Those trapped in poverty often find themselves spending all their hard-earned money on essentials – their existence defined by a constant struggle to scrimp and save,[5] unable to progress much beyond a mindless repetition of subsistence on a wage treadmill where there is often too much of the month left at the end of the

1 *Brass In Pocket* by The Pretenders. Written by Christine Hynde and James Honeyman-Scott
2 *Paradise City* by Guns N' Roses. Written by Saul Hudson, William Rose, Jeffrey Isbell, Michael McKagan and Steven Adler
3 *Money For Nothing* by Dire Straits. Written by Mark Knopfler and Gordon Sumner
4 *The Message* by Grandmaster Flash And The Furious Five. Written by Clifton Chase, Edward Fletcher, Melvin Glover and Sylvia Vanterpool
5 *Just Who Is The 5 O'Clock Hero* by The Jam. Written by John Weller

money, which is spent before it's earned.[1] Poverty compels some to borrow money outside mainstream lending channels, often at extortionate and iniquitous interest rates, pulling them deeper into a grinding cycle of full-time debt and making them slaves to predatory loan sharks and hire purchase.[2] When weighed down by the heft of debt repayments, life can become an endless struggle to keep one's head above the financial water. Such is the ease of drowning during hard times[3] that some try to keep from going under[4] by resorting to radical (sometimes desperate) measures to break this relentless cycle, such as a *Move Away*[5] from their roots to the bright light[6] allure of major cities, or any place promising financial buoyancy. The highlight in the headlights of Tracy Chapman's *Fast Car*[7] was that a ticket to anywhere was preferable to staying put. The simplistic and deceptive allure of seeing distant lands as an escape from economic hardship (leave to achieve – and for better pay)[8] continues to tempt many to relocate in search of opportunity.

The Pet Shop Boys went looking for the money only to end up living with love.[9] Inevitably, lyrics link money (a 'resource' in evolutionary terms) with love and relationships. A relationship can be an enormous personal investment – loving can come at a high cost[10] – with life-long consequences. For example, pregnancy, childbirth and raising children as a fully engaged parent entails a substantial

1   *I Got You Babe* by UB40 and Chrissie Hynde. Written by Salvatore Bono
2   *Walls Come Tumbling Down!* by The Style Council. Written by John Weller
3   *Saddle Up* by David Christie. Written by Philo Robinson and Jacques Pépino
4   *Walking In The Sunshine* by Bad Manners. Written by Brian Tuitt, Andrew Marson, Paul Hyman, Douglas Trendle, David Farren, Christopher Kane, Louis Cook, Alan Sayag and Martin Stewart
5   *Move Away* by Culture Club. Written by Roy Hay, George O'Dowd, Michael Craig, Jonathan Moss and Philip Pickett
6   *Desire* by U2. Written by Paul Hewson, Adam Clayton, David Evans and Laurence Mullen Jr
7   *Fast Car* by Tracy Chapman. Written by Tracy Chapman
8   *Rollin' Home* by Status Quo. Written by John David
9   *What Have I Done To Deserve This?* by Pet Shop Boys with Dusty Springfield. Written by Neil Tennant, Christopher Lowe and Alta Willis
10 *Temptation* by Heaven 17. Written by Glenn Gregory, Ian Craig Marsh and Martyn Ware

commitment of time, effort and resources unparalleled in the natural world; to do this right can take a great deal of money.[1] Consequently, it's not surprising that some women of child-bearing age may, for sound evolutionary reasons, gravitate towards men who can provide the requisite resources and support so that both mother and children can survive and flourish. Thankfully, in advanced societies, women are free to bear children and procure their resources. However, biologically and lyrically, some women still find men with money appealing, while others, such as Neneh Cherry, take a more defiant stance, declaring that no such man can win her affection.[2] Likewise, while marriage should provide non-monetary mutual enrichment, some cannot resist the opportunity to marry for money.[3] Echoing Shakespeare's *King Lear*, Gwen Guthrie sings that there will be no romance without finance because nothing from nothing leaves, well, nothing.[4] Romance in pursuit of finance will leave your heart permanently clenched.

Although not driven by procreation, the Pet Shop Boys neverthe-less displayed a mercenary streak through their love of being bought whatever they needed and by having their rent covered.[5] That a tenant should love having the rent paid comes as no great surprise.

Madonna's *Material Girl*[6] was equally pragmatic, declaring that the one with the hard cash is Mr Right. Prince took the opposite (predominantly male) view, saying that to be his girl didn't require monetary riches.[7] These contrasting viewpoints raise a question: is a life rich in love more fulfilling than the faked passion of luxury?[8]

1   *Got My Mind Set On You* by George Harrison. Written by Rudolph Clark
2   *Buffalo Stance* by Neneh Cherry. Written by Neneh Karlsson, Cameron McVey, James Morgan and Philip Ramacon
3   *Gloria* by Laura Branigan. Written by Umberto Tozzi, Giancarlo Bigazzi and Trevor Veitch
4   *Ain't Nothin' Goin' On But The Rent* by Gwen Guthrie. Written by Gwen-dolyn Guthrie
5   *Rent* by Pet Shop Boys. Written by Neil Tennant and Christopher Lowe
6   *Material Girl* by Madonna. Written by Peter Brown and Robert Rans
7   *Kiss* by Prince And The Revolution. Written by Prince Nelson
8   *What's The Colour Of Money?* by Hollywood Beyond. Written by Jamie Rose and Mark Rogers

Duo Mel and Kim were, appropriately, in two minds about the answer, declaring on one track that you would be better off living in love than luxury,[1] while on another suggesting that money (along with fun and love) was the solution.[2]

Other nobler songs proclaim that money isn't everything.[3] Despite widely held beliefs to the contrary, the correlation between a rise in happiness and a rise in income disappears at surprisingly modest levels of wealth and comfort: accumulating wealth to excess (especially when only for its own sake, long after the dopamine hit has passed) fails to guarantee endless extra happiness or relief from stress. You can't buy happiness, runs the argument, and love's not for sale,[4] more effusively described in *High Energy*[5] as beyond the purchasing power of all the gold in Fort Knox. Lyrically, when love is around, money becomes superfluous. While the unhappy rich do not have the comfort of believing that money will resolve their problems, they do have the financial resilience, opportunity and agility to try to buy their way out of any knotty entanglement of unhappiness.

Money only buys limited happiness because happiness is a state of mind, not a commodity. (Although often ephemeral, you can choose to increase and control the factors that create and contribute to feeling happy.) Happiness is an 'inside job' involving elements such as how you choose to think about what life has given you, or by engaging in activities that bring you great pleasure (especially those that nurture social connectedness or that help others), or where you can align your internal values with your external actions, or through activities that allow you to feel sensations deeply in the present moment. Many believe they must change and improve

1   *Showing Out (Get Fresh At The Weekend)* by Mel and Kim. Written by Michael Stock, Matthew Aitken and Peter Waterman
2   F.L.M. by Mel and Kim. Written by Michael Stock, Matthew Aitken and Peter Waterman
3   *Run Runaway* by Slade. Written by Neville Holder and James Lea
4   *To Be With You Again* by Level 42. Written by Mark King and Rowland Gould
5   *High Energy* by Evelyn Thomas. Written by Ian Levine and Jacques Pépino

their external circumstances (the need for more money, a better job, more fulfilling relationships, different possessions . . .) before they can achieve happiness and success. The opposite is often true: attaining happiness invites all forms of success, and as your inner life improves, so does the rest of your life.

Beyond love and happiness, the lyrics suggest that money can't buy beauty[1] (the 1980s was a time before cosmetic procedures were readily affordable, although great beauty still eludes most cosmetic outcomes), time (but you can sell your soul for a song)[2] or the right kind of human company, should you be a *Stool Pigeon*[3] (aka a police informer – not to be confused with a pigeon stool).

Sound advice? A penny for your thoughts?[4] (note how 500 years of inflation have eroded and devalued this idiom to near worthlessness). For many, money's role as a stepping stone to pursue something more meaningful has become obscured as money has taken control of their lives.[5] Building a healthy relationship with money – one where you retain control – is essential to reduce financial stress. In terms of monetary sound advice, that's about as sound as a pound[6] (and where will this idiom stand after another 500 years of inflation?).

In market-centred economies and societies, some see the excessive accumulation of money (wealth well beyond meeting your needs) as a marker of success. It is not, nor is the accumulation of tawdry or pointless possessions[7] a measure of self-worth or a mark of competency. Analysing spending patterns on non-essentials may help reveal hidden priorities. You can liberate a part of your life when you reject the need and reduce the price you pay when trying

1   *Puss 'N Boots* by Adam Ant. Written by Stuart Goddard and Marco Pirroni
2   *Manchild* by Neneh Cherry. Written by Neneh Karlsson, Robert del Naja and Cameron McVey
3   *Stool Pigeon* by Kid Creole and The Coconuts. Written by Thomas Browder
4   *Lavender* by Marillion. Written by Derek Dick, Mark Kelly, Steven Rothery, Peter Trewavas and Ian Mosley
5   *What's The Colour Of Money?* by Hollywood Beyond. Written by Jamie Rose and Mark Rogers
6   *Anfield Rap (Red Machine In Full Effect)* by Liverpool F.C. Written by Craig Johnston
7   *We Take Mystery (To Bed)* by Gary Numan. Written by Gary Webb

to impress[1] either those you know or those you don't know. After years of relentless hard work, chronic and excessive stress (which can suppress neuroplasticity and increase mood disorders), long hours and time spent away from family and friends, many find that the sacrifices they made to amass wealth at the expense of health fails to deliver an acceptable dividend. Such disillusionment is a common hidden cost where monetary gain is the sole or dominant extrinsic reward motivator in a working life. Being rich transcends monetary accumulation: your unique riches surpass any monetary value.[2]

If you are fortunate enough to have some spare money or time, invest in yourself (you are already adept at this by choosing to buy and read this book) and in the people, experiences or causes that matter to you. To achieve your financial goals, save and invest only in areas you know and understand; diversify your investments and allow them to grow for as long as is prudent. For lifestyle spending, always live within your means, which means budgeting ruthlessly.

The highwayman offered his victims a stark choice: your money or your life.[3] Too many are willing to sacrifice or debase their lives in the obsessive desire and frenzied pursuit of wealth (plutomania). Achieving spiritual balance through your unique personal mission, accumulated knowledge and experience, deep personal relationships and an appreciation of nature, beauty and music is far more enriching than any bank balance (most money in your bank and building society accounts is intangible, existing electronically rather than physically). You cannot buy what truly matters: love, time or a virtuous life philosophy offering meaning and purpose that celebrates, appreciates and relishes the sensations that the gift of life brings.

To paraphrase Greek philosopher Epicurus, you add to your riches when you subtract from your desires.

1   *The Harder I Try* by Brother Beyond. Written by Michael Stock, Matthew Aitken and Peter Waterman
2   *You're The Best Thing* by The Style Council. Written by John Weller
3   *Stand And Deliver* by Adam And The Ants. Written by Stuart Goddard and Marco Pirroni

NEW

Are you keen to begin something new?[1] The allure of the new is an old and well-worn song theme that describes a fresh start, a new perspective,[2] and a way to reignite curiosity, spark adventure and renew optimism.

Start something new[3] rings out an optimistic, enthusiastic and upbeat tone: new year, new day, new you, New York? (where you can make a new start).[4] Pop songs regularly explore the intoxicating excitement and promise of a new relationship, especially when this serves as a gateway to infuse new meaning[5] and new hope[6] into an old life.

According to the Pointer Sisters, heaven awaits at their door.[7] Janus, the Roman deity and door supervisor to Heaven, is the guardian of all portals and gateways, presiding over the entrance or beginning of all new things, such as a new year, hence 'January'. Janus is two-faced: one face looks back on the old, the other looks forward to the new. Having two sides to the same record reflects the inherent vacillating duality of human nature – that other side inside you.[8] A well-balanced (and typically flawed) life is a complex mosaic of thoughts, emotions and behaviours. Consequently, it's common to feel conflicting emotions co-existing within us, especially during stressful times when the emotional mix can gather within your head:[9]

1   *Wild World* by Maxi Priest. Written by Steven Georgiou
2   *The Living Years* by Mike + The Mechanics. Written by Brian Robertson and Michael Rutherford
3   *How 'Bout Us* by Champaign. Written by Dana Walden
4   *Theme From New York, New York* by Frank Sinatra. Written by Fred Ebb and John Kander
5   *Suddenly* by Billy Ocean. Written by Keith Alexander and Leslie Charles
6   *Love Changes (Everything)* by Climie Fisher. Written by Dennis Morgan, Simon Climie and Robert Fisher
7   *Jump (For My Love)* by Pointer Sisters. Written by Gary Skardina, Martha Sharron and Stephen Mitchell
8   *Behind The Groove* by Teena Marie. Written by Richard Rudolph and Mary Brockert
9   *Walking In The Rain* by Modern Romance. Written by David Jaymes and Michael Mullins

wise/foolish, focused/vague, cautious/impulsive, courageous/faint-hearted, generous/greedy, unbiased/prejudicial, hopeful/pessimistic, enthusiastic/apathetic, certain/doubtful, deferential/disrespectful, dependable/unreliable, lively/listless, concise/verbose and relaxed/anxious. It is natural to experience lighter, brighter days in new ways alongside heavier, darker days in old ways because you are, after all, only human.[1] Don't feel guilty about having the occasional bad day. The collective song themes highlight how a rounded life involves a delicate balancing act, particularly in relation to many of the inner/outer life self-care basics, including the interplay between rest/exertion (rest feels best and is more intense after exertion), work/leisure and exercise/diet (remembering that you can't exercise your way out of a poor diet). Managing these aspects can help tip the scales in your favour.

Visual artists understand how the balance and interplay of light and dark, colour, and subject matter combine to enhance the emotional effect of their work. Aural artists regularly use a song's bridge to add a new element of interest, banishing predictability.

In Eastern philosophy, the idea of two complementary but opposing forces – yin and yang – transcends human characteristics to include concepts such as light/dark. This ancient philosophy can offer a new way to view the balance and harmony present/absent in your life.

This double-sided discrepancy extends beyond the individual. For example, medical research has enabled humankind to understand and synthesise new life-saving antibiotics while simultaneously and unnecessarily contributing to the threat of antibiotic resistance. A daft situation,[2] snap The Piranhas.

Similar folly applies to environmental issues, such as habitat destruction, loss of biodiversity, the incautious application of chemicals, wasteful water practices, human-induced climate change and

1 *Something About You* by Level 42. Written by Michael Lindup, Philip Gould, Mark King, Rowland Gould and Waliou Badarou
2 *Tom Hark* by The Piranhas. Written by Rupert Bopape and Robert Grover

wasted food.[1] On this latter point, somewhere between one-quarter and one-third of world food production (often grown in topsoil subjected to unsustainable overproduction practices – where the soil has cracked its back)[2] is lost to waste, while there is hunger and malnutrition in the mouths of millions. An equally crazy situation[3] arises from our profligate throwaway society that pollutes the very world we all depend upon for survival. To tackle personal and societal challenges requires new ways of thinking, such as removing the restrictive barriers of traditional, compartmentalised 'silo' thinking that hold you inside,[4] to allow interconnected systems (such as music and well-being) to interact freely. It also calls for the imaginative application of new technologies and the wisdom to apply good old-fashioned common sense.

Your brain imbues the shiny and new[5] – such as cutting-edge trends – with a mesmeric and exciting appeal, as with the fascination with new fashion.[6] Newness extends to many aspects of life, including the emergence of life-changing ideas or events, a new day[7] or listening to new music. Biologically, novelty's sheen attracts your attention because it activates your innate survival instinct to evaluate the potential to either help and reward or hinder and harm. Detecting novelty is an evolved trait.

Sound advice? Pop songs can deliver a new sound, time or place,[8] but this is nothing new.[9] As the 2,000-year-old *Book of Ecclesiastes*

1   *Sowing The Seeds Of Love* by Tears For Fears. Written by Roland Orzabal and Curt Smith
2   *Muscle Bound* by Spandau Ballet. Written by Gary Kemp
3   *I Should Be So Lucky* by Kylie Minogue. Written by Michael Stock, Matthew Aitken and Peter Waterman
4   *Where The Streets Have No Name* by U2. Written by Paul Hewson, Adam Clayton, David Evans and Laurence Mullen Jr
5   *Like A Virgin* by Madonna. Written by Thomas Kelly and William Steinberg
6   *Wee Rule* by Wee Papa Girl Rappers. Written by Charles Cochrane, Hamish MacDonald, Samantha Lawrence and Sandra Lawrence
7   *The NeverEnding Story* by Limahl. Written by Giovanni Moroder and Keith Forsey
8   *Foolish Beat* by Debbie Gibson. Written by Deborah Gibson
9   *I Feel Like Buddy Holly* by Alvin Stardust. Written by Michael Batt

reminds us, "there is no new thing under the sun". While little may be genuinely new (much is reinvention or repackaging, as with the concept of 'conspicuous consumption' associated with the 1980s, but first described in 1899 by economist and social scientist Thorstein Veblen), unearthing something fresh remains thrilling, especially where this involves discovering novelty in the familiar or when searching for a new connection or direction.[1]

The search for something new[2] often necessitates letting go of the old, stale or entrenched. Newness – whether an idea, product or process – has the potential to disrupt (as with the introduction of CDs), often provoking resistance. Keeping an open and active mind enables you to open new doors and find something new to engage with, so continue to pose fresh questions and look for new angles and insights. When you challenge yourself to strive for improvement, learn new skills and broaden your range of interests, you help maintain and enhance brain health. Both novelty and variability are important in creating new memories.

Try to embrace new challenges and change enthusiastically rather than avoid them out of fear or habit. Robin Beck implored you to reach out, explore and muster fortitude for new, *First Time* experiences.[3] To do this, you need to push and stretch the pliable boundaries of your comfort zone, which requires an element of character-building personal courage, itself an attribute of human adaptability.

Musically, the beat goes on: there's always something new to keep your ears engaged and the tables turning,[4] even if the tables have long since turned on the fortunes of record players (call it new

1   *(Keep Feeling) Fascination* by The Human League. Written by John Callis and Philip Oakey
2   *The War Song* by Culture Club. Written by Roy Hay, George O'Dowd, Michael Craig and Jonathan Moss
3   *First Time* by Robin Beck. Written by Gavin Spencer, Thomas Anthony and Terence Boyle
4   *And The Beat Goes On* by The Whispers. Written by Leon Sylvers, Stephen Shockley and William Shelby

technology).[1] Discovering new musical genres, new bands or listening to familiar music with fresh ears can open new worlds. Marcel Proust described how music helped him descend into his inner self to discover new things through what he called the "sonorous tide".

There's no need to wait until *New Year's Day*[2] (especially if you are prone to waking up on the first of January feeling tired and hungover) to start afresh on your manifesto for personal reinvention: change can begin wherever you are. Trying something new might be as simple as learning a new skill, breaking an old or unhelpful habit or varying your routine, or as radical as starting a new life in a new land. It's not about waiting for another day[3] or a new or perfect moment in a new setting. There is no right time or place: the time is right now,[4] and the place is right here.

Your new life is waiting to begin,[5] so it's time to start a new theme.

OPEN-MINDEDNESS

Angry Anderson dreamt of finding an open mind.[6] To be open-minded is to see in a world of blindness.[7] Open-minded people possess a malleable growth mindset rather than the rigid obstinacy of a fixed mindset. Open minds relish opportunities to explore and experience new challenges, eager to broaden their intellectual bandwidth and welcome fresh ideas, feelings and perspectives that nurture

1   *The Circus* by Erasure. Written by Vincent Martin and Andrew Bell
2   *New Year's Day* by U2. Written by Paul Hewson, Adam Clayton, David Evans and Laurence Mullen Jr
3   *The Captain Of Her Heart* by Double. Written by Felix Haug and Kurt Meier
4   *So Cold The Night* by The Communards. Written by Richard Coles and James Somerville
5   *Behind The Groove* by Teena Marie. Written by Richard Rudolph and Mary Brockert
6   *Suddenly* by Angry Anderson. Written by Gary Anderson, Andrew Chicon and Kevin Beamish
7   *All I Want Is You* by U2. Written by Paul Hewson, Adam Clayton, David Evans and Laurence Mullen Jr

growth. Openness enhances problem-solving and decision-making skills because of the readiness to consider diverse sources of information and viewpoints (often stemming from a willingness to engage in constructive dialogue). Those with open minds can draw creative inspiration from alternative and unexpected sources, such as introducing transformative sound advice into their lives using song themes from the top 10 hits of the 1980s. Open minds think about it,[1] propounded Tears For Fears.

Howard Jones urged listeners to challenge predetermined notions, consider the other side's viewpoint (display empathy) and cast aside mental shackles.[2] To free your soul, Soul II Soul advised raising (and thereby opening) your mind.[3]

Sound advice? Yes. You can find sound advice and lyrical depth from all music genres. A willingness to let open ears feed an open mind vastly expands the pool of perspectives, possibilities, experiences and emotions, making each song like a piece of art: if it works for you, that's all that matters. Nurturing openness liberates your thinking by keeping your mind agile and helping to decalcify your thoughts, thus preventing stagnation.

Bob Marley reminded us that we each have a mind of our own.[4] Keeping that mind open doesn't involve relinquishing critical, independent thinking; on the contrary, it demands discernment and vigilance. Being receptive to new thoughts, viewpoints and emotions can make you vulnerable to manipulation and deceit that blow in uninvited when the doors of a mind are left open.

Having an open mind doesn't mean that your worldview is susceptible to vacillation, nor does it imply you accept everything without question. Instead of erecting rigid defensive barricades around intransigent beliefs, treat your worldview as a dynamic

1   *Sowing The Seeds Of Love* by Tears For Fears. Written by Roland Orzabal and Curt Smith
2   *New Song* by Howard Jones. Written by John Jones
3   *Get A Life* by Soul II Soul. Written by Trevor Romeo and Hayden Browne
4   *Could You Be Loved* by Bob Marley and The Wailers. Written by Robert Marley

collection of evolving ideas to be objectively probed and tested as you encounter and accumulate new information, ideas and experiences. Challenge, elevate and trust your thoughts to free your soul and keep your mind open, flexible and receptive to explore the abundant sources of inspiration and perspectives the world has to offer.

OPTIMISM

Let's be optimistic,[1] let's find the good,[2] seek the silver lining and make the best of every situation.[3] Optimism is the belief that expected outcomes will be positive, that *Things Can Only Get Better*[4] and that grey skies will turn blue.[5] Optimists view setbacks as external vectors, temporary (or one-off) hurdles that offer the opportunity to experiment, improve and become more resilient in the move onward and upward. Optimists look up[6] because *The Only Way Is Up*.[7] Musicians try to capture optimism's bright, light, upbeat vibe by using major keys when creating their pop songs.

Rod Stewart sang that optimism was his best defence.[8] Optimists benefit from fully functioning immune systems, improved cardio-vascular function (translating to a lower risk of heart attacks), more effective pain management, quicker recovery times and more stable mental health than pessimists. Unsurprisingly, optimists live up to about 15% longer (they certainly expect to enjoy many more years), or perhaps pessimists die prematurely, which is how a pessimist would see it. The right level of optimism has an infectious quality

1   *Love Resurrection* by Alison Moyet. Written by Genevieve Moyet, Steven Jolley and Anthony Swain
2   *I Have A Dream* by ABBA. Written by Göran Andersson and Björn Ulvaeus
3   *Layla* by Derek And The Dominoes. Written by Eric Clapton and James Gordon
4   *Things Can Only Get Better* by Howard Jones. Written by John Jones
5   *F.L.M.* by Mel and Kim. Written by Michael Stock, Matthew Aitken and Peter Waterman
6   *Two Hearts* by Phil Collins. Written by Philip Collins and Lamont Dozier
7   *The Only Way Is Up* by Yazz and The Plastic Population. Written by George Jackson and John Henderson
8   *Baby Jane* by Rod Stewart. Written by Roderick Stewart and Jay Davis

and improves social connections, as people are drawn to and uplifted by the presence of optimists. For both optimists and pessimists, their beliefs often become self-fulfilling prophecies.

The songs are careful not to confuse optimism with Pollyannaism, where individuals choose to live in *The Land Of Make Believe*[1] – a *Fantasy Island*[2] where you can be just what you want to be,[3] success is guaranteed, and nothing ever gets you down.[4] Such thinking is irrational and self-deluding. The naive but commonly held over-optimism of 'Dr Everything'll Be All Right'[5] (possibly a nod to the incurable optimism of Dr Pangloss from Voltaire's *Candide*) reflects an 'optimism bias' that, without hard work, talent or practical application can lead to entirely wishful and unrealistic expectations, inadequate risk assessment and subsequent disappointment. The same applies to relationships, where one overly optimistic party may summarily dismiss or suppress negative feelings. Realism builds resilience and enhances the quality of your problem-solving and decision-making abilities.

Sound advice? Yes – as a state of mind[6] realistic optimism can improve outcomes and your mental and physical health, provided the correct checks and balances are in place. Should you use the word 'poptimism'? No – you'll never need it.[7]

When optimism becomes your default mindset, it sets you on a positive trajectory, gently lifting you on a thermal of hope and expectation while keeping you tethered to reality. This positive state of mind shields you from living under the weight of cynics or doomsters.[8] If the voice of doom and gloom emanates from within

1   *The Land Of Make Believe* by Bucks Fizz. Written by Andrew Hill and Peter Sinfield
2   *Fantasy Island* by Tight Fit. Written by Martinus Duiser and Pieter Souer
3   *Americanos* by Holly Johnson. Written by William Johnson
4   *Jump* by Van Halen. Written by Edward Van Halen, Alex Van Halen, Michael Anthony and David Lee Roth
5   *Let's Go Crazy* by Prince And The Revolution. Written by Prince Nelson
6   *It's A Hard Life* by Queen. Written by Freddie Mercury
7   *Everybody Wants To Rule The World* by Tears For Fears. Written by Roland Orzabal, Ian Stanley and Christopher Hughes
8   *New Song* by Howard Jones. Written by John Jones

you, examine the evidence, then challenge it. Optimism is not about taking refuge from or denying reality, or living in a fantasy where the warmth of the future always eclipses the permafrost of the past, where everything is perfect all the time. Life's path is rarely straight and smooth: with many a twist and turn,[1] it's a long road strewn with rocks on which you will, at times, stumble;[2] after a fall, there can be only one way to go.[3]

Optimism enables you to make the most of every day[4] and focus your energy and attention on what matters. It unleashes resourcefulness, helping you to find quick, clever and effective solutions that help you circumvent any immediate or anticipated obstacles. Optimism also enables you to access and tap into the power of your unconscious mind, unlocking further opportunities and instilling an unwavering belief that you know you can make it.[5]

When life throws its random array of difficulties and unexpected challenges your way (as it will), don't accept them as fate. Instead, let your musical choices bring a much-needed lift of life-affirming joy, a shaft of light[6] that will illuminate the gloom and light the way for optimism and renewed hope. Balance is, as ever, essential as excessive optimism can easily tilt into unrealistic over-optimism, where over-confidence can lead to a harmful sense of invincibility and arrogance. Temper optimism with realism to achieve a happy and healthy mindset. The additional injection from the octane of optimism in your life can fuel self-belief, motivation and persistence, giving you the edge to succeed.

1   *He Ain't Heavy, He's My Brother* by The Hollies. Written by Sidney Russell and Robert Scott
2   *Could You Be Loved* by Bob Marley and The Wailers. Written by Robert Marley
3   *C'est La Vie* by Robbie Nevil. Written by Robert Nevil, Duncan Pain and Mark Holding
4   *Wham Rap! (Enjoy What You Do)* by Wham! Written by George Michael and Andrew Ridgeley
5   *St. Elmo's Fire (Man In Motion)* by John Parr. Written by David Foster and John Parr
6   *Cat Among The Pigeons* by Bros. Written by Nicholas Graham and Thomas Watkins

PARENTAL ADVICE

As a song theme, parental advice involves the timeless guidance passed down through generations rather than offering everyday parenting tips.

Songs that deliver parental advice often begin with the words "mama said", reflecting maternal *Intuition*[1] and experience about love and life. Mama's advice? *You Can't Hurry Love*[2] – be patient, save yourself[3] and choose carefully, warning that a lie can easily be seen as true.[4] Motherly advice also includes not rushing to be older and to live your life[5] as it is far too precious to waste[6] and don't stay out late with the wrong crowd.[7] As you might expect, mama's advice, rooted in care, is consistently sensible, solid and sound.

Lyrical advice from papa is thinner on the ground but does include the man-to-boy guidance to show true strength by walking away from confrontation – you don't have to fight to be a man,[8] advised Kenny Rogers. Advice heeded? No. As Howard Jones noted in *Look Mama*,[9] while parents can dispense advice, children often lack the wisdom to take it. He also points out that each child's path is unique; children are not carbon copies of their parents.

Sound advice? Yes. Parental advice is usually sound as it's gleaned from life experience, serving as a repository of guidance that embodies the song themes promoting health, well-being and personal growth: moderate alcohol consumption, eat healthily, prioritise sleep, maintain physical fitness, nurture and cherish relationships,

1   *Intuition* by Linx. Written by David Grant and Peter Martin
2   *You Can't Hurry Love* by Phil Collins. Written by Brian Holland, Lamont Dozier and Edward Holland
3   *It's Different For Girls* by Joe Jackson. Written by David Jackson
4   *Billie Jean* by Michael Jackson. Written by Michael Jackson
5   *Mama Used To Say* by Junior. Written by Robert Carter and Norman Giscombe Jr
6   *Alphabet St.* by Prince. Written by Prince Nelson
7   *Shaddap You Face* by Joe Dolce. Written by Joseph Dolce
8   *Coward Of The County* by Kenny Rogers. Written by Billy Edward Wheeler and Roger Bowling
9   *Look Mama* by Howard Jones. Written by John Jones

be open-minded, stay curious, embrace change, seek truth, respect others, learn from mistakes, strive for excellence, be passionate, build resilience, stay positive, try to make both yourself and the world a better place . . .

In both songs and life, parental advice is well-meaning and positive. However, actions speak louder than words – children are far more likely to emulate their parents' behaviour than heed their advice. Try to set a good example, and *Papa Don't Preach*,[1] especially where your child perceives advice as just another burdensome layer of parental expectation or passive-aggressive criticism (where your mother is never satisfied).[2] In *Girls Just Want To Have Fun*, for example, the mother questions her daughter about when she intends to start living her life the right way,[3] subtly hinting at the tension between advice and expectation.

Effective parenting involves more than the safe delivery of children into the world. Parents naturally want the best for their offspring so that they can grow to lead happy, healthy, fulfilled and fully engaged lives, complete with core values and a range of mental tools and techniques that enable them to make the right choices independently (or perhaps with just a gentle nudge from mama). For those on the cusp of adulthood, parental advice can sometimes feel like personal criticism.[4] Parents should try to be unconditionally supportive, loving (but not suffocating) and ever-present role models who guide and help develop the necessary skills and values their offspring need to thrive rather than being endless critics of their children's choices. Parents should take the advice to control only what lies within their sphere of influence.

One strength of informed advice and feedback dispensed by parents (and sometimes close friends) is its honesty, although it can

1   *Papa Don't Preach* by Madonna. Written by Brian Elliot and Madonna Ciccone
2   *When Doves Cry* by Prince. Written by Prince Nelson
3   *Girls Just Want To Have Fun* by Cyndi Lauper. Written by Robert Hazard
4   *Criticize* by Alexander O'Neal. Written by Alexander O'Neal and Garry Johnson

sometimes be detonative. Parents are willing – or at least prepared – to tell it like it is,[1] *Straight Up*,[2] without the usual filters of spin or social politeness. Such candid, productive dialogue is valuable because we regularly overlook or harbour blind spots regarding our shortcomings and hidden assumptions; sometimes, we need others to reveal truths we'd rather ignore.

While insightful song lyrics can deliver sound advice, they can never be a surrogate parent, even one who sounds like a stuck record.

PASSION

The word "passion" has roots in suffering, specifically that endured by Christ between the Last Supper and his crucifixion, as captured in works such as J.S. Bach's *St Matthew Passion*. As a song theme, passion represents a deep inner drive or an all-consuming enthusiasm for something you love doing. Conveniently, the 1980s had its very own passion poster kid, taken from the soundtrack of the 1983 film *Flashdance*, asserting that you can make things happen by pursuing your passion.[3]

Sound advice? A passionate yes: following a passion imbues life with meaning and purpose. But there's still much to unpack. First, before your fiery passion can set the world alight, you need to know your passion,[4] which can take time to find and crystallise. Most people don't possess a single, all-consuming, burning passion. Unearthing it may require a good rummage or a deep delve through childhood memories to identify and unlock the activities, interests and causes that made you feel truly happy, energised, fulfilled and alive, where, deep inside, something stirred.[5] Your passion need

1   *Buffalo Stance* by Neneh Cherry. Written by Neneh Karlsson, Cameron McVey, James Morgan and Philip Ramacon
2   *Straight Up* by Paula Abdul. Written by Elliot Wolff
3   *Flashdance . . . What A Feeling* by Irene Cara. Written by Giovanni Moroder, Keith Forsey and Irene Escalera
4   *Prove Your Love* by Taylor Dayne. Written by Seth Swirsky and Arnold Roman
5   *Rip It Up* by Orange Juice. Written by Edwyn Collins

not be centred solely on taking delight but, like a raging internal fire,[1] can be stoked by a surge of righteous indignation in the face of a blood-boiling injustice, mistreatment or cruelty that enrages and incenses[2] you enough to want to dedicate your time and energy to right a wrong. Passion propels change, but if you don't possess an internal incendiary streak, look to your unique strengths or consider what others frequently seek your advice on to reveal your hidden talent. Sometimes, even the tiniest spark can ignite a cognitive *Chain Reaction*,[3] revealing a calling that draws on your internal fire.[4]

Once found, the next step is to commit to extensive research, reality checks and physical action, such as volunteering, seeking advice from those already working in the field, enrolling on a course, joining a club[5] or society or working part-time within a related discipline. Taking your passion on a real-world test drive will reveal whether you possess the natural aptitude, courage of conviction and unique talents and attributes required to ensure that practising and pursuing your passion will inspire, elevate and instil in you a feeling of effortless freedom, joy and full engagement once the nuts-and-bolts reality of mastering that passion kicks in. And if you choose to be who you feel you must be, can you make your all-embracing passion pay its way? For many who follow their passion – especially hobby-based ventures – it is more a labour of love[6] that gives them a life, if not a living. The primary motivator for pursuing what you love to do should be your love of doing it – applying your passion and skill – rather than expecting vast financial gain. Those driven by intrinsic passion can sustain their inspiration and enthusiasm

1   *Love Changes (Everything)* by Climie Fisher. Written by Dennis Morgan, Simon Climie and Robert Fisher
2   *Drowning In Berlin* by The Mobiles. Written by Christopher Downton, Adrian Blundell and Russell Madge
3   *Chain Reaction* by Diana Ross. Written by Barry Gibb, Robin Gibb and Maurice Gibb
4   *Look Away* by Big Country. Written by William Adamson
5   *Left To My Own Devices* by Pet Shop Boys. Written by Neil Tennant and Christopher Lowe
6   *You Take Me Up* by Thompson Twins. Written by Thomas Bailey, Alannah Currie and Joseph Leeway

for longer, thus creating more time for themselves to succeed than those motivated by money alone. However, be prepared for financial uncertainty and instability and factor into your equation the cost of lost earnings and benefits from deviating from a conventional career path.

No one can teach you the essence of passion, but you can shape, develop and cultivate it, which forms the next step. Even history's standout figures, such as the familiar classical music composers, were driven to relentless practise to improve and innovate their innate skills. Although we are all born with a capacity for music, genius is never delivered fully formed. OMD noted that their obsession is their creation,[1] highlighting the necessity to find balance for your passion. Avoid allowing passion's energetic fire to burn out of control[2] and become a harmful obsession; your desire to succeed (especially when you have relinquished something of value to pursue it) means starting is easy, but you can't stop.[3] Melomania is a condition whereby great passion and enthusiasm for music become obsessive. Obsessions such as melomania are harmful because they shut out and abandon other essential facets of a rounded life, such as love and relationships, family and friends. Strive for a healthier balance by setting a series of smaller, progressive goals rather than fixating on achieving one big win at any cost.

The next significant challenge is sustaining your passion when there's always something else thrown in your way.[4] Once ignited, it's easy to burn brightly but rapidly through passion's initial energy of exuberance, leaving your resources depleted in the face of the inevitable challenges, frustrations and obstacles on your path. At this point, you might find that your new life is not as endlessly

1   *Souvenir* by Orchestral Manoeuvres In The Dark. Written by Paul Humphreys and Martin Cooper
2   *Dancing On The Floor (Hooked On Love)* by Third World. Written by William Clarke
3   *Cry Wolf* by A-ha. Written by Pål Waaktaar Gamst and Magne Furuholmen
4   *Love Will Save The Day* by Whitney Houston. Written by Antoinette Colandero

motivating and fulfilling as you had hoped, and what once moved you now makes you stand still.[1] This is where hard work and consistent effort will help you persevere, funnel your passion and forge it once more into motivation. Persistence, perseverance, fortitude and tenacity are all crucial, as are self-discipline and the ability to resist the temptation to compromise. In short, stay committed to your goal and don't give up trying.[2]

What if you fail the first hurdle and remain unable to unearth a passion that will become the backbone of your life? If you can't pinpoint what you would love to do, try to love what you already do. And hating (with, of course, a passion) what you already do makes it feel like hard work, so contemplate making a change before all your precious time, energy and positivity drain away into the sands of regret of a life gone by.[3] Strong negative feelings about your work can leach harmful toxins into all other compartments of your life.

Alternatively, you may find yourself so overwhelmed by a multitude of passions that they collide within you[4] such that you can't make up your mind[5] about which path to pursue. The result is passion paralysis. However, the beauty of the quest to find, develop and sustain a passion is that it can integrate into – and thereby bring vitality to – all areas of life, throughout life. You are more likely to excel if your life is full of passion[6] because passion generates its own sustainable energy, especially when you do something you love to do and, using your natural talent, you do it well. Infectious passion can make things happen and, in the process, enrich your day, your life and the days and lives of those around you.

As sound advice goes, that's a lot for one poster.

1   *I Don't Wanna Dance* by Eddy Grant. Written by Edmond Grant
2   *Ol' Rag Blues* by Status Quo. Written by Alan Lancaster and Keith Lamb
3   *Dancing With Tears In My Eyes* by Ultravox. Written by William Currie, Christopher Allen, James Ure and Warren Cann
4   *For Your Eyes Only* by Sheena Easton. Written by William Conti and Michael Leeson
5   *Purple Rain* by Prince And The Revolution. Written by Prince Nelson
6   *When Will I Be Famous?* by Bros. Written by Nicholas Graham and Thomas Watkins

PHYSICS

Physis, the Greek goddess of nature's origin and order, embodies a form far removed from the matter and particles that make mortal humans. The immutable laws of physics govern the interactions of the subatomic particles that make humans human, so, in essence, the laws of physics govern you.

The Time Warp[1] song introduces another dimension. Einstein's space-time continuum describes time as the fourth dimension, inseparably interwoven into the three spatial dimensions of length, width and height. Much like words and music, space and time intertwine. Given the importance of time within songs, it warrants a dedicated entry (it's about time too).[2]

Ascend vertically by about 100 kilometres and you'll find yourself in space. As physics shows, all life is but a transient moment in space,[3] but how scientifically accurate are the physics-based references? Lionel Richie suggests you should believe in yourself because you're a shining star.[4] Whether a shining star or not, you, as a carbon-based human – along with everything else that exists, has existed or will ever exist – are created from only 92 naturally occurring elements, many of which can only be forged by nuclear fusion reactions that occur within the crucible of extreme temperatures and pressures found within massive stars in the seconds following their explosive death. Or there goes a supernova,[5] as Frankie Goes To Hollywood said (a supernova should not be confused with a Vauxhall Nova, a 'hot hatch' from the 1980s, which was far from being either hot or super). 'You are a dying star' or 'You are a conscious, temporary assemblage of waste nuclear material that evolved as part of the

---

1   *The Time Warp* by Damian. Written by Richard Smith
2   *There It Is* by Shalamar. Written by Charmaine Sylvers, Dana Meyers and Nidra Beard
3   *Woman In Love* by Barbra Streisand. Written by Barry Gibb and Robin Gibb
4   *Say You, Say Me* by Lionel Richie. Written by Lionel Richie
5   *Welcome To The Pleasuredome* by Frankie Goes To Hollywood. Written by Peter Gill, William Johnson, Mark O'Toole and Brian Nash

swansong of an ancient apocalyptic cosmic explosion' may lack lyrical beauty, but it is an incredible fact of physics. You are stardust.

According to ABC, whether stars collide is up to you.[1] Thanks to gravity's cosmic orchestration, stars and galaxies do collide, such as the impending collision between our galaxy (the Milky Way) and our nearest galactic neighbour, Andromeda, but this has nothing – nothing at all[2] – to do with what you or anyone else may decide. It's astrophysics that can predict and explain far-future cosmic collisions.

The universal theme of love and relationships is often metaphorically tied to the universe – both are, for example, out there awaiting discovery. Two of a billion stars[3] could describe the relationship in a binary star system, where a pair of stars orbit around a common centre of gravity. Elton John wondered whether a gender-neutral *Nikita*[4] counted the stars. If so, he/she should expect a stiff neck as there are approximately 2,500 visible stars in our night sky, only a minuscule fraction of what may be a billion trillion stars in the two trillion galaxies in the observable universe. Alas, despite the scope of these scintillating numbers, nothing is written in the stars[5] about your romantic destiny. Elsewhere, Dionne Warwick sang of love being stronger than the universe,[6] but what strength does the universe possess beyond the aptly named 'strong force', only displayed at an *Atomic*[7] level? The universe is undoubtedly immense, but the Thompson Twins' claim that they can travel to eternity[8] is misplaced;

1   *All Of My Heart* by ABC. Written by Martin Fry, Mark White, Stephen Singleton and David Palmer
2   *I Owe You Nothing* by Bros. Written by Nicholas Graham and Thomas Watkins
3   *Rio* by Duran Duran. Written by Simon Le Bon, Nigel Taylor, Roger Taylor, Andrew Taylor and Nicholas Bates
4   *Nikita* by Elton John. Written by Elton John and Bernard Taupin
5   *Woman* by John Lennon. Written by John Lennon
6   *Heartbreaker* by Dionne Warwick. Written by Barry Gibb, Robin Gibb and Maurice Gibb
7   *Atomic* by Blondie. Written by Deborah Harry and James Mollica
8   *Doctor! Doctor!* by Thompson Twins. Written by Thomas Bailey, Alannah Currie and Joseph Leeway

it's not eternity[1] because eternity isn't a place. Conceptually, you may be able to travel for an almost infinite amount of time, but, as Iron Maiden assert, comprehending infinity is hard to do.[2] Also hard to understand are the multi-dimensions of string theory or the gravity-defying weightless love described in *Walking On The Moon*,[3] known to amateur physicists and romantics as Sting theory. Entanglement (it's not easy to explain)[4] is equally strange, coming from the always-strange microworld of quantum mechanics, where two separate particles exist as a bonded pair regardless of how far apart they are. Spandau Ballet noted that bonds made together are strong,[5] so could this concept of pair bonding from the realm of physics be extended to explain the intense love that two people feel, however how far apart?[6] No.

Returning to our solar system, the RAH Band reported violent storms in the asteroid belt.[7] Astronomers believe that this belt, located between Mars and Jupiter, comprises vestigial rubble from the formation of our early solar system. However, this rocky material cannot accrete into fully formed planets because of the immense gravitational influence that our solar system's oldest and largest planet, Jupiter, has in stirring up the neighbourhood. Some 66 million years ago, this belt was home to the 10-kilometre-wide asteroid that, again under the influence of Jupiter, this time in a more impish mood, decided to relocate into what is now the Gulf of Mexico, effectively ending the reign of the non-avian dinosaurs, extinguishing three-quarters of all life on Earth and creating a niche that became the starting point for human evolution. Back in the asteroid belt, there's no atmosphere and, therefore, no weather. The

1   *He Ain't No Competition* by Brother Beyond. Written by Michael Stock, Matthew Aitken and Peter Waterman
2   *Infinite Dreams* by Iron Maiden. Written by Stephen Harris
3   *Walking On The Moon* by The Police. Written by Gordon Sumner
4   *Baby, I Love You* by Ramones. Written by Harvey Spector, Eleanor Greenwich and Joel Adelberg
5   *Muscle Bound* by Spandau Ballet. Written by Gary Kemp
6   *Two Hearts* by Phil Collins. Written by Philip Collins and Lamont Dozier
7   *Clouds Across The Moon* by RAH Band. Written by Richard Hewson

only 'weather' in the near vacuum of space is solar wind – charged particles that stream forth from the Sun – that sometimes pepper our planet with enough intensity to disrupt and damage satellites and power grids, despite the protection usually afforded by Earth's magnetic field. And while spotlighting matters solar, *Walking On Sunshine*[1] is impossible as sunlight is merely waves of electromagnetic radiation. However, feeling a little sunshine on your face[2] can bring joy, inspiration and vital vitamin D synthesis, all without the added inconvenience of sunshine's shadowier side: instant radiation.[3]

Soul II Soul tell us that the Sun's rays are yellow.[4] However, our Sun's rays are white. The clue to why this confusion arises comes from Chrissie Hynde's channelling of Isaac Newton's experiments from 1672 when she sang about splitting like refracted light.[5] It is not The Pretenders who act prismatically, but rather the Earth's layered atmosphere that sometimes causes sunlight to be separated into its constituent colours when viewed from our planet's surface. Similarly, our personalities, identities and motivators are like the hidden spectrum within the white light of sunshine in search of a suitable prism through which they can shine and reveal themselves.

In *The Final Countdown*,[6] we learn that astronauts (etymologically, 'star sailors', from the Greek) are embarking on a voyage to Venus, but they still have many light years to go. Venus, our nearest and brightest planetary neighbour, is made of material similar to Earth, is almost equal in size and mass and has gravity similar to our own, making it a promising destination. Physics warns us otherwise. The primary problem posed by our pearlescent planetary

1 *Walking On Sunshine* by Katrina And The Waves. Written by Kimberley Rew
2 *Where The Streets Have No Name* by U2. Written by Paul Hewson, Adam Clayton, David Evans and Laurence Mullen Jr
3 *Chain Reaction* by Diana Ross. Written by Barry Gibb, Robin Gibb and Maurice Gibb
4 *Keep On Movin'* by Soul II Soul featuring Caron Wheeler. Written by Trevor Romeo
5 *Don't Get Me Wrong* by The Pretenders. Written by Christine Hynde
6 *The Final Countdown* by Europe. Written by Rolf Larsson

cousin – more of an evil twin – is meteorological, or as *Doctorin'*
The House[1] might describe it, we have a hot one. Venus' dense
swirling clouds are formed from sulphuric acid, contributing to
a surface temperature of about 460 degrees Celsius – hot enough
to melt lead. The atmospheric pressure on this burning hell is 92
times that on Earth. Landing on volcanic Venus would be the final
touchdown, swiftly followed by the final crushdown and then the
final meltdown. Additionally, the light reflected off the clouds from
this bringer of light (as the Greeks referred to it) reaches the Earth
in less time than it takes to listen to Europe's song, meaning that
travel to Venus is achievable within months rather than the many
light years the song suggests. Maybe all this talk of *Venus*[2] simply
mirrors Bananarama's song about the mythical Roman goddess of
love rather than referring to the second planet from the Sun.

Red Box unpack further confusion with talk of our globe having
corners,[3] while Midnight Oil ask the burning question about how we
are able to dance on an Earth that turns.[4] The answer lies in physics:
the dancers, along with everything else on the planet's surface, move
at the same constant speed relative to the Earth's rotation (1,675km/h
at the equator), rendering the dizzying rotational speed impercep-
tible. If that leaves your head in a spin,[5] here are more numbers to
make you dizzy with delight: while the world keeps turning,[6] the
Earth itself is on its annual 940 million kilometre orbit around the
Sun (at about 107,000km/h), and our solar system revolves around
the centre of the Milky Way at about 828,000km/h. (At our galaxy's
centre – about 27,000 light years away from the outer Orion 'arm'
where Earth resides – is a B-flat-sound-emitting supermassive black

1   *Doctorin' The House* by Coldcut featuring Yazz and The Plastic Population.
    Written by Yasmin Evans, Jonathan More and Matthew Cohn
2   *Venus* by Bananarama. Written by Robert van Leeuwen
3   *Lean On Me (Ah-Li-Ayo)* by Red Box. Written by Simon Toulson-Clarke
4   *Beds Are Burning* by Midnight Oil. Written by Robert Hirst, James Moginie
    and Peter Garrett
5   *Feels Like I'm In Love* by Kelly Marie. Written by Raymond Dorset
6   *Cat Among The Pigeons* by Bros. Written by Nicholas Graham and Thomas
    Watkins

hole called Sagittarius A*, with a mass about four million times that of our Sun.) Our galaxy, along with its estimated 200 billion stars, is barrelling through an expanding universe at about 2,000,000km/h. As you read these mind-expanding sentences in apparent stillness, you are hurtling through space at many hundreds of kilometres per second. Even for the only species known to be able to comprehend and contemplate its place in the universe, the strange and complex world of physics can sometimes be hard to understand.[1]

Sound advice? Landscape remind us that Einstein formulated $E = mc^2$.[2] Assuming that 'E' signifies 'energy' and not 'ecstasy', and 'mc' represents 'mass multiplied by the constant speed of light' and not 'master of ceremonies', this equation stands as a rare truth in a world where much of the lyrical advice has a short half-life. Unsurprisingly, physics-related references seldom undergo rigorous scientific scrutiny, including the Socratic-like questioning of peer review (see the Q&A theme).

Some physicists postulate that we might inhabit a multiverse, where infinite universes exist, of which this one is ideal. If true, a flawless version of you exists somewhere out there.

When it comes to love, Venus is far from perfect. Why? It's the chemistry,[3] it's the biology, but worse of all, it's the physics.[4]

POSITIVITY

Pop songs treat positivity and optimism as discrete ideas. Positivity focuses on feeling happy, hopeful and confident in the present, while optimism is the belief and expectation that future outcomes will be favourable. Positivity involves taking conscious control and responsibility for your thoughts (including challenging the default negativity

1   *Crying* by Don McLean. Written by Roy Orbison and Joe Melson
2   *Einstein A Go-Go* by Landscape. Written by Richard Burgess, John Walters, Andrew Pask, Christopher Heaton and Peter Thoms
3   *Together We Are Beautiful* by Fern Kinney. Written by Ken Leray
4   *Star Trekkin'* by The Firm. Written by John O'Connor, Grahame Lister and Rory Kehoe

of opinion-based criticism from your inner voice to make it more constructive, motivational and useful), actions, diet, exercise, sleep and leisure time: you are the one in control.[1] Accepting autonomy over your thoughts and actions allows you to make constructive change, raising your motivation and energy levels. The reverse is also true: failing to take control can result in your thoughts and actions starting to take control of you.

As with passion, the authentic virtuous circle of good feelings, actions and energy flowing from positivity is contagious. A laser-like focus on what you gain from what you do helps maintain clarity and direction. According to Stevie Wonder, acting with positivity can take you to the brightest star[2] (let's hope he wasn't referring to Venus).

Neneh Cherry encourages us to emphasise the positive.[3] However, most people harbour a natural default bias that leans towards negativity, often noticing (and remembering) what's wrong and seeing the danger[4] rather than what's right and seeing the opportunity. As with fear, this negativity bias serves as an evolutionary survival protection adaptation (to promote positivity here, think of it as a protective guardian angel), a throwback to a time when being primed to spot potential threats and take the requisite evasive action was crucial for survival. Losses usually outweigh gains – misjudging a threat could cost you your life. Thus, you are, in part, the living result[5] at the end of a long chain of survivors – ancestors who paid attention to avoid loss. While it's beneficial to focus on the positive, you should not entirely banish or suppress all that is neutral or negative, or fail to acknowledge reality. For example, feeling acute

---

1   *Like A Prayer* by Madonna. Written by Madonna Ciccone and Patrick Leonard
2   *Master Blaster (Jammin')* by Stevie Wonder. Written by Stevie Wonder
3   *Manchild* by Neneh Cherry. Written by Neneh Karlsson, Robert del Naja and Cameron McVey
4   *Obsession* by Animotion. Written by Holly Erlanger and Michael Des Barres
5   *I Can't Stand Up For Falling Down* by Elvis Costello And The Attractions. Written by Allen Jones and Homer Banks

pain[1] or unhappiness indicates that something is wrong and needs addressing. As you are attuned to specific threats, treat the sound of any negative messages as a siren[2] alerting you to the need to confront that negativity. Focus on finding positive solutions rather than fixating on the problem.

Sound advice? Whitney Houston's soulful paean to the 1988 Seoul Olympics began with her desire to be the best she could be every day.[3] Some find this inspiring, others toe-curlingly corny. For the latter, positivity can curdle and turn negative, even toxic, such as with the proliferation of misplaced New Age platitudes and affirmations that demand that you magically unblock the free flow of cosmic energy to cure all ills. Positivity can sometimes oversimplify complex issues without the benefit of gaining insight, or it may involve suppressing rather than acknowledging negative thoughts and emotions. Such thinking was surprisingly prevalent during the self-help boom of the 1980s. Remnants persist, often from those who mean well but fail to recognise that life is not always great. However, the songs do not promote the benefits of unrealistic or endless positivity (with its potential to disappoint, frustrate or add an extra layer of burden), instead preferring to focus on finding ways to tip the balance in your favour. When viewed in the light of positivity, opportunities appear sharply focused and seem simple to take. When used judiciously, positivity can help you be at your best, ensuring you make every day count.

If you lean towards having a restrictive and strange default reaction[4] – one that favours oppressive negativity (where, for example, your first response is always to find fault or complain) rather than liberating positivity – you will need to practise techniques to cleanse your mind of self-sabotaging thought patterns. When you

1   *Heartache* by Pepsi & Shirlie. Written by Iris Folwell and Tambi Fernando
2   *New Moon On Monday* by Duran Duran. Written by Simon Le Bon, Nigel Taylor, Roger Taylor, Andrew Taylor and Nicholas Bates
3   *One Moment In Time* by Whitney Houston. Written by Albert Hammond and John Bettis
4   *Heart* by Pet Shop Boys. Written by Neil Tennant and Christopher Lowe

feel negativity begin to creep in, challenge those thoughts so that they help rather than hinder you.

No Doubt About It.[1] Another technique to reframe your thinking is to treat rational doubt as a potential ally, not a harmful adversary. Examine the questions that natural doubt raises and ask yourself whether there is any evidence to back this uncertainty or if this doubt offers valuable feedback that you could use to your advantage. A complete absence of doubt can lead to unquestioning and even reckless over-confidence, while endless waves of doubt[2] will impede progress. Once again, seek to balance positive presence with negative absence.

Howard Jones's positively titled song, *Things Can Only Get Better*, reminds us that sceptics can't stop us from achieving our goals.[3] Ensuring an abundant supply of positivity[4] helps sustain morale and motivation, boosts mood, energises, increases resilience, bolsters confidence, improves productivity and outcomes, and reduces stress and anxiety (which in turn helps to fortify your immune system, lower your blood pressure and generally contribute to improved physical health).

Maintaining a positive outlook on significant aspects of life – such as relationships, health and fitness, and ageing – offers multiple benefits. For example, maintaining a positive attitude toward ageing could add more than seven years to your life over those who harbour negative, pessimistic views. To cultivate positivity, find the time and space to be grateful for life's little things,[5] those seemingly inconsequential aspects you barely take notice of,[6] such as the aroma of

---

1   *No Doubt About It* by Hot Chocolate. Written by David Hayes, Michael Burns and Steven Glen
2   *Lessons In Love* by Level 42. Written by Wally Badarou, Mark King and Rowland Gould
3   *Things Can Only Get Better* by Howard Jones. Written by John Jones
4   *Get A Life* by Soul II Soul. Written by Trevor Romeo and Hayden Browne
5   *What Have You Done For Me Lately* by Janet Jackson. Written by James Harris, Terry Lewis and Janet Jackson
6   *Suddenly* by Billy Ocean. Written by Keith Alexander and Leslie Charles

fresh coffee, the sensation of a barefoot walk on a lawn,[1] the gentle warmth of the sun,[2] the song of a lark,[3] the texture of bark, the shape of clouds or the way that a shaft of light illuminates a dancing mote of dust (which might just be a micrometeorite, a speck of cosmic dust that predates our solar system). These little things can mean so much,[4] so take a moment to observe and appreciate them by focusing on your senses rather than your thoughts; cumulatively, they can contribute valuable enrichment in a positive life.

One way to embrace the best moments in life[5] is to count your blessings before you count your sheep – that is, to cultivate gratitude by writing a daily bedtime diary. Before kissing the day goodnight, [6]take a moment to mentally scan your day to seek out, reflect upon and savour any silver linings, listing your best or most pleasant experience(s), including your top achievement, and why this matters to you: 'Today, I'm grateful for . . .' Some days will yield obvious accomplishments, while on most other days, your focus will be on smaller, often overlooked moments of joy, contentment and happiness, which can help reduce stress levels and bring you a sense of calm. During your day, open your eyes and take a good look around;[7] be as specific as possible when selecting your standout moments. As this daily habit develops, you'll learn to actively and outwardly explore opportunities to focus your attention on the details of the look, touch, sound and smell of the commonplace and seemingly unremarkable to unveil a hidden splendour, an exquisite beauty or a

1   *Kayleigh* by Marillion. Written by Mark Kelly, Ian Mosley, Steven Rothery, Peter Trewavas and Derek Dick
2   *When I Fall In Love* by Nat King Cole. Written by Edward Heyman and Victor Young
3   *You'll Never Walk Alone* by The Crowd. Written by Richard Rodgers and Oscar Hammerstein
4   *Feel So Real* by Steve Arrington. Written by Steven Arrington and India Arrington
5   *Jump To The Beat* by Stacy Lattisaw. Written by Michael Walden and Anukampa Walden
6   *Night Birds* by Shakatak. Written by William Sharpe and Roger Odell
7   *Just An Illusion* by Imagination. Written by Ashley Ingram, Leslie John, Steven Jolley and Anthony Swain

simple pleasure that exists in abundance and plain sight to all those willing to open their eyes and see.[1] The superficially ordinary can be extraordinary: when you look closely at what you see,[2] you'll find that the more you look, the more you see. You'll discover evidence of the extraordinary all around you when you train yourself to recognise golden moments; you may even transform your entire perspective on the world. Beauty is a constant: for Byron, music existed in all things. Nature, in particular, yields precious treasures,[3] so access to the natural world – even the most modest garden or public green space (which emit phytoncides, a natural form of immunity-enhancing aromatherapy) – will help you to count your blessings, cherish the moment[4] and rewire your brain for positivity. It's too easy to take for granted the abundance of good that already exists in your life, especially if you enjoy good health and strong, fulfilling relationships.[5] Nurturing gratitude for many of life's 'ordinary' aspects and recognising that every day holds something special can help you become more self-aware and develop a balanced perspective. For Roman philosopher Cicero, gratitude was the root of other virtuous behaviour, including kindness, generosity and compassion. Furthermore, your diary entries may even cross the porous membrane between wakefulness and sleep to seed positive and pleasant dreams.

The Three Degrees reminded us how easy it is to forget what you ought to say,[6] so positivity should include the appreciation of others, which you might routinely – but inadvertently – overlook.

1   *Xanadu* by Olivia Newton-John and Electric Light Orchestra. Written by Jeffrey Lynne
2   *The NeverEnding Story* by Limahl. Written by Giovanni Moroder and Keith Forsey
3   *Chain Reaction* by Diana Ross. Written by Barry Gibb, Robin Gibb and Maurice Gibb
4   *Upside Down* by Diana Ross. Written by Bernard Edwards and Nile Rodgers
5   *I Should Have Known Better* by Jim Diamond. Written by Graham Lyle and James Diamond
6   *My Simple Heart* by The Three Degrees. Written by Dominic King and Frank Musker

It's too easy for the little things to slip your mind.[1] The more open your antennae, the more receptive you'll become to tune into the power of positivity and the easier it will be to remain appreciative, happy and relaxed. This openness will, in turn, help you to connect more deeply with others (and with nature), build better relationships, become more resilient and improve your physical and mental health. Ultimately, you'll realise the significance and importance of life's fleeting, intangible moments.

Q & A

Ready? Sitting on the edge of your seat?[2] Let's start by comparing two short sentences: Sound advice. Sound advice? Sitting on the end of a sentence, the question mark distinguishes a statement from a direct question, without which, *How Will I Know.*[3] Appropriately, the absence of a question mark in this song title raises a question: *Why.*[4] *What Have I Done To Deserve This?*[5] The answer to that question is unknown.[6] Whitesnake kept searching for an answer but didn't find what they were looking for.[7] *Wouldn't It Be Good*[8] if all song titles that ask direct questions included a humble question mark at the end?

Where are we going with this?[9] First, let's go back in time[10]

---

1   *Always On My Mind* by Pet Shop Boys. Written by Wayne Head, Francis Zambon and John Christopher Jr
2   *Another One Bites The Dust* by Queen. Written by John Deacon
3   *How Will I Know* by Whitney Houston. Written by George Merrill, Shannon Rubicam and Michael Walden
4   *Why* by Carly Simon. Written by Nile Rodgers and Bernard Edwards
5   *What Have I Done To Deserve This?* by Pet Shop Boys with Dusty Springfield. Written by Neil Tennant, Christopher Lowe and Alta Willis
6   *The Look Of Love* by ABC. Written by Martin Fry, Mark White, Stephen Singleton, David Palmer and Mark Lickley
7   *Here I Go Again* by Whitesnake. Written by David Coverdale and Bernard Marsden
8   *Wouldn't It Be Good* by Nik Kershaw. Written by Nicholas Kershaw
9   *The Living Daylights* by A-ha. Written by Pål Waaktaar Gamst and John Barry
10 *I Feel Like Buddy Holly* by Alvin Stardust. Written by Michael Batt

to the cradle of civilisation, ancient Greece. Socrates employed a teaching technique that involved asking a series of probing, rapid-fire questions that challenged the foundational beliefs of some of his students. This approach encouraged them to articulate quickly and engage in critical thinking, reason and logic when formulating their answers. The Socratic method of thoughtful questioning is still used today in some law schools, as well-structured questions can help clarify and organise thoughts, often opening doors to the mind in the relentless pursuit of truth. By applying this Socratic method to self-enquiry, you can challenge the answers you give about yourself, allowing you to explore and expose the root causes of your concerns.

Fast-forward to the 1980s. Questions asked within pop songs – Socratic or otherwise – implant intrigue into listeners' minds. As any good barrister will concur, the phrasing and form of a question can determine how you mentally search for evidence when formulating an answer. What lurks for the unwary is the danger of becoming caught in a trap:[1] having arrived at your answer (even if prompted by a leading question that taints your reply with the questioner's bias), you inadvertently shut out other possibilities, convinced that there can only be one solution.[2] Even when other compelling possibilities come beating at your door,[3] you will likely turn them away because they don't align with the shape of your new-found answer. To counter this potential pitfall, maintain an open mind and remember that many valid answers may exist.

Think you know all the answers?[4] No one does. Acknowledging that you do not or cannot possibly know all the answers is an important realisation, and it's why some answers come with a

1   *Suspicious Minds* by Fine Young Cannibals. Written by Mark James
2   *One Vision* by Queen. Written by Brian May, Freddie Mercury, Roger Taylor and John Deacon
3   *The Living Years* by Mike + The Mechanics. Written by Brian Robertson and Michael Rutherford
4   *Say You, Say Me* by Lionel Richie. Written by Lionel Richie

question mark[1] (punctuation for which we should be grateful). At any age, you can ask deeply profound, often deceptively simple – even childlike – questions (as many songs do), which may take a lifetime to answer: What do I want?[2] Where do hopeless sinners go?[3] Must life be full of sorrow?[4] What's the meaning of life?[5]

In the quest for answers,[6] should you turn to pop songs? While acknowledging that some look to the bottle for answers, Madness didn't care much about the question.[7] Whitney Houston believed the answers were up to her.[8]

What's Love Got To Do With It.[9] Whitney Houston suggests entrusting the answer to your heart.[10] Questions usually flow freely before, during, and (potentially) after a relationship to help quell any doubt or confusion: Do you feel for me?[11] *Don't You Want Me.*[12] *Do You Really Want To Hurt Me*[13] (not including question marks really hurts).

Sound advice? Questions, questions.[14] Humankind has always craved answers to deep, probing questions. There will always be more questions than answers; the artist's role is to reflect and then

1   *The Reflex* by Duran Duran. Written by Simon Le Bon, Nigel Taylor, Roger Taylor, Andrew Taylor and Nicholas Bates
2   *Beat Dis* by Bomb The Bass. Written by Pascal Gabriel and Tim Simenon
3   *One Love/People Get Ready* by Bob Marley and The Wailers. Written by Robert Marley and Curtis Mayfield
4   *More Than I Can Say* by Leo Sayer. Written by Jerry Allison and Sonny Curtis
5   *Get A Life* by Soul II Soul. Written by Trevor Romeo and Hayden Browne
6   *Burning Heart* by Survivor. Written by Frank Sullivan III and James Peterik
7   *Madness (Is All In The Mind)* by Madness. Written by Christopher Foreman
8   *One Moment In Time* by Whitney Houston. Written by Albert Hammond and John Bettis
9   *What's Love Got To Do With It* by Tina Turner. Written by Terence Britten and Graham Lyle
10 *Love Will Save The Day* by Whitney Houston. Written by Antoinette Colandero
11 *I Feel For You* by Chaka Khan. Written by Prince Nelson
12 *Don't You Want Me* by The Human League. Written by John Callis, Philip Oakey and Philip Wright
13 *Do You Really Want To Hurt Me* by Culture Club. Written by Roy Hay, George O'Dowd, Michael Craig and Jonathan Moss
14 *To Cut A Long Story Short* by Spandau Ballet. Written by Gary Kemp

raise challenging questions, not provide answers. To elicit interesting and insightful answers, ask open questions that stimulate thought and encourage the sharing of ideas and opinions. Typically, these questions begin with "when", "where", "why", "what", "who" or "how". For example, instead of asking the closed question, "Did you enjoy the latest album?" consider the more open question, "What did you enjoy about the latest album?" Likewise, "How may I be of help?" invites a specific answer unlike the closed question, "May I help?" The beauty of asking thoughtful questions is that they can generate answers that initiate meaningful discussion and further insightful questions. This approach may unveil fresh evidence to challenge preconceived ideas and result in new thoughts and perspectives, so continue questioning any answers. Asking the right questions identifies you as a fully engaged, effective thinker interested in and listening actively to the speaker rather than passively accepting what you hear or only concerned about how you intend to respond. Good listeners ask questions to help maintain, enrich and expand the natural flow of a conversation.

One of the first questions we ask as children is one of the most potent: "Why?" (Alas, all too soon, many children believe they have all the answers.) The Kids From Fame were right to keep asking themselves why;[1] understanding the 'why' behind your actions helps reveal the true motives and values that drive them. Equally, it's easy to judge others' behaviours without first questioning and understanding the motivation behind their actions.

The answers to the questions you ask yourself[2] come from within, not from a bottle or by popping a pill. Listen closely[3] to the automatic questions you ask yourself, such as, "How could I be so foolish?" Try to make internal Q&A sessions more positive and productive by shifting the focus and asking: "What can I learn from this?" "How

1   *Starmaker* by The Kids From Fame. Written by Bruce Roberts and Carole Bayer
2   *In Your Eyes* by George Benson. Written by Daniel Hill IV and Michael Masser
3   *The Time Warp* by Damian. Written by Richard Smith

can I ensure this doesn't happen again?" "What can I do better next time?" "What leads me to think this way?" The right questions can unlock valuable insight and foster understanding. Look for an answer – and there will be an answer[1] – rather than at what might damage or diminish your self-esteem. One tip to protect your self-esteem is to frame these questions in the second person, substituting the "I" and "me" for "you" in the examples above.

Many questions remain unanswered:[2] *When Will I Be Famous?*[3] No, not that one. The big, unanswered question raised earlier that may have piqued your interest concerns the meaning of life, so here's Soul II Soul's answer to that question:[4] discover the answer yourself by being discerning, unbiased and a valuable contributor to your group.[5] You might consider adding a sense of purpose, too.

Yes, it's crazy to ask,[6] but it's tough to live without you,[7] so please always remember to use the question mark.

RELIGION

Who am I? Why am I here? How do I fit into the world? Where do I come from? Is there any meaning to my life? What happens when I die? Profound questions about existence have been asked throughout history, especially during the chaos and vagaries of adolescence when the young must address and navigate new challenges, changes, anxieties and fears. Across time and all cultures, religion has sought to answer these fundamental questions and to

1   *Let It Be* by Ferry Aid. Written by John Lennon and Paul McCartney
2   *Don't Know Much* by Linda Ronstadt featuring Aaron Neville. Written by Barry Imberman, Cynthia Weil and Thomas Snow
3   *When Will I Be Famous?* by Bros. Written by Nicholas Graham and Thomas Watkins
4   *Can't Wait Another Minute* by Five Star. Written by Susan Sheridan and Paul Chiten
5   *Get A Life* by Soul II Soul. Written by Trevor Romeo and Hayden Browne
6   *Leave A Light On* by Belinda Carlisle. Written by Richard Nowels Jr and Ellen Shipley
7   *Nothing's Gonna Change My Love For You* by Glenn Medeiros. Written by Gerald Goffin and Michael Masser

give life meaning, direction and structure through beliefs, rituals (such as those surrounding births, deaths and marriages) and codes of ethics to live by – for example, lead us not into temptation.[1] For the devout, religion offers salvation and the promise of a blissful eternal afterlife, while others are comforted by the belief that there's a saviour of us all.[2]

Echoing Hamlet, Pebbles asks whether to believe or not to believe.[3] Some believe that music's ability to express the complexity and vulnerability of an immortal soul proves the existence of a higher spiritual force. For the faithful, your god is real, your creator and a guiding presence that helps you make sense of your life and the world. By extension, life in the absence of religion would be chaotic, full of fear (of death, the unknown, being alone in your hour of need, social isolation, loss and unfocused identity) and devoid of meaning.

Throughout history, every culture has developed forms of music and religious practice. Some theories suggest that religion emerged in response to the human desire to live in settled agricultural communities, enabling the growth of cultures and their attendant religious traditions. Others posit that the need to feed those assembled for religious ceremonies – including musical rituals – sparked agricultural development.

Bonnie Tyler swore that she could feel someone, somewhere, watching her.[4] The concept of all-seeing, all-knowing deities or ancestral spirits watching over everything you do every minute of the day,[5] passing judgement on all your actions (whether seen or unseen by others) and offering the reward of heaven or the punishment of eternal hell (or their cultural equivalents) would be of great use in expanding human societies. Madonna, too, knew about the power

1   *Temptation* by Heaven 17. Written by Glenn Gregory, Ian Craig Marsh and Martyn Ware
2   *Flash* by Queen. Written by Brian May
3   *Girlfriend* by Pebbles. Written by Kenneth Edmonds and Antonio Reid
4   *Holding Out For A Hero* by Bonnie Tyler. Written by James Steinman and Dean Pitchford
5   *Is There Something I Should Know?* by Duran Duran. Written by Simon Le Bon, Nigel Taylor, Roger Taylor, Andrew Taylor and Nicholas Bates

of a stare.[1] When you live under the belief that an all-seeing eye is looking down at you,[2] it pays to collaborate, cooperate and conform. The sensation that someone's watching you[3] remains palpable – in the case of Rockwell's song, *Somebody's Watching Me*,[4] to the point of paranoia.

Others argue that, within nascent cultures, there was a need to fill the void left by an incomplete understanding of a complex world. The creation of conceptual constructs involving omniscient, omnipotent gods was thus a logical, inevitable consequence of the evolving complexity of human consciousness. Today, some continue to draw great reassurance from their belief in miracles[5] (events inexplicable under the laws of nature or science) and the thought that they live in a purposefully designed world guided and governed by a higher power. Religion brings comfort and certainty to creatures driven as much by emotion as by reason.

For millennia, virtually all practitioners and vessels of religion – priests, shamans and witch doctors from across the world and throughout different belief systems and cultures - have harnessed music as an integral part of their ceremonies, prayers and healing rituals. Beethoven described music as the divine messenger between heaven and human. "Dearly beloved, we are gathered here today ..."[6] But what do our more modern rock gods and high priests of princely pop preach to their equally enthralled congregations of like-minded devoted worshipers and disciples to have in their impassioned musical sermons? *Faith*,[7] because it's foundational[8] and, with faith alone,

1   *Crazy For You* by Madonna. Written by John Bettis and Jonathan Lind
2   *Geno* by Dexys Midnight Runners. Written by Kevin Archer and Kevin Rowland
3   *Every Breath You Take* by The Police. Written by Gordon Sumner
4   *Somebody's Watching Me* by Rockwell. Written by Kennedy Gordy
5   *Manchild* by Neneh Cherry. Written by Neneh Karlsson, Robert del Naja and Cameron McVey
6   *Let's Go Crazy* by Prince And The Revolution. Written by Prince Nelson
7   *Faith* by George Michael. Written by George Michael
8   *Love Of The Common People* by Paul Young. Written by John Hurley and Ronnie Wilkins

Jah can be your guide[1] (Jah being the Rastafarian name for God). When you're *Livin' On A Prayer*,[2] you may need a little divine intervention,[3] not forgetting that God moves in mysterious ways,[4] far beyond our puny capacity to understand any universal master plan. "There's a divinity that shapes our ends", mused Hamlet. Believers often attribute mysterious celestial intervention[5] to explain away seemingly senseless, randomly tragic events, whether intentional or natural. ABBA sang of dice-throwing gods;[6] Einstein famously disagreed, contending that God does not play dice with the universe.[7]

It's natural during adverse or bewildering times to feel the need for a little help from above[8] (or anywhere else) through daily prayer.[9] However, given divine omniscience (where *Heaven Knows I'm Miserable Now*),[10] you shouldn't have to pray[11] because your god already knows all your thoughts. If reciting ten Hail Marys[12] to the Madonna doesn't appeal, you could praise and thank the Lord[13] through something *Like A Prayer*[14] that involves singing and chanting

1   *Amigo* by Black Slate. Written by Anthony Brightley, Chris Hanson, Cledwyn Rogers, Desmond Mahoney, Elroy Bailey and Keith Drummond
2   *Livin' On A Prayer* by Bon Jovi. Written by John Bongiovi Jr, Richard Sambora and John Barrett
3   *Love Resurrection* by Alison Moyet. Written by Genevieve Moyet, Steven Jolley and Anthony Swain
4   *Sister* by Bros. Written by Matthew Goss, Luke Goss and Nicholas Graham
5   *There Must Be An Angel (Playing With My Heart)* by Eurythmics. Written by Ann Lennox and David Stewart
6   *The Winner Takes It All* by ABBA. Written by Göran Andersson and Björn Ulvaeus
7   *Einstein A Go-Go* by Landscape. Written by Richard Burgess, John Walters, Andrew Pask, Christopher Heaton and Peter Thoms
8   *The Power Of Love* by Huey Lewis and The News. Written by Hugh Cregg III, Christopher Hayes and John Colla
9   *Say Say Say* by Paul McCartney and Michael Jackson. Written by Paul McCartney and Michael Jackson
10 *Heaven Knows I'm Miserable Now* by The Smiths. Written by Steven Morrissey and John Maher
11 *Baby I Don't Care* by Transvision Vamp. Written by Nicholas Sayer
12 *Mary's Prayer* by Danny Wilson. Written by Gary Clark
13 *One Love/People Get Ready* by Bob Marley and The Wailers. Written by Robert Marley and Curtis Mayfield
14 *Like A Prayer* by Madonna. Written by Madonna Ciccone and Patrick Leonard

with a Christian rhyme.[1] Taking a musical approach aligns with the proverb proclaiming that the one who sings (well) prays twice.

Regardless of whether you were born into a culture of faith and worship (living with a crucifix on the wall)[2] or you quickly acquired religion[3] through personal adversity or divine revelation (such as encountering architectural angels),[4] a posthumous judgement day[5] arrives for believers whose names are recorded in the Book of Life,[6] the moment when you get to meet your maker.[7] After death, Doctor & The Medics believed they would ascend to the *Spirit In The Sky*,[8] while U2 sang of a belief in the kingdom come.[9] Irene Cara thought she would make it to heaven[10] where she would reside, in the words of Hazel O'Connor, for ever and ever. Amen.[11]

Other artists express scepticism. Phil Collins questions why the Lord says nothing about the plight of the homeless in society,[12] while former Catholic schoolboy Neil Tennant asks for forgiveness for his shameful life[13] in a lyric that concludes with a partial recital in Latin of the Confiteor – a prayer confessing sins – on a song that ascended all the way to number 1.

John Lennon invited us to imagine and contemplate a world

1   *Mistletoe And Wine* by Cliff Richard. Written by Jeremy Roche, Leslie Gannagé-Stewart and Keith Strachan
2   *Labelled With Love* by Squeeze. Written by Glenn Tilbrook and Christopher Difford
3   *Breakthru* by Queen. Written by Roger Taylor, Freddie Mercury, Brian May and John Deacon
4   *You Can Call Me Al* by Paul Simon. Written by Paul Simon
5   *Move Away* by Culture Club. Written by Roy Hay, George O'Dowd, Michael Craig, Jonathan Moss and Philip Pickett
6   *The Evil That Men Do* by Iron Maiden. Written by Adrian Smith, Paul Dickinson and Stephen Harris
7   *The Clairvoyant* by Iron Maiden. Written by Stephen Harris
8   *Spirit In the Sky* by Doctor & The Medics. Written by Norman Greenbaum
9   *I Still Haven't Found What I'm Looking For* by U2. Written by Paul Hewson, Adam Clayton, David Evans and Laurence Mullen Jr
10 *Fame* by Irene Cara. Written by Dean Pitchford and Michael Gore
11 *Eighth Day* by Hazel O'Connor. Written by Hazel O'Connor
12 *Another Day In Paradise* by Phil Collins. Written by Philip Collins
13 *It's A Sin* by Pet Shop Boys. Written by Neil Tennant and Christopher Lowe

without heaven, hell or religion.[1] What if you don't need religion[2] or the Bible[3] filled with its fanciful tales about 40 days and 40 nights[4] or those who walk on water?[5] For non-believers, a universe arising spontaneously and randomly is just as awe-inspiring as a miraculous one crafted by a divine creator. Even if you believe that religion is little more than a supernatural irrational mass delusion, you still have a role to play in helping to build a better, more interdependent world, where, for all life, heaven can be a place on Earth.[6] As for your existence, always insist on life before death.

Sound advice? Religion, encompassing over 4,000 faiths, is a broad church. However, most songs from the 1980s that reference religion primarily focus on Christianity (think of all those songs on the theme of Christmas), with only occasional nods to the other four major faiths, such as the Buddha's call to stop sericulture.[7] The forcefulness of religious advice varies according to the intensity of belief held by the songwriter, performer or preacher. Pop songs are more reflective than prescriptive. Ultimately, the decision to believe remains deeply personal.

A compilation box set album of CDs featuring every top 10 hit from the 1980s (200 of which reached number 1) would straddle many genres, be written over many years, and cover numerous narratives and themes that reflect diverse viewpoints. This collection would enable the listener to distil advice and guidance about living a good life, applicable across all eras. The impressive longevity and sales figures from the *Now!* compilation albums reflect demand for such a product. The publishing world has a religious equivalent to this

1   *Imagine* by John Lennon. Written by John Lennon and Yoko Ono
2   *You Take Me Up* by Thompson Twins. Written by Thomas Bailey, Alannah Currie and Joseph Leeway
3   *I Want Your Sex* by George Michael. Written by George Michael
4   *Billie Jean* by Michael Jackson. Written by Michael Jackson
5   *We Close Our Eyes* by Go West. Written by Peter Cox and Richard Drummie
6   *Heaven Is A Place On Earth* by Belinda Carlisle. Written by Richard Nowels Jr and Ellen Shipley
7   *Being Boiled* by The Human League. Written by Philip Oakey, Martyn Ware and Ian Craig Marsh

musical anthology: the Bible. With global sales exceeding five billion, the Bible is the best-selling and most translated book of all time, with a print run dating back to the advent of the printing press: "In the beginning was the word"[1] (John 1:1). The Bible - from the Greek *ta biblía* meaning 'the books' - is a compilation of stories and parables that cover multiple genres written by various authors over about 1,000 years. As with the insights of ancient Greek philosophers and the words of Shakespeare, the life advice and verbal imagery from way back in Biblical times[2] applies to any time, even secular times, and has entered and shaped popular culture. For example, the Bible may have been the first written source of "the writing on the wall"[3] (Daniel chapter 5) that has since become idiomatic. Other song phrases with biblical origins include "stranger in a strange land"[4] (Exodus 2:22); "land of milk and honey"[5] (Exodus 3:8, among many other citations); "promised land"[6] (Genesis - the first book of the Bible, not the rock band - 12:7); "flesh and blood"[7] (Ephesians 6:12); "tongues of fire"[8] (Acts 2:3); "skin and bones"[9] (Job 19:20); references to "manna"[10] (Exodus 16 and many others); *I Have A Dream*[11] (Isaiah

---

1   *Eighth Day* by Hazel O'Connor. Written by Hazel O'Connor
2   *Pink Cadillac* by Natalie Cole. Written by Bruce Springsteen
3   *(I've Had) The Time Of My Life* by Bill Medley and Jennifer Warnes. Written by Donald Markowitz, Franke Previte and John DeNicola
4   *We Didn't Start The Fire* by Billy Joel. Written by William Joel
5   *The Message* by Grandmaster Flash And The Furious Five. Written by Clifton Chase, Edward Fletcher, Melvin Glover and Sylvia Vanterpool
6   *King* by UB40. Written by James Brown, Alistair Campbell, Robin Campbell, Earl Falconer, Norman Hassan, Brian Travers, Michael Virtue and Terence Wilson
7   *Human* by The Human League. Written by James Harris and Terry Lewis
8   *The Power Of Love* by Frankie Goes To Hollywood. Written by William Johnston, Peter Gill, Mark O'Toole and Brian Nash
9   *Food For Thought* by UB40. Written by James Brown, Alistair Campbell, Robin Campbell, Earl Falconer, Norman Hassan, Brian Travers, Michael Virtue and Terence Wilson
10 *Food For Thought* by UB40. Written by James Brown, Alistair Campbell, Robin Campbell, Earl Falconer, Norman Hassan, Brian Travers, Michael Virtue and Terence Wilson
11 *I Have A Dream* by ABBA. Written by Göran Andersson and Björn Ulvaeus

40:4-5); "suffer little children"[1] (Matthew 19:14); *Wings Of A Dove*[2] (Psalm 68:13); and "love is better than wine"[3] (Song of Solomon 1:2).

For billions of devout followers, religion holds crucial meaning, bringing joy, community, belonging, usefulness and (particularly during times of uncertainty) ritual comfort and solace. Religion may offer health benefits for both body and mind, helping believers to live longer, despite the promise in some religions of a blissful eternal afterlife. However, questioning one's faith is a natural part of the human experience, especially for adolescents who often wrestle with internal struggles. If, after exploration, you believe that what you feel is a lie[4] – that religion deceives you – then it's valid to reject it, even if choosing a secular path is a more formidable challenge. (*It's A Miracle*[5] that religions endure despite extensive scientific explanation.) Sidestepping religion doesn't mean embracing nihilism. While the vast, cold universe feels nothing about the fleeting moment[6] of your existence or indeed that of anyone or anything, meaning can still exist as an empowering internal creation; you believe in yourself rather than in external forces.

For Sister Sledge, music was a salvation,[7] while rock and roll was the closest Aztec Camera could get to heaven.[8] The devotion of some hardcore music fans shows that music shares many sacred qualities with religious experiences, all without the threat of eternal damnation. The songs within this theme are far from the ashes of happy-clappy campfire songs left behind after the devil has made off

1   *Ship Of Fools* by Erasure. Written by Vincent Martin and Andrew Bell
2   *Wings Of A Dove* by Madness. Written by Graham McPherson and Cathal Smyth
3   *Kiss Me* by Stephen "Tin Tin" Duffy. Written by Stephen Duffy
4   *Chant No. 1 (I Don't Need This Pressure On)* by Spandau Ballet. Written by Gary Kemp
5   *It's A Miracle* by Culture Club. Written by Roy Hay, George O'Dowd, Michael Craig, Jonathan Moss and Philip Pickett
6   *Is This Love?* by Alison Moyet. Written by Genevieve Moyet and David Stewart
7   *Lost In Music* by Sister Sledge. Written by Nile Rodgers and Bernard Edwards
8   *Somewhere In My Heart* by Aztec Camera. Written by Roddy Frame

with all the hottest tunes. Music's transcendent power can connect us to something greater, be it a deity, the universe or the essence of humanity. Without the grip of numinous music to link us to the divine, religion's hold on the human heart would significantly diminish.

REPUTATION

Reputation is a curious concept: it's yours, yet you don't fully own it. It's a part of your identity, yet it exists separately. You retain a gatekeeping influence over its shape through your actions, yet you do not – and cannot – have absolute control over the beliefs and opinions that others hold about you. Reputation resembles a delicate glass sculpture: it requires skill, time, consistency and effort to blow and grow it into the desired shape while remaining fragile and susceptible to a single knock that could leave you picking up the pieces[1] from your shattered world.[2] The shards from a broken reputation can be hazardous.

Bobby Brown questioned why he was unable to live a life free from what others say.[3] Reputation evolved and persists because it reflects traits valued within human societies. For thousands of years, humans lived together in small community groups, typically numbering about 150 individuals (the Dunbar number, from the *Friends* theme), where everyone knew each other and group survival depended on the cooperation of collective work. Emergent societies needed a mechanism to protect against freeloaders. Reputation provided just such insurance, helping to lubricate society's cogs to ensure smooth interactions. Social pressure to comply and conform by being observed and judged by others for transgressions remains a powerful influence on human behaviour. By contrast, acting honestly

1   *Every Time You Go Away* by Paul Young. Written by Daryl Hohl
2   *A Groovy Kind Of Love* by Phil Collins. Written by Carole Bayer and Toni Wine
3   *My Prerogative* by Bobby Brown. Written by Robert Brown, Edward Riley and Gene Griffin

and decently when unobserved remains a cornerstone of personal integrity.

Tracey Ullman asked a follow-up question: why should approval from others matter?[1] Others' opinions count because they influence our social standing, credibility, trustworthiness and potential desirability as a sexual partner and parent. Even if you don't care what people say,[2] humans generally harbour a sensitivity about negative information: tarnished reputations linger. In today's society, anti-social behaviour by a few inconsiderate and thoughtless individuals (some of whom wear their sullied reputation as a twisted badge of honour) can unfairly damage the reputation of an entire cohort, perpetuating crude one-dimensional stereotypes of inaccurate and assumed common characteristics, and even, in some cases, weakly justifying discrimination. For example, not every youngster is reckless and feckless, not every older man is curmudgeonly and cantankerous, and not every pop star is a prima donna, either post- or pre-Madonna.

Some relish the opportunity to dig up dirt[3] and spread rumour[4] and sordid details[5] through the grapevine,[6] especially when their competitors transgress social norms. In every culture, and now increasingly online, many devote considerable amounts of their conversational time to tracking friends and social connections through gossip and rumour. Unfettered talk about reputation – often little more than hints or unsubstantiated allegations[7] – can turn gossip's embers into a raging inferno of exaggeration and misinformation. When someone goes too far with their gossip and rumour[8]

1 *They Don't Know* by Tracey Ullman. Written by Kirsty MacColl
2 *Whenever You Need Somebody* by Rick Astley. Written by Michael Stock, Matthew Aitken and Peter Waterman
3 *Private Investigations* by Dire Straits. Written by Mark Knopfler
4 *Cuddly Toy* by Roachford. Written by Andrew Roachford
5 *Ashes To Ashes* by David Bowie. Written by David Jones
6 *I Heard It Through The Grapevine* by Marvin Gaye. Written by Barrett Strong and Norman Whitfield
7 *You Can Call Me Al* by Paul Simon. Written by Paul Simon
8 *April Skies* by The Jesus And Mary Chain. Written by William Reid and James Reid

in a deliberate attempt to burn down another's reputation via verbal arson, they may be partly motivated by one of the most corrosive and negative emotions: jealousy. One game played by jealous people[1] involves selling you jealous lies.[2] Those with jealous tongues often possess jealous ears (selective hearing) and jealous eyes within which lurks deep-seated irrationality and resentment – where they hate you just for existing.[3] However, transforming harmless chatter into damaging reputational harm through sharp-tongued loose talk[4] is a perilous pastime because the rumour-monger risks undermining their credibility should idle chatter escalate into malice, which it's prone to do. Michael Jackson, a man whose real-world reputation was subject to intense courtroom scrutiny, sang about how razor tongues in motor mouths churn out lies.[5]

Sound advice? Sonia insisted she shouldn't let rumour sway her opinion.[6] Reputation's strange duality means it can be both significant and insignificant. Many songs take the view that you need not – and should not – allow the thoughts and opinions of others to shape a life that's true to you. Pop stars and some prominent philanthropic corporations understand the value of reputation and have become adept at crafting (usually bolstering) their reputation and 'brand' value as they attempt to build loyalty and expand their reach.

Other songs brush aside any talk on the street,[7] caring little for what others say.[8] Yet, it's a facet of human nature that, at least to

1   *Our Lips Are Sealed* by Fun Boy Three. Written by Jane Wiedlin and Terence Hall
2   *Nothing Can Divide Us* by Jason Donovan. Written by Michael Stock, Matthew Aitken and Peter Waterman
3   *Wonderful Life* by Black. Written by Colin Vearncombe
4   *Don't Stand So Close To Me* by The Police. Written by Gordon Sumner
5   *Wanna Be Startin' Somethin'* by Michael Jackson. Written by Michael Jackson
6   *Listen To Your Heart* by Sonia. Written by Michael Stock, Matthew Aitken and Peter Waterman
7   *My One Temptation* by Mica Paris. Written by Michael Leeson, Stephen Waters and Peter Vale
8   *Somewhere In My Heart* by Aztec Camera. Written by Roddy Frame

some degree, you do care about your reputation, especially during the first half of your life. Modern life, particularly the technological advancements since the 1980s, is far removed from the vast swathe of time over which we evolved. Most people now live in large impersonal cities where virtually instantaneous online connectivity distorts the traditional role once played by reputation within societies, including the obsession to curate a reputation and public persona among people you don't know or will never meet. Bigots will continue to hate you despite never having met you,[1] so it's essential to maintain some perspective regarding what is being said about you by people who don't know you or only know you superficially.

The power of cruel words[2] to sully a nascent reputation, especially attacks and slurs that traduce the sexual fidelity of women (where, historically, the social ramifications of a stained reputation could be life-changing), is enough not only to temporarily derail a vulnerable life but also, in extreme cases of abuse, cause that life to be cut tragically short. Unjustified trampling on someone's reputation often reveals more about the perpetrator's character than it does about the target of their malice.

Your reputation is not built on future intentions but develops naturally from the unique characteristics and qualities displayed as part of your personality. You should not look to form your identity based on what passes through the subjective eyes, minds or mouths of others. Fun Boy Three concur, suggesting you give no credence to what others say.[3] To be affected by negative sentiment about your reputation usually requires you to open a door and allow such comments to blow in. The solution is simple: close the door,[4] particularly if you don't like the look or sound of malicious or obsequious

1   *People Are People* by Depeche Mode. Written by Martin Gore
2   *Breakaway* by Tracey Ullman. Written by Sharon Lee Myers and Sharon Sheeley
3   *Are Lips Are Sealed* by Fun Boy Three. Written by Jane Wiedlin and Terence Hall
4   *Gotta Pull Myself Together* by The Nolans. Written by Benjamin Findon, Robert Puzey and Michael Myers

comments about you or your reputation from social media. One perk of ageing (sitting just ahead of cheaper car insurance) is naturally caring less about how others view you (the diminished need for external validation) and your reputation, allowing you to stay true to who you are.

RESPECT

Respect comprises three main strands. The first is recognising, admiring and appreciating someone's unique abilities, accomplishments or qualities.[1] You don't have to admire the individual or their output to respect their contribution. For example, if Prince's music is not to your liking, you can still respect and acknowledge the musicianship, lyrics, performance, work ethic, creativity and production influences he brought to popular culture during the 1980s. Most people appreciate some acknowledgement for their efforts.

The second aspect of respect involves treating others with dignity, recognising and valuing their intrinsic worth as fellow humans. This involves showing kindness, compassion, empathy and an openness to others' views, feelings, opinions and wishes. By respecting others' rights and traditions, we foster harmonious inclusivity, support and cooperation while minimising friction and disagreement. Howard Jones showed respect for his mother by refraining from trying to change her actions.[2]

The third strand is self-respect. *Prince Charming*[3] lived up to his name with his regal advice to respect yourself and all others. Bruce Willis reminded us that if you fail to *Respect Yourself*,[4] no one else will give a "good cahoot" (you probably know what this means, even though it means nothing).

1   *Girl You Know It's True* by Milli Vanilli. Written by William Pettaway Jr, Sean Spencer, Kevin Liles, Rodney Holloman and Kayode Adeyemo
2   *Look Mama* by Howard Jones. Written by John Jones
3   *Prince Charming* by Adam And The Ants. Written by Stuart Goddard and Marco Pirroni
4   *Respect Yourself* by Bruce Willis. Written by Luther Ingram and Bonny Rice

Sound advice? There's a clear message:[1] A *Little Respect*,[2] especially self-respect, goes a long way. But what exactly is self-respect, and how do you cultivate it? Self-respect involves treating yourself with the same kindness, compassion and empathy you extend to others. The ability to accept, take pride in and value who you are also requires taking responsibility for your thoughts and actions. With self-respect comes confidence (by dispelling self-doubt) that empowers you to embrace change, usher in the new and withstand setbacks with enhanced resilience.

When you respect others, they are more likely to reciprocate, even in relationships as delicate as that between parent and child. A desire to listen and collaborate and the careful use of language – such as "I admire your tenacity . . . ", "How would you feel about . . . " and "I forgive you for . . . " – are simple ways to build mutual respect and make others feel valued.

Forgiveness is transformative because it garners and builds all-round respect by enabling you to choose (without requiring any change in others) to untie painful emotional knots, allowing you to release yourself from any internal resentment, hurt, bitterness and anger, helping sever the link between revenge and justice (revenge isn't justice). Forgiveness is hard to dispense because it's often easier and simpler to cling to the burden of negative emotions and to hold on to grudges than to release and replace them with compassion, empathy and a desire to understand others' actions. Forgiveness does not right a wrong – words cannot be unsaid, actions cannot be undone (in pop songs, this usually involves relationship infidelity) – but it remains a positive response and a tool (but not a weapon) that allows you to break the perpetual cycle of bitterness and tension. Forgiveness frees you from the grip of the past without changing it, granting you some control over reshaping the future by offering everyone a chance to move forward. Although it requires a degree

1 *Islands In The Stream* by Kenny Rogers and Dolly Parton. Written by Barry Gibb, Robin Gibb and Maurice Gibb
2 *A Little Respect* by Erasure. Written by Vincent Martin and Andrew Bell

of humility, forgiveness – including self-forgiveness – always comes from a position of strength.

SELF-RELIANCE

Self-reliance is about trusting your skills, abilities, adaptability and resourcefulness. Whitney Houston adds that self-reliance is (as its name implies) about learning to depend on yourself[1] – trusting your skills, abilities, adaptability and resourcefulness – rather than relying on others (including the state and institutions) to get things done. John Parr urged perseverance because only you can do what you need to do.[2] In popular song culture, self-reliance projects positive personal empowerment. However, self-reliance may sometimes conflict with faith in divine providence for those with strong religious beliefs. It's crucial to differentiate self-reliance from the self-centred individualism prevalent in (but not exclusive to) the 1980s, with its attendant lack of empathy and cooperation.

In the opening of his sermon song *Let's Go Crazy*,[3] Prince reminded us that we are on our own. As you'll spend your entire life in your own company, it's good to learn how to rely on yourself to get things done, make decisions and take control.[4] Bobby Brown reiterates part of the theme from *On My Own* in his song *My Prerogative*[5] when he sings that he doesn't need others' consent to make decisions. Bucks Fizz urge you to trust your judgement when making decisions and not to allow others to make up or change your mind for you,[6]

1   *The Greatest Love Of All* by Whitney Houston. Written by Michael Masser and Linda Creed
2   *St. Elmo's Fire (Man In Motion)* by John Parr. Written by David Foster and John Parr
3   *Let's Go Crazy* by Prince And The Revolution. Written by Prince Nelson
4   *On Our Own* by Bobby Brown. Written by Antonio Reid, Kenneth Edmonds and Daryl Simmons
5   *My Prerogative* by Bobby Brown. Written by Robert Brown, Edward Riley and Gene Griffin
6   *Making Your Mind Up* by Bucks Fizz. Written by Andrew Hill and John Danter

Sound advice? Yes. Self-reliance empowered many pop stars to enjoy their creative freedom, allowing them to explore, grow and develop personally and musically as their careers blossomed. This self-reliance distinguishes them from the more 'manufactured' acts burdened by their dependence on external validation.

George Harrison understood that, by focusing his mind, he could achieve his goal.[1] The songs encourage self-reliance, but so too did many of the policies of Thatcherism throughout the 1980s, and they were not always universally embraced. While the songs promote self-reliance, they often lack the practical 'show me how'[2] steps necessary for its implementation. Developing self-reliance entails accepting and taking responsibility for your actions and resisting the urge to assign blame when things go wrong (a surprisingly common occurrence in the pop songs of the 1980s, particularly regarding relationship breakdowns). When you stop externalising responsibility – and viewing yourself as a victim – you gain greater control over your life and its trajectory. If you always blame others for your failures, you should equally always credit others for your successes.

When you live a *Good Life*,[3] life thrives. To date, you've already met and overcome many challenges. You weren't born with your current level of accomplishment – you have carved out that success for yourself. Self-reliance builds on your ability to recognise and refine the skills and mental strategies you've used to face challenges, thereby arming yourself with an effective coping mechanism to deal with future uncertainties. This desire to develop yourself will help you adapt and develop practical survival skills,[4] along with the cognitive ability to work out where to find and how to employ any

1   *Got My Mind Set On You* by George Harrison. Written by Rudolph Clark
2   *Back To Life (However Do You Want Me)* by Soul II Soul featuring Caron Wheeler. Written by Trevor Romeo, Caron Wheeler, Paul Hooper and Simon Law
3   *Good Life* by Inner City. Written by Kevin Saunderson, Shanna Jackson and Roy Holmon
4   *Eye Of The Tiger* by Survivor. Written by Frank Sullivan III and James Peterik

new information, much as you are doing now by reading this book.

Choose to engage in practical tasks such as cooking, gardening and sewing rather than endlessly outsourcing them. By dedicating time to these activities, you'll reap the mindful pleasure, enjoyment and satisfaction that comes from relying on the labour of your own hands. This hands-on approach will help you become an active player (rather than a passive payer) in your life. Learning to cook from scratch nurtures creativity and adaptability while supporting a healthier, more balanced diet that favours nutrition while minimising highly processed foods. You can reduce food miles and bolster the local economy by choosing seasonal, locally sourced ingredients. Krush were confident that you will further "dig this"[1] because the positive and therapeutic effects multiply if you have the time, space and inclination to become an *Ace Of Spades*[2] and start growing some of your fruit and vegetables. Growing some of your food will help to feed your sense of self-reliance and improve your mood (by reducing stress), increase your self-esteem and improve your fitness. Being literally in touch with the ground[3] allows you to connect (or reconnect) hands-on with the living, natural world of soil and plants, exposing you to beneficial soil bacteria that can enhance the diversity of your microbiome. In a beautiful symbiosis, the garden tends to the gardener as much as the gardener tends to the garden.

Quality sleep, a healthy diet and regular exercise are the central pillars vital for *Body and Soul*.[4] They lie at the heart of the quest to help your body care naturally for itself from within. Similarly, feeding your brain with a mind diet rich in a variety of wholesome mental nutrition and stimulation (including social connections) enhances cognitive function. Although your brain accounts for

1   *House Arrest* by Krush. Written by Cassius Campbell, Mark Gamble and Ruth Oram
2   *Ace Of Spades* by Motorhead. Written by Edward Clarke, Ian Kilmister and Philip Taylor
3   *Hungry Like The Wolf* by Duran Duran. Written by Simon Le Bon, Nigel Taylor, Roger Taylor, Andrew Taylor and Nicholas Bates
4   *Body And Soul* by Mai Tai. Written by Eric van Tijn and Jochem Fluitsma

only about 2% of your body weight, it snaffles about 20–25% of the energy derived from your calorie intake. Working together as one,[1] the inseparable body-brain double act can help you achieve what you once thought impossible, giving your confidence and self-reliance a tremendous boost.

As you acquire experience, fortitude and mental robustness over the years, you may also develop some economic resilience by whittling down the unnecessary indulgences of consumerism to focus on your core needs. What you must continue to own are your thoughts and actions. Like most desirable traits, self-reliance requires conscious effort, especially in a world (particularly online) that – sound advice aside – loves to dictate how you should think and what you should do and own.

In our modern interconnected societies, we have come to rely on one another[2] through established infrastructure instead of living like isolated *Islands In The Stream*. However, to paraphrase John F. Kennedy, rather than asking what society can do for you, consider what you can do for yourself and then for society. Much like the safety message in a pre-flight safety briefing, you must prioritise your well-being before assisting others.

SHAKESPEARE

William Shakespeare (1564-1616) was the nation's favourite bard. 'Bard' originally described an ancient Celtic order of roaming minstrel poets who sang (usually to the accompaniment of a small harp) their self-composed verses celebrating battle victories, recounting traditional or historical events, or imparting knowledge of laws or religious teachings in what was a predominantly preliterate age. To leave a lasting impression on their audiences, these musical poet-singers crafted their verses to be as engaging and entertain-

1   *Come Into My Life* by Joyce Sims. Written by Joyce Sims
2   *Islands In The Stream* by Kenny Rogers and Dolly Parton. Written by Barry Gibb, Robin Gibb and Maurice Gibb

ing as possible, much like contemporary lyricists. Such traditions helped transmit cultural knowledge from person to person and from generation to generation, which serves as a reminder of the origin of the word 'lyrics' from Chapter I.

"To steal his sweet and honeyed sentences" (*Henry V*). Shakespeare's mastery of capturing and articulating profound insights into the human condition has inspired many modern-day lyricists to borrow his phrases (knowingly or not) to give voice to their thoughts and feelings. Tina Turner informs us that there's a fitting phrase;[1] a few examples of phrases first recorded by the Bard that fit seamlessly into top 10 lyrics from the 1980s include: "Love is blind" from *The Merchant Of Venice* used in *Islands In The Stream*[2] (Shakespeare freely borrowed, embellished and retold the work of others, including Aristotle, Seneca, Plutarch and the Bible; here he's borrowed the image of the blindfolded Cupid, the Roman God of Love); "Forever and a day" from *As You Like It* used in *Baby I Don't Care*;[3] "Break the ice" from *The Taming Of The Shrew* used in *Ashes To Ashes*;[4] "Lend me your ears" from *Julius Caesar* used in *With A Little Help From My Friends*;[5] "Salad days" from *Antony and Cleopatra* used in *Gold*;[6] and "Pure as the driven snow" from both *The Winter's Tale* and *Hamlet* used in *White Lines (Don't Don't Do It)*,[7] where 'snow' serves as contemporary slang for cocaine.

Hamlet is often hailed as the greatest play ever written. The complex Prince of Denmark, a man more inclined towards introspective thought than deed, has inspired extensive analysis. Sigmund Freud drew upon Hamlet to help explain his psychoanalytic theories

1   *What's Love Got To Do With It* by Tina Turner. Written by Terence Britten and Graham Lyle
2   *Islands In The Stream* by Kenny Rogers and Dolly Parton. Written by Barry Gibb, Robin Gibb and Maurice Gibb
3   *Baby I Don't Care* by Transvision Vamp. Written by Nicholas Sayer
4   *Ashes To Ashes* by David Bowie. Written by David Jones
5   *With A Little Help From My Friends* by Wet Wet Wet. Written by John Lennon and Paul McCartney
6   *Gold* by Spandau Ballet. Written by Gary Kemp
7   *White Lines (Don't Don't Do It)* by Grandmaster & Melle Mel. Written by Melvin Glover and Sylvia Vanterpool

about human nature, as our thoughts can be used to assess the unconscious mind. Hamlet's pensive line, "There is nothing either good or bad, but thinking makes it so", possibly inspired by Seneca's idea that we are not so much affected by actual events but by our opinions of them, provides an ideal starting point to evaluate your own experiences.

Inspired by Hamlet's famous soliloquy on existential angst, B.A. Robertson's song *To Be Or Not To Be*[1] claims Shakespeare is his sort of guy, though it's hard to imagine what the Bard guy would have thought of rhyming "Barbadian" with "Stratford-on-Avion". Lo! is that the sound of someone spinning in their grave in the Holy Trinity Church in Stratford-upon-Avon, the one whose epitaph famously warns, "And curst be he that moves my bones"?

While contemplating interred bones, heavy metal band Iron Maiden's hit *The Evil That Men Do*[2] draws its titular inspiration from *Julius Caesar*: "The evil that men do lives after them; the good is oft interred with their bones."

Frankie Goes To Hollywood sang of a world that was their oyster.[3] Molluscs transform an annoying and worthless irritant into a beautiful and precious pearl. Shakespeare was the first to write about the idiomatic *Pearl In The Shell*[4] in his play *The Merry Wives Of Windsor*.

To believe or not to believe?[5] is the question Pebbles ponders about her boyfriend's honesty and integrity, and many scholarly minds have pondered in relation to Shakespeare's religious leanings. Along with his Elizabethan audiences, Shakespeare was well acquainted with the Bible, though he was wily enough to avoid creating difficulties for himself through overtly biblical borrowings

1   *To Be Or Not To Be* by B.A. Robertson. Written by Brian Robertson
2   *The Evil That Men Do* by Iron Maiden. Written by Adrian Smith, Paul Dickinson and Stephen Harris
3   *Welcome To The Pleasuredome* by Frankie Goes To Hollywood. Written by Peter Gill, William Johnson, Mark O'Toole and Brian Nash
4   *Pearl In The Shell* by Howard Jones. Written by John Jones
5   *Girlfriend* by Pebbles. Written by Kenneth Edmonds and Antonio Reid

during religiously intolerant times. As with so much in his life, Shakespeare's religious beliefs remain an enigma.

Music be the food of love,[1] according to Musical Youth, borrowing from the opening scene from *Twelfth Night*: "If music be the food of love, play on." Love, with over 2,000 mentions in Shakespeare's canon, plays a central starring role, much like it does for lyrists in the 1980s. In a line sung not by Shakespears Sister but by another 1980s 'Shaky' icon, Shakin' Stevens, we encounter forbidden love,[2] the central predicament of Shakespeare's most influential play on the lyrics of the 1980s: *Romeo and Juliet*.[3] As the world's best-known pre-internet teenage couple, star-crossed lovers Romeo and Juliet embody the emotional fervour of romance. Many songs from the 1980s drop Romeo's name, including those by Madonna,[4] Ottawan[5] and Sinitta.[6]

Not everyone delights in old drama; Transvision Vamp, for one, asked to be excused from the plays.[7] As an alternative to the plays, Shakespeare's 154 sonnets (14-line poems) offer a shorter, more accessible gateway into his artistry. Many of Shakespeare's most intense sonnets relate – and are still relatable – to the complexities of love and relationships; most are addressed to a man. 'Sonnet', from the Latin *sonus* (sound), fittingly reflects these 'little sounds' of intense emotion.

Sonnet advice? A line that glistens from *Gold*[8] tells of a play for today. Shakespeare, born over 450 years ago, based many of his plays on universally relevant themes, such as love, power, ambition

1 *Pass The Dutchie* by Musical Youth. Written by Leroy Sibbles and Donat Mittoo
2 *Cry Just A Little Bit* by Shakin' Stevens. Written by Robert Heatlie
3 *Romeo And Juliet* by Dire Straits. Written by Mark Knopfler
4 *Cherish* by Madonna. Written by Madonna Ciccone and Patrick Leonard
5 *Hands Up (Give Me Your Heart)* by Ottawan. Written by Daniel Bangalter and Jean Kluger
6 *Toy Boy* by Sinitta. Written by Michael Stock, Matthew Aitken and Peter Waterman
7 *Baby I Don't Care* by Transvision Vamp. Written by Nicholas Sayer
8 *Gold* by Spandau Ballet. Written by Gary Kemp

and jealousy. His unique command and playfulness[1] with "words, words, words" (*Hamlet*) established him as the most quoted author in the OED (with approximately 33,300 quotations, with nearly 1,600 from *Hamlet* alone). His words and influence permeate and endure in modern pop songs, the individual dramas of lived-in lives and the wider theatre of the world around us. *The Complete Works Of Shakespeare* is issued as standard reading material (alongside the story-packed Bible, providing a brace of books covering the whole human condition) to the hypothetical castaways on Radio 4's long-running (since 1942) *Desert Island Discs*, along with their choice of eight pieces of music. Although some critics dismiss pop music as generating more heat than light (another nod to *Hamlet*), it remains a favoured genre because castaways can pack so much relatable and pleasurable content into a small space. The discs that matter most are not those that make the castaway sound cultured but rather those that imbue and reinforce cherished memories (the MEAMs from *The Intro*) – happy or poignant – connecting the castaway to other people, moments and places that infuse their life with significance. *Forget Me Nots*.[2] You should consider creating a playlist that stimulates cherished personal memories as insurance in the event you find yourself cast away on an island of neurodegeneration.

Great themes and words, along with the emotions, thoughts and feelings they conjure (whether from pop songs, plays or poems), are timeless, universal and malleable. Engaging with Shakespeare's work enables us to block out humanity's incessant noise to hear only the finest expressions of thought and speech.

"The rest is silence" (*Hamlet*).

SOCIETY

Margaret Thatcher's infamous sound bite, "There's no such thing as

1   *Now Those Days Are Gone* by Bucks Fizz. Written by Andrew Hill and Nichola Martin
2   *Forget Me Nots* by Patrice Rushen. Written by Fred Washington Jr, Patrice Rushen and Theresa McFaddin

society," made during an interview with *Women's Own* magazine in October 1987, has become a part of political folklore. Thatcher's view was that too many individuals looked to the government and society to solve their problems instead of first looking to themselves (self-reliance and personal responsibility). Thatcher did not advocate for a government or society absolved from responsibility but emphasised that entitlement comes with obligations: society is not about take with no give.[1]

Amid the blithe hedonism and rampant excess of the 1980s, especially within large cities, a few songs attempted to tackle socio-political and socio-economic issues. In *Ghost Town*,[2] The Specials painted a haunting picture of urban decay and social unrest, depicting the youth as abandoned by governments. The Fine Young Cannibals highlighted the struggles and stark disparities of big city life – such as hunger (cannibalism aside) and homelessness.[3] Thatcher's brand of popular neoliberal capitalism, particularly the sale of one-and-a-quarter million council houses to former tenants, led to higher levels of both home ownership and homelessness. To nudge the growing homelessness problem out of public sight and to hide the failure to tackle its root cause, the destitute found themselves constantly moved on.[4] The Treasury raised billions of pounds from one-off sales of such national assets, while society's poorest (the bottom 10% of earners) experienced a real-term decline in income. Society's citizens, whether willing or not, increasingly became cogs in consumer-driven capitalism, free to make choices in a competitive market despite the cost to social cohesion.

Prince questioned society's seemingly absurd spending priorities, noting that while people were dying for want of money to buy food, governments sent men to the Moon[5] (although, at that time,

1   (I Just) Died In Your Arms by Cutting Crew. Written by Nicholas Eede
2   Ghost Town by The Specials. Written by Jeremy Dammers
3   Johnny Come Home by Fine Young Cannibals. Written by David Steele and Roland Gift
4   Another Day In Paradise by Phil Collins. Written by Philip Collins
5   Sign O' The Times by Prince. Written by Prince Nelson

a decade-and-a-half had passed since the last human-landing lunar visit). Aside from crewed missions promoting national prestige rather than science (robots are far better suited for space exploration), this is not a societal choice between meeting basic human needs or pursuing grand ventures exploring space, but instead involves budgeting to accommodate both: we need to provide for inner space (social welfare) and outer space (exploration) to fulfil their respective roles in advanced, modern societies.

Sound advice? Paul Weller's typically forthright conclusion in *Going Underground*[1] was to reject everything society had to offer. Regardless of whether you want or like what's on offer, everyone forms a constituent link in a societal chain. Through social osmosis, we all absorb ideas, values and expectations – along with their accompanying pressures – relating to education, love, marriage, parenthood, divorce, money, work and beyond. Pop music possesses a rare power to reflect societal themes and offer a fleeting respite from societal realities.

Shout To The Top.[2] Politics shapes society, and, in turn, society helps individuals organise their lives to meet and manage struggles and challenges while re-engineering difficulties to prevent recurrence. Aristotle believed that political structures (including laws) played a role in organising society, creating an environment conducive to virtuous living. To effect positive change in modern societies – whether promoting recycling or addressing loneliness among an ageing population – voters in a democracy must communicate their needs and priorities to their elected political representatives at both national and local levels. Investing in infrastructure, community spaces and public services, such as libraries, sports halls and day-care centres, fosters societal integration, not separation. Thoughtful urban planning can align thinking with policy to encourage healthier lifestyles, create safe and secure neighbourhoods and protect the environment. Integrating themes remains essential to both sound advice and effective political thinking.

1 *Going Underground* by The Jam. Written by John Weller
2 *Shout To The Top* by The Style Council. Written by John Weller

Inequality of opportunity within society increases the potential for friction, harm, insecurity and unhappiness. Nordic nations such as Norway and Sweden show that reducing disparities creates higher-functioning societies. Effective checks and balances are needed to maintain societal equilibrium, serve common ideals (such as justice) and meet basic, everyday needs, such as ensuring clean air through environmental protection policies.

UB40 sang of the right to freedom and to build their society.[1] How societies are built and developed, including providing safety nets to catch and help those in greatest need – overlooking no one[2] – is a mark of advancement and commitment to its citizens, especially where policies provide permanent solutions over temporary fixes. In a cover of another song, socially conscious UB40 sang of helping those in need and showing them the way.[3]

Both society and music provide individuals with a way to connect to something greater than themselves. In an attempt to simplify, compartmentalise and tidy a fragmented and complicated world, societies often employ the shorthand convenience of labels, especially in fields such as medicine and mental health. However, zealously labelling life's natural but mild ups and downs as mental health issues risks diluting the significance of, and diverting limited resources from, more serious psychological conditions, or it may overlook cases that require urgent care.

Other societal labels, such as 'elderly', 'unemployed' or 'disabled', affect mindsets, often in a negative way that reinforces differences and limitations. Even if you refuse to apply a single surface label to yourself, others may struggle to resist the temptation of easy, stereotypical categorisation. It can be hard to remove a label that others stick on you. However, as the pop song themes remind us, each person's multi-stranded identity is far too deep, complex and

1   *Sing Our Own Song* by UB40. Written by Alistair Campbell, Robin Camp-bell, Brian Travers, Earl Falconer, Norman Hassan and Michael Virtue
2   *Harvest For The World* by The Christians. Written by Ernest Isley, O'Kelly Isley Jr, Ronald Isley, Rudolph Isley, Marvin Isley and Christopher Jasper
3   *I Think It's Going To Rain Today* by UB40. Written by Randall Newman

layered to be reduced to a single, specific label that conveys any meaningful accuracy. If society repeatedly tries to assign a label to you, don't allow any restricted expectations inherent in that stereotype to pigeonhole or limit who you are or what you can achieve.

TIME

To understand the enigmatic nature of time, you'll need to take your time.[1] Time matters, which is why it is the most frequently used noun in the English language. The Greeks personified time through three mythological entities: Cronos, Kairos and Aion. Cronos, infamous for castrating his father with a flint sickle, marrying his sister and devouring his newborn children in a graphic demonstration of how time consumes all, represents familiar, linear clock time. Kairos represents that fleeting, opportune moment for decision or action when everything seems possible. Aion embodies unbounded, eternal time that has given rise to the word 'aeon'. Unsurprisingly, tyrannical Cronos, who was to suffer the same dethroning by his (uneaten) son, Zeus, finds no home in the theme on *Parental Advice*, but his name does live on through the chronicles of history in time-related words such as 'chronology', 'chronic' and 'synchronous'. With its intangible but constant presence, temporal thinking has captivated our attention for quite some time.

Jumping to 1988 (for this is our time),[2] Stephen Hawking published *A Brief History Of Time*, a book exploring cosmology from the Big Bang (the day without a yesterday and widely accepted as the beginning of time, the echoey ripples of which we can still detect on our planetary shores as cosmic background radiation some 13.75 billion years later: *Echo Beach*[3] – far away in time). This

1   *Stand Up For Your Love Rights* by Yazz. Written by Yasmin Evans and Timothy Parry

2   *All The Things She Said* by Simple Minds. Written by James Kerr, Charles Burchill and Michael MacNeil

3   *Echo Beach* by Martha And The Muffins. Written by Mark Gane

tome on time – a hard read[1] – spent considerable time on *The Times* bestseller list, but how many of the reported 25 million buyers took the time to read the book remains a timeless mystery. Those readers reaching Chapter Nine, *The Arrow of Time*, could reflect on how time's river 'flows' irreversibly, irresistibly and entropically in one ageing direction – forward into the future: time's moving on.[2]

Carl Sagan, the esteemed astronomer and presenter of the landmark 1980 television documentary *Cosmos*, wrote the introduction to Hawking's book. The word cosmos, derived from the Greek for 'order', emerged from its antonym, chaos, the void at the dawn of time.

One quirk of space-time makes astronomy akin to visual archaeology. The immense distances in space create the opportunity to see (but not travel) back in time by using a simple technique that doesn't require a sophisticated sci-fi time machine: on a clear, moonless night, stare into space.[3] Although nothing known can travel faster than light, the speed and distance that light can travel in a year are finite. Light can travel no more than 5.88 trillion miles a year (a light year), meaning that, for example, when you look at the Andromeda galaxy (our nearest galactic neighbour and visible to the naked eye), it's like looking back about 2.5 million years, the point in time at which the light that lands on your retina began its long journey. This light has been travelling for ten times longer than modern humans – *Homo sapiens* – have been walking our planet. Access to the most powerful space telescope would allow you to see back to the 'cosmic dawn', when stars – and subsequently the heavier elements – first formed, about 250 to 350 million years after the Big Bang (which was neither big nor involved a bang). Back on Earth, the passage of enough time can oversee the splitting and drifting of continents,

---

1   *Straight Up* by Paula Abdul. Written by Elliot Wolff
2   *Southern Freeez* by Freeez. Written by Peter Maas, John Rocca and Andrew Stennett
3   *I Guess That's Why They Call It The Blues* by Elton John. Written by Elton John, Bernard Taupin and David Johnstone

the creation and crumbling of the mightiest of mountains[1] and the evolution and extinction of entire species, including our own.

If you could turn back time,[2] you would violate the immutable universal laws of physics, alter causality and be able to remember the future, which would be something weird.[3] Fortunately, you can't change the laws of physics.[4] What properties did lyricists, aside from theoretical physicists like Queen's Brian May, bestow upon the concept of time? Common lyrical observations are that time (when having fun) flies,[5] is fleeting,[6] passes by[7] and rolls on.[8] In a pop career, it can take many years to become an overnight success.

What time is it?[9] Thanks to the power of the Babylonians[10] and their adoption of the easily divisible base-60 numerical system, we measure chronological time in hours, minutes and seconds. If you're trying to tell the time on a watch without hands,[11] you are either in a dream or looking at the face of a watch that tells absolute time, because absolute time doesn't exist. As Einstein determined, time is relative.

When you hear a ticking clock,[12] that's time as it slips away.[13] Your perception of time slips and shifts, as indeed does the actual passage of time, depending on the proximity of a significant source

1   *The Unforgettable Fire* by U2. Written by Paul Hewson, Adam Clayton, David Evans and Laurence Mullen Jr
2   *If I Could Turn Back Time* by Cher. Written by Diane Warren
3   *Ghostbusters* by Ray Parker Jr. Written by Ray Parker Jr
4   *Star Trekkin'* by The Firm. Written by John O'Connor, Grahame Lister and Rory Kehoe
5   *Can't Stay Away From You* by Gloria Estefan and Miami Sound Machine. Written by Gloria Estefan
6   *The Time Warp* by Damian. Written by Richard Smith
7   *Cherish* by Kool And The Gang. Written by Robert Bell, Ronald Bell, James Bonnefond, George Brown, Charles Smith, James Taylor and Curtis Williams
8   *Hold On Tight* by Electric Light Orchestra. Written by Jeffrey Lynne
9   *Doctorin' The House* by Coldcut featuring Yazz and The Plastic Population. Written by Yasmin Evans, Jonathan More and Matthew Cohn
10 *Orinoco Flow* by Enya. Written by Enya Brennan and Roma Ryan
11 *These Dreams* by Heart. Written by Bernard Taupin and Martin Page
12 *Alone* by Heart. Written by William Steinberg and Thomas Kelly
13 *We Close Our Eyes* by Go West. Written by Peter Cox and Richard Drummie

of gravity (so, theoretically, your brain ages at a slightly different rate from your feet because your feet are marginally closer to the centre of the Earth) and how fast the observer is moving relative to something else – as explained by Einstein's theory of special relativity. Although time may appear to be an equal possession, it is, in fact, relative to the person measuring it. Assuming that not even the busiest person's speed of life reaches close to the speed of light (despite what they may claim), and you do not have access to super-accurate caesium-based atomic clocks, why is there a change in the perceived rate of the passage of time from the sensation in the time-abundant young that time stands still[1] to the feeling that, as we accumulate years, time rushes onwards?[2] The proportional theory – more descriptive than explanatory – suggests that each day lived represents an ever-smaller fraction of one's overall lifespan, creating a feeling that time accelerates with age. Another theory (again not from Einstein) posits that the multiple new stimuli encountered by the young (up until the age of about 25) are processed and laid down rapidly as new memories in a process that causes the perception of time to slow down because the more new memories the brain forms, the more time the brain assumes has elapsed. In more experienced middle-aged brains, the production of new memories slows as there are fewer new markers in time as life becomes settled and more routine. This reduction in new stimuli, coupled with a decrease in the brain's processing efficiency, results in a slower rate of memory formation, thereby causing the perception that time speeds up with age.

A red alert and panic bells[3] may trigger another time-warping phenomenon when your body generates an adrenaline rush during a life-or-death moment that causes your internal clock to accelerate, allowing you to take in potentially vital extra information, making the external world appear as though you're watching it in

1   *Straight Up* by Paula Abdul. Written by Elliot Wolff
2   *Absolute Beginners* by The Jam. Written by John Weller
3   *99 Red Balloons* by Nena. Written by Jörn-Uwe Fahrenkrog-Petersen, Carlo Karges and Kevin McAlea

slow motion.[1] This time dilation phenomenon seems to alter time perception even after the rush has passed[2] because strong fear-based memories have evolved a different neural architecture that embeds them deeper into your mind than everyday memories. The disorientating fog that descends with depression or addiction can similarly disrupt internal clocks, as can being immersed, engrossed and engaged passionately in the 'flow' of pleasurable activities, the supersaturation of which can absorb you with such intensity that you lose track of time and your days feel as if they roar on by.[3] Conversely, watching the clock as its hands crawl slowly around[4] can make it feel like time drags on.[5] Without any stimulating activity to engross and engage your mind and lay down new memories, you'll perceive time as passing slowly by,[6] weighing heavily upon you as if in punishment for your boredom.

What do the lyrics say about love and the perception of time? Van Halen suggest that only time will tell if love stands the test of time.[7] Hmm, again, not Einstein. Is there anything more insightful? How about the notion that every minute spent with the right person is the right time,[8] or, for a *Woman In Love*,[9] time has no measure? If you find in love that there is a measure of time, and you're being metered and sold to by the hour,[10] then it's not love but commerce. Love is a priceless gift, freely given.

1   *Take My Breath Away* by Berlin. Written by Thomas Whitlock and Giovanni Moroder
2   *Gold* by Spandau Ballet. Written by Gary Kemp
3   *Don't Talk To Me About Love* by Altered Images. Written by Clare Grogan, John McElhone, Stephen Lironi and Anthony McDaid
4   *When We Were Young* by Bucks Fizz. Written by Warren Harry
5   *Anything For You* by Gloria Estefan and Miami Sound Machine. Written by Gloria Estefan
6   *9 To 5* by Sheena Easton. Written by Florrie Palmer
7   *Why Can't This Be Love* by Van Halen. Edward Van Halen, Michael Anthony, Samuel Hagar and Alex Van Halen
8   *Something's Gotten Hold Of My Heart* by Marc Almond featuring Gene Pitney. Written by Frederick Cook and Roger Greenaway
9   *Woman In Love* by Barbra Streisand. Written by Barry Gibb and Robin Gibb
10 *Welcome To The Pleasuredome* by Frankie Goes To Hollywood. Written by Peter Gill, William Johnson, Mark O'Toole and Brian Nash

Does love change over time, making us strangers or allowing us to grow closer?[1] And what of time's healing power should love's touch turn cold?[2] (It's said to just take time.)[3] Grinding grief for the loss of love or of a loved one creates a situation where our emotions overshadow everything else, warping or suspending our perception of time. Allowing the flow of time to create distance between such events is one way to help dissipate grief's paralysing venom.

Whether you wish, hour to hour, to chase time,[4] pass time[5] or even challenge time's doors,[6] what other time-related advice do the songs impart? Without hesitating, Elton John suggests living for every second,[7] while Kool And The Gang urges that every moment be cherished.[8]

As a finite resource, time is precious[9] and what is precious holds value. While you cannot buy time,[10] you can spend it wisely and consciously, just as you do with your money. When you *Find The Time*,[11] allocate some for pleasure,[12] including scheduling those activities and techniques that help bring happiness and fulfilment. Shakespeare's eponymous *Richard II* lamented how wasted time was wasting him, a sentiment echoed by Whitesnake's sound decision

1   *In Your Eyes* by George Benson. Written by Daniel Hill IV and Michael Masser
2   *(Feels Like) Heaven* by Fiction Factory. Written by Edward Jordan and Kevin Patterson
3   *Hard Habit To Break* by Chicago. Written by Steven Kipner and John Lewis Parker
4   *What Have I Done To Deserve This?* by Pet Shop Boys with Dusty Springfield. Written by Neil Tennant, Christopher Lowe and Alta Willis
5   *Bedsitter* by Soft Cell. Written by David Ball and Peter Almond
6   *A Kind Of Magic* by Queen. Written by Roger Taylor
7   *I Guess That's Why They Call It The Blues* by Elton John. Written by Elton John, Bernard Taupin and David Johnstone
8   *Cherish* by Kool And The Gang. Written by Robert Bell, Ronald Bell, James Bonnefond, George Brown, Charles Smith, James Taylor and Curtis Williams
9   *Time (Clock Of The Heart)* by Culture Club. Written by Roy Hay, Michael Craig, Jonathan Moss and George O'Dowd
10 *Somewhere In My Heart* by Aztec Camera. Written by Roddy Frame
11 *Find The Time* by Five Star. Written by Paul Gurvitz and Nicholas Trevisick
12 *Wings Of A Dove* by Madness. Written by Graham McPherson and Cathal Smyth

not to waste any more time.[1] Morrissey questioned why he should spare his valuable time for those indifferent to whether he's dead or alive.[2] Why indeed.

Alison Moyet chose not to forget.[3] Dendrochronology, the science of investigating events over time by studying annual growth ring patterns in ancient trees, allows us to identify significant moments from the archive of change collected and stored within the natural world, such as notably cold winters or major volcanic eruptions. Music, too, can get you to wear its ring.[4] Because music unconsciously embeds itself into the yearly growth rings of your life, it can serve as a gateway to access other associated memories, emotions and feelings laid down at the same time in individuals whose usual path to recollection or cognitive focus is no longer available, those memories having been washed away by the devastating flood of neurodegeneration.

Sound advice? It's only a matter of time[5] before time sweeps all away. Music, however, can often feel beyond the realm of time, able to withstand the current. Time may confine the best pop songs – their themes and the sound advice captured within – to about four minutes (coincidentally for those living in the 1980s, the same time as the warning siren of a nuclear attack), yet these songs possess a timeless quality, remaining as relevant in the 1980s as they will be in the 2080s; music will endure to give us strength.[6] During those powerful but fleeting minutes when you feel lifted out of yourself

1   *Here I Go Again* by Whitesnake. Written by David Coverdale and Bernard Marsden
2   *Heaven Knows I'm Miserable Now* by The Smiths. Written by Steven Morrissey and John Maher
3   *Is This Love?* by Alison Moyet. Written by Genevieve Moyet and David Stewart
4   *I Got You Babe* by UB40 and Chrissie Hynde. Written by Salvatore Bono
5   *When You Come Back To Me* by Jason Donovan. Written by Michael Stock, Matthew Aitken and Peter Waterman
6   *It's Alright* by Pet Shop Boys. Written by Paris Robinson, Marshall Jefferson and Duane Pelt

or are so engrossed, immersed and *Lost In Music*,[1] little else seems to matter. Away from the welcomed brevity of pop songs (where it's necessary to make a long story short),[2] innovative Russian composer Igor Stravinsky pithily noted that too much music finishes long after it has ended. With music, what matters is not the time it takes to listen to it but how long you spend thinking about what you have heard after it has finished playing.

John Parr sang about how everyone has their time.[3] Marcus Aurelius, Roman Emperor between 161 and 180, wrote in his philosophical collection of reflections on life, *Meditations*, how brief – almost momentary – is the time allocated to you when set against the vast expanse of time. Aurelius was right. Each of us has but *One Moment In Time*,[4] which, with care and good fortune, is a lifespan of about 80 years, set against a universe that has existed for about 13.75 billion years (a mighty long time)[5] and will continue for billions more years after your candle has burnt to nought. Unless you believe in an eternal soul that, through reincarnation, has and will always exist, all you have is this moment,[6] a fleeting instance that comes with a guaranteed expiry. As your time burns down, you will reach the point where what is left becomes less than what has already gone, increasing the value of what remains. You should welcome this remorseless inevitability as it will enable you to prioritise effectively, help you create special moments and allow you to spend what time you have left on what matters most to you – typically the relationships with those you love and care for. Philosopher Martin Heidegger noted that awareness of our finite existence imbues life with authenticity and purpose.

1   *Lost In Music* by Sister Sledge. Written by Nile Rodgers and Bernard Edwards
2   *I Can Make You Feel Good* by Shalamar. Written by Howard Hewett, Renwick Jackson and William Shelby
3   *St. Elmo's Fire (Man In Motion)* by John Parr. Written by David Foster and John Parr
4   *One Moment In Time* by Whitney Houston. Written by Albert Hammond and John Bettis
5   *Let's Go Crazy* by Prince And The Revolution. Written by Prince Nelson
6   *Need You Tonight* by INXS. Written by Andrew Farriss and Michael Hutchence

So little time,[1] remarked the brothers Gibb. Everyone has obligations that voraciously devour their time. Work is particularly ravenous. If the clock rules your life or you are unable to fathom out what consumes your time, some simple time recording can help to show you what bites deepest into time's jugular, sucking out your energy. With this information, you can reallocate your time and reset your priorities around goals that will help you do more of what you do best. Aim to structure your time to play to your strengths (which may entail ceasing the urge to do everything by saying no to some time-consuming tasks that overload you or by reserving allotted times during your day for specific activities, such as checking emails). Additionally, try arranging your day to work in harmony with your chronotype – the natural rhythm of your alertness and energy, which varies depending on the time of day, light exposure, age and genetic components. (Having a mix of morning/evening/neutral chronotypes may have evolved as a survival strategy, ensuring that someone is always awake and alert to warn of danger.) Tackling your most difficult and important tasks during your optimal working time – when you are most alert – maximises productivity. If you cannot identify your best time, consider tackling your most challenging task first, thinking of it as energising rather than depleting. Effective time management involves striking the right balance.

Don't Waste My Time[2] is sound advice: wasted time is lost, never to be re-found, recovered or refunded. It's good to prioritise time on the people you love and the activities you love doing, but be wary of letting time bleed out on pointless and unnecessary tasks or succumbing to ennui. When you think you've time to kill,[3] you're the one who's dying. When you're killing time recovering from alcohol over-consumption, you are, in effect, dying twice. A particularly potent hangover – one where you wake

1   *You Win Again* by Bee Gees. Written by Barry Gibb, Robin Gibb and Maurice Gibb
2   *Don't Waste My Time* by Paul Hardcastle. Written by Paul Hardcastle
3   *The Riddle* by Nik Kershaw. Written by Nicholas Kershaw

up to find your mouth is dry[1] – can feel like a double dose of death.

If you regularly say to yourself, "There's no time for . . . ",[2] you may be externalising your decisions by suggesting that something else is more important, that other priorities consume your attention, often at the behest of others. If this is the case, be honest with yourself and accept that your priorities deserve to drive your day (although this may be challenging as an employee with contractual obligations). Phil Collins sang of the need to find time.[3] Ideally, find or make time for your most pleasurable and nourishing activities, including setting aside regular time for your mental and physical health, exercising, reading, family and friends, enjoying music, sleeping, and simply being yourself.

Shakin' Stevens failed to find time to fix his shingles.[4] It's always wiser to find or make time to maintain and improve the roof over your physical and mental health rather than be forced to find time when the burdensome leaks of illness drop in unexpectedly upon you. Making time for preventative health measures is an investment in your future by helping to build personal resilience.

As Kylie Minogue noted, it's easy to think you have for ever, and all you need is time.[5] However you choose to use it, you're perpetually running out of time[6] because you can only spend it, not deposit it for later use. Try to make every second count[7] by maximising each day because how you spend your ever-diminishing lifetime will help determine who you are and who you will become.

1   *Fantastic Day* by Haircut One Hundred. Written by Nicholas Heyward
2   *Eighth Day* by Hazel O'Connor. Written by Hazel O'Connor
3   *You Can't Hurry Love* by Phil Collins. Written by Brian Holland, Lamont Dozier and Edward Holland
4   *This Ole House* by Shakin' Stevens. Written by Carl Hamblen
5   *Got To Be Certain* by Kylie Minogue. Written by Michael Stock, Matthew Aitken and Peter Waterman
6   *She Drives My Crazy* by Fine Young Cannibals. Written by Roland Gift and David Steele
7   *Temptation* by Heaven 17. Written by Glenn Gregory, Ian Craig Marsh and Martyn Ware

As Ovid observed, time devours all such that, before you know it, it's the end of time.[1]

TRUTH

Want to know the truth?[2] In theory, pursuing truth to deepen and enrich your understanding of the world seems straightforward and virtuous: all you need do is be true.[3] In reality, however, truth can be more elusive. Illuminating the truth often casts dark shadows where lies may lurk.

Eighth Wonder claimed the only truth is that we are always telling lies.[4] Fun Boy Three considered whether this should come as a surprise.[5] Distinguishing truth from lies is surprisingly tricky because lying is so prevalent – Madonna reckons that a mendacious man can tell a thousand lies[6] – and, in a day, you may hear up to 200 fibs, although this could be one of them. Given so many people freely forgo the truth in everyday life, including crucially to themselves, The Human League suggest you shouldn't be surprised by someone's lies.[7] Our propensity to forfeit truth and start telling *Little Lies*[8] begins – appropriately – when we are little. Among adults, a lack of self-honesty often underlies the manipulation of the truth as people seek to deflect blame and criticism away from themselves and on to others. Shalamar admitted to

1   *Come Back And Stay* by Paul Young. Written by Jack Lee
2   *Infinite Dreams* by Iron Maiden. Written by Stephen Harris
3   *Somewhere In My Heart* by Aztec Camera. Written by Roddy Frame
4   *I'm Not Scared* by Eighth Wonder. Written by Neil Tennant and Christopher Lowe
5   *Our Lips Are Sealed* by Fun Boy Three. Written by Jane Wiedlin and Terence Hall
6   *Live To Tell* by Madonna. Written by Madonna Ciccone and Patrick Leonard
7   *Open Your Heart* by The Human League. Written by Philip Oakey and John Callis
8   *Little Lies* by Fleetwood Mac. Written by Christine McVie and Eduardo Quintela De Mendonca

complaining even when they knew they've only themselves to blame.[1]

Inspired by Shakespeare, Pebbles asks whether to believe or not to believe?[2] The Human League (once again) believe in the truth, despite lying a lot.[3] Truth is fundamental in many belief systems because followers must have complete faith in religious exposition. However, delivering unadulterated truth can have repercussions, so you may instead have to rely on degrees of truthfulness – where the truth may need a touch of "rearranging",[4] at least according to The Human League (what with this band and truth?). The degree of truthfulness varies, depending on the time, place and circumstances: in a courtroom, only the truth, the whole truth and nothing but the truth will suffice, while in informal social interactions, you may be more attuned to others' feelings and therefore use tact and diplomacy rather than risk disharmony or conflict that full disclosure of the raw truth might incite. *Sometimes*,[5] as acknowledged by Erasure, full disclosure can hit as hard as any internal pain, suggesting that the truth may yield little or no comfort.[6]

Openness and transparency establish trust and credibility, strengthen relationships, bolster reputation and enhance understanding. Disregarding the truth, however, can erode that credibility and trust, weaken bonds and foster corrosive feelings of betrayal, mistrust and anger, all of which can damage reputation. Michael Jackson sang that knowing the truth protects you from being hurt,[7] while many songs long to break free from lies,[8] for the truth instead

1   *Dead Giveaway* by Shalamar. Written by Joseph Gallo, Leon Sylvers III and Marquis Dair
2   *Girlfriend* by Pebbles. Written by Kenneth Edmonds and Antonio Reid
3   *Love Action (I Believe In Love)* by The Human League. Written by Philip Oakey and Ian Burden
4   *(Keep Feeling) Fascination* by The Human League. Written by John Callis and Philip Oakey
5   *Sometimes* by Erasure. Written by Vincent Martin and Andrew Bell
6   *Careless Whisper* by George Michael. Written by George Michael and Andrew Ridgeley
7   *Wanna Be Startin' Somethin'* by Michael Jackson. Written by Michael Jackson
8   *I Want To Break Free* by Queen. Written by John Deacon

to be said,[1] however cruel or unkind. The pursuit of truth may be arduous, but choosing to tell the truth requires less cognitive effort than circumlocution (using many words where fewer would suffice in a deliberate attempt to evade or be vague) or spinning over-elaborate yarns that necessitate remembering what you said to whom and when. Trusting that someone is telling you the truth also demands less cognitive effort as it liberates you from exploring and scrutinising all the potential falsehoods that a suspected lie would entail. Cognitively (and sidestepping any moral imperative), the truth sets you free, while lies bind you to a complex narrative.

Just An Illusion?[2] A song may convey the whole truth, a kernel of truth or be entirely fictitious. Some choose to believe the promises they hear in the songs of the past[3] because they want what they hear to be true. And if some promise, advice or reassurance successfully projects an aura of authenticity, you are more likely to believe it. An emphatic John Lennon wanted to tell Yoko Ono over and over again[4] how he felt about her. Repetition, so prevalent in pop song construction because of its rhythmic power and appeal, can straighten a twisted untruth to make it seem credible; this is known as the illusion of truth – where a lie is told so often it can appear to be the truth.[5] The more often you are exposed to the lie, the more normalised the belief becomes: the Associates pleaded with us not to start saying this for fear they would begin believing it.[6] This illusion of truth is how propaganda spreads its pernicious wings. Tears For Fears questioned why we should believe one (usually reductive) headline,[7] while The Jam denounced

1 *True* by Spandau Ballet. Written by Gary Kemp
2 *Just An Illusion* by Imagination. Written by Ashley Ingram, Leslie John, Steven Jolley and Anthony Swain
3 *Here I Go Again* by Whitesnake. Written by David Coverdale and Bernard Marsden
4 *Woman* by John Lennon. Written by John Lennon
5 *Billie Jean* by Michael Jackson. Written by Michael Jackson
6 *Party Fears Two* by Associates. Written by William MacKenzie and Alan Rankine
7 *Everybody Wants To Rule The World* by Tears For Fears. Written by Roland Orzabal, Ian Stanley and Christopher Hughes

the promises of democratically elected leaders that turn to rust.[1]

Sam Brown expressed disbelief that she had been lied to.[2] What characteristics do these skilled manipulators and contaminators of truth possess to make their lies so believable? Often, they are attractive individuals and natural performers who can look you in the eye, generate a sincere smile and speak fluently and confidently (while not sounding overly rehearsed). They can perpetrate the most convincing lies by making you give them the benefit of the doubt. Interestingly, many pop performers from the 1980s closely fit this description.

Sound advice? Yes, it's the truth,[3] provided you are willing to believe what the lyrics tell you. The Style Council wished we could see that there's no truth,[4] which accords with the idea of truth relativism - that truth is not absolute, only subjective relative to your frame of reference. Expanding on philosopher Karl Popper's ideas, you cannot categorically confirm that sound advice is true, but you can accept it as such if it can withstand bombardment from new knowledge and information that could disprove it.

Queen envisioned neither black nor white.[5] Far from always being a chessboard of monochrome, truth and lies often exist as a fusion. For Iron Maiden, the truth was harsh: a lake of fire will burn your soul.[6] Speaking the truth calls for thoughtfulness. Sometimes, a well-intended and harmless truth in a shade of grey - a white lie - may be appropriate to spare someone's feelings (and can be easier to swallow than the truth),[7] to avoid embarrassment or to turn down the heat under that soul-boiling lake of

1 *Going Underground* by The Jam. Written by John Weller
2 *Stop!* by Sam Brown. Written by Bruce Brody, Samantha Brown and Gregg Sutton
3 *(I've Had) The Time Of My Life* by Bill Medley and Jennifer Warnes. Written by Donald Markowitz, Franke Previte and John DeNicola
4 *My Ever Changing Moods* by The Style Council. Written by John Weller
5 *One Vision* by Queen. Written by Brian May, Freddie Mercury, Roger Taylor and John Deacon
6 *Can I Play With Madness* by Iron Maiden. Written by Adrian Smith, Paul Dickinson and Stephen Harris
7 *I'll Fly For You* by Spandau Ballet. Written by Gary Kemp

fire. A white lie may involve consciously reshaping or not fully disclosing specific details to maintain harmony or avert unnecessary conflict. Plato described the decision to distort the truth to protect the recipient's soul (such as where a parent shields their child from a brutal truth) as a 'noble lie'. Most lies are self-serving.

However much you wish a song's narrative to be a version of the truth, it may be far closer to a work of fiction and only loosely based on actual events. A shadowy lie may be thrown in sharp relief when you shine the bright, piercing searchlight of truth on any subject, exposing previously concealed fault lines within that truth. Avoiding the harsh glare of truth can inadvertently render it more incomprehensible.[1]

Lie, lie, lie is what Wet Wet Wet say you do.[2] Lies like to wear layers, dressing themselves in nuance and camouflage, including deceit, denial, delusion, circumvention, omission, suppression and spin. Consequently, when someone tells you a lie, their narrative may lack personal pronouns, refer to others in the third person, employ negative language or adopt an oversimplified structure, all of which ease the extra cognitive burden on the liar's brain. Understandably, it's difficult to reflect nuance in a short pop song, while the bare truth loves to go naked[3] (a concept popularised by Shakespeare's 'naked truth' from *Love's Labour's Lost*; Shakespeare borrowed the idea of *nuda veritas* from the Roman fable about the time when Truth and Falsehood went bathing, and Falsehood, emerging first from the water, dressed in Truth's clothes. In contrast, Truth opted to remain naked rather than wear the clothes of Falsehood). In all honesty,[4] the songs are far from a lost cause on the theme of truth:

---

1   *Lay All Your Love On Me* by ABBA. Written by Göran Andersson and Björn Ulvaeus
2   *Wishing I Was Lucky* by Wet Wet Wet. Written by Graeme Clark, Thomas Cunningham, Neil Mitchell and Mark McLachlan
3   *Go Wild In The Country* by Bow Wow Wow. Written by David Barbarossa, Leigh Gorman, Malcolm McLaren and Matthew Ashman
4   *Take Me To Your Heart* by Rick Astley. Written by Michael Stock, Matthew Aitken and Peter Waterman

as Morrissey says, when it rings true, it's hard not to quote you.[1]

UNITY

Aristotle emphasised that altruistic love was the essence of unity in all things, while for Alison Moyet, unity keeps us from falling apart.[2] While *Anyone Can Fall In Love*,[3] true love is about a commitment to remain united, despite romantic love's propensity to split and splinter. In a social and political context, unity is a way to voice collective needs and establish a shared identity so that life can be made better.[4]

When *We All Stand Together*,[5] we create change. Unity in lyrics and life takes many forms, from a trade union to a romantic union, from choirs singing[6] in praise of religion to the oneness of all.[7] Freddie Mercury dreamt of hope and unity.[8] As Queen's frontman, Mercury achieved greater success than with his solo ventures, illustrating how unity, artistic 'flow' and the dynamic creativity forged within the crucible of a band (but prone to slip into creative tension) can feed off one another to elevate and complement each other's performance so that ultimately they stand stronger together.[9] A unified band must deliver more than the sum of its individuals, or there's little value in remaining together.

1   *The Last Of The Famous International Playboys* by Morrissey. Written by Steven Morrissey and Stephen Street
2   *Love Resurrection* by Alison Moyet. Written by Genevieve Moyet, Steven Jolley and Anthony Swain
3   *Anyone Can Fall In Love* by Anita Dobson and The Simon May Orchestra. Written by Simon May, Leslie Osborne and Donald Blackstone
4   *Holiday* by Madonna. Written by Curtis Hudson and Lisa Stevens
5   *We All Stand Together* by Paul McCartney and The Frog Chorus. Written by Paul McCartney
6   *Like A Prayer* by Madonna. Written by Madonna Ciccone and Patrick Leonard
7   *Happy Birthday* by Stevie Wonder. Written by Stevie Wonder
8   *One Vision* by Queen. Written by Brian May, Freddie Mercury, Roger Taylor and John Deacon
9   *We Are The World* by USA For Africa. Written by Michael Jackson and Lionel Richie

Let's Stay Together.[1] In nature, individuals within a species often instinctively congregate, learning how to live together,[2] as there's safety and strength in numbers, as seen in starling murmurations. In humans, unity transcends survival, offering joy, comfort, support and companionship. However, unity through congregation only becomes effective when all participants are committed to learning and adhering to a shared set of fundamental rules to ensure they give each other what's needed to survive.[3]

Shalamar celebrated being united.[4] The intensity of unity felt amid the tumult of a crowded stadium, cathedral, theatre or concert hall - often described as an invisible 'energy' created by the atmosphere - is palpable and far surpasses the experience of watching the same events at home on television. This intense bonding experience is what makes live music so compelling. Shared laughter[5] is also socially unifying (and contagious, thanks to mirroring). Rhythm - particularly from shamanic and tribal drumming, singing and chanting - can help engender a sense of unity, synchronise movements (including breathing and heart rates) and even induce trance-like states.

Sound advice? All together now,[6] the advice holds up. Unity has power[7] akin to a societal glue capable of transforming the 'I' of the individual to the 'we' of the collective so that we are stronger when

1   *Let's Stay Together* by Tina Turner. Written by Albert Greene
2   *Walking In The Rain* by Modern Romance. Written by David Jaymes and Michael Mullins
3   *Ebony and Ivory* by Paul McCartney and Stevie Wonder. Written by Paul McCartney
4   *A Night To Remember* by Shalamar. Written by Charmaine Sylvers, Dana Meyers and Nidra Beard
5   *Against All Odds (Take A Look At Me Know)* by Phil Collins. Written by Phil Collins
6   *Best Years Of Our Lives* by Modern Romance. Written by David Jaymes
7   *Walls Come Tumbling Down!* by The Style Council. Written by John Weller

united.[1] When unified, we can make it.[2] As one,[3] we can bridge gaps, build relationships, foster understanding and muster the strength to succeed by pooling and harnessing members' unique and diverse talents, skills and expertise as we move toward a common goal. The fractured political opposition during the 1980s (where parties were riven with division and insurrection) and the fleeting lifespans of many pop groups across all decades underscores the difficulty of channelling idealistic aims because of the internal conflicts and power struggles arising when personal ambition, clashing temperaments and inflated egos readily disrupt harmony, creating disunity and fragmentation.

Humans evolved to connect, collaborate and innovate through the realisation that when pulling together[4] we can get somewhere.[5] Cultural knowledge is an especially useful tool because our brains are adept at remembering and emulating processes, behaviours and ideas, especially those passed down through a linear, logical three-act narrative (stories with a clear beginning, middle and end). Unity is essential when pursuing ambitious goals where the objective, by scale or ambition, surpasses what individual endeavour can accomplish alone. Harvesting bountiful yet vulnerable crops, exploring space or constructing cathedrals ('cathedral thinking' is a term used to describe projects with a far-reaching vision that will benefit future generations) all rely on a vast melting pot of skills, talent and experience. By working together, it's possible to build a dream.[6]

Together We Are Beautiful.[7] Some artists who performed at Live Aid in the 1980s exemplified unity by setting aside personal differences (being in a band can sometimes lead to a sense of diminished

1 *If Only I Could* by Sydney Youngblood. Written by Claus Zundel, Michael Staab, Sydney Ford and Ralf Hamm
2 *Blow The House Down* by Living In A Box. Written by Albert Hammond and Marcus Vere
3 *My Love* by Julio Iglesias featuring Stevie Wonder. Written by Stevie Wonder
4 *My Oh My* by Slade. Written by Neville Holder and James Lea
5 *Fast Car* by Tracy Chapman. Written by Tracy Chapman
6 *Nothing's Gonna Stop Us Now* by Starship. Written by Albert Hammond and Diane Warren
7 *Together We Are Beautiful* by Fern Kinney. Written by Ken Leray

individuality and a constraint on personal expression) to unite and raise millions of pounds for famine relief. Unity and solidarity often emerge in response to shared outrage, adversity or exclusion.

In USA For Africa's collective anthem to help alleviate poverty, they called for the world to unite.[1] Artistic unity helps to amplify a message, address a problem and advocate for transformative change. The arc of human history curves relentlessly towards greater unity, which is essential when grappling with pressing global-scale challenges and consequences, such as those stemming from existential climate change. However, as we pursue ever-greater unity, we must remain vigilant against the pitfalls of groupthink, where the hivemind can trample over or suppress individual creative contributions or opinions, particularly those dissenting voices.

The science touched upon to analyse song themes highlights how much of our knowledge accumulates and evolves through continual revision and refinement, often constructed incrementally (usually laboriously) through synergy and collaboration. The meticulous process of observing, waiting and recording is only sporadically punctuated by an Archimedean "eureka!" shaft of revelatory scientific breakthrough or overturning insight, often made by those on a mind-wandering break from complete immersion in their specialist subject. Similarly, individuals can build fulfilling, multifaceted lives with the mutual support, assistance and encouragement of others.

All matter in the universe vibrates. Music, too, is a form of vibration (see *Biology*). While music may not be the foundational element of a unifying theory of everything, it can provide a sense of solidarity that transcends linguistic, cultural and temporal boundaries, making it a potent unifying force in our lives.

WISHES

Wishes are expressions of our desires or hopes that, if fulfilled or

---

1   *We Are The World* by USA For Africa. Written by Michael Jackson and Lionel Richie

realised (however improbable), would bring immediate gratification. Chrissie Hynde's public declaration of her wish became the *Talk Of The Town*.[1] Wishes often indicate and reveal your innermost cravings, those private mental flights of fancy that are unlikely to materialise through planning, effort and action alone. Unlike the determination and perseverance inherent in willpower that can progressively nudge you ever closer to a long-term goal through incremental, well-defined steps, wish fulfilment relies on miraculous external factors to jump directly to attaining that goal. With regular use, willpower develops and strengthens, which is not the case if you spend your life wishing.[2]

"Wish I was somewhere"[3] sang Bryan Ferry. Grammarians remind us that when expressing a hypothetical wish, we should use the subjunctive form: 'I wish I were . . . ' not 'I wish I was . . . '. As for finding grammatical compliance with pop songs, for what wishes are worth, good luck.[4]

With their fantastical nature and detachment from reality, wishes regularly attach themselves to symbols of luck and superstition, such as wishing on a four-leaf clover[5] (the four leaves represent faith, hope, love and luck – how bizarre),[6] on a star, on a dream or on a rainbow.[7] Others *Knock On Wood*[8] for luck or pray their wishes will come true.[9] Kirsty MacColl wished upon two shooting stars, only to discover they were orbiting satellites.[10] She might have fared better

1   *Talk Of The Town* by The Pretenders. Written by Christine Hynde
2   *Wishing (If I Had A Photograph Of You)* by A Flock Of Seagulls. Written by Alister Score, Frank Maudsley, Michael Score and Paul Reynolds
3   *Over You* by Roxy Music. Written by Bryan Ferry and Philip Targett-Adams
4   *A Winter's Tale* by David Essex. Written by Michael Batt and Timothy Rice
5   *Foolish Beat* by Debbie Gibson. Written by Deborah Gibson
6   *The Reflex* by Duran Duran. Written by Simon Le Bon, Nigel Taylor, Roger Taylor, Andrew Taylor and Nicholas Bates
7   *Wishing On A Star* by Fresh 4 featuring Lizz E. Written by Billie Rae Calvin
8   *Knock On Wood/Light My Fire* by Amii Stewart. Written by Eddie Floyd and Stephen Cropper
9   *Peace On Earth/Little Drummer Boy* by David Bowie and Bing Crosby. Written by Ian Fraser, Larry Grossman, Alan Kohan, Harry Simeone, Katherine Davis and Henry Onorati
10 *A New England* by Kirsty MacColl. Written by Stephen Bragg

using a down-to-earth *Wishing Well*,[1] into which people still drop coins in exchange for a making wish; such custom may hark back to the Neolithic practice of offering precious metals and sacrificial objects to life-giving waters. Some people believe so strongly in the power of charms and superstitions that the resulting boost they give to their confidence from these placebos can yield a measurably positive effect on some outcomes.

According to Madonna, the arrival of an *Angel*[2] after she had wished for it could not be a mere coincidence. Only it could (if angels existed). Random outcomes and coincidence, governed by the mathematics of probability, explain those instances where you wish for something to happen, and it subsequently materialises. Marillion suggest we call it synchronicity.[3] The human brain possesses an innate ability to spot synchronicity, patterns and order as it seeks to look for and make associations and connections between what it sees and what it already knows or has previously encountered. Pattern recognition evolved as a survival strategy, allowing all the sensory information you continually gather to predict the probability of an event occurring based on experience. Coincidences (including those seemingly against all odds)[4] inevitably arise, even in our data-drenched modern-day information age, and are subsequently imbued with symbolism, meaning and significance, often interpreted as signals of fate, destiny or divine communication. Rather than concentrating on the rare occasions when a wish coincidentally aligns with reality (explicable by probability), don't forget to acknowledge the countless times when a wish failed to yield any meaningful outcome.

1   *Wishing Well* by Terence Trent D'Arby. Written by Terence Trent Howard and Sean Oliver
2   *Angel* by Madonna. Written by Madonna Ciccone and Stephen Bray
3   *Incommunicado* by Marillion. Written by Derek Dick, Mark Kelly, Ian Mosley, Steven Rothery and Peter Trewavas
4   *Solid* by Ashford & Simpson. Written by Nickolas Ashford and Valerie Simpson

"Your wish is my command"[1] Perhaps the best-known dispenser of wishes is the genie from *Aladdin And The Magic Lamp*. Rubbing this magic lantern, Madonna suggests, will make your dreams come true.[2] For those who prefer fantasy over euphemism, the genie grants three wishes, often centred on the themes found within pop songs: love, happiness, peace, wealth, fame . . . However, when songwriters add a negative twist, wishes can display a darker, more sinister side, such as the wish not to have been born,[3] to sink without a trace[4] or to be wished away.[5]

Sound advice? However much you may wish it were otherwise, the advice fails the soundness test. Endlessly wishing on the stars[6] runs the risk of entanglement in superstition.[7] Practices that funnel the credulous down the mind-narrowing straits of superstition are little more than a legacy stemming from a lack of understanding. Louis Pasteur said that chance favours the prepared mind, so recognise and pay attention to the opportunities that unfold and present themselves to you. This strategy is far more productive than going through life wishing for luck.[8]

The lesson from the tale of Tithonus (see *Ageing*) is that you need to be careful what you wish for, echoed by T'Pau's warning not to wish too hard in case those wishes are fulfilled.[9] In Shakespeare's *Henry IV*, a wish is said to be the father to a thought – you are more likely to believe something if you wish it were so; Texas describe

1   *You To Me Are Everything* (*The Decade Remix 76/86*) by The Real Thing. Written by Christian Gold and Michael Denne
2   *Dear Jessie* by Madonna. Written by Madonna Ciccone and Patrick Leonard
3   *Live It Up* by Mental As Anything. Written by Andrew Smith
4   *Grey Day* by Madness. Written by Michael Barson
5   *Wouldn't It Be Good* by Nik Kershaw. Written by Nicholas Kershaw
6   *Causing A Commotion* by Madonna. Written by Madonna Ciccone and Stephen Bray
7   *Waiting For A Star To Fall* by Boy Meets Girl. Written by George Merrill and Shannon Rubicam
8   *Wishing I Was Lucky* by Wet Wet Wet. Written by Graeme Clark, Thomas Cunningham, Neil Mitchell and Mark McLachlan
9   *China In Your Hand* by T'Pau. Written by Carol Decker and Ronald Rogers

this as what you see is what you wish it to be.[1] All such thoughts are *Wishful Thinking*[2] – where hope swamps reason and reality.

Central to the sound advice within this book is the concept of volition – the power to make, choose or determine your own decisions to help transform your life. The Latin root of 'volition' is *volo*, meaning 'I wish'. If your wishes help clarify your priorities and drive your motivation, you'll need to strike the happy medium between the uplifting joy and happiness that comes from visualising hope and the fulfilment of those wishes against the perpetual disappointment and disillusionment of holding unrealistic expectations that rely on luck or fate to achieve them. Remember to appreciate what you already have rather than lose gratitude to the endless anticipation of wishing for a better future.

Elton John's sensible advice was to neither wish your life away nor expect it to last for ever.[3]

WORDS

Billy Ocean reflected on how a thousand words may be insufficient to express oneself,[4] which explains why the average adult native English speaker has a vocabulary approximately 20 to 35 times larger than this. Yet, within an average pop song, a thousand words are sufficient to convey an image of how others think, feel and act. And what's a pop song devoid of words? An instrumental. And how many instrumentals topped the charts in the 1980s? None. (Songs featuring only words – a cappella – fared slightly better.) Words are thus an indispensable constituent of pop songs and a convenient and effective way to uplift, motivate and empower you

1   *I Don't Want A Lover* by Texas. Written by John McElhone and Sharleen Spiteri
2   *Wishful Thinking* by China Crisis. Written by Gary Daly and Edmund Lundon
3   *I Guess That's Why They Call It The Blues* by Elton John. Written by Elton John, Bernard Taupin and David Johnstone
4   *Suddenly* by Billy Ocean. Written by Keith Alexander and Leslie Charles

to take incremental steps that collectively can transform your life. As Elton John suggested, if the words of a song make sense, they should form a part of your life.[1]

"In the beginning was the Word"[2] (John 1:1), and words are powerful. Soft Cell's words were dynamite,[3] while other sources of words of wisdom[4] enable the stone-cold dead[5] to communicate with the still-warm living, even offering advice on what you should do.[6] Words express, evoke, convey and interlink thoughts, feelings and ideas from one person to another, often eliciting potent emotional responses. Great orators – philosophers, priests, politicians and poets – have long relied on the power of words to move minds and uphold their positions.[7]

If Midge Ure were a poet (or a pyromaniac), he would express love through burning words.[8] If music paints the broad-brush language of emotion, the lyrics add the finer-detailed language of love.[9] Many, however, will be familiar with the awkwardness of being caught tongue-tied[10] in a mouth trap,[11] unable to get the words out,[12] and everything you intended to say ends up trapped within circuitry.[13] At other times, there may be thoughts and feelings you cannot express[14] – the ineffable – that elude the capture of words. Ineffability is most apparent during the delicate days of adolescence when burgeoning new feelings often outgrow the concurrent vocabulary with which

1   *Sad Songs (Say So Much)* by Elton John. Written by Elton John and Bernard Taupin
2   *Eighth Day* by Hazel O'Connor. Written by Hazel O'Connor
3   *Torch* by Soft Cell. Written by Peter Almond and David Ball
4   *Let It Be* by Ferry Aid. Written by John Lennon and Paul McCartney
5   *Town Called Malice* by The Jam. Written by John Weller
6   *Wordy Rappinghood* by Tom Tom Club. Written by Martina Weymouth, Charlton Frantz and Steven Stanley
7   *De Do Do Do, De Da Da Da* by The Police. Written by Gordon Sumner
8   *If I Was* by Midge Ure. Written by Daniel Mitchell and James Ure
9   *The Best* by Tina Turner. Written by Michael Chapman and Holly Erlanger
10 *Who's That Girl?* by Eurythmics. Written by Ann Lennox and David Stewart
11 *Stutter Rap (No Sleep Til Bedtime)* by Morris Minor And The Majors. Written by Anthony Hawksworth
12 *Everywhere* by Fleetwood Mac. Written by Christine Perfect
13 *Automatic* by Pointer Sisters. Written by Brock Walsh and Mark Goldenberg
14 *Rip It Up* by Orange Juice. Written by Edwyn Collins

to articulate them; this is the prime time and space for pop music to step in to help the young find their voice.

Words may be taken as token by someone bound tightly in sorrow.[1] For others in the cold grip of grief, carefully chosen words can mean so much,[2] bringing warmth and serenity,[3] sometimes immediately, sometimes later upon quiet reflection.

Given that what you say matters,[4] what if words fail to come easily to you?[5] As rapping demonstrates, the more words you know, the better your flow; the more you read, the more words you'll know to fulfil your needs. *Stairway To Heaven*[6] warns us to proceed with caution, as some words have double meanings. Two meanings? If only it were that simple. Some words – contronyms (or 'Janus' words – see the theme on *New*) – have two opposite meanings dependent on context (such as 'sanction'), while other words – homonyms – have different (often multiple) meanings that also depend upon context, despite sharing the same spelling and sound, such as 'rock' and 'roll', 'band' and 'set'. The second edition of the OED, published in 1989, lists 430 shades of meaning for the word 'set', requiring 60,000 words of explanation. The long, convoluted history of word usage shows how words can go up, down, forward and backward.[7]

Although highly versatile, there's a limit to what words can say.[8] Some emotions remain inaccessible to words, evading capture by the most skilled and articulate lyricists, novelists and playwrights, adolescent or otherwise. What should you do when words are not

1 *Do You Really Want To Hurt Me* by Culture Club. Written by Roy Hay, George O'Dowd, Michael Craig and Jonathan Moss
2 *Divine Emotions* by Narada Michael Walden. Written by Michael Walden and Jeffrey Walden
3 *All I Ask Of You* by Cliff Richard and Sarah Brightman. Written by Andrew Lloyd Webber, Charles Hart and Richard Stilgoe
4 *The War Song* by Culture Club. Written by Roy Hay, George O'Dowd, Michael Craig and Jonathan Moss
5 *Words* by F.R. David. Written by Eli Fitoussi
6 *Stairway To Heaven* by Far Corporation. Written by James Page and Robert Plant
7 *Train Of Thought* by A-ha. Written by Pål Waaktaar Gamst
8 *A Letter To You* by Shakin' Stevens. Written by Dennis Linde

enough,[1] and you cannot express how you feel?[2] When someone's void of sadness is too deep to fill or the crushing weight of grief too heavy to lift, there may be no need for words at all, least of all the temptation to administer a heavy dose[3] that, despite good intentions, may hinder not help. Where a feeling is so strong as to be impervious to words, or there are no words to describe a sensation,[4] simply let time and space go about their silent and restorative work. View such silence in challenging moments as a time, space and opportunity for meaningful thoughts to arise and organise rather than a socially awkward gap to fill. When supporting others, being present to simply sit or stand alongside someone in silent companionship – recognising that 'silent' is an anagram of 'listen' – can be more value and comfort than risking verbal trespass into the private realm of grief: at such times, you can say more by speaking less.

In its various forms, silence can communicate beyond loss and grief; Madness pondered how, without words, so much can be said.[5] When you share a deep connection with someone, you can see and hear the silent words spoken by their eyes;[6] you need only physical proximity and eye contact for a powerful expression of understanding to pass between you. Madonna agrees, telling us no words are needed when eye to eye.[7] The Pet Shop Boys noted that words mean little when someone special is lying beside you.[8] 'Lying' is a homonym.

In contrast, employees, especially those forced to endure endless meetings endemic within large enterprises (where words are taken

1   *Hold Me Now* by Johnny Logan. Written by Seán Sherrard
2   *I Need Love* by LL Cool J. Written by James Smith, Bobby Ervin, Darryl Pierce and Dwayne Simon
3   *Manchild* by Neneh Cherry. Written by Neneh Karlsson, Robert del Naja and Cameron McVey
4   *First Time* by Robin Beck. Written by Gavin Spencer, Thomas Anthony and Terence Boyle
5   *It Must Be Love* by Madness. Written by Claudius Siffre
6   *Blow The House Down* by Living In A Box. Written by Albert Hammond and Marcus Vere
7   *Crazy For You* by Madonna. Written by John Bettis and Jonathan Lind
8   *Rent* by Pet Shop Boys. Written by Neil Tennant and Christopher Lowe

in minutes and time is taken in hours), will recognise situations where everyone's talking, but no meaningful words are said.[1] If the talking continues, they're still unlikely to get anywhere.[2] When no more words are left[3] – or at least no valuable or insightful ones – it's time for *facta, non verba*, for actions to speak louder than words[4] and a chance to show what you say when words are not enough.[5] For example, you may agree with every word of sound advice within this book, but those words only hold value if you use them as a catalyst to inspire concurrent action, without which nothing changes.

If you can find the words to say what you want to say,[6] are words dangerous? Potentially, yes. Burning words[7] can harm, hurt and humiliate. Even ignoring intentionally inflammatory language, it is easy to use the heat of words to forge swords capable of inflicting injury ranging from superficial scratches to the deep and gruesome gashes of verbal violence. When wielded carelessly or thoughtlessly (as opposed to deliberately with precision), weaponised words can wound,[8] and speaking daggers (from *Hamlet*) can both inflict immediate pain and open an entry route for infection. Chris de Burgh reckoned that only a word or two could break a heart,[9] while Sinitta acknowledged that even little things she says can cause hurt.[10] A single word – a shibboleth – may betray you, while a *Four Letter Word*[11]

1   *Nobody Told Me* by John Lennon. Written by John Lennon
2   *They Don't Know* by Tracey Ullman. Written by Kirsty MacColl
3   *Can't Take My Eyes Off You* by Boys Town Gang. Written by Robert Crewe Jr and Robert Gaudio
4   *Say It Again* by Jermaine Stewart. Written by Walter Sigler and Carol Davis
5   *Prove Your Love* by Taylor Dayne. Written by Seth Swirsky and Arnold Roman
6   *Breakout* by Swing Out Sister. Written by Andrew Connell, Corinne Drewery and Martin Jackson
7   *Do You Really Want To Hurt Me* by Culture Club. Written by Roy Hay, George O'Dowd, Michael Craig and Jonathan Moss
8   *If I Could Turn Back Time* by Cher. Written by Diane Warren
9   *Missing You* by Chris de Burgh. Written by Christopher Davison
10   *Right Back Where We Started From* by Sinitta. Written by Vincent Edwards and Pierre Tubbs
11   *Four Letter Word* by Kim Wilde. Written by Reginald Smith and Richard Smith

may deeply offend some listeners.

Sound advice? In a word, yes. You can shape your world through the unconscious use of words to form your thoughts and the more deliberate selection of the words in your speech. Words make humans human, while language (along with its 5,500-year-old spin-off, writing) is arguably the most significant achievement in human civilisation (and may explain the dominance of our species), allowing us to share knowledge, ideas and skills across generations. Philosopher Ludwig Wittgenstein argued that how we use words to experience and categorise the world means that the limits and structure of language dictate the limits of our perception of reality: you can only describe what you have the words to describe. It can, for example, be challenging to verbalise the multiple hues of a single colour that your eye can easily discern. Music, too, can help free you from the constraints of words.

They might only be words,[1] but if you mean what you say[2] and recognise that words shape your world and define your life, then what you say and how you say it is of fundamental importance and requires responsible use. For example, the words you use to describe ageing or disability (both regularly weighed down with negative connotations and messaging) will affect your perspective, including how you think about and approach your old age. Similarly, words deployed in the 'war' against certain illnesses are frequently encased in aggressively masculine and militaristic metaphors, such as the 'fight', 'conquering' and either 'winning' or 'losing' the 'battle'. In another example, consider the relative weight and differing implications you attach to 'child-free' over 'childless'. There remains a worthwhile incentive to employ positive, carefully chosen words, as the exposure effect of some words can influence behaviour, so, for example, talking about old age may affect your posture. When you incorporate 'inner' into 'winner' and select appropriate words for any internal self-talk, you can positively affect your ability to interpret and deal with any challenge.

1   *One More Night* by Phil Collins. Written by Philip Collins
2   *Heart* by Pet Shop Boys. Written by Neil Tennant and Christopher Lowe

Because words are influential (seldom are they neutral, and even when they are, that neutrality conveys a message), it's important to define words and concepts that are meaningful to you. For example, many obsess over pursuing and attaining happiness without knowing whether they ever achieve it. They may miss their target because concepts such as happiness are difficult to measure objectively, but primarily because they have not defined accurately what 'happiness' means to them on their terms (for some, happiness may involve complete relaxation and doing nothing, while for others it's about being highly stimulated). The same applies to words such as 'success',[1] 'health' and 'wealth'. Once you've added your unique flavour requirements to these terms, you'll have a clearer perspective on how to frame and pursue your goals. If you struggle to define a goal positively, consider using their negative equivalents (failure, ill-health, poverty . . .) as a source of motivation.

In *Clouds Across The Moon*, the intergalactic operator urges the cosmic callers to be as brief as possible.[2] There's no room for prolixity (the pouring forth of superfluous words) within intergalactic telephone calls, pop songs or your life's script. (A couple of notable exceptions here are the words invented by Lionel Richie for the bridge in *All Night Long (All Night)*[3] fashioned to both sound African and fit the available music, and practically the whole of *The Riddle*,[4] claimed by Nik Kershaw to be lyrical gibberish created to successfully dovetail with the tune, showing that even a dose of *Double Dutch*[5] can sometimes make sense.) The constraints inherent in a pop song compel the lyricist to distil their silky words[6] and

1   *Sign Of The Times* by The Belle Stars. Written by Clare Hirst, Jennie Matthias, Judy Parsons, Lesley Shone, Miranda Joyce, Sarah-Jane Owen and Stella Barker
2   *Clouds Across The Moon* by RAH Band. Written by Richard Hewson
3   *All Night Long (All Night)* by Lionel Richie. Written by Lionel Richie
4   *The Riddle* by Nik Kershaw. Written by Nicholas Kershaw
5   *Double Dutch* by Malcolm McLaren. Written by Malcolm McLaren and Trevor Horn
6   *Ain't Nothin' Goin' On But The Rent* by Gwen Guthrie. Written by Gwendolyn Guthrie

thoughts to land with clarity, effectiveness and a dash of passion. In the meantime, the message from music speaks a universal cross-cultural international language of emotion that transcends words, requiring neither a passport nor a translator; when words end, music begins.

WORK

Many full-time working lives follow a monotonous, exhausting pattern: insufficient sleep, a fraught commute, long and hassle-filled days, a fraught commute home, insufficient sleep. Rinse and repeat for 40 years or even more, should life expectancy and retirement age continue to ratchet upwards. If this or a similar pattern has become the routine[1] of the only adult life you know,[2] it's remarkable you make it through your days.[3] Such a repetitious, unrewarding and unhealthy existence arises when the long hours you dedicate to work inadvertently take centre stage to become the dominant (or only) theme in your life. Fiddler's Dram could make themselves feel ill just by thinking about work at the mill.[4] But surely work and working practices in the 1980s were so vastly different from today that the lyrics are as obsolete as the mill's machinery or the bygone days of heavy industry, given that the work has moved away and the factories largely disappeared?[5] By the 1980s, manufacturers had outsourced much of the laborious eight-days-a-week[6] means of production to the world's cheaper labour regions.

For city-centre commuters, the songs from the 1980s tunnel their

1 *She's Got Claws* by Gary Numan. Written by Gary Webb
2 *Wishing I Was Lucky* by Wet Wet Wet. Written by Graeme Clark, Thomas Cunningham, Neil Mitchell and Mark McLachlan
3 *Love Will Save The Day* by Whitney Houston. Written by Antoinette Colandero
4 *Day Trip To Bangor (Didn't We Have A Lovely Time)* by Fiddler's Dram. Written by Deborah Cook
5 *The Circus* by Erasure. Written by Vincent Martin and Andrew Bell
6 *Let's Go All The Way* by Sly Fox. Written by Gary Cooper

attention upon one mode of transport: the (early) train[1] (often late). Commuting by rail should be straightforward, were it not for the delays, cancellations, chronic overcrowding and expense, all of which generate a great deal of strain when taking the train,[2] derailing the working day before it's even begun, all with the grim prospect of a repeat return performance. Resigning themselves to this daily exertion[3] as part of their hollowed-out lives, it's understandable why commuters seem jaded and joyless. Unsurprisingly, a correlation exists between the length of your sedentary commute and many negative aspects of physical and psychological health, from elevated blood pressure to chronic, time-bomb-ticking stress.

Rockwell's protagonist considered himself average, leading an average life, working 9 to 5, albeit at a cost.[4] Office doors may have replaced factory gates, but what happens, 9 To 5,[5] when it is just another day at work?[6] Ennui, too often. Martha And The Muffins describe filling their days with boring and monotonous work as an office clerk,[7] prompting the question: what's it all for?[8] One reason why people remain tethered to a working life that isn't working for them is simple: they work to survive,[9] clinging to the financial security that comes with a regular income – even if only a pittance[10] where they're left holding handfuls of nothing,[11] scant gain for enduring excessive pain[12] – from a world of

1 *Manic Monday* by The Bangles. Written by Prince Nelson
2 *Fantastic Day* by Haircut One Hundred. Written by Nicholas Heyward
3 *Stop!* by Sam Brown. Written by Bruce Brody, Samantha Brown and Gregg Sutton
4 *Somebody's Watching Me* by Rockwell. Written by Kennedy Gordy
5 *9 To 5* by Sheena Easton. Written by Florrie Palmer
6 *Train Of Thought* by A-ha. Written by Pål Waaktaar Gamst
7 *Echo Beach* by Martha And The Muffins. Written by Mark Gane
8 *Footloose* by Kenny Loggins. Written by Kenneth Loggins and Dean Pitchford
9 *You Take Me Up* by Thompson Twins. Written by Thomas Bailey, Alannah Currie and Joseph Leeway
10 *That's Livin' Alright* by Joe Fagin. Written by David Mackay and Ken Ashby
11 *All Cried Out* by Alison Moyet. Written by Genevieve Moyet, Steven Jolley and Anthony Swain
12 *Labour Of Love* by Hue And Cry. Written by Gregory Kane and Patrick Kane

work offering limited social benefit, little meaning or any sense of accomplishment.

This all sounds desperately uninspiring. At least beleaguered workers can rely on - and deserve the support, respect and attention of - management to help them make the best of their long and hard-working days. Well, not so, according to The Jam, as endless worker/management friction leads them to conclude that there must be more than this to life.[1] Perhaps instead, after a long and illustrious career, you can reflect with pride upon your working legacy. However, the Specials suggested that those working within the Rat Race[2] know they're wasting their time. Big Country assigned a figure to the unavailing toil[3] of sweat and tears that fails to leave a trace: 50 years.[4]

Sound advice? The negative sentiment expressed in work-related songs is striking: for many, the relentless struggle and drudgery of working life does not work. Work needs a thorough appraisal (although not all essential workplace qualities can be measured, monitored and managed through blunt, rigid and time-consuming box-ticking performance indicators; for example, it is hard to bottle the intangible essence of pop song creativity).

The Wham Rap! (Enjoy What You Do)[5] succinctly captured much about the essence of work in the 1980s: working 9 to 5 could leave you feeling barely alive, yet still conscious enough to hear the sound of countless fellow commuters switching off for work. The song's chorus reflects its title, asking whether people enjoy what they do and, if not, advises them to end their working life before their working life ends them. Research indicates that in the 1980s - and still today - too few engage fully with their work (the switching-off

1   Just Who Is The 5 O'Clock Hero by The Jam. Written by John Weller
2   Rat Race by The Specials. Written by Roderick Byers
3   Love Resurrection by Alison Moyet. Written by Genevieve Moyet, Steven Jolley and Anthony Swain
4   Wonderland by Big Country. Written by William Adamson, Mark Brzezicki, Anthony Butler and Bruce Watson
5   Wham Rap! (Enjoy What You Do) by Wham! Written by George Michael and Andrew Ridgeley

noted by Wham!) and, in some strange quarters,[1] one in four employees actively disengage from their employment, choosing to work in a state of resentment, not contentment. Despite a reduction in harmful emissions from heavy industry, many workplaces retain a dangerously toxic atmosphere.

The lyrical expression 'nine to five' is often shorthand for tediously unfulfilling work undertaken solely for a means-to-an-end pay packet and the eagerly anticipated weekend. Meanwhile, many long-hour professionals can only dream of working as little as a five-day, 35-hour week, as the intense demands of their looming deadlines, excessive workloads and professional responsibilities can make it feel more like a 35-hour day. The outcome is a *Dead Giveaway*:[2] stress and sleep deprivation. Heavy hearts often accompany heavy eyelids, especially within corporate cultures where everything is deemed urgent in the belief that urgency creates efficiency but where endless, frenetic busyness has become confused and conflated with productivity. Please hurry.[3] Okay, various UK productivity data (output divided by the hours worked) suggest that output levels remain stubbornly stagnant while busyness levels increase. Always in a rush,[4] where nothing slows you down,[5] the endless to-do list tasks of busyness are worn by some as a badge of honour and status, despite being the antithesis of savouring the moment, reflective thoughtfulness and living for the day;[6] sometimes the joy is in being, not doing. Socrates warned of the barrenness of busy lives. For those suffering work-related stress and pressure, busyness – especially the mundane or manufactured type – can turn every hour into a time-compressed,

---

1   *The War Song* by Culture Club. Written by Roy Hay, George O'Dowd, Michael Craig and Jonathan Moss
2   *Dead Giveaway* by Shalamar. Written by Joseph Gallo, Leon Sylvers III and Marquis Dair
3   *Come Back And Stay* by Paul Young. Written by Jack Lee
4   *Rock 'N' Roll* by Status Quo. Written by Francis Rossi and Bernard Frost
5   *Our House* by Madness. Written by Cathal Smyth and Christopher Foreman
6   *Burning Bridges (On And Off And On Again)* by Status Quo. Written by Francis Rossi and Andrew Bown

heated rush[1] that runs the risk of becoming so bloated and swollen that, at its splitting point, it can overwhelm and stress all those who encounter its noxiousness. The resulting physical and mental burnout means the annual UK loss of working days attributable to stress and exhaustion runs into the millions. Excessive busyness in the ceaseless race to a deadline also results in workers making avoidable, costly and reputationally damaging mistakes. Being too busy with pressing but meaningless activities to enjoy the richness of life – especially family life and engaging with your passions – is a common regret that the long-since retired articulate when reflecting on their working lives and one which you should listen to and learn from. Where possible, slow down and deepen your focus on what matters and what you want to do rather than rushing to complete a never-ending list of tasks you think need doing. Reducing the pace of life may allow you to savour and enjoy the spice of life.[2]

In the early 1980s, *karoshi* was *Big In Japan*,[3] a phenomenon illustrating the deadly consequences of overwork and job-related exhaustion. The lesson here is that if you do not look out for, listen to and acknowledge bodily warning signals (such as perpetual exhaustion etched onto faces)[4] that tell you to slow down, nature will do this for you, often without your consent, sometimes permanently.

Heaven 17 suggested that we cannot continue living this way.[5] Why do people live like this?[6] Is it to satisfy a desire to be a power glutton[7] – the thrill of a hit from inhaling your ego while on a power trip – or does it conceal deeper insecurities? Some undoubtedly

1   *Slow Hand* by Pointer Sisters. Written by John Bettis and Michael Clark
2   *Let's Groove* by Earth, Wind & Fire. Written by Maurice White, Wanda Vaughn and Wayne Vaughn
3   *Big In Japan* by Alphaville. Written by Bernhard Gößling, Frank Sorgatz and Hartwig Schierbaum
4   *Mad World* by Tears For Fears. Written by Roland Orzabal
5   *Temptation* by Heaven 17. Written by Glenn Gregory, Ian Craig Marsh and Martyn Ware
6   *Keep On Movin'* by Soul II Soul featuring Caron Wheeler. Written by Trevor Romeo
7   *I Won't Let The Sun Go Down On Me* by Nik Kershaw. Written by Nicholas Kershaw

revel in and lust after the allure of power, authority, prestige and the material trappings that accompany high pay and commercial success. However, our culture too readily defines the whole person only by their work, turning it into the centrepiece of their identity. Coupling identity with work can bring the dual dangers of an inflated sense of entitlement and indispensability and, should they lose their 'prestigious' position, a collapse in the pillars of identity, dignity, purpose and meaning. Some even subsume their identity from their corporate employers, making the end of that association particularly challenging.

For workers lower down the power hierarchy, the focus is often on the struggle to make a living, not a life. A lack of autonomy can make workers feel frustrated, despondent, overmanaged, overworked and undervalued. Why stay? Many feel *Trapped*[1] by their circumstances, by in-work poverty or by the debt their salary allows them to incur, especially to cover high rent or a mortgage for accommodation in which they do little but spend time trying to sleep on HP beds.[2] Additionally, they feel unable to leave to achieve because of the constraints of the specialised nature of their work. Such workers often have little job security, explaining why they comply rather than complain, even in the face of clear exploitation, to avoid running the risk of losing their job: they dare not *Rock The Boat*.[3]

Some are hardwired to do as others do.[4] As a result, they sleepwalk straight from university into full-time corporate careers, often with little thought (but considerable debt) about why they should conform to fit into a system that they know will deliver an uneven trade-off on their work/life balance sheet. When you let others dictate and define your career path – where you follow the conventional, well-trodden route into the world of work, especially when tracing the trajectory

1   *Trapped* by Colonel Abrams. Written by Donald Abrams and Marston Freeman
2   *Young Guns (Go For It)* by Wham! Written by George Michael
3   *Rock The Boat* by Forrest. Written by Waldo Holmes
4   *Big Apple* by Kajagoogoo. Written by Steven Askew, Nicholas Beggs, Stuart Neale and Jeremy Strode

of the traditional professions where familial obligations and expectations loom large – the result may be safe, secure and predictable, but could leave you feeling as unfulfilled, full of regret and trapped as those without the benefit or advantage of professional qualifications. The Kids From Fame sang of the only life they've known without being able to call it their own.[1] In Shakespeare's *Hamlet*, Polonius offers his son a snippet of advice above all others: "To thine own self be true." Your life, especially your working life, should not revolve around fulfilling others' expectations or performing a role from a script that is not your own. Instead, be courageous and start living a life written by you, for you and on your terms.

Some work for the fun of it.[2] For a fortunate few, such as dramatist and composer Noel Coward, work is more fun than fun, furnishing their life with meaning, purpose, enjoyment and financial security. In these cases, it's not work[3] but a vocation, a *Labour Of Love*,[4] where the calling is the passion and the work a mission, making it feel like anything but real work. For those who struggle to find their calling, what counts is not the type of work you do but the spirit in which you do it.

Bros had other things that they wanted to do.[5] If you want your work to be more aligned with your life, you'll need to fit your work around that life rather than shoehorn your life around the constant needs of your work. To start, visualise your ideal working life; get your *Senses Working Overtime*[6] (the sight, sound, smell and feel) to corral and create a picture with as much vivid detail as possible. Visualisation is a way to see what you thought was unachievable as achievable. This exercise will allow you to set objectives, clarify your priorities and help you decide and focus on what steps you need to

1   *Starmaker* by The Kids From Fame. Written by Bruce Roberts and Carole Bayer
2   *Everything She Wants* by Wham! Written by George Michael
3   *Modern Love* by David Bowie. Written by David Jones
4   *Labour Of Love* by Hue And Cry. Written by Gregory Kane and Patrick Kane
5   *Drop The Boy* by Bros. Written by Nicholas Graham and Thomas Watkins
6   *Senses Working Overtime* by XTC. Written by Andrew Partridge

take or adjustments you need to make to enjoy and be fulfilled by the work that interests you the most.

What if you already have it all but still feel unsatisfied?[1] If you've achieved all the traditional trappings of a successful career but still don't feel like your life is a success, redefine what, to you, success means. In pursuit of high achievement, you may have blunted the very edge of those qualities that contributed to your initial success. Redefine the terms that describe your role, ensuring they are positive and motivating. Remember to attach the meaning of success to your whole life, not just your working life.

Whatever job you do and at whatever level, you are more likely to find your labour valuable and worthwhile (having purpose and meaning) if you can align your unique and natural skills, strengths and beliefs with your work. This alignment applies more directly to work that involves helping others. Contributing to others' happiness benefits those you serve and will make you feel better about yourself. (The reverse is also true: you won't feel better about yourself by engaging in behaviour that makes others feel worse.) Aptitude and attitude together sing a powerful duet.

One notable change in working practice since the 1980s is the rise of mobile technology, complete with promises of freedom and flexibility. Alas, though, some confusion has infiltrated the roles in this technologically manacled *Master And Servant*[2] relationship, blurring the boundaries between work and home and making you endlessly reachable, on-call *All Day And All Of The Night*,[3] relentlessly shadowed by the blue hue of screen light. 'Full-time' has intensified and encroached to become 'all-time'. To counteract this permanent 'on' mode, which can make you socially absent even when you are physically present, try giving 100% to your work when working, but then detach the distracting and cognitively costly umbilical

1   *My One Temptation* by Mica Paris. Written by Michael Leeson, Stephen Waters and Peter Vale
2   *Master And Servant* by Depeche Mode. Written by Martin Gore
3   *All Day And All Of The Night* by The Stranglers. Written by Raymond Davies

cord of technology so that you can focus on your personal life. Some work-related issues and problems resolve themselves without your constant input and oversight. When away from your work, you should be just that, rather than preparing and waiting to start the next round of work. While working, try taking regular breaks between concentrated bursts of activity across the day; breaks are essential, not indulgent, and allow you to recharge, refocus, boost creativity and reduce fatigue (and thus the likelihood of making mistakes). Outside work, rest, be it in the evenings, at weekends or during holidays, should be total and complete. Returning to work feeling refreshed will feed back positively via enhanced performance and productivity in both your work and your broader life.

Another change from the 1980s is in the structure of careers. The familiar rigid, well-defined, predictable and linear career ladder has given way to greater flexibility and more emphasis on creating a more individual career matrix. The cost of this extra flexibility is greater career precariousness.

Sister Sledge felt alive after quitting their 9 to 5,[1] but you must carefully evaluate your options before deciding to move on. Quitting work is easier sung than done, so take time to think it through carefully[2] before executing your plan. If you can find the courage and strength[3] to say, "I *Quit*",[4] ensure that it's part of a rational, considered strategy rather than an impetuous act that you might come to regret as the bills inexorably roll in. If changing your work is a step too far, explore ways to reimagine and re-engineer how you do your current work to make it more meaningful and engaging. When you can incorporate your innate talents and personal values into your work, you are more likely to find joy in that work, making you happier and, by extension, healthier and more productive. Whatever your path, your work will occupy a significant proportion of your

1   *Lost In Music* by Sister Sledge. Written by Nile Rodgers and Bernard Edwards
2   *I Beg Your Pardon* by Kon Kan. Written by Barry Harris and Joseph Souter
3   *Babe* by Styx. Written by Dennis DeYoung
4   *I Quit* by Bros. Written by Nicholas Graham and Thomas Watkins

lifetime, so it is worthwhile to learn to love – or at least try to like by taking some pride in – what you do. Try to make your work an ally rather than an adversary with which you need to battle endlessly.

WORRY

Wouldn't It Be Good, reflected Nik Kershaw, to live free from any cares?[1] If the prospect of living without a care[2] would bring you sleepless nights and worried days,[3] you're more a worrier than a warrior. Worry is that tight knot of anxiety, unease or uncertainty formed when ordinary thoughts stagnate or fixate and circulate on real or imagined troubles or difficulties to the point where they start turning toxic. The accumulation of corrosive toxins inflicts harm and alters the course from standard 'linear' thinking (think-resolve-move on) by twisting thoughts into endlessly churning circles that perpetuate in ever-tightening, tail-chasing,[4] loops. The Thompson Twins observed that you won't get far if you move in circles.[5] Worry caught in circles[6] that spins around your head[7] neither solves the problem nor permits progress.

Worry can also act like a thought microscope, mentally magnifying small triggers (often rooted in deep-seated but exaggerated or irrational fears) that subsequently appear much larger and more dramatic than they objectively are. These powerful and enlarged images sear onto the worrier's retina so that the same worry overlays and casts a spectral shadow over everything else the viewer sees. Chronic worrying, especially when compounded by other stressors like drugs or alcohol, is pernicious because, cumulatively, it becomes

1   *Wouldn't It Be Good* by Nik Kershaw. Written by Nicholas Kershaw
2   *The Wanderer* by Status Quo. Written by Ernest Maresca
3   *I Won't Run Away* by Alvin Stardust. Written by John Williams
4   *Could Have Told You So* by Halo James. Written by Raymond St. John
5   *You Take Me Up* by Thompson Twins. Written by Thomas Bailey, Alannah Currie and Joseph Leeway
6   *Time After Time* by Cyndi Lauper. Written by Cynthia Lauper and Robert Hyman
7   *Your Love Is King* by Sade. Written by Helen Adu and Stuart Matthewman

mentally paralysing and exhausting (prompting Kate Bush to advise an over-worried Peter Gabriel to rest his head)[1] and physically taxing, manifesting as debilitating symptoms such as muscular tension (when you're already tense,[2] the last thing you need is another pain in the neck),[3] compromised immunity, disturbed or stolen sleep (from problems that are deep),[4] fatigue, irritability and digestive issues. The substantial cognitive burden of excessive worry can allow caustic anxiety to seep into and corrode every aspect of your life.

According to the *Bad Boys*[5] of Wham!, we cannot help but worry. Hardwired within our brains, worry serves as a survival mechanism honed by generations who came before,[6] enabling us to navigate a world of challenges and hazards using the better-safe-than-sorry[7] principle. This mechanism may explain why worry is so widespread and anxiety is the most common mental disorder. Protective and productive, heritable worry allowed our rational ancestors to identify any warning signals and potential threats and then take appropriate – usually evasive – action, such as running from danger.[8] The experience and acceptance of some degree of stress are thus natural components of living a full life. A life devoid of stress is unlikely to stretch and challenge you. However, when your focus becomes over-focus, when worry spreads from what matters to what doesn't, it can infuse once-manageable stress levels with exaggerated intrusive thoughts that distort and transform your worry into more poisonous anxiety, leaving you feeling overwhelmed. Irrational thinking

1   *Don't Give Up* by Peter Gabriel and Kate Bush. Written by Peter Gabriel
2   *Patience* by Guns N' Roses. Written by Steven Adler, Michael McKagan, Jeffrey Isbell, William Rose and Saul Hudson
3   *I Quit* by Bros. Written by Nicholas Graham and Thomas Watkins
4   *Love Will Save The Day* by Whitney Houston. Written by Antoinette Colandero
5   *Bad Boys* by Wham! Written by George Michael
6   *Blue Monday* by New Order. Written by Gillian Gilbert, Peter Hook, Stephen Morris and Bernard Sumner
7   *Take On Me* by A-ha. Written by Magne Furuholmen, Morten Harket and Pål Waaktaar Gamst
8   *Goodbye Stranger* by Pepsi & Shirlie. Written by Iris Folwell, Tambi Fernando and Wayne Brown

patterns can then quickly spiral out of control. For example, if you worry about something and nothing catastrophic happens, you might falsely assume that your fretting prevented disaster, allowing worry to gnaw at you perpetually. Instead of letting worry strain your brain,[1] try bending your brain[2] by forcing it to retrain.

When you feel the pressure[3] from worry descend upon you, take a moment to reflect on the strategies and techniques that could help lighten this dead weight from your ever-worrying mind[4] as a way to retrain thinking patterns so that they become more constructive. The most direct lyrical advice to support this comes from the a cappella song *Don't Worry, Be Happy*[5] in which Bobby McFerrin emphasises that while you should expect some difficulties to arise, worrying only doubles your troubles. The titular advice is said to have originated from a saying by Indian mystic Meher Baba, who claimed both to be an avatar (an earthly manifestation of a deity) and to have lived with the shrieks of nothing[6] – that is, in silence – for the final 44 years of his life. A shrieking silence[7] is as unlikely a source of inspiration for a pop lyric as any.

One practical way to forget your worries[8] is to use the positive diffusing filter of distraction and absorption (without resorting to online trivia) to provide respite from, or even jettison, worry. Positive distraction and absorption from engagement with creative activities, hobbies and interests aim to reverse the inward-directed focus of your mind outward and away from worry. Quick and easy distractions include listening to music (especially songs with themes that hold meaning for you, allowing what you hear to help

---

1   *Rapture* by Blondie. Written by Deborah Harry and Christopher Stein

2   *New Song* by Howard Jones. Written by John Jones

3   *Loco In Acapulco* by The Four Tops. Written by Philip Collins and Lamont Dozier

4   *The Sun Always Shines On T.V.* by A-ha. Written by Pål Waaktaar Gamst

5   *Don't Worry, Be Happy* by Bobby McFerrin. Written by Robert McFerrin Jr

6   *Ashes To Ashes* by David Bowie. Written by David Jones

7   *Banana Republic* by The Boomtown Rats. Written by Patrick Cusack and Robert Geldof

8   *Rhythm Of The Night* by DeBarge. Written by Diane Warren

play away any worry),[1] reading for pleasure (only 10 minutes a day can be beneficial, but ideally aim for at least 30 minutes, which could help you to live longer and boost feelings of self-esteem and life satisfaction) or expressing yourself through writing. Carving out 10-15 minutes a day to write down, release, express and explore your inner-most thoughts and emotions – both positive and negative – in a free-flowing and uncensored way (with permission to disregard spelling and grammar) is a simple yet effective way to begin to understand yourself and to unburden your mind of worry or compulsive thoughts. More active ways to iron out the creases of worry include a gentle head-clearing stroll in a green space to appreciate the sights and delight in the sounds of nature to a trip 'downtown' (for Petula Clark, all the hustle and bustle helped to ease worry).[2] Movement – whether a full workout, a stroll outdoors, an impromptu hop, skip and *Jump To The Beat*[3] around the kitchen to a favourite tune, a standing shakedown or stretch, or even a hearty laugh – can help discharge any pent-up physical tension and mental worry. It's less about the activity and more about causing you – in a good sense – to be driven to distraction,[4] lifting both your spirits and your attention from past or future concerns to focus instead on something enjoyable in the present. Although effective at managing symptoms, distraction does not address the root causes of worry.

A similar and sane piece of advice comes from *Madness (Is All In The Mind)*:[5] live day by day instead of getting caught up in worries about tomorrow. Worry naturally assumes the role of the shadow of future uncertainty; therefore, if you live for the day[6] – that is, fully absorbed in the present – you can alleviate stress by detaching

1   *Take On Me* by A-ha. Written by Magne Furuholmen, Morten Harket and Pål Waaktaar Gamst
2   *Downtown '88* by Petula Clark. Written by Anthony Hatch
3   *Jump To The Beat* by Stacy Lattisaw. Written by Michael Walden and Anukampa Walden
4   *Is This Love?* by Alison Moyet. Written by Genevieve Moyet and David Stewart
5   *Madness (Is All In The Mind)* by Madness. Written by Christopher Foreman
6   *O L'Amour* by Dollar. Written by Vincent Martin and Andrew Bell

and distancing yourself from your worries and refusing to allow your mind to brood and fret over a future that may never come to pass. Learning to live for the moment[1] will help you manage and tolerate uncertainty.

Another quick and easy way to focus on the present, calm yourself, find contentment and dampen worry is to allocate a portion of your 22,000 daily breaths to slow, deep, conscious breathing (see the theme on *Exercise*).

When faced with momentous life decisions, such as whether to marry, divorce, change careers, relocate, start a family . . . , ensure you take the time to consider fully all the options rather than making a snap decision. Taking time for consideration is not an excuse for procrastination (the Latin etymology means 'to put forward until tomorrow') over minor, inconsequential decisions, as this doubles your cognitive load: first, you must decide to delay your decision, then you are still left with a decision to make, only now under added time pressure. Procrastination robs you of the present in return for an uncertain future.

Sound advice? A jamming Stevie Wonder suggests one answer is to allow the air to flow through your fingers to carry away your worries.[2] (Another mindful technique involves imagining placing all your worries on a cloud and then watching as it drifts away on a gentle breeze; alternatively, visualise your worries as grains of sand able to slip effortlessly through your fingers.)[3] The lyrical advice to distract yourself and practice mindfulness can help dissipate your worries, allowing your restless mind to press the pause button. Before this, you should decide to take control and grab hold[4] of your worries. Taking control and managing your worries will help

1   *I Need Your Lovin'* by Alyson Williams. Written by Frederick Gordon and Vincent Bell
2   *Master Blaster (Jammin')* by Stevie Wonder. Written by Stevie Wonder
3   *Oh Diane* by Fleetwood Mac. Written by Lindsey Buckingham and Richard Dashut
4   *Sexual Healing* by Marvin Gaye. Written by Marvin Gaye Jr and Odell Brown Jr

you become productive, for example, when it compels you to focus and prepare for an upcoming overseas holiday. Such 'worries' often have practical solutions that you can break down into smaller, more manageable steps and decisions. For that overseas trip, check and arrange vaccinations, book flights and accommodation, explore the best payment options, research local customs, and so on. However, if you allow it, productive worry can accumulate to reach a critical tipping point, becoming counterproductive and leaving you feeling overwhelmed with all that you still need to do, especially if you are prone to leaving everything to the last minute.

Thin Lizzy noted many reasons to worry.[1] By identifying and acknowledging the specific triggers that spark your worry (money, work, health, relationships, *Killer On The Loose* . . .), you can take simple and appropriate action to help alleviate them. For example, if an annual bill requiring a sizeable one-off payment triggers worry about cash flow, consider arranging smaller monthly payments instead. Recognising your triggers also helps identify problematic or recurring thought patterns, which you can change. If, for example, you notice that your inner voice has a negative reflex response, try to coach yourself to reframe these responses by following any negative remark with a pausing comma and then a positive, perception-changing, follow-on statement that includes an action or solution: if 'a', then 'b' – "If my train is delayed [add the comma and the positive planned response], then I'll have extra time to enjoy reading my book."

Other lifestyle changes that help counteract worry include those that you should already adopt for the benefit of your general health: take regular outdoor exercise; eat a balanced and sensible diet; limit your intake of stimulants (ditching nicotine) and diuretics (drinks that dehydrate your body by forcing it to excrete water, such as alcohol and excessive amounts of caffeine); try to see the funny side

1 *Killer On The Loose* by Thin Lizzy. Written by Philip Lynott

of life (incorporating some silliness and restoring laughter[1] is a great way to banish worry, diffuse tension, enhance pain tolerance, boost general health – particularly heart health – and give your brain a welcome shot of both endorphins and serotonin); take measures to ensure you get a good night's sleep (see the *Dreams* theme); and talk to a trusted friend or relative (open your mind to fresh perspectives). Cultivating good relationships helps manage natural stress hormones by restoring equilibrium rather than allowing chronic stress to build and disrupt life. Mindful meditation always beats mindless medication. An equally calming, pleasant and gratifying way to smooth and soothe your mind is to listen to your favourite music, not as background noise,[2] but up front and centre.

Understanding risk can also help you to manage worry, particularly unproductive hypothetical concerns centred on the perceived uncertainty of an outcome that may never arise – usually the worst-case scenario. It is futile to worry about remote possibilities (or expose yourself to the constant exploitative drip, drip sources of this negative information) about which there is either little evidence or nothing you can do to influence or control the outcome, such as the fear of global annihilation from an asteroid strike or the eruption of a supervolcano. The fear of the consequences of such risks can become grossly exaggerated and bloated out of all proportion, leaving some worriers feeling powerless, frustrated and vulnerable.

For risks within your sphere of influence, preparation helps you to challenge and confront your fears rather than only think of them negatively. Some worrying global issues, such as human-induced climate change, can feel pervasive and insurmountable. Those who believe there is nothing they can do will do nothing. If such issues fall within your sphere of concern, take some action,[3] such as directing your purchasing power towards more climate-friendly

1   *New Beginning (Mamba Seyra)* by Bucks Fizz. Written by Michael Myers and Tony Gibber
2   *Radio Ga Ga* by Queen. Written by Roger Taylor
3   *Prove Your Love* by Taylor Dayne. Written by Seth Swirsky and Arnold Roman

options. By taking action, you can become a positive force for change – and ultimately a force for good – that will boost your sense of empowerment by helping to alleviate what you once thought was an overwhelming or demoralising problem. And, as Simple Minds recognised, one step leads to another.[1] When you decide to take practical action and break down large tasks into a series of smaller, progressively manageable steps, it helps you to gradually challenge, confront and subsequently overcome (through exposure) some of the fears at the root of worry. When taking action, remember to do the first things – or the worst things – first.

If you have challenged irrational evidence with rational thinking and constructive action but remain unable to banish worry or are still prone to excessive or escalating worrying about issues that you can't let go of,[2] try compartmentalising your thoughts. For example, set boundaries that only allow you to worry for a limited, scheduled time, restricted to specific days; to start, you might designate 15 to 30 minutes at, say, 18:30 every other day or slot your scheduled time to worry[3] into any 'dead' time such as during a passive commute. Assure yourself that you will not engage with worry outside your strictly allotted worry time.

YOUTHFULNESS

Youthfulness covers that fleeting, carefree, exhilarating and emotionally intense phase of life through which, as a fledgling, you fly on your one-way migration from dependence to independence. The Housemartins wondered if you were ready for the time of your life,[4] as this journey's thrilling moments of unbridled exuberance

1   *Sanctify Yourself* by Simple Minds. Written by James Kerr, Charles Burchill and Michael MacNeil
2   *Chequered Love* by Kim Wilde. Written by Reginald Smith and Richard Smith
3   *Cry Wolf* by A-ha. Written by Pål Waaktaar Gamst and Magne Furuholmen
4   *Caravan Of Love* by The Housemartins. Written by Ernest Isley, Christopher Jasper and Marvin Isley

and euphoria are often considered the best days you will have.[1] This elevated state may help explain why society is so mesmerised by – and often fetishises – youthfulness. However, what many overlook about this ostensibly idealistic time is that such heightened joy often counterbalances having to live constantly *Under Pressure*.[2] As KISS commented, the tightly wound need to release steam.[3] This persistent and sometimes intense push-and-pull pressure arises from the high expectations and associated stress, uncertainty and anxiety that young people face as they strive to acquire educational qualifications, build their skill base, carve out and project their developing sense of identity, seek social acceptance and integration, manage financial responsibilities, develop relationships within new social circles and embrace their burgeoning desire for liberty, exploration and independence – the will to be free.[4] Amid the need to jump through so many hoops, it's fortunate that the young still possess fully functioning knees.

With so many wide-open doors into life,[5] youthful potential and optimism seem boundless. Inevitably, a few will attempt to squeeze in *Too Much Too Young*,[6] only to become ensnared by the premature arrival of the web of adult responsibilities. Conversely, a few airlings passively embrace the lightness of being gifted by youthfulness, allowing them to blithely drift like downy feathers caught on a breeze,[7] without course, direction or a care in the world.[8]

1   *Each Time You Break My Heart* by Nick Kamen. Written by Madonna Ciccone and Stephen Bray
2   *Under Pressure* by Queen and David Bowie. Written by Roger Taylor, Freddie Mercury, John Deacon, Brian May and David Jones
3   *Crazy Crazy Nights* by KISS. Written by Adam Mitchell and Stanley Eisen
4   *I'll Find My Way Home* by Jon and Vangelis. Written by John Anderson and Evángelos Papathanassíou
5   *The Sun Goes Down (Living It Up)* by Level 42. Written by Michael Lindup, Mark King, Philip Gould and Waliou Badarou
6   *Too Much Too Young* by The Specials featuring Rico. Written by Jeremy Dammers and Lloyd Tyrell
7   *A Little Peace* by Nicole. Written by Bernd Meinunger, Paul Greedus and Ralph Siegel
8   *More Than This* by Roxy Music. Written by Bryan Ferry

Mike + The Mechanics suggested that each generation tends to blame the preceding one.[1] Without a unified voice to defend their interests, it's common for the youth of any generation to come under scrutiny, often becoming an easy target for media-driven outrage. As in every phase of life, a small percentage of persistently stubborn malcontents can skew and negatively taint wider society's perception of entire cohorts. The 1980s were rife with moral panic (reminiscent of the Decadent movement a century before), with various factors blamed for deviant youthful behaviour, including the ready availability of drugs, video 'nasties' (on either VHS or Betamax), glue-sniffing, the disintegration of traditional nuclear families and, of course, the nefarious, corrupting and character-diluting influence of contemporary pop music on impressionable young minds. Wider society (regularly stoked by sensationalist newspaper headlines) assumed that the youthful desire to watch video nasties or to listen to 'inappropriate' song lyrics was symptomatic of the disease and decay in moral and societal values. Both then and now, there was concern that the imagery and language that fed directly into young, malleable minds would desensitise them, allowing questionable or twisted values to be implanted and promoted. However, each new generation needs the space to rebel, reject mainstream political ideology and explore and experiment with alternative viewpoints. Societies need to acknowledge these needs. Like individuals, each generation needs music for its identity;[2] in the run-up to the 1980s, this gave rise to cultural movements such as punk rock. Musical choice provides the recalcitrant young with a sense of agency and control that may be missing from other areas of their lives designed, defined and dominated by adults. It is not so much the genre of music that matters, but what you do with it (play it loud, play it often) and the subsequent connection and empowerment it yields. If the prevailing musical culture is met with fear, unease or disdain

1   *The Living Years* by Mike + The Mechanics. Written by Brian Robertson and Michael Rutherford
2   *I'd Rather Jack* by The Reynolds Girls. Written by Michael Stock, Matthew Aitken and Peter Waterman

by the established adult world, it might well have achieved at least one of its aims.

Junior spoke of those who, in trying to bypass youthful insecurities, attempt to vault straight into early adulthood by acting older to come of age sooner.[1] The lyrics often describe this as trying to see through the eyes of the old[2] before their time.[3] Some cultures proudly celebrate the transition from girl to woman and boy to man; these changes are biologically incremental rather than falling conveniently on a specified date, even if the celebratory event or legal milestone passed on certain birthdays does occur on a specific day. Naturally and inevitably – with or without ceremonial recognition – youthfulness metamorphoses into the next phase of life. Spandau Ballet sang of the slow eating away of their salad days[4] (without a munching mollusc in sight), while Bucks Fizz noted ruefully in *When We Were Young*[5] that, following the passing of youth, comes the collection of age.

During the 1980s, lyricists imbued the cult of youthfulness with distinct traits. For example, the tone in *Young Guns (Go For It)*[6] is (as the bracketed words suggest) assertive and self-assured, as indeed it is in *Wham Rap! (Enjoy What You Do)*,[7] in which George Michael affirms his desire to have fun and stay young. This underlying sense of youthful confidence and astuteness to anticipate and avoid adult pitfalls (such as erosion of the self) is also featured in *Come On Eileen*.[8]

1   *Mama Used To Say* by Junior. Written by Robert Carter and Norman Giscombe Jr
2   *An Innocent Man* by Billy Joel. Written by William Joel
3   *Young At Heart* by The Bluebells. Written by Robert Hodgens and Siobhan Fahey
4   *Gold* by Spandau Ballet. Written by Gary Kemp
5   *When We Were Young* by Bucks Fizz. Written by Warren Harry
6   *Young Guns (Go For It)* by Wham! Written by George Michael
7   *Wham Rap! (Enjoy What You Do)* by Wham! Written by George Michael and Andrew Ridgeley
8   *Come On Eileen* by Dexys Midnight Runners and The Emerald Express. Written by Kevin Rowland, James Paterson, Kevin Adams and Michael Billingham

Aristotle believed the young were prone to excessively and vehemently overdoing everything – loving and hating far *Too Much*[1] – their lives corralled more by impassioned feelings than by reason. Bryan Ferry highlighted the predicament of being too young to reason but too old to dream.[2] Within the neuron-pruned and changing circuitry of young brains, and particularly so in impulsive, risk-taking adolescent men, resides the bravado of invincibility, both physical and emotional: Feargal Sharkey cautioned about the high risk of getting hurt because the emotionally callow still need to learn.[3] *When You're Young And In Love*[4] the heady mix of idealism, innocence and naivety means that, in matters of the heart, you are often open, exposed and foolish, prone to making mistakes,[5] all at a time when emotional intensity is amplified to super-pitched levels, felt as never before or never again.[6] Such love is remembered long after the aftermath of inconsolable heartbreak and shattered teenage dreams.[7] The Smiths wondered how such sorrowful words could come from one so young.[8] Gary Numan thought the answer was emotional fragility and brittleness, rendering the young susceptible to breakage.[9]

Level 42 pointed out that these years of change can add to a sense of confusion.[10] Coming across as distant, detached or withdrawn from mainstream society (often accompanied by feelings of being the

---

1 *Too Much* by Bros. Written by Matthew Goss, Luke Goss and Nicholas Graham
2 *Slave To Love* by Bryan Ferry. Written by Bryan Ferry
3 *A Good Heart* by Feargal Sharkey. Written by Maria McKee
4 *When You're Young And In Love* by The Flying Pickets. Written by Van McCoy
5 *Perfect* by Fairground Attraction. Written by Mark Nevin
6 *Frankie* by Sister Sledge. Written by Denise Rich
7 *Robert De Niro's Waiting* by Bananarama. Written by Sara Dallin, Siobhan Fahey, Keren Woodward, Steven Jolley and Anthony Swain
8 *Sheila Take A Bow* by The Smiths. Written by John Maher and Steven Morrissey
9 *We Are Glass* by Gary Numan. Written by Gary Webb
10 *Something About You* by Level 42. Written by Michael Lindup, Philip Gould, Mark King, Rowland Gould and Waliou Badarou

odd one out,[1] an outsider, or a square peg in a round hole)[2] may be facets of a coping strategy to help deal with the discombobulation and fragility of this challenging time of flux, or as a consequence of the youthful search for greater independence and identity. Or both. The uncertainty surrounding identity can lead some young people to grow inward towards darkness rather than upward towards the light, preferring to withdraw or seek refuge in the safety and security of a secret internal place.[3]

Sound advice? Navigating youth is a unique personal odyssey. The songs provide helpful guideposts in this new and changing emotional landscape, showing that others have been there before,[4] and lived to tell the tale. As with other themes, you must experience both the highs and the lows to fully appreciate each for what it is and to know that your current situation and emotional state are not permanent. Despite the novelty of what you might encounter at any age, you're not the first to experience these feelings, especially the hurt.[5]

While boasting about how wonderful he was, Kid Creole's song character sang of being at his peak.[6] Between the ages of 18 and 25, you reach many of life's peaks, including cognitive prowess (such as flexible and adaptable thought and excellent memory retention), female attractiveness to men, muscle strength, immune system efficacy (and thus fewer chronic diseases) and, at age 23, your first peak in life satisfaction. *Best Years Of Our Lives?*[7] For

1   *Misfit* by Curiosity Killed The Cat. Written by Martin Volpeliere-Pierrot, Julian Brookhouse, Miguel Drummond, Nicholas Thorp and Tobias Andersen
2   *Wedding Bells* by Godley & Creme. Written by Kevin Godley and Laurence Crème
3   *Take My Breath Away* by Berlin. Written by Thomas Whitlock and Giovanni Moroder
4   *Breakfast In Bed* by UB40 with Chrissie Hynde. Written by Donald Fritts and Edward Hinton
5   *Love Will Save The Day* by Whitney Houston. Written by Antoinette Colandero
6   *I'm A Wonderful Thing, Baby* by Kid Creole and The Coconuts. Written by Thomas Browder and Peter Schott
7   *Best Years Of Our Lives* by Modern Romance. Written by David Jaymes

some, undoubtedly yes. With so many vivid and memorable 'firsts' happening between the ages of 15 and 25, favourable autobiographical memories peak during these years. Psychologists refer to this period of enhanced self-defining recollection as the 'reminiscence bump', which includes favourable feelings – heightened recognition, preference and emotional responses – towards the pop music, books and films you consumed during this formative time. Those beyond a youthful 25 may start to feel a little nervous that their best years have passed by[1] but fret not because, by the time you reach your late sixties, your u-shaped life-satisfaction curve will have made a triumphant return from its mid-life nadir to reach a second peak.

Within popular legend, the Fountain of Youth possesses magical restorative powers for those no longer required to show ID to verify their age. Similarly, bathing in Madonna's fountain of gold prevents you from growing old.[2] However, it is not all plain bathing. Many involuntarily caught in the spray of youth feel angst caused by the turbulence of their liminal voyage of exploration and self-discovery, often wishing they could fast-forward their life to hasten the escape from the berth of childhood and its trappings. Yet, before they know it, those days are gone.[3]

Bronski Beat's *Smalltown Boy*[4] knew he couldn't find the answers to the questions he sought while living at home. Youth is a time of transformative change for body, brain and life, and it soon dawns upon you – for better or worse – that life will never again be the same.[5] Much of that change involves grasping a new-found desire for independence and raising the anchors of childhood from their former moorings – home life, school, friends, neighbourhoods, ways

---

1   *Total Eclipse Of The Heart* by Bonnie Tyler. Written by James Steinman
2   *Dear Jessie* by Madonna. Written by Madonna Ciccone and Patrick Leonard
3   *Now Those Days Are Gone* by Bucks Fizz. Written by Andrew Hill and Nichola Martin
4   *Smalltown Boy* by Bronski Beat. Written by Steven Forrest, James Somerville and Lawrence Cole
5   *You Came* by Kim Wilde. Written by Kim Smith and Richard Smith

of thinking – leaving the past behind[1] and setting sail towards new, broader horizons. This de-anchoring process risks leaving behind an essential essence of who you are from a time when others loved and liked you for simply being you[2] – the who-you-are rather than the what-you-do (when you fulfil an identifiable, labelled role, stuck on you by society and usually directly linked to your career choice).

Caught in this whirlwind of change,[3] it is hardly surprising that the young can feel all churned up inside.[4] The cognitive changes that contribute to many youthful characteristics are complex and can make every day seem like life is both up and down.[5] While youthfulness may heighten and refine musical rhythm, it also batters the natural circadian rhythm, disrupting and distorting lifestyles; it's akin to someone placing a super-strong magnet next to a young person's internal biological clock so that they may watch the mayhem ensue.

Young brains are developing brains. Brain regions mature at different rates, with the rational decision-making prefrontal cortex being notably tardy, a lag that leaves some youngsters lacking in considered judgement and perspicacity. Reward centres within youthful brains are particularly susceptible to the allure of feel-good dopamine. This susceptibility can set into overdrive impulsive, risky and reward-driven behaviour, especially under the influence of peer pressure or among those attempting to display sexual attractiveness via signalling and swagger to showcase their genetic fitness and desirable traits (such as confidence, fearlessness and general vitality) to both rivals and potential mates. These dance-with-danger[6] traits

1 *Starmaker* by The Kids From Fame. Written by Bruce Roberts and Carole Bayer
2 *Roses Are Red* by The Mac Band featuring The McCampbell Brothers. Written by Antonio Reid and Kenneth Edmonds
3 *My Ever Changing Moods* by The Style Council. Written by John Weller
4 *Long Hot Summer* by The Style Council. Written by John Weller
5 *Midas Touch* by Midnight Star. Written by June Watson Williams and Boaz Watson
6 *Domino Dancing* by Pet Shop Boys. Written by Neil Tennant and Christopher Lowe

evolved to reward independence in the necessary step outside the comfort zone of home life. Occasionally, a good scare can jolt invincible-feeling youngsters into adopting precautionary ratcheting-down measures in a way that a thousand words of sound parental advice will not. Negative experiences can be brutal teachers: you must take (and likely fail) the test (you'll find no answers without taking chances)[1] before learning harsh lessons about how the world works. When teetering close to the edge,[2] some may topple. However, these characteristics are common biological traits of youth, not personal flaws. The brain's remarkable plasticity at all ages means that it, and the thoughts it generates, can always change for the better.

Although usually unfairly overshadowed by the apparent darker downsides, try not to overlook the brighter and more positive characteristics displayed by the young. Intellectual acuity (especially the capacity to swiftly acquire and readily absorb new information and skills) and acumen enable youngsters to embrace fresh ideas and alternative viewpoints. Some youngsters feel compelled to channel their headstrong energy, drive and enthusiasm to effect positive, meaningful change and use their firmly held values and ideals to address and rectify injustices. Even youthful impatience to get things done can help keep everyone feeling strong.[3] These are all commendable qualities. Every phase of life carries pros and cons; what matters here is knowing what they are and how to maximise natural talent and youthful vivacity.

Those for whom the leaves of change have already dropped[4] – where autumn's breeze has removed summer's leaves[5] – can leverage their experience to guide, support and encourage those currently on

1   F.L.M. by Mel and Kim. Written by Michael Stock, Matthew Aitken and Peter Waterman
2   *Close (To The Edit)* by Art Of Noise. Written by Anne Dudley, Gary Langan, Jonathan Jeczalik, Paul Morley and Trevor Horn
3   *Through The Barricades* by Spandau Ballet. Written by Gary Kemp
4   *Who's Leaving Who* by Hazell Dean. Written by Markus Spiro and Horst Nussbaum
5   *The Bitterest Pill (I Ever Had To Swallow)* by The Jam. Written by John Weller

their turbulent and parabolic paths to show them how to think about the best ways to become resilient to, and overcome, the inevitable obstacles, struggles, setbacks and difficulties that arise. This guidance might involve imparting advice or sharing experience and insights on processes such as calculated risk-taking, problem-solving or how to repair *Broken Wings*[1] by taking what was wrong and helping to make it right. The rise and fall[2] in the personal landscape of life adds captivating interest to the journey.

Potential has no expiry date. To help younger people identify, unleash and maximise their potential, you first need to listen deeply and actively (that is, with open ears and an open, non-judgemental mind that grants space for young individuals to express themselves freely), recognise inherent (or dormant) qualities and believe in that individual and the unique abilities and energy they possess. Try to instil in the young the self-belief and confidence to allow them to enjoy being themselves in a world where competitive (digitally hyper-curated) comparison with others is all too easy but all too often an unhelpful catalyst and amplifier of difference. The only meaningful comparisons are those that gauge personal progress – comparing how you are now with how you were in the past. Regardless of who you are, as the years continually wash over you, they erode the jagged edges formed by the ups and downs of youthfulness until life begins to level out in a smoother, calmer, more predictable way.

1   *Broken Wings* by Mr Mister. Written by Richard Page, Steven George and John Lang
2   *One Moment In Time* by Whitney Houston. Written by Albert Hammond and John Bettis

CHAPTER VI

The Outro

EVERYTHING from the Big Bang to bird bones brought us to the brink of the 1980s. Having rung in the tunes and wrung out the themes from our dedicated decade, it's time for the reflective outro, the start of the end.[1]

By its nature, sound advice sounds familiar, with its emphasis on balance and moderation, resilience and adaptation, personal responsibility, forming and maintaining good habits, adopting a positive mindset and continuous learning. If any ideas sparked into life from the song themes have made sense to you,[2] consider them *Food For Thought*.[3] However, before delving into further mental sustenance, let's reflect on a few pieces of less palatable advice. For example, the catchy tune from *Get Outta My Dreams, Get Into My Car*[4] conceals unsettling undertones: get into my car ... get in the back seat ... touch my bumper. While contemplating stranger danger,[5] we should be thankful the word 'car' wasn't replaced with the more sinister-sounding 'van', 'pick-up' or 'boot'.

In British English car-speak, 'boot' refers to what Americans

1 *Who's Leaving Who* by Hazell Dean. Written by Markus Spiro and Horst Nussbaum
2 *Love On Your Side* by Thompson Twins. Written by Thomas Bailey, Alannah Currie and Joseph Leeway
3 *Food For Thought* by UB40. Written by James Brown, Alistair Campbell, Robin Campbell, Earl Falconer, Norman Hassan, Brian Travers, Michael Virtue and Terence Wilson
4 *Get Outta My Dreams, Get Into My Car* by Billy Ocean. Written by Leslie Charles and Robert Lange
5 *My One Temptation* by Mica Paris. Written by Michael Leeson, Stephen Waters and Peter Vale

call the 'trunk'; both signify a confined storage space. The chilling suggestion in *Living Doll*[1] is to lock up your crying living doll (the one with the real hair) in a trunk to keep her all to yourself. Made in '59,[2] this number 1 hit earned acclaimed songwriter Lionel Bart an Ivor Novello Award for best song. Comic Relief recorded their entertaining 1986 cover, which, upon lyrical deconstruction, offers little comic relief.

Grammy-nominated Cyndi Lauper recalls driving all night, creeping into your room, waking you up and making love to you, only then asking whether this was all right with you.[3] Consent comes first.

The noxious lyric injected by Alice Cooper suggests the protagonist's motive for inflicting pain on a woman was to hear her scream his name, which is *Poison*,[4] however you choose to take it.

There, There My Dear[5] offers no soothing reassurance with its suggestion that the only means of effecting change is to shoot the men who hold power. Such incitement does not sit well with modern sensibilities.

Changing tack, you know that life can be cruel[6] and you may feel especially aggrieved if unfairly singled out by life's broken wheel of fortune[7] (round and round it goes, but where it stops, nobody knows).[8] One example might be if you are overlooked for an

1   *Living Doll* by Cliff Richard and The Young Ones featuring Hank Marvin. Written by Lionel Begleiter
2   *Driving In My Car* by Madness. Written by Michael Barson
3   *I Drove All Night* by Cyndi Lauper. Written by William Steinberg and Thomas Kelly
4   *Poison* by Alice Cooper. Written by Vincent Furnier, John Barrett and John McCurry
5   *There, There My Dear* by Dexys Midnight Runners. Written by Kevin Archer and Kevin Rowland
6   *Kids In America* by Kim Wilde. Written by Reginald Smith and Richard Smith
7   *The Bitterest Pill (I Ever Had To Swallow)* by The Jam. Written by John Weller
8   *Abracadabra* by Steve Miller Band. Written by Steven Miller

opportunity, knowing that your worst is better than another's best;[1] this feels unfair.[2] Assuming there is no prejudice or correctable bias to call out (ageism, sexism, racism, nepotism . . .), reframing can help put such matters into perspective. For example, by accepting that such problems and issues are transitory, ask yourself how you will feel about them in one, five or ten years. Such temporal distancing helps prevent short-term overreaction as you realise and accept that although life is good, it's not necessarily fair.[3] The song themes show that the inevitability of adversity, setbacks and challenges related to love and relationships (possibly marriage and divorce), educational attainment, work, money, reputation, friends and other aspects of a balanced life are just that – part of a balanced life, and thus a part of your growth and development. It's not personal. The universe did not evolve to conspire against you to dole out adverse treatment (even if an imperfect human has done so); there is always more to the joy and wonder of life than your problems, difficulties or frustrations. It is not worth wasting valuable time and energy dwelling on past personal injustices or plotting some ultimately futile, all-consuming, weapons-grade retaliation, which does little more than reduce you to the same level as the wrongdoer. Seneca wrote how a calm mind robs misfortune of its strength and burden, while Janet Jackson pointed out that we only get to live one life,[4] so use it positively and constructively, learn lessons and keep moving on.[5] *C'est La Vie.*[6]

The rapid pace of technological change during and since the 1980s has rendered some pop culture references to contemporary technology obsolete, such as the telegrams (discontinued in 1982)

1   *Open Your Heart* by The Human League. Written by Philip Oakey and John Callis
2   *Wonderful Life* by Black. Written by Colin Vearncombe
3   *White Wedding* by Billy Idol. Written by William Broad
4   *What Have You Done For Me Lately* by Janet Jackson. Written by James Harris, Terry Lewis and Janet Jackson
5   *Welcome To The Pleasuredome* by Frankie Goes To Hollywood. Written by Peter Gill, William Johnson, Mark O'Toole and Brian Nash
6   *C'est La Vie* by Robbie Nevil. Written by Robert Nevil, Duncan Pain and Mark Holding

mentioned in *One Step Further*.[1] Staying with telecommunications, the notion of sitting and waiting at home by the phone[2] (worse still, most landline telephones were usually in a communal area such as a hallway, allowing everyone to listen in on private conversations) makes little sense in today's world of mobile telephony. Likewise, references to ghetto blasters,[3] turning dials on a radio[4] and even lowering a needle onto a record[5] are now largely out of date.[6]

The same technological advancements that revolutionised pop music production and consumption in the 1980s have continued to evolve and shape the sound of music in the intervening years. The digitisation of music (a whir of zero, zero,[7] one, one)[8] enabled audio file compression and the availability of an almost limitless selection of online songs, supplanting the tactile precision and sonically satisfying rituals associated with a 'physical' music collection: the crackle, hiss and scratch of a needle touching down on vinyl, the loading of cassette tapes (often following a quick loosening shake) into players or the careful ceremony of placing a CD into the player tray. More recently, we've been drawn into the stream.[9] Streaming platforms have entirely restructured how people buy and listen to pop music, altering the very shape of songs. Frequently, specially selected teams write digital-age songs designed for the media on which they are consumed. As a result, those wonderfully lush, anticipation-building half-minute-long instrumental intros once commonplace on songs

1   *One Step Further* by Bardo. Written by Simon Jefferies
2   *Say Say Say* by Paul McCartney and Michael Jackson. Written by Paul Mc-Cartney and Michael Jackson
3   *Theme From S-Express* by S'Express. Written by Mark Moore and Pascal Gabriel
4   *Find My Love* by Fairground Attraction. Written by Mark Nevin
5   *Pump Up The Volume* by M/A/R/R/S. Written by Martyn Young and Steven Young
6   *I'd Rather Jack* by The Reynolds Girls. Written by Michael Stock, Matthew Aitken and Peter Waterman
7   *1999* by Prince. Written by Prince Nelson
8   *One Vision* by Queen. Written by Brian May, Freddie Mercury, Roger Taylor and John Deacon
9   *Something About You* by Level 42. Written by Michael Lindup, Philip Gould, Mark King, Rowland Gould and Waliou Badarou

across many genres, such as *Total Eclipse Of The Heart*,[1] *Stairway To Heaven*,[2] *Blue Monday*,[3] *Sweet Child O' Mine*,[4] *One Vision*,[5] *It's A Sin*,[6] *The Power Of Love*[7] and *Billie Jean*[8] are now a rarity. Factors contributing to this change include listeners' shorter attention spans[9] (the preference for more immediate gratification has led to shorter songs with faster tempos rather than a gradual build-up to a crescendo), the ease of track skipping, and the need to capture listener attention for 30 seconds to trigger a micropayment. Nowadays, shorter songs (with intros roughly half the length of those from the 1980s, and studio-produced outro fade-outs almost entirely vanished) are composed to be front-loaded, often jumping straight into the chorus, as this is the quickest and easiest way to hook a listener's perceived shorter working memory (only 'perceived' because today's world is strewn with numerous competing and tempting sources of stimuli vying for – and fragmenting – your attention, rather than being definitive proof of diminishing or drifting attention spans).[10] In the 1980s, the chorus was written as an emotional response to the preceding narrative verses, although the more modern musical mantra of 'Don't bore us, get us to the chorus' first appeared in print as early as the 1980s.

The influence of technology on the sound of the 1980s is undeniable. In the context of the millennia over which music has existed, the first phonograph music recordings – making sound solid – are

1   *Total Eclipse Of The Heart* by Bonnie Tyler. Written by James Steinman
2   *Stairway To Heaven* by Far Corporation. Written by James Page and Robert Plant
3   *Blue Monday* by New Order. Written by Gillian Gilbert, Peter Hook, Stephen Morris and Bernard Sumner
4   *Sweet Child O' Mine* by Guns N' Roses. Written by Steven Adler, Michael McKagan, Jeffrey Isbell, William Rose and Saul Hudson
5   *One Vision* by Queen. Written by Brian May, Freddie Mercury, Roger Taylor and John Deacon
6   *It's A Sin* by Pet Shop Boys. Written by Neil Tennant and Christopher Lowe
7   *The Power Of Love* by Huey Lewis and The News. Written by Hugh Cregg III, Christopher Hayes and John Colla
8   *Billie Jean* by Michael Jackson. Written by Michael Jackson
9   *You Can Call Me Al* by Paul Simon. Written by Paul Simon
10 *I Beg Your Pardon* by Kon Kan. Written by Barry Harris and Joseph Souter

relatively recent, having emerged only a century before the start of the 1980s. Early gramophones allowed 10-inch shellac records (shellac is a natural resin secreted by the lac beetle) rotating at 78 revolutions per minute ('rpm') to deliver about three minutes of recorded sound, which remains the best explanation for the duration of pop songs. By the mid-twentieth century, record manufacturers reduced the rpm to run at a different speed,[1] which explains references to old 45s,[2] such as Alvin Stardust's fumble through his 45s.[3] The 45 gave birth to the 7-inch vinyl single, although the 'single' was actually a 'double' as it could accommodate tracks on both sides. When manufacturers increased the diameter of vinyl to 10 or 12 inches and further reduced the rpm to 33⅓, the 'Long Play' or 'LP' record was born, which became the standard format for albums until the commercial launch of compact discs in 1982. Vinyl LP aficionados perceive that their medium of choice delivers a richer, warmer and superior sound over modern formats. However, the true marvel of modern technology lies not in sound quality but in song accessibility and the ease with which you can integrate your musical choices into everyday life. The storage capacity of many portable electronic devices allows you to carry songs by the thousands and access tracks by the millions (most popular streaming services hold over 100 million tracks), ensuring you can always listen to music that caters to your needs, from relaxation to motivation.

As music morphed from 'house' to 'mouse', it increasingly needed to adhere to a formula for commercial sales success (these formulae are continually measured, analysed and refined through continuous data harvesting by streaming algorithms). This shift to market-driven tunes poses a risk to the narrative-rich ballad that once connected listeners to songwriters via *Heart And Soul*.[4] What sound advice will future listeners discover when analysing today's songs in 40 or 50 years? In the 1980s, aspiring to make great pop music meant you

1   *Addicted To Love* by Robert Palmer. Written by Robert Palmer
2   *Real Gone Kid* by Deacon Blue. Written by Richard Ross
3   *I Feel Like Buddy Holly* by Alvin Stardust. Written by Michael Batt
4   *Heart And Soul* by T'Pau. Written by Carol Decker and Ronald Rogers

had the chance to make the top 10, make a living and – potentially – make a difference. However, music moulded to fit a modern industry sales template is unlikely to achieve these aims. The significant commercial pressure within the cost-intensive music industry to replicate a winning formula is high, stifling musical innovation and limiting audience exposure to new or diverse sounds. Yet, such patterns and pressures are not entirely new. Over the decades, many bands have built their careers by applying a musical formula, giving their fans the music they wanted or (more cynically) convincing them that the music they got was the music they wanted. Having carved out their niche, some bands came to develop and 'own' a signature sound and thus maintained a consistent musical status quo. Status Quo may come to mind as a rock band known to have an instantly recognisable and distinctive signature sound, charting over 60 times (a record for a band in UK chart history), with 22 of their tracks entering the top 10. Their 87 appearances on *Top of the Pops* is also a record. Their formula worked for them just as it did for songwriters and producers Stock, Aitken and Waterman. From the mid-1980s, this trio sold over 40 million, often soundalike, records. The lesson here is that in life, try to find and refine the multiple components of a winning formula that works for you.

Inside Out.[1] Just as a CD is laser-read from the inside out, any personal transformation must start from within. As Madonna suggests, begin with your head.[2] A balanced, well-rounded and harmonious life is far more likely to arise through intention than by chance, especially when you harness the array of remarkable abilities of your subconscious mind. Some extraordinary skills are innate, while others are acquired; collectively, they can create and shape your life to make you what you want to be.[3] From its lofty podium, your subconscious adeptly orchestrates your body, enabling you to perform numerous complex yet routine actions almost effortlessly

1   *Inside Out* by Odyssey. Written by William Rae
2   *Express Yourself* by Madonna. Written by Madonna Ciccone and Stephen Bray
3   *Don Quixote* by Nik Kershaw. Written by Nicholas Kershaw

(think of riding a bicycle or driving a car) without overloading your brain. Your subconscious is non-discriminatory (it dutifully accepts and believes everything you tell it) so that, once imprinted, it executes good and bad habits with equal conscientiousness. Our evolution has made us hard-wired creatures of habit, as habit lends us a sense of control. When habit supersedes willpower (a challenging process that can take months for your brain to lay down new neural pathways), subsequent behaviour can become a *Hard Habit To Break*.[1] With time and effort, you can master this mechanism to adopt virtuous behaviours and abandon detrimental ones. To wire new neural pathways and let your mind physically alter its structure, you must stimulate and activate those neurons that create, implement and maintain those pathways. Back with your behaviour, if you want to break a habit, just drop it.[2] If you cannot immediately drop it, try in the short term to substitute it for more mindful, healthier alternatives: with nutrition, for example, swap biscuits for a handful of nuts, vegetable oil for extra virgin olive oil (ideally filtered and stored in a dark glass bottle), white wine for red wine, and refined white bread/pasta/rice for wholefood (wholegrain, wholewheat and brown). In your wider life, consider swapping some of your weekly 20 hours of music listening for potentially transformative top 10 tunes from the 1980s.

Integrating small but positive lifestyle adjustments into your routine helps to counteract the weight of decision fatigue (choice overload) and guides you to find, design and build a better life. Remember to be realistic when managing your expectation levels; as you strive for a better life, you will find pearls of perfection, which is a better aim than expecting a life of perfection (especially that promoted by narcissistic social media) that is unrealistic, unattainable and against which you will always fall short. The benefits from improving your physical and mental habits will flow effortlessly into

1   *Hard Habit To Break* by Chicago. Written by Steven Kipner and John Lewis Parker
2   *Drop The Boy* by Bros. Written by Nicholas Graham and Thomas Watkins

all other areas of your life because your physical and mental health are double-A sides of the same record. Some detrimental habits will hold you back, so uprooting vices and planting virtues in their stead is a worthwhile endeavour.

As with so much about your body's functionality (and the functionality of life in general), many themes overlap, intertwine and integrate, often in lockstep. This interconnectedness exists because they are mutually beneficial – each reinforces the other, such as with the positive effects of exercise on sleep and sleep on exercise. A balanced, harmonious life involves drawing and plaiting many threads from each theme to create a single, strong, yet flexible golden thread that surpasses the sum of its individual strands. As its creator, you get to choose the design of those strands.

Opting for what you know and feel is right, such as when you accept and take responsibility for yourself and your emotions instead of assigning blame to external vectors, doesn't drain your life of its colour and vitality but, on the contrary, amplifies it in vibrant, multi-layered ways. Another intricately intertwined theme that runs through the centre of the thread of life is how you internally control, interpret, respond, react, view and approach the uncontrollable external narratives, events, circumstances and problems that wage their continual assault against you and your goals. Taking charge and responsibility for your thoughts, feelings and behavioural responses to these assaults empowers you to choose how you wish to represent them and how often you mentally re-form and replay them. When you can recognise, evaluate and challenge your thoughts, you can reframe and reverse any negative narrative attached to them so that you reclaim your sense of control. Your thoughts will acquire a new, beneficial look. The Pointer Sisters describe how they went from feeling sad to feeling exhilarated.[1] Similarly, you can reframe what you once thought of as worry and convert it into feelings of challenge, excitement and expectation, as these contrasting emotional states share comparable physiological characteristics (likewise with

1   *Automatic* by Pointer Sisters. Written by Brock Walsh and Mark Goldenberg

musical goosebumps and feeling some kinds of fear).[1] Some thrive on challenges that fortify, enliven and enrich their lives. In *All's Well That Ends Well*, Shakespeare commented on our ability to find solutions from within: "Our remedies oft in ourselves do lie."

Life's golden thread is woven into a larger tapestry of time. Although no historical era monopolises pop song themes, echoes from long ago[2] readily reverberate down Greek Street.[3] And with good reason: ancient Greece was the first well-documented and significant civilisation, laying many foundations for subsequent Western cultures, especially that of the Roman Empire. The Greeks shaped and informed our present through their pioneering ideas, influence and teachings on language, art and culture, politics and democracy, architecture, philosophy and numerous scientific discoveries, inventions and improvements, such as those in cartography, medicine and mathematics. The archaeological signature left behind on remnants of Greek cultural calling cards suggests their world (along with other ancient Mediterranean civilisations) was one steeped in music, illustrating the timeless nature of some human experience – where nothing is new.[4]

With time, the meaning of words can warp and distort, sometimes twisting entirely free from their etymological moorings. Today, for example, the term 'epicure' describes someone who indulges in the pleasures of the stomach through fine food and drink and, more broadly, delights in a decadent and indulgent lifestyle where the destination is recreation.[5] However, this pleasure principle is a corruption of the teachings of Greek philosopher Epicurus, who,

1   *Lay All Your Love On Me* by ABBA. Written by Göran Andersson and Björn Ulvaeus
2   *Xanadu* by Olivia Newton-John and Electric Light Orchestra. Written by Jeffrey Lynne
3   *Chant No. 1 (I Don't Need This Pressure On)* by Spandau Ballet. Written by Gary Kemp
4   *Maneater* by Daryl Hall & John Oates. Written by Daryl Hohl, John Oates and Sara Allen
5   *Respectable* by Mel and Kim. Written by Michael Stock, Matthew Aitken and Peter Waterman

while acknowledging that sensual pleasure was indeed a natural aim and the highest good, espoused that one should seek pleasure through a code of simple, ascetic living. Epicurus believed that a life of simplicity and moderation would expel disturbances from your mind and pain from your body, leaving you free to revel in tranquillity.

Epicurus encouraged his pupils to learn by rote, especially memorised mottos, slick slogans or perhaps even a snippet from a top 10 ode. One catchy declaration integral to Epicurean philosophy was *Dum vivimus vivamus*. With Latin roots,[1] you may think that this means nothing to you[2] (at least it's not all Greek - another nod to Shakespeare, this time from *Julius Caesar*). The motto translates as: "While we live, let us live." You likely already possess all the indispensable ingredients to live well and be well. There are no secrets[3] to bringing transformative advice to life: it involves the gradual accumulation of sound advice, such as that extracted from pop song themes. Some topics, especially sleep, exercise, diet and attitude, exert a disproportionately large influence, but every theme contributes to building a balanced, rounded life. Drawing on pop song themes offers a simple, novel and relatable way to engage and remind you of advice you may already know but which has struggled to take root in your life, crowded out or overshadowed by other thoughts that invade and occupy your mind.

Elaine Paige and Barbara Dickson remind us that nothing lasts for ever.[4] All life, matter and soul in the universe will ultimately reach a necessary and natural end.[5] Until then, let the sound advice inspired by the song themes be a rudder that steers your course,

1   *Blue Jean* by David Bowie. Written by David Jones
2   *Vienna* by Ultravox. Written by William Currie, Christopher Allen, James Ure and Warren Cann
3   *Wishful Thinking* by China Crisis. Written by Gary Daly and Edmund Lundon
4   *I Know Him So Well* by Elaine Paige and Barbara Dickson. Written by Göran Andersson, Timothy Rice and Björn Ulvaeus
5   *Kayleigh* by Marillion. Written by Mark Kelly, Ian Mosley, Steven Rothery, Peter Trewavas and Derek Dick

allowing you to make a series of adjustments that will bring about positive change, helping you to find what you are looking for.[1] It seems apt that a sentiment from a 1980s song should provide the profound closing words – the lyrical setting sun – drawn from *Clouds Across The Moon*:[2] it's the end.

sound.advice.80s@gmail.com

1   *Causing A Commotion* by Madonna. Written by Madonna Ciccone and Stephen Bray
2   *Clouds Across The Moon* by RAH Band. Written by Richard Hewson